December 1997 –
Merry Christmas Kathy,
from Rob, Andrea, Dan + Rose

D0579732

December 1997 –
Merry Christmas Kathy,
from Rob, Andrea, Dan + Rose

The Book of

CHRISTIAN
CRAFTS

The Book of
CHRISTIAN CRAFTS

50
Beautiful Projects
that Celebrate
Christian Themes

DEBORAH
MORGENTHAL

Lark Books

Art Director: Dana Irwin

Production: Dana Irwin and Elaine Thompson

Illustrations and Production Assistance: Bobby Gold

Photograpy: Richard Babb

Library of Congress Cataloging in Publication Data
Morgenthal, Deborah, 1950-
     The book of Christian crafts : 50 beautiful projects that celebrate
Christian themes / Deborah Morgenthal. -- 1st ed.
     p. cm
     Includes index.
     ISBN 1-57990-008-9
     1. Bible crafts. 2. Handicraft. I. Title.
BS613.M57 1997   97-15487
745.5'088'204--dc21   CIP

10 9 8 7 6 5 4 3 2 1

Carved wood; made in Taiwan

First Edition

Published by Lark Books
50 College St.
Asheville, NC 28801, US

© 1997, Lark Books

Distributed by Random House, Inc., in the United States, Canada, the United Kingdom, Europe, and Asia

Distributed in Australia by Capricorn Link (Australia) Pty Ltd., P.O. Box 6651, Baulkham Hills Business Centre, NSW 2153, Australia

Distributed in New Zealand by Tandem Press Ltd., 2 Rugby Rd., Birkenhead, Auckland, New Zealand

Printed in Hong Kong

ISBN 1-57990-008-9

C O N T E N T S

Articles of Faith

As the year 2000 approaches, more and more Americans are looking to religion to help them make sense of the increasingly complex social and moral issues that confront us all. According to a 1996 Gallup Organization survey, more Americans said that religion played a role in their lives today than did 10 years ago. Church attendance has remained constant and has risen among teenagers. It is becoming more commonplace for people from all walks of life, including politicians, actors, athletes, writers, and the neighbor down the street, to talk about God and religion.

This "trend"—if that is what this phenomenon is—may come as no surprise to you. For me, the turn and returning of friends, colleagues, and family members to churches, synagogues, and Buddhist retreats, is a source of wonderment, and was, in part, a catalyst for this book. The art director, Dana Irwin, and I dreamed up this book with the certain feeling that the timing was right to offer crafters the chance to express their Christian faith and their creativity at the same time.

To transform a dream into a reality, we commissioned 31 talented designers to create projects using a wide range of today's most popular craft techniques, including sewing, appliqué, embroidery, cross stitch, needlepoint, decorative painting, woodworking, and jewelry-making using beads and polymer clay. We believe this diversity of materials and techniques makes *The Book of Christian Crafts* a resource you will enjoy using for many years.

The book features projects for beginners and more experienced crafters. However, because of space constraints, we are not able to explain the basic techniques required to make some of the projects. For instance, we have not included illustrations of the embroidery and needlepoint stitches used in the book. For that information, you will have to refer to books that focus on just that subject. Then you will be able to return to this book and follow the instructions for making a specific item.

Putting *The Book of Christian Crafts* together has been a joy. It has afforded me the chance to reflect on the meaning of the symbols and practices that the different projects bring to life and to inhabit sacred spaces in the middle of my hectic working day. It is in this spirit that we offer these articles of faith to you.

Mark Strom hand carved this six-foot soft maple sculpture, titled Mary Holding the Christ Child, *for the St. Francis Assisi Catholic Church, in Raleigh, North Carolina*

Before You Start

Whether you are a beginner or an experienced crafter, it is always a good idea to read the instructions all the way through once or even twice before you launch into making the project. In fact, many successful crafts people imagine themselves going through each step as they read the instructions. If a certain step doesn't make sense to you, try it out with a scrap of material or even a piece of paper. Written instructions can come to life when you rehearse them in this manner. Make sure you have all the materials and tools required for the project before you begin.

TRANSFERRING PATTERNS ONTO FABRIC

There are several ways that you can transfer a design onto your fabric.

1. Tracing: The easiest method (especially good for thin fabrics) is to trace the pattern on directly using a water-soluble pen or very fine pencil. Simply draw or trace the design onto a piece of tracing paper or thin white paper and tape it to a window. Then tape the fabric on top and trace the pattern onto it.

2. Dressmaker's carbon paper: This special fabric carbon comes in different colors so that you can select one that will clearly show on your fabric. Draw, trace, or photocopy the pattern. Place the fabric on a clean, flat surface and tape it down with making tape. Place the carbon paper face down on the fabric and use tape to secure it. Place the pattern on top and tape it down. Use a ballpoint pen to trace carefully over the pattern.

3. Making a transfer: Transfer pencils may not wash out, so this method is only appropriate on fabric if the technique (embroidery, for instance) will completely cover the marks. Start by tracing the design onto a sheet of thin tracing paper. Turn the tracing over and trace the back with the transfer pencil. Press the fabric, pin the transfer in place (transfer-pencil side down), and press slowly using a hot iron (do not use a steam setting).

TRANSFERRING PATTERNS ONTO WOOD AND OTHER SURFACES

First make a photocopy of the pattern, enlarged to the desired size. On the backside of the paper, rub white or colored pastel pencil all around the edges of the pattern. Position the paper, pastel pencil side down, on the surface you want the pattern to appear. With a hard pencil or ink pen, trace over the pattern. When you remove the paper, you should see the outline of the pattern on the surface.

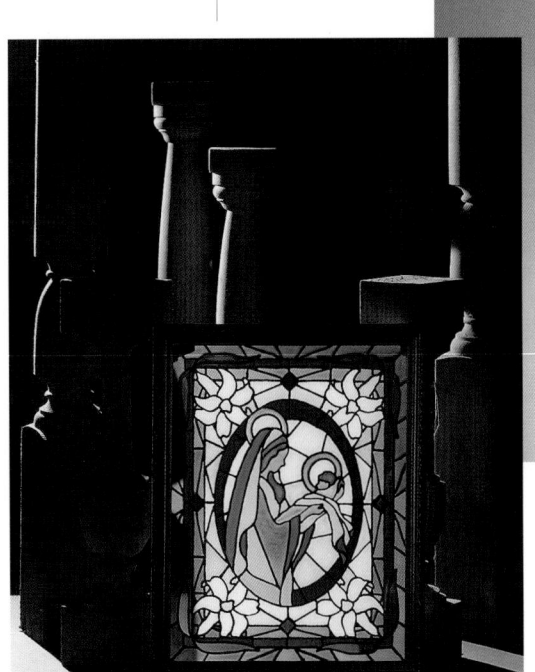

Left, Scandinavian Cross, page 100; center, Faux Stained Glass Madonna and Child, page 90; right, Silk Vest with Gold Medallions, page 18

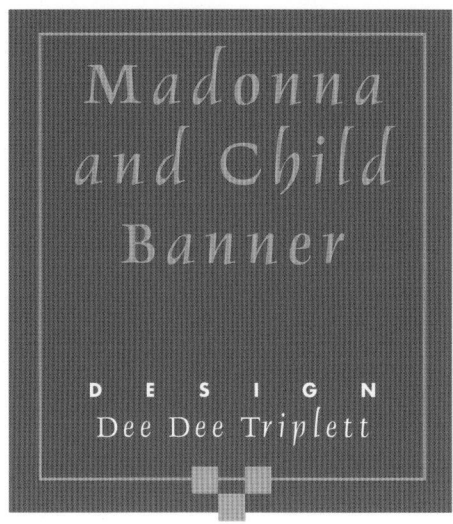

Madonna and Child Banner

DESIGN
Dee Dee Triplett

SIZE
12" (31cm) x 22" (56 cm)

THIS STUNNING MADONNA AND CHILD BANNER SHIMMERS WITH LIGHT, THANKS TO DEE DEE TRIPLETT'S ARTFUL BLENDING OF RICH VELVETEEN AND METALLIC FABRICS.

❧ Materials and Tools

⅔ yd. (62 cm) navy cotton velveteen (background)

14" x 9" (36 x 23 cm) dark red velveteen (Madonna back layer)

14" x 9" (36 x 23 cm) soft blue velveteen (Madonna top layer)

2 pieces of polyester lining, each 14" x 9" (36 x 23 cm)

7" x 6" (18 x 15 cm) dark purple velveteen (Jesus back layer)

7" x 6" (18 x 15 cm) medium purple velveteen (Jesus top layer)

2 pieces polyester lining, each 7" x 6" (18 x 15 cm)

6 inches (15 cm) gold silk/metallic fabric (halos)

6 inches (15 cm) fusible web

4" x 4" (10 x 10 cm) flesh-colored synthetic suede (faces)

sewing thread to match velveteen

very fine invisible thread

gold metallic thread

3 feet (1 m) of ⅛" (.5 cm) brass rod

❧ Instructions

1. The banner has flaps on the top edges which, when folded to the back, form a casing for the brass hanger. Prepare the pattern for the banner background using the measurements indicated in figure 1. Place two layers of navy velveteen right sides together. Pin or baste. Sew as shown on figure 1, leaving one top flap open to turn. Clip the corners and turn the fabric right side out.

2. Enlarge the patterns for Madonna and Jesus (figure 2, page 123) onto tracing paper. Label the tracing paper patterns on the right side and cut them all out. (Pattern lines are seam lines.)

3. For the velveteen body and face shapes: Sew one layer of one pattern and then the other. For each layer of each pattern, place the velveteen right side up, the lining right side down on top of the velveteen (colors indicated in the materials list), then place the pattern piece right side up on top of the lining. Pin to hold the layers. With your sewing machine set on 15–17 stitches per inch [2.5 cm]—(1.5 on computer machines) and a fine needle in the machine (size 11 or smaller), sew all

the way around each body shape. Cut each pattern out, leaving a generous ⅛" (.5 cm) seam allowance. Clip the curves. Very carefully cut a slit in the lining only and turn the layer right side out. (Sewing all the way around these shapes assures smooth curves and no frayed edges when appliquéing.) Repeat for all layers. Pin the face shapes onto the body forms and appliqué them in place.

4. Halos: Fold the gold silk/metallic fabric in half and fuse the two halves together with fusible web. Use a pressing cloth to avoid melting the fabric. Cut the two halos out of the fused metallic.

5. Appliqué Madonna's top layer to the bottom layer: Newer sewing machines have a blind hem stitch. To appliqué these shapes by machine, use navy thread in the bobbin and invisible thread in the needle. Stitch "in the ditch" next to the layer, being sure the machine catches the top layer when the needle swings sideways. Repeat for Jesus's two layers. Pin Madonna's layers to the background, with the halo under all the layers. Appliqué. Repeat for Jesus, positioning his halo on top of her layers.

Using the gold metallic thread, machine-stitch the radial lines in both halos.

6. Bend the brass wire to form the hanger. Fold the flaps over the wire to the back of the banner, and hand-stitch in place.

Figure 1

9

Embroidered Christening Dress

DESIGN
Peggy Cable McClure

PERSONALIZE A VERY SPECIAL CHRISTENING DRESS BY FOLLOWING THE DESIGN CREATED BY PEGGY MCCLURE, FEATURING AN EMBROIDERED CROSS AND MEANDERING FLOWERS.

▪ Materials and Tools

handmade or purchased christening dress and baby bonnet

embroidery floss in white and blue (or pink, for a girl)

water soluble marker or very fine pencil

tracing paper

embroidery hoop wrapped in white twill tape

embroidery needle

#26 tapestry needle

sharp scissors

▪ Instructions

1▪ Transfer the pattern on page 124 onto the lower portion of the dress using method #1. Replace the "ABC" with the appropriate initials. Then transfer just the horizontal portion of the floral design around the bottom of the dress and on the bonnet. Place the portion of the fabric with the cross design on it into the embroidery hoop.

2▪ Begin with the cross, using the tapestry needle and white floss. Shadow work embroidery is basically a closed herringbone or double back-stitch. A right-handed person will work from right to left, and a left-handed person will work from left to

Designer Reflections

When doing shadow work embroidery, keep your face work stitches as uniform as possible. The stitches should be large enough to lay flat on the fabric. If they are too small, they will resemble knots. One-tenth of an inch is about the perfect shadow work stitch.

right. The stitch is a "stab" stitch, using the backstitch and the back cross-over stitch.

Cut the thread 18" to 22" (46 to 56 cm) long and use a single strand. (You may use a "waste" knot to secure your thread.)

Begin to stitch, as shown in figure 1:

Up at A, down at B. Cross under on back to C. Up at C, down at D.

Cross under to E. Up at E, down at F-A. Cross under to G. Up at G, down at H-C. Continue until you have finished the cross motif.

Turn the fabric over. Lace extra white threads using the cross-over herringbone stitch to make the cross as solid-looking as possible.

3· Move the fabric as necessary in the embroidery hoop. Stitch the leaves with a lazy daisy stitch. Stitch the stems with a stem stitch. Lastly, stitch the remainder of the design with a satin stitch.

Figure 1

Painted clay; made in Peru

Child's
Quilt and
Pillow
Cover

DESIGN
Karyn Sanders

dear Lord
hear and bless thy
Beasts and singing birds
and guard with tenderness
Small things that have no words

SOFT AS BUNNY'S FUR, THIS DELIGHTFUL QUILT AND PILLOW SET, DESIGNED BY KARYN SANDERS, IS SURE TO CAPTIVATE AND CUDDLE A VERY SPECIAL CHILD.

❖ Materials and Tools

polar fleece:

2½ yds. (2.3 m) cream

1 yd. (91.4 cm) blue

¾ yd. (69 cm) yellow

½ yd. (46 cm) green

¼ yd. (23 cm) each of available colors, such as black, gray, terracotta, tan and red

pearl cotton thread in black

water-soluble fabric marker

washable fabric glue

embroidery hoop, 8" to 10" (21 to 26 cm) adjustable

#22 chenille embroidery needle

stretch needle for sewing machine

cellophane tape

ruler

appliqué scissors

pillow supplies:

standard size pillow

water-soluble fabric stabilizer

pinking shears or pinking blade on a rotary cutter

❖ Instructions

MAKING THE PILLOW

1. Tape several sheets of paper together so that you wind up with one piece of paper that measures 21" x 27" (53 x 69 cm). Write out the prayer with a black marker. Draw your own "critters" on paper using the photograph as a guide. Cut out the shapes and tape them to the paper that has the lettering on it. Lay transparent sheets of water-soluble fabric stabilizer over the paper and pin to hold in place. Trace the words and the outlines of the creatures onto the fabric stabilizer. Unpin the paper.

2. Cut out a piece of cream-colored polar fleece 21" x 27" (53 x 69 cm).

Place the fabric stabilizer on top with the lettering right side up. To hold the stabilizer in place, pin and then baste around the perimeter, and then vertically and horizontally in a grid pattern, 3" to 4" (8 to 10 cm) apart.

3. Open the embroidery hoop as much as possible. Starting at the left corner, place the hoop on the fleece and the stabilizer, being careful not to tear the stabilizer. With a double-strand of black pearl cotton, fill in the lettering, using a chain stitch. Outline the "critters" with a basting stitch using sewing thread: this will mark their placement for the appliqué (step 4).

4. *Embroidery:* All stitches are single-thread unless otherwise indicated. Use the paper patterns as templates to cut out the critters that belong on the pillow; refer to the photograph for the appropriate color polar fleece to use. Lightly glue them in place over the outlines you basted onto the pillow. Cut out the other elements of the creatures' bodies and glue them on. Embroider the antenna first, then appliqué and embroider all the pieces, using your choice of stitches.

Eight long stitches, emanating from the center in the shape of a spoke, form the spider's base. The web is a backstitch, wrapping itself around the individual spokes. Backstitch between the spokes to form the spiral shape.

5. *Pillow sham construction:* For the back of the sham, cut two pieces of cream-colored polar fleece, 16" x 21" (41 x 54 cm). Overlap these pieces in the back so that, together, they measure 20" x 27" (51 x 69 cm). Pin them, wrong sides together, to the embroidered front of the pillow. Topstitch around the perimeter 2" (5 cm) in. Trim the edges with a rotary cutter or pinking shears and insert the pillow.

MAKING THE BLANKET

6. Cut out two pieces of cream-colored polar fleece each, 31½" (80 cm) x 45" (114 cm).

Draw the tree, sun, creatures, and other patterns on paper, using the photograph as a guide. Lay transparent sheets of water-soluble fabric stabilizer over the paper patterns and pin to hold in place. Trace the outlines of the patterns onto the fabric stabilizer. Unpin the paper. Position the sheets of fabric stabilizer on top of one of the pieces of cream fleece, with the marked sides up. To hold the stabilizer in place, pin and then baste around the perimeter, and then vertically and horizontally in a grid pattern, 3" to 4" (8 to 10 cm) apart.

Outline the patterns with a basting stitch, using sewing thread to mark their placement for the appliqué.

7. *Embroidery:* All stitches are single-thread unless otherwise indicated. Use the paper patterns as templates to cut out the elements that belong on the blanket; refer to the photograph for the appropriate color fleece to use. Lightly glue the pieces in place over the outlines you basted on. Cut out the other elements of the creatures' bodies and glue them on. Appliqué and embroider all the pieces to the fleece, using your choice of stitches.

8. *Construction:* After you have completed the front of the quilt, place it on the back piece, wrong sides together, and topstitch ½" (1.5 cm) away from the edge.

9. *Checkered border:* Cut out 34 squares, each 2" x 2½" (5 x 6.5 cm), from the cream fleece, and 30 squares of the same size from the blue fleece (or a color of your choice). To wrap the corners, cut four blue pieces of fleece as shown in figure 1. Measure and mark the fabric 2" (5 cm) in all around the perimeter. Place one of the corner wrap pieces on a 2" (5 cm) mark. Wrap the rest of the piece around to the back and wrap the small corner piece around to the front; tuck in place under the front, lightly glue, and pin. Take a white square and butt it up alongside the corner piece; glue and pin in place. Continue in this manner until the border is completely covered. If necessary, you can overlap the pieces.

Loosen the tension on your sewing machine's pressure foot to accommodate the thickness of the fleece. Adjust the stitch length to the longest stitch. Sew the front of each square by stitching down one side and then jumping over to the next square, making sure that the squares are tightly butted to each other as you sew.

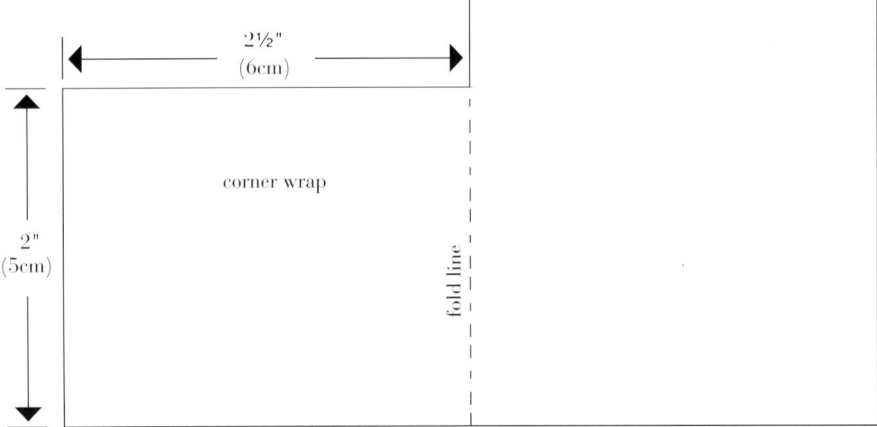

2½"
(6cm)

corner wrap

2"
(5cm)

fold line

Figure 1

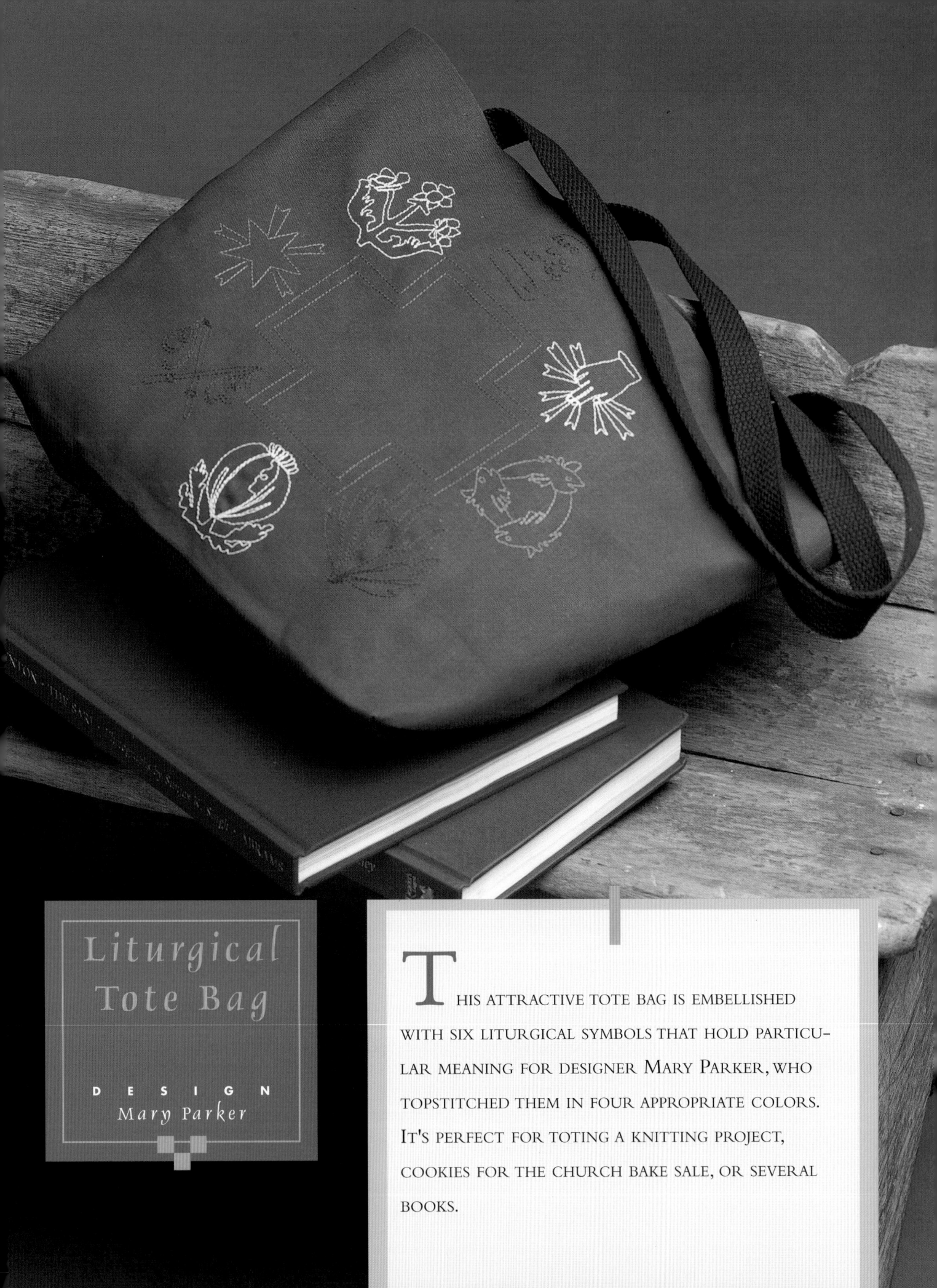

Liturgical Tote Bag

DESIGN
Mary Parker

THIS ATTRACTIVE TOTE BAG IS EMBELLISHED WITH SIX LITURGICAL SYMBOLS THAT HOLD PARTICULAR MEANING FOR DESIGNER MARY PARKER, WHO TOPSTITCHED THEM IN FOUR APPROPRIATE COLORS. IT'S PERFECT FOR TOTING A KNITTING PROJECT, COOKIES FOR THE CHURCH BAKE SALE, OR SEVERAL BOOKS.

Materials and Tools

½ yd. (45.7 cm) sturdy cotton fabric

⅓ yd. (31 cm) white cotton fusible interfacing

½ yd. (45.7 cm) lining fabric

3 yds. (2.7 m) webbing

sewing thread to match tote fabric

topstitching weight thread to match tote fabric

white, red, purple, and green sewing thread

white, red, purple, and green topstitching weight sewing thread

iron-on transfer pen or pencil

large-eyed hand-sewing needle

Instructions

I ▪ Trim the cotton fabric to 36¾" x 18" (93.3 x 45.7 cm). Using straight pins, mark a 12" (30.5-cm) square that will be the design area on the front of the tote. Refer to figure 1 on page 17 for placement.

2 ▪ Cut a 12" (30.5-cm) square from the white cotton fusible interfacing and fuse it to the wrong side of the tote bag fabric in the 12" (30.5-cm) square that you marked with pins in step 1. Follow the manufacturer's directions for fusing.

3 ▪ Select liturgical designs that are meaningful to your denomination or use the patterns on page 125, and arrange them in a pleasing pattern within the 12" (30.5-cm) square.

4 ▪ Make a photocopy of your design and use the iron-on transfer pen or pencil to mark over the design. Following the manufacturer's directions, transfer the design to the white interfacing that you have fused in place.

5 ▪ Wind the topstitching weight thread onto the bobbin and place the sewing thread in your sewing machine needle. You will need to loosen your needle tension. To find the best tension, experiment by fusing leftover interfacing onto scraps of tote bag fabric. Stitch with the interfacing side facing up and examine the underside of your fabric. This is the side that will show on the outside of your finished tote bag. When you are satisfied with the tension, stitch all the designs on your tote bag in the appropriate colors. You will stitch with the interfacing side up, following the lines you transferred in step 4. After completing each design, use the large-eyed hand-sewing needle to pull the heavier topstitching threads through to the interfacing side and tie these off against the other threads.

6 ▪ Cut three rectangles from the cotton rectangle as shown in figure 2. Note the location of the bottom and side seams and mark the center bottom seam as shown.

7 ▪ Place the right sides of the tote together and sew the side and bottom seams with a ⅜" (1-cm) allowance. This will leave two unjoined areas at the bottom corners of your tote (figure 3). Insert both index fingers into one of these corners and pull the fabric taut so that the unsewn portion from the bottom meets that from the side. Pin this in place; then sew a ⅜" (1-cm) seam. Repeat on the other corner.

8 ▪ At the top of the tote, turn under 2½" (6.4 cm) of fabric to the inside (wrong side). Press but don't sew.

9 ▪ Cut the webbing into two equal lengths. With the tote still inside out, shape one piece of webbing into a U and tuck each end into the seam allowance at the bottom of the tote, placing each end 4" (10.2 cm) from the center of the bottom seam. Don't twist the webbing; the same side should be pinned at both ends. Continue pinning the webbing against the wrong side of the tote fabric in

parallel lines up to the edge of the hem at the top. Allow enough ease in the webbing that it doesn't pull the tote fabric. When you reach the hem on each side, pin the webbing only to the hem, not through to the outer fabric. Release all of the pins except those holding the webbing to the hem. Then repeat on the other side of the tote with the second piece of webbing.

I0 ▪ Stitch the webbing only to the hem area on both sides of the tote. Then hand-baste the ends of the webbing back under the seam allowance at the bottom.

II ▪ Cut the lining fabric as shown in figure 2, but decrease the length from 18" (46 cm) to 13¾" (35 cm). With right sides together, start at the top and sew 3" (7.6 cm) of the side seam with a ⅜" (1-cm) seam allowance. Press the seam open and turn the lining right side out.

I2 ▪ With the right sides of the tote and lining together, match the seams. Align the raw edges along the top of the tote and lining and sew a ⅜" (1-cm) seam. Press the seam toward the lining.

I3 ▪ Turn the lining; then with the right sides together, stitch 3" (7.6 cm) of the side seam from the bottom corner. Press open. Pull the bottom of the lining through the unsewn middle area of the side seam and with the right sides together, stitch the bottom seam. Then stitch the open corners as you did for the tote in step 7 above.

I4 ▪ Turn the lining right side out and fit it into the tote. Hand-baste the bottom seams of the tote and lining together.

I5 ▪ Open the tote and stand it upright. With a piece of chalk, mark the area that forms the bottom of the tote. Hand-baste the webbing in place where it crosses under the chalk line; then stitch over the chalk line on your machine. Also stitch ¼" (6 mm) on each side of the center seam. This will

Figure 1

Figure 2

side seam

unjoined   bottom seam   unjoined

Figure 3

secure the handles and ensure that the lining and tote stay together.

16. Slipstitch the side seam of the lining completely closed.

▪ Designer Reflections

The designs I chose for the tote bag (starting at the 12 o'clock position and proceeding counter-clockwise) include a scroll representing Advent (the start of the Church year) with the beginning of the phrase, in Latin, "Behold a Virgin shall conceive and bear a Son;" a rose bush symbolizing Christmas; a star representing Epiphany; scourges for Lent; a pomegranate symbolizing Easter; tongues of flame representing Pentecost; three intertwined fishes for Trinity Sunday; and the hand of God representing All Saints Day. I embroidered these designs in the color that would be used for altar cloths and vestments in the Episcopal Church I attend. I placed them in a counter-clockwise direction to remind myself not to be in such a hurry to perform the everyday tasks of life and meet temporal deadlines that I forget what is really important—the eternal.

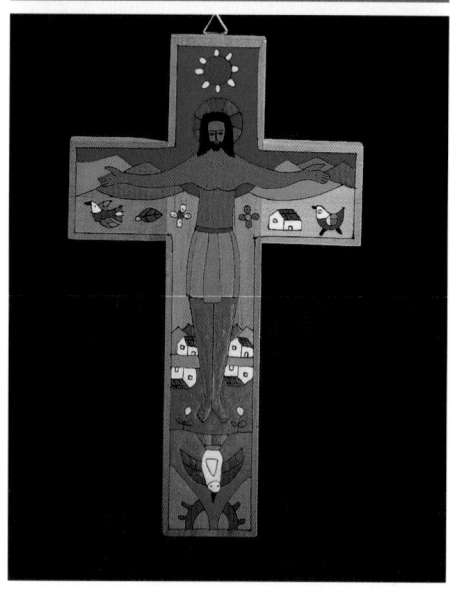

Painted wood; made in El Salvador

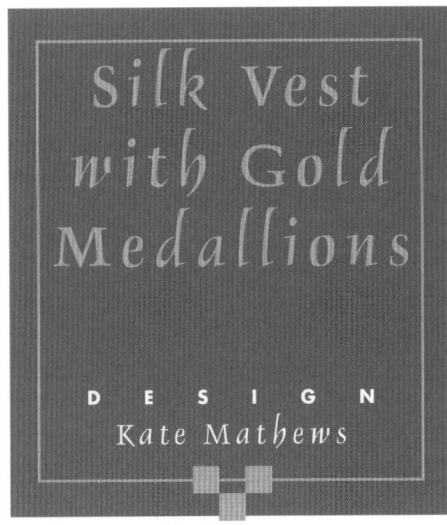

Silk Vest with Gold Medallions

DESIGN
Kate Mathews

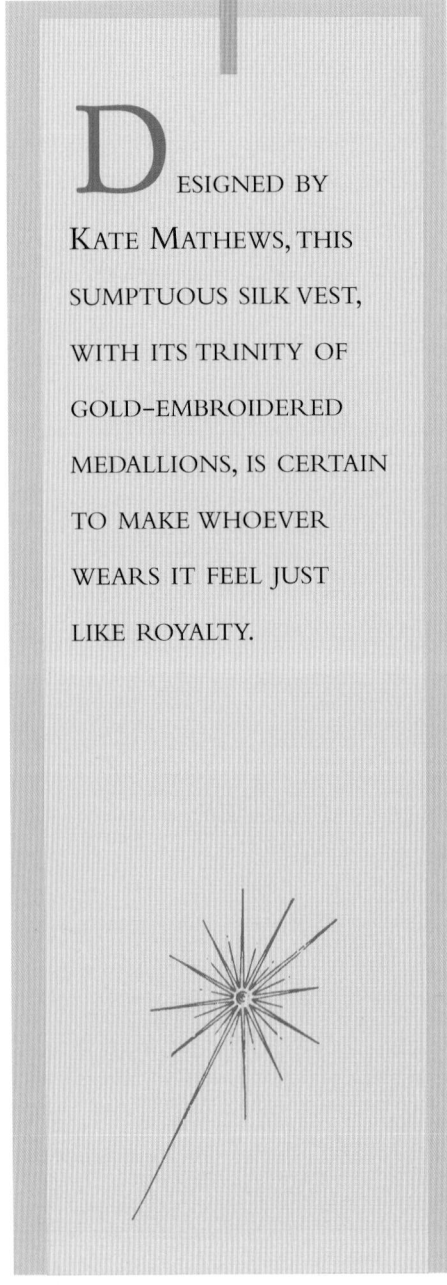

DESIGNED BY KATE MATHEWS, THIS SUMPTUOUS SILK VEST, WITH ITS TRINITY OF GOLD-EMBROIDERED MEDALLIONS, IS CERTAIN TO MAKE WHOEVER WEARS IT FEEL JUST LIKE ROYALTY.

✜ Materials and Tools

dartless vest pattern★

1¾ yds. (1.6 m) silk, 45" (1.1 m) wide for the vest★★

2 yds. (1.85 m) lining, 45" (1.1 m) wide

2 yds. (1.85 m) flannelette for the underlining

½ to 1 yd. (46 to 91 cm) sandwashed silk for the medallions

lightweight fusible woven interfacing

nonwoven sew-in medium-weight interfacing

bias or stay tape

thread to match fabric

gold metallic machine embroidery thread

sewing machine embroidery needle

open-front or embroidery sewing machine foot

★The designer used the pattern from *Making Your Own Great Vests* by Carol Parks (Sterling/Lark, 1995).

★★The designer used hand-painted silk crepe.

✜ Instructions

ALTERING THE PATTERN

1▪ Add 12" (30.5 cm) in length at the center back hemline. Add 8" (20.5 cm) in length at the side seams.

2▪ Blend a curving line to smoothly connect the center back, side seams, and center front opening at the hemline.

3▪ Make up a quick muslin to be sure you like the length, curved hem, and overall look.

PREPARING THE FABRIC

4▪ Pre-wash and dry the flannelette *twice* (use hot water and a hot dryer). 5. Cut out the pattern from the vest silk, the lining, and the pre-washed flannelette.

6▪ Baste the flannelette pieces to the wrong side of the silk pieces; you will treat them as one during sewing.

ASSEMBLING THE VEST

7▪ With right sides together, baste and stitch the vest fronts to the vest back at the shoulders. (*Tip:* Basting the seams together before stitching keeps the lining fabric from sliding.) Press the seams open.

8▪ With right sides together, baste and stitch the lining fronts to the lining back at the shoulders. Press the seams open.

9▪ To stabilize the front edges of the vest, cut the bias or stay tape to match the front opening seam lines of the pattern pieces. Baste or stitch over the vest seam lines ½" (1.25 cm) from the edge.

10▪ With right sides together, stitch the vest to the lining at the front opening edges and neckline, around the armholes, and across the lower back. Leave the side seams unsewn.

11▪ Trim and grade the seam allowances, clip the curves where necessary, and press the seams toward the lining.

12▪ To keep the lining from rolling to the outside of the garment, understitch the seam allowances to the lining (figure 1).

Figure 1

13▪ Turn the vest right side out through one of the side seams (figure 2, page 20). Press.

Figure 2

Figure 3

14. Stitch the vest back to the vest front at the side seams as far as possible, keeping the lining free. Press the seam open as far as possible.

15. Fold the lining seam allowances under and press; slip stitch the lining side seam closed (figure 3).

MAKING THE MEDALLIONS

16. Cut squares out of medallion fabric, lining, both interfacings, and flannelette big enough for the embroidered motifs, plus the surrounding unembroidered fabric, plus seam allowances on all four edges. Cut a second square out of flannelette. (The designer cut 4" (10 cm) squares for small medallions and 7½" (19 cm) squares for the large medallion.) Set the lining squares aside.

17. Fuse the lightweight interfacing to the wrong side of the medallion fabric.

18. Baste both layers of flannelette and the medium-weight interfacing to the wrong side of the fabric. The sandwiched layers are in this order: fabric, fused lightweight interfacing, flannelette, flannelette, and medium-weight interfacing.

19. For the small medallions, trace or thread-mark the interwoven cross design (figure 4) onto the right side of the small squares. Using gold thread, machine embroider the interwoven crosses on the right side of the squares, using a wide zigzag stitch. Loosen the bobbin tension slightly; set the stitch width to 3¾ to 4; set the stitch length to the appliqué setting or to almost zero. Do not backstitch with metallic thread.

20. For the large medallion, trace the circle and cross design (figure 5) on the wrong, interfacing side of the large square. Machine embroider the design on the wrong side, using a straight stitch. Adjust the stitch length until you like the way it looks.

Figure 4, actual size

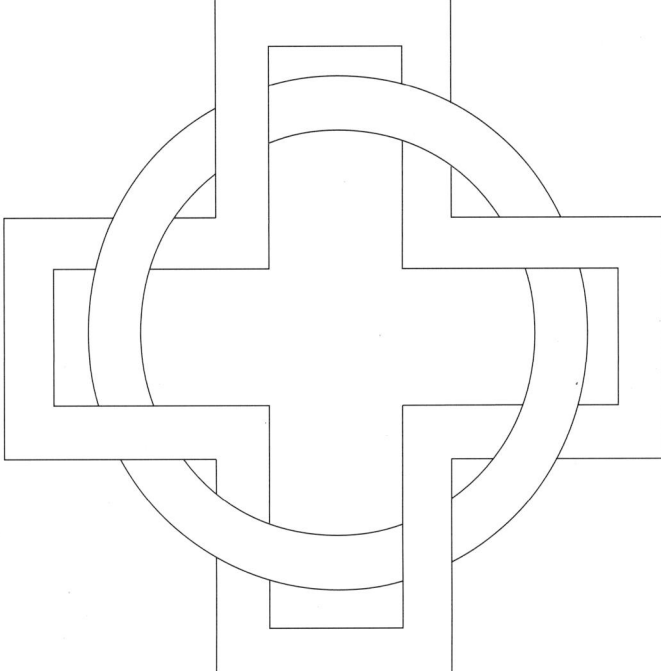

Figure 5, actual size

21· To finish all the squares, trim the medium-weight interfacing close to the embroidery and grade the two layers of flannelette.

22· With right sides together, stitch the squares of lining fabric to the medallions with a ½" (1.25 cm) seam allowance, leaving a small opening. Trim the seams, turn right side out through the opening, and steam or press very lightly. Slip stitch the small opening closed.

ATTACHING THE MEDALLIONS TO THE VEST

23· Experiment with the placement of the medallions on the vest until you like their positions; pin in place.

24· Sew them on as invisibly as possible, catching only the lining/backing of the medallions and the fabric/flannelette of the vest.

DESIGN
Mary S. Parker

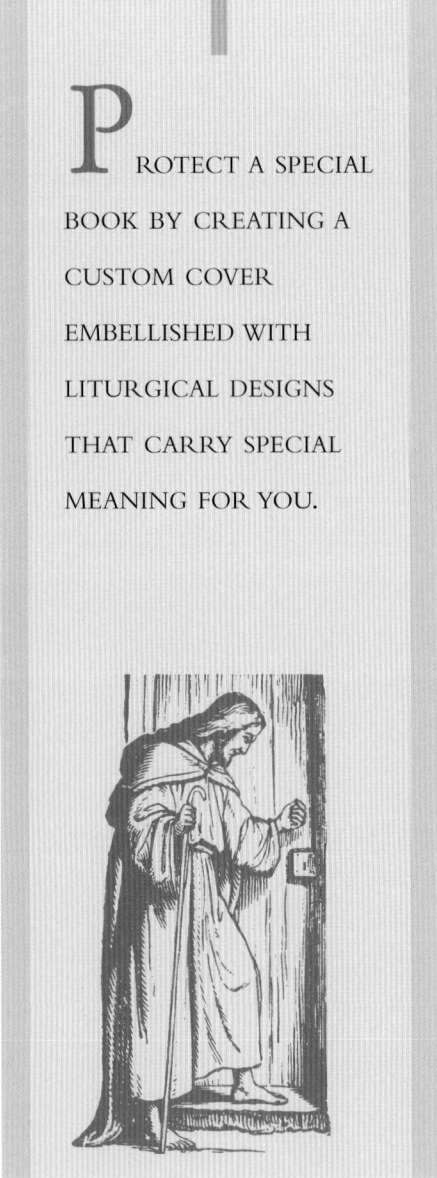

PROTECT A SPECIAL BOOK BY CREATING A CUSTOM COVER EMBELLISHED WITH LITURGICAL DESIGNS THAT CARRY SPECIAL MEANING FOR YOU.

⁛ Materials and Tools

raw silk or other fashion fabric; ¼ yd (23 cm) will be enough for most small bibles or prayer books

white cotton fusible interfacing (same quantity as book cover fabric)

iron-on transfer pen or pencil

sewing thread to match fabric

gold decorative heavy-weight thread (normally used in serger loopers)

ribbon

⁛ Instructions

1▪ Measure the height and width of your bible or prayer book from the front edge, around the closed spine, and to the back edge. Draw a rectangle this same height and width. Add 6" (15 cm) to the width of this rectangle and 2" (5 cm) to the height of this rectangle. Use the enlarged rectangle to cut out your fashion fabric.

2▪ Cut the interfacing to the size of the smaller original rectangle, and fuse it to the wrong side of the fashion fabric, leaving a 1" (2.5-cm) margin around the top and the bottom of the fabric and a 3" (7.5-cm) margin on both sides of the fabric. Follow the manufacturer's directions for fusing.

3▪ Select liturgical designs that are meaningful to you and your denomination or use the patterns on page 126. Arrange them in an attractive pattern that will fit on the front cover. The three designs used here are the "CHI RHO" (the first two letters of the name Christ in Greek); the Trefoil, interwoven with an equilateral triangle (a double symbol of the Trinity); and the ALPHA and OMEGA (used by many Christian denominations to represent the infinitude and eternity of God).

4▪ Make a photocopy of your design, and use the iron-on transfer pen or pencil to mark over the design. Place your pattern at the extreme right edge of the interfacing that you have fused to the wrong side of your fabric. (This will position the design so that it appears on the front cover.) Transfer the design to the interfacing according to the manufacturer's directions.

5▪ Wind the top-stitching weight thread on the bobbin, and place the regular weight sewing thread in your sewing machine needle. You will need to loosen your needle tension. To find the best tension, experiment by fusing leftover interfacing onto scraps of the fabric you are using. Stitch with the interfacing side facing up, and examine the underside of these test pieces until you achieve a pleasing stitch on the underside of your fabric. This is the side that will show on the outside of your finished book cover. When you are satisfied with the tension, stitch all the designs on your cover. Leave a tail of thread when beginning and ending each design; bring these through to the wrong side of the fabric and tie off as you finish sewing each design.

6▪ Fold the front and back edges of the cover under ¾" (2 cm) with the wrong sides together, and press. Keeping these edges folded under, turn the edges an additional 2" (5 cm) to the other side (you will now have the right sides of the fabric together), and press. Stitch a ¾" (2-cm) seam along both the top and bottom of each edge when the right sides of the fabric are folded towards each other. Test fit the book cover while it is still wrong side out. If the cover requires adjustment, make it on the back cover so that the design on the front cover will not be distorted. Press the rest of the top and bottom of the cover under ¾" (2 cm).

7▪ To create bookmarks, sew strips of ribbon to the upper hem of the cover.

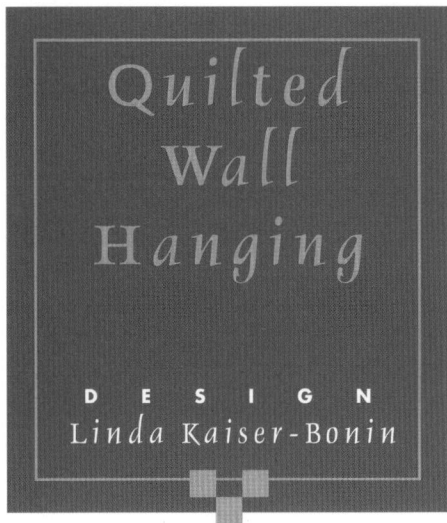

Quilted Wall Hanging

DESIGN
Linda Kaiser-Bonin

SIZE
19" x 19" (49 x 49 cm)

❖ Materials and Tools

15½" x 15½" (40 x 40 cm) light blue fabric for background

¼ yd. (23 cm) complementary print fabric for border

¼ yd. (23 cm) print or solid fabric for edge binding

24" x 24" (61 x 61 cm) piece of fabric for backing

5" x 16" (13 x 41 cm) scrap of fabric for hanging sleeve

⅓ yd. (31 cm) white fabric for dove and banner

scrap of beige fabric for dove's beak

4" x 10" (10 x 26 cm) piece of green fabric for leaves

1" x 10" (2.5 x 26 cm) strip of brown fabric for branch

⅓ yd. (31 cm) navy blue felt for letters

low-loft batting: a 20" x 20" (51 x 51 cm) piece, a 7" x 7" (18 x 18 cm) piece, and a 4" x 10" (10 x 26 cm) piece

small black button

sewing thread in white, green, brown, beige, and navy blue

16" (41 cm) length of dowel, ½" (1.5 cm) in diameter

24" (62 cm) decorative ribbon or string

❖ Instructions

1▪ From the border fabric, cut four strips, each 2½" x 19½" (6.5 x 50 cm). Sew the four border pieces onto the blue square, right sides together, with ¼" (1 cm) seam allowances. Miter the corners.

2▪ Center the finished top piece onto the largest piece of batting and secure with pins or basting stitches. (The batting serves as a stabilizer for the machine appliqué.)

3▪ Enlarge all the pattern pieces (page 126) on a copier as indicated.

4▪ Cut out the patterns for the dove. Use them as templates for cutting out the dove's body, tail, and head from both the white fabric and the medium-sized piece of batting. *Do not cut the wing yet.* Cut out the upper and lower beaks from the beige fabric. Cut out the branch from the brown fabric and fold it in quarters width-wise.

5▪ Place the dove's body, tail, and head (both the white fabric and the batting) on the blue background and pin in place. Position the beak pieces and the branch, and pin in place. Satin stitch the upper beak and the branch, and then the lower beak, using matching threads. Satin stitch the dove pieces to the background. With a straight stitch, outline the tail and body shapes several times.

6▪ Trace the wing pattern onto two pieces of white fabric and one piece of batting but do not cut them out. Layer the batting between the two pieces of white fabric, with the wrong sides of the fabric against the batting. Satin stitch on the traced lines. Cut out the wing, being careful not to cut any stitches. With straight stitches, add detail to the wing shape. Hand-tack the wing to the dove's body.

7▪ The leaves are done the same way as the wing, using two pieces of green fabric layered with batting. Satin stitch around the traced leaf shape, adding detail with straight stitching. Cut out the leaves and attach them to the branch.

8▪ Cut out a 2" x 20" (5 x 51 cm) strip of white fabric. From the navy blue felt, cut out the letters. Sew them to the white strip with matching blue thread. Satin stitch the edges of the white strip and cut the ends with a v-cut. Hand-stitch the strip to the banner.

9▪ To create a quilted look, stitch around the dove, the branch, and the leaves directly onto the blue background. Sew on the dove's black eye.

10▪ For the edge binding, cut four strips of fabric, each 1" x 19½" (2.5 x 50 cm). Fold the strips in quarters widthwise and sew them on.

11▪ Make a hanging sleeve from the 5" x 16" (13 x 41 cm) piece of fabric. Sew a narrow hem on each 5" (13 cm) side. With right sides together, sew the fabric lengthwise. Turn, center the sleeve on the back top of the wall hanging, and whipstitch in place. Place the dowel through the sleeve. Tie a length of colored ribbon to each end of the dowel and tie the two ends together. Now the ribbon can be hung from a decorative hook.

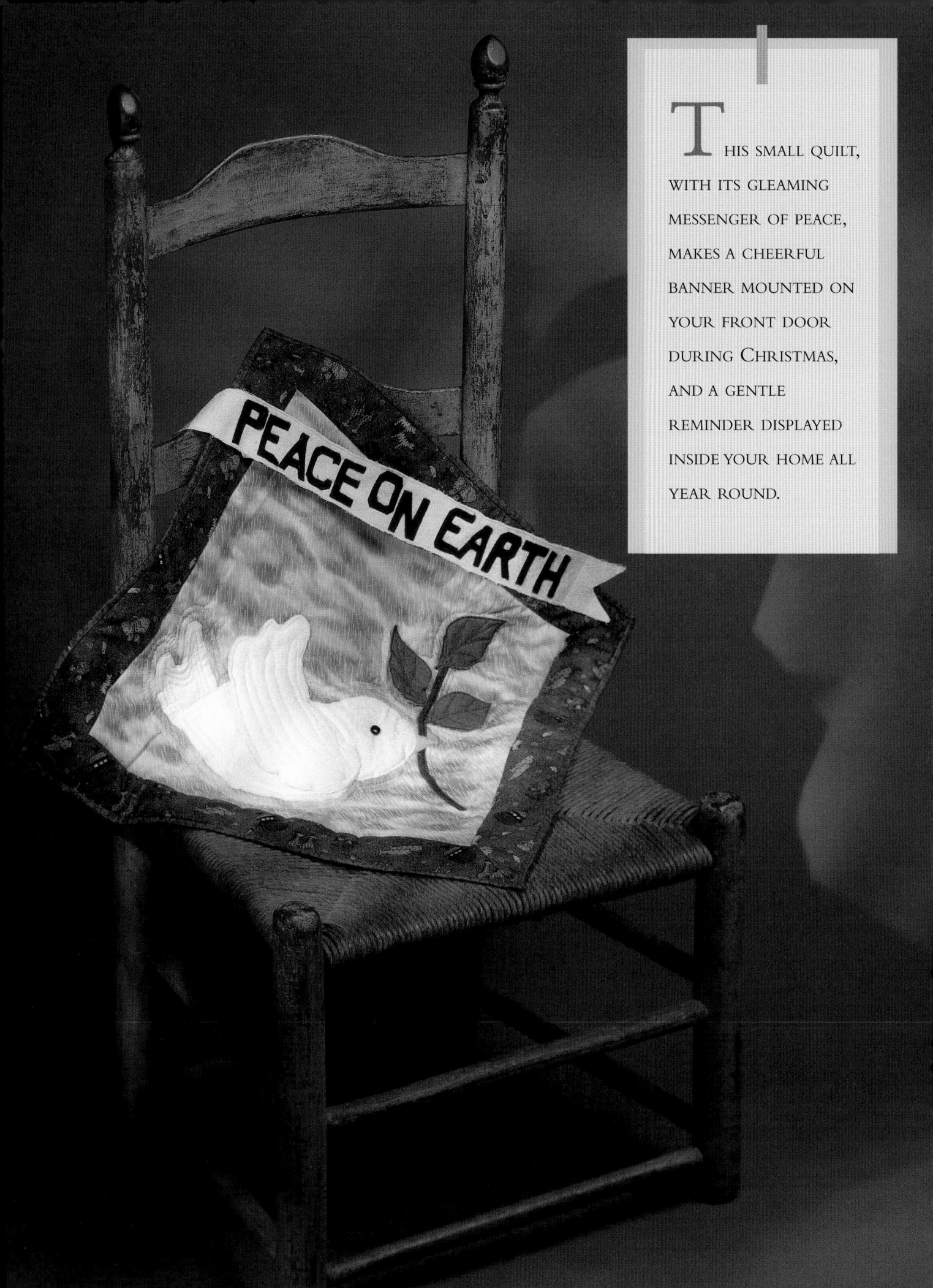

THIS SMALL QUILT, WITH ITS GLEAMING MESSENGER OF PEACE, MAKES A CHEERFUL BANNER MOUNTED ON YOUR FRONT DOOR DURING CHRISTMAS, AND A GENTLE REMINDER DISPLAYED INSIDE YOUR HOME ALL YEAR ROUND.

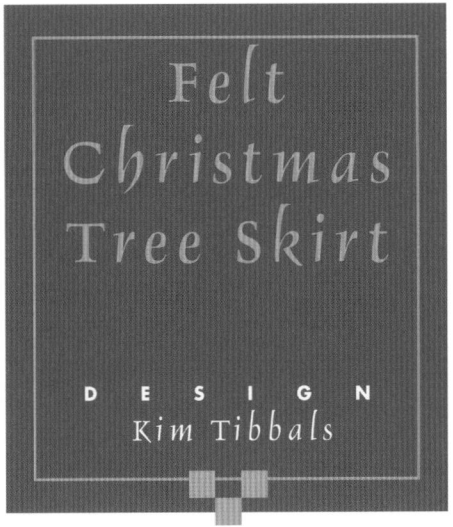

Felt Christmas Tree Skirt

DESIGN
Kim Tibbals

SIZE
60" (1.5 m) diameter

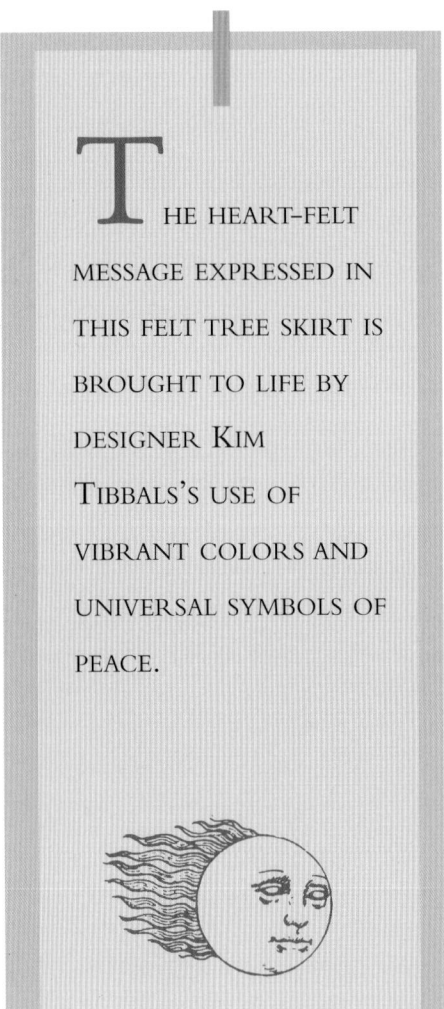

THE HEART–FELT MESSAGE EXPRESSED IN THIS FELT TREE SKIRT IS BROUGHT TO LIFE BY DESIGNER KIM TIBBALS'S USE OF VIBRANT COLORS AND UNIVERSAL SYMBOLS OF PEACE.

⁍ Materials and Tools

$3\frac{1}{3}$ yds. (3.2 m) royal blue felt

1 yd. (92.5 cm) white felt (dove)

$\frac{2}{3}$ yd. (62 cm) red felt ("P" and "e")

$\frac{1}{3}$ yd. (31 cm) yellow felt ("e")

$\frac{1}{2}$ yd. (46 cm) purple felt ("A")

$\frac{1}{3}$ yd. (31 cm) turquoise felt ("c")

$\frac{1}{2}$ yd. (46 cm) green felt (olive leaves)

$\frac{1}{3}$ yd. (31 cm) light brown felt (olive branches/stems)

20 or more wooden stars, 1"-2" (2.5-5 cm)

4-5 yds. (3.7-4.6 m) red cord, $\frac{3}{4}$" (2 cm) wide

3 yds. (2.75 m) gold metallic cord (width of 6-strand DMC)

1 yd. (92.5 cm) gold metallic cord, about $\frac{1}{2}$" (1.5 cm) wide

gold metallic thread (used for ALL stitching)

temporary white fabric marker

gold metallic craft paint

scissors

pinking shears

yardstick

straight pins

electric drill with $\frac{1}{16}$" (2-mm) drill bit

paintbrush

large-eyed needle

hot-glue gun and glue sticks

fray retardant

⁍ Instructions

1⁃ Fold the royal blue felt in half widthwise and cut it into two 60" (1.5 m) squares. Using pinking shears, cut each square into a 60" (1.5 m) circle. (Fold a square in half and mark the center point on the fold with a pin. Placing one end of a yardstick at the center point, pivot around this point, marking with pins or temporary

26

marker at the 30" (77 cm) mark as you go; this becomes your cutting line.) Repeat with the other square.

2· Mark and cut the center-circle opening for both blue circles by repeating the yardstick pivoting procedure, marking at the 3" (8 cm) mark as you pivot. Cut with pinking shears.

3· Make three button loops from scraps of blue felt by using pinking shears to cut three strips, each 1¼" x 7" (3.5 x 18 cm). Fold in half lengthwise and stitch ¼" (1 cm) in from the raw edges. Fold in half widthwise and stitch across the raw edges.

4· Enlarge the pattern on page 127. Cut out all the pieces, using the materials list as a guide. (*Tip:* You may want to number the olive leaves and the wing pieces to ensure correct placement.)

5· Beginning with the letters in the word "Peace," position the pieces on one of the blue felt circles; starting with the "A" helps to determine the best placement. Lay down the olive stem and the leaves (all the leaves should be on top of the stem). Pay careful attention to whether or not the leaves fall in front of or behind different portions of the letters "P" and "e." Also note how the "P" hooks the "e." Next, position the pieces of the dove, noting the overlapping layers on the wings and the position of the head and beak in relation to the olive stem. Stand back and look at your work to be certain you are keeping things in proportion and allowing enough space between the last "e" in "Peace" and the dove's wing tip to create the words "on earth" with the red cording. If not, move the pieces closer together as needed. When you are satisfied, pin all the pieces in place.

6· Right after the last "e" in "Peace," write "on earth" on the blue felt circle, using the white marker. Glue the red cord along this path at necessary intervals. Work slowly and carefully; if you do have a glue accident, you can always cover the drip with a wooden star. Use fray retardant to seal the cord ends.

7· Stitch the pieces into place using a ¼" (1-cm) seam. Sew the letters first. In cases where overlap occurs, peel back the uppermost piece to allow the underlying piece to be fully stitched in place, then reposition the overlapping piece and stitch it in place. In cases where this becomes too complicated, it may be necessary to break your stitching line and continue on the other side of the overlapped piece (as is the case with the olive leaves entwined with the letters "p" and "e.") After all the letters are stitched, stitch the olive stem, pulling back the overlapping ends of the leaves, then go back and stitch all the leaves in place. Stitch the dove and its wings last. Cut a 1" (2.5 cm) circle of blue felt for the dove's eye and glue it in place.

8· Pin the second blue circle to the back of the appliquéd one, aligning the raw edges. Create the back opening by drawing a line from the center to the outer edge (possibly through the tip of the dove's wing). Cut through both thicknesses with pinking shears. Pin the open edges together. Place the button loops along the back opening, slip the raw edges between the two felt layers, and pin in place. Stitch the two circles together along all open edges, using a ½" (1.5 cm) seam allowance.

9· Make buttons from the wooden stars by drilling two holes in each, ¼" (1 cm) apart. Paint them with gold metallic paint. When dry, place them on the tree skirt in a random pattern, being sure to use three for the closing. Using the large-eyed needle and the thin gold cord, insert the needle down through one hole in the star, through the first layer of blue felt, and then up through the second hole in the star. Tie a knot and knot both ends of the cord.

10· Make a simple bow out of the thicker gold cord and knot both ends. Glue it onto the olive branch.

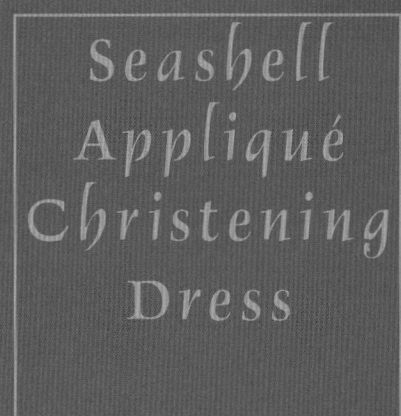

Seashell Appliqué Christening Dress

DESIGN
Karyn Sanders

A CIRCLE OF SEASHELLS, SYMBOLIC OF ST. JOHN THE BAPTIST, GRACES THE HEMLINE OF THIS BEAUTIFUL CHRISTENING DRESS, DESIGNED BY KARYN SANDERS.

❖ Materials and Tools

pattern for christening dress and baby bonnet

required quantity of fabric for slip

required quantity of sheer fabric plus ½ yd. (46 cm) for hem facing (voile was used here)

½ yd. (46 cm) fabric in a contrasting color for the shell appliqué★

scrap of fabric, 8" to 10" (21 to 26 cm) wide and as long as the circumference of the bottom of the skirt

DMC embroidery floss to match shell fabric

sewing thread to match christening gown

#26 tapestry needle

hand-sewing needle

water-soluble fabric marking pen

small sharp scissors

embroidery hoop, 8" x 10" (21 x 26 cm)

craft knife

light-weight cardboard

awl

ruler

★ The designer used an extra ½ yd. (46 cm) of voile which she tea dyed to a medium shade.

⋮ Instructions

1· Press and starch the sheer fabric you have selected. Following the pattern you have purchased, cut out and construct the slip, bodice, and skirt. Leave the hem of the skirt unfinished.

2· Making sure that the hem is even, use the water-soluble fabric marker to mark ½" (1.5 cm) up from the edge of the skirt's hem. You should have a continuous line around the circumference of the skirt.

3· In order to have room to place the embroidery hoop below the hemline, baste onto the hem the long scrap fabric measuring 8" to 10" (21 to 26 cm); you will remove this later.

4· Make 16 to 20 copies of the shell pattern (figure 1) on a copier, enlarging it to the desired size. Cut the shells out and place them on the hemline to determine how many shells your skirt bottom will accommodate. If you need to, you can overlap the shells slightly. Use a straight pin to mark the position of each shell, then set the paper shells aside.

5· To create a template, mount one of the paper shells onto light-weight cardboard and trim around the shell. Use the awl to punch three holes

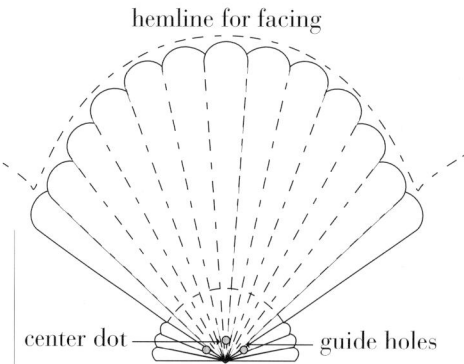

hemline for facing

center dot — guide holes

Figure 1

where indicated. Each hole should be large enough to accommodate the tip of the fabric marker.

6· On the right side of the sheer fabric, starting in the front, place the template where one of your pins is placed, on the line you have drawn at the hem. Mark around the template and through the holes. (These holes are guides for the shell's vertical segment lines.) Repeat this process until the entire hem in encircled with shells.

7· You will have to freehand draw the vertical segment lines. Start at the bottom part of the curve and, with a ruler, angle a line down to the center dot. Continue to draw lines to the bottom of the shell. Fill in the smaller parts of the shell sides. All of these lines will be your stitching lines.

8· From the colored fabric, cut two strips 5½" (14 cm) wide and long enough, when placed end to end, to encircle the bottom of the skirt. Sew them together end to end. Press the seams open and place the strip inside the skirt, ¼" (1 cm) below the hem mark, with the seams inside. The colored strip should fit perfectly, with no gapping. Baste the top and bottom of the strip in place. Attach the embroidery hoop to the center front. Make sure that both fabrics are straight and smooth in the hoop; attach the front first and work towards the back.

9· Backstitch the outline of the shell shape, then backstitch the segment lines. To end a thread, weave it

through the stitches on the wrong side. (Try to keep the back of the fabric free of stray threads, as they will show through the front.) When you have completed embroidering the shell motif, remove the hoop and the extra strip you basted in place at the bottom of the hem.

10· Hand-wash the skirt to remove the markings. Roll the skirt in a towel to remove the moisture. Press on the wrong side with the right side facing the towel. Use the small scissors to trim the colored fabric around the outside of the shell design, close to the stitching line. Be careful not to cut the stitches.

11· For the inside facing, cut two ½ pieces of fabric, 6" (15 cm) wide, with a ¼" (1-cm) seam, which, when placed end to end, encircle the bottom of the skirt. Press open and place right sides together. Sew the hem ¼" (1 cm) below the hand-stitching on the shells. Press the hem seam open. Turn it to face towards the inside and press. Working from the inside out, slip the skirt onto an ironing board. Trim the facing so it conforms to the scallop shape, leaving ⅛" to ¼" (3 mm to 6 mm) for the hem. Clip the curves, turn the edges under, and pin. The facing creates a shadow effect and also encloses all the stitches to keep everything neat inside. Slipstitch the hem in place with thread that matches the skirt. Press and attach the skirt to the bodice.

Noah's Ark Vest

DESIGN
Peggy Cable McClure and Rebecca Freeman

MOTHER, PEGGY, AND DAUGHTER, REBECCA, COMBINED THEIR CONSIDERABLE TALENTS TO DESIGN THIS ELEGANT VEST, AND DRESSED UP AN OTHER-WISE WILD BUNCH (NOAH WENT ON AHEAD TO RESERVE A TABLE).

▸ Materials and Tools

vest pattern in your size

1 yd. (91.4 cm) black fabric

1 yd. (91.4 cm) lining

1½ yds. (1.4 m) lightweight interfac-ing

synthetic suede scraps—brown, tan, beige, gold, gray-blue, offwhite

machine-embroidery thread

2½ yds. (2.3 m) black braid, with seam allowance attached

3 black frog closures

DMC floss in gold, black, brown, and white

paper-backed fusible web

small black seed beads

tear-away paper stabilizer or freezer paper

zigzag sewing machine

▸ Instructions

1▪ Cut out the vest fabric and lining, according to the needs of your vest pattern. Cut out the same amount of lightweight interfacing. Fuse the inter-facing to the wrong side of the outer vest fabric, following the manufactur-er's directions.

2▪ Seam up the sides of the vest and lining, and press the seams open. Turn under a ⅝" (2.5-cm) seam allowance on the lining shoulder seams, and press.

3▪ Enlarge the pattern pieces (pages 32 and 128) on a copier to the desired sizes and trace them onto paper-backed fusible web. If you want the design to face "left," be sure to flip the design, then trace the design facing "right."

4▪ Position the animals and the ark on the vest, using the photograph as a guide. Follow the manufacturer's directions when fusing the animals and ark. With synthetic suede, you need to place a sheet of paper between the iron and the pattern piece.

5. Appliqué around each pattern piece using a zigzag stitch set at a very short length and a slightly less than medium width. Use an open-toe or clear appliqué foot. Always place a piece of tear-away paper stabilizer or freezer paper underneath.

Designer Reflections

Here are two special notes on appliqué that will give your work a professional look. First, if your zigzag machine has a needle position option, leave the needle in the *down* position. Second, when raising the pressure foot to continue the pattern piece in a curve: If the pattern curves to the *right*, stop the needle in the *left* position; if the pattern piece curves to the *left*, stop the needle in the *right* position.

6. Sew the seed beads in place for eyes.

7. Make the manes with DMC floss by backstitching and leaving a loop. For the giraffe's mane, cut the loops.

8. Stitch the black braid around the outer edges of the vest.

9. Place the lining to the vest, right sides together. Stitch around the edges, leaving the shoulder seams free. Trim, turn through the shoulder seams, and press.

10. Place front to back, right sides together at the shoulder seams. Stitch, keeping the lining free. Press the seams open, and, by hand, slip stitch the shoulder seam closed. Press and hand-stitch the frog closures to the vest front.

Holy
Greeting
Cards

DESIGN
Terry Taylor

THERE ARE NO SET RULES OR DIRECTIONS FOR CREATING THESE GORGEOUS CARDS, DESIGNED BY TERRY TAYLOR. THEY ARE CREATED SPONTANEOUSLY AND DEPEND ON THE MATERIALS AT HAND.

❖ Materials and Tools

blank greeting cards and matching envelopes

small pieces of decorative paper

mica

brass screen wire

sheer ribbon

small seed beads

accent beads

metallic and silk threads

mat board

acetate

assorted holy medals, crucifixes, jewelry findings

white craft glue

jewelry glue

images to photocopy

gold leaf

adhesive size

paintbrush

beading needle

NOTE ABOUT THE MATERIALS

The materials listed above were used to make the cards shown in the photograph. They are provided here to guide you in selecting materials for the cards you want to make.

❖ Instructions

Here are some general tips for making these cards.

CARDS WITH PHOTOCOPIED IMAGES

Use line drawings taken from an encyclopedia of saints. Copy selected images on paper or on acetate. Images copied on acetate can be glued onto decorative papers and attached to the cards and embellished as desired. Use images on paper and layer them under mica, brass screen wire, or sheer ribbon.

SMALL COLLAGES

Small pieces of mat board covered with decorative papers make great bases for attaching charms or holy medals with Christian themes. When you are satisfied with the base, attach the charm to the board with bead glue, allow it to dry, and then embellish with beads and metallic thread. When you are satisfied with the look, glue the mat board to the card.

BEADING ON CARDS

Sewing beads directly onto images and the cards themselves can lend a very special touch to your cards. Use either beading thread or decorative metallic or silk threads. If you are sewing beads to small collages, the threads are hidden when you glue the collage to the card. If you are sewing directly onto the card, you may not wish to see the thread when you open the card. This is easily solved by gluing a decorative paper to the inside of the card to cover the stitching.

A NOTE ON BEADED CARDS & CARDS WITH RELIEF COLLAGES

The postal service charges extra for mail that exceeds the general postal requirements for first class mail. Be prepared to use extra postage. Also, a small scrap of "bubble wrap" or some other type of packing material to cover the beaded portion is an excellent idea. If you have taken the time and trouble to create this type of card, take the time and trouble to ensure that the recipient gets an undamaged card.

❖ Designer Reflections

I like the look of images on paper layered under mica, brass screen wire, or sheer ribbon. It brings to mind the screened portion of the confessional or how sacred relics appear under glass.

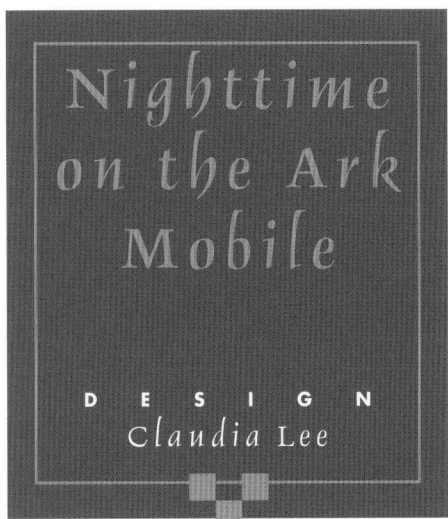

Nighttime on the Ark Mobile

DESIGN
Claudia Lee

SIZE
36" (91.4 cm) long
when fully assembled

❖ Materials and Tools

assorted good-quality papers

several pieces of high-quality medium-weight interfacing

good-quality paper glue

newspaper

acrylic gloss medium

waxed paper

dimensional paints, black or colors (squeeze-bottle with pointed tip)

cotton swabs

assorted colorful buttons and beads

sequins and rhinestones

blender

strainer or colander

containers to hold pulp (one for each color)

scissors

fiberglass screening

sponge

paintbrush, 1" (2.5 cm) wide

wire cutters

length of wire

needle and thread

ice pick or awl

monofilament

❖ Instructions

1 ▪ When making your paper, don't use too much glossy paper, such as magazine pages, and be sure to remove any staples or plastic. To keep the colors bright, group together similar colors; if you combine dissimilar colors, you will wind up with a muddy gray. If you are recycling all white papers, you can make them different colors by adding pieces of construction paper to the mix.

2 ▪ Tear the papers into small pieces about the size of a large coin and soak them well in water. After filling the blender three-quarters full of water, add a handful of the soaked paper. Make sure the lid is on tight! Turn on the blender and mix, using short bursts. If the motor sounds strained, stop the blender, remove some of the pulp, and add more water. Process again.

3 ▪ When the pulp is as smooth as oatmeal or finer, it is ready. Pour it through a strainer into a container. Repeat this process until you have enough pulp for this project. Process each color separately.

4 ▪ Draw the simple patterns on paper, making them as large as you want. All component parts of the mobile are made from two thicknesses of paper. Cut out *two* of all parts, except the windows—you will need *eight* of these.

5 ▪ Transfer each pattern piece to a piece of interfacing. Cut each pattern piece slightly larger than the outline. Immerse one of the fabric patterns in water and squeeze out the excess. Then smooth out the excess and spread the fabric pattern on a flat surface.

6 ▪ Place a small handful of soggy pulp (don't squeeze out the water) on the fabric and fill in the pattern. Place a piece of fiberglass screen on top and apply steady pressure with the sponge, squeezing out as much water as you can. This helps bond the fibers and reduces shrinkage. Remove the screen and set the piece aside to dry.

Continue in this manner until you have completed all the pieces. When the pieces are completely dry, remove the interfacing.

7 ▪ Now you can glue the pieces together. First, glue the two cabin pieces together. Place the glued cabin on a work surface and position the roof, hull, door, windows, and one set of waves. When you are pleased with the arrangement, pencil lightly where each piece goes. Glue the pieces in place and let dry. Turn the finished ark face down and repeat the process with the duplicate set of ark pieces and the four remaining windows, using the finished side of the ark as a guide. The placement of these pieces does not have to exactly match their position on the other side. Glue the front and the back of the ark together and let dry. Now glue together the two sides of the rest of the mobile.

8 ▪ Lay all the glued parts on newspaper. One at a time, coat one side of each piece with a layer of gloss medium, and then immediately place it on wax paper to dry. Don't let the wet pieces dry on the newspaper or they will stick! The pieces will be dry in 10 to 15 minutes. Then give all the pieces a second coat. When that coat is dry, turn the pieces over and apply two coats on the other side.

9 ▪ When the pieces are thoroughly dry, you can begin to embellish them.

Outline the glued edges with dimensional paints; you can use black as in the photograph, or experiment with different colors. Use these paints to decorate all the pieces and to add features to the fish. These paints occasionally will splatter out, or you may accidentally smear them with your hand. Because you've covered the pieces with an acrylic coating, you can easily clean up any mishaps with a wet cotton swab. You can also use a swab to erase an embellishment you don't like. Dimensional paints need several hours to dry. Test them by touching very lightly for tackiness. Don't rush them. When the paint is completely dry, turn all the pieces over on a fresh

THIS WHIMSICAL MOBILE IS BLESSED WITH VIBRANT COLOR AND QUIET HUMOR. "NOAH AND ALL THE ANIMALS ARE INSIDE THE ARK SLEEPING," EXPLAINS DESIGNER CLAUDIA LEE (AND BESIDES, WHO WANTS TO MAKE ALL THOSE ANIMALS?).

piece of waxed paper, and decorate the other side. When both sides are dry, glue on the beads, rhinestones, sequins, and buttons.

10· Assembling the mobile: On a large work surface, lay out all the pieces the way you want them. The key to making a mobile is balance; if you hang a piece on the right side, you will need to hang a piece of about the same size on the left side.

To give your mobile a strong center of support, add a wire rod to the first, largest rainbow or it will bend from the weight of supporting the other pieces. Cut the wire to the size you need, gently bend it to conform to the rainbow shape, and tack it on in several places with a needle and thread.

Using an awl or ice pick, pierce a hole in the areas where you will tie the pieces together with monofilament. Starting at the top, tie the rainbow pieces together. Hold them up; if they hang in a satisfactory way, continue by tying on the moon, star, and lightning bolt. Corrections and adjustments can be made to any part at any time.

Ark Switch Plate

Additional Supplies

piece of handmade paper that is larger than the finished ark

double switch plate and screws

craft knife

⊱ Instructions

Cut out only one of each pattern piece. The spaces for the switches will be the windows. Arrange the pieces to your liking. Place the double switch plate on top of the arranged pieces to make sure the ark is large enough to hide the plate. Mark where the plate will go. Glue all the pieces together to form the ark. Place the ark on the large piece of handmade paper and trace the shape. Cut out the ark shape and glue it to the back of the other ark. Cut out the windows with a craft knife. Apply two coats of gloss medium to the front. Coat the back once. Glue the switch plate to the ark and let dry. Decorate the front with dimensional paints. Poke holes for the screws and hang the fish with a length of monofilament.

Ark Clock

Additional Supplies

clock parts (available in craft-supply stores)

Instructions

The clock is made in the same manner as the switch plate but without cutting out holes for windows. You can adjust the size of the ark to suit the size of the clock parts.

Choose one or all three of these important symbols, and make your own colorful gift or greeting cards, designed by Laura Sims.

⊹ Materials and Tools

good-quality blank cards and matching envelopes

acrylic paints

tracing paper

pencil

gum erasers

craft knife

❖ Instructions

1 ▪ Draw a single image on the end of a gum eraser. (You can draw a design freehand or trace the symbols from the photograph and enlarge or reduce on a copier.)

2 ▪ Cut away the rubber around the design.

3 ▪ Dip the carved eraser in the paint and use it to decorate the cards and envelopes.

Prayer Journal

DESIGN
Gwen Diehn

SIZE
6¼″ x 6″ (16 x 15 cm)

THIS HANDSOME HANDMADE BOOK, DESIGNED BY GWEN DIEHN, IS THE PERFECT PLACE TO RECORD SPIRITUAL PASSAGES OR DAILY MEDITATIONS AND PRAYERS. EASY TO MAKE, YOU CAN DECORATE IT WITH A FAVORITE CHRISTIAN SYMBOL.

❖ Materials and Tools

medium-weight paper, such as typing or copier paper (white or colored)★

2 sheets of decorative paper for end papers and concertina guard★★

2 sheets of chipboard or other medium-weight cardboard★★★

several yds. of waxed cotton thread to match color of book pages★★★★

fabric to cover the book★★★★★

thin colored ribbon, 6" (15 cm) longer than the height of pages

acrylic gel medium

fabric-treatment spray

PVA glue

gold acrylic paint

straight needle

scissors

metal yardstick

triangle

craft knife

several paper clips

awl

cardboard scraps

waxed paper

2 paintbrushes, flat and fine-tipped

soft graphite pencil

★When determining the size paper to purchase, remember that each sheet will be folded in half. The pages in the journal shown here are 6" x 11" (15 x 28 cm), which means that, when folded, each page is 6" x 5½" (15 x 14 cm). The journal shown here has 48 sheets. When these are folded, the journal has 192 pages, counting both sides of each page.

★★This paper needs to be relatively strong because it will be used to help hold the text pages to the cover. It needs to be as tall as the pages of the book. To determine the width, add two times the width of a single page, plus 2" (5 cm) for every 8 sheets of paper, minus 2" (5 cm). In the journal shown here, the 48 sheets are folded in 6 signatures or groups of folded pages. This was the formula used to determine the width of the decorative paper: 5½" + 5½" + 2" + 2" + 2" + 2" +2" + 2"- 2" = 21" (15 + 15 + 5 + 5 + 5 + 5 + 5 + 5 - 5 cm = 54 cm).

★★★Needs to be ¼" (1 cm) and ½" (1.5 cm) wider than the pages. You will also need a piece for the spine of the book, the same height as the cover boards and approximately 1" (2.5 cm) wide. The width will be determined after the pages have been sewn together. These cover boards are 6¼" x 6" (16 x 15 cm) each and the spine board is 6¼" x ½" (16 x 1.5 cm).

★★★★Measure a length of thread for each signature (group of 8 sheets) and add a couple of extra lengths.

★★★★★ Enough to cover both covers and the spine and to allow a 1" (2.5 cm) border all around. This cover cloth is 14" x 8" (36 x 21 cm).

❖ Instructions

I ▪ Fold the individual sheets in half, then crease the folds, and slip the sheets inside one another.

2 ▪ Now you will make a concertina guard to protect the sheets of paper and to help bind them to the cover boards. Lay the piece of heavy decorative paper on the cutting surface with the decorative surface facing down. Measure and cut the strip so that it is exactly as high as the signature pages. To determine the width, add twice the width of the signature pages plus 2" (5 cm) for every signature MINUS 2" (5 cm).

Place one folded signature along the left edge of the concertina paper (figure 1 on page 44). To make the paper easy to fold, use the triangle, ruler, and a paper clip to *score* a line straight along the right side edge of the signature on the concertina paper.

Move the triangle 1" (2.5 cm) to the right and score another line 1" (2.5 cm) to the right of the first line.

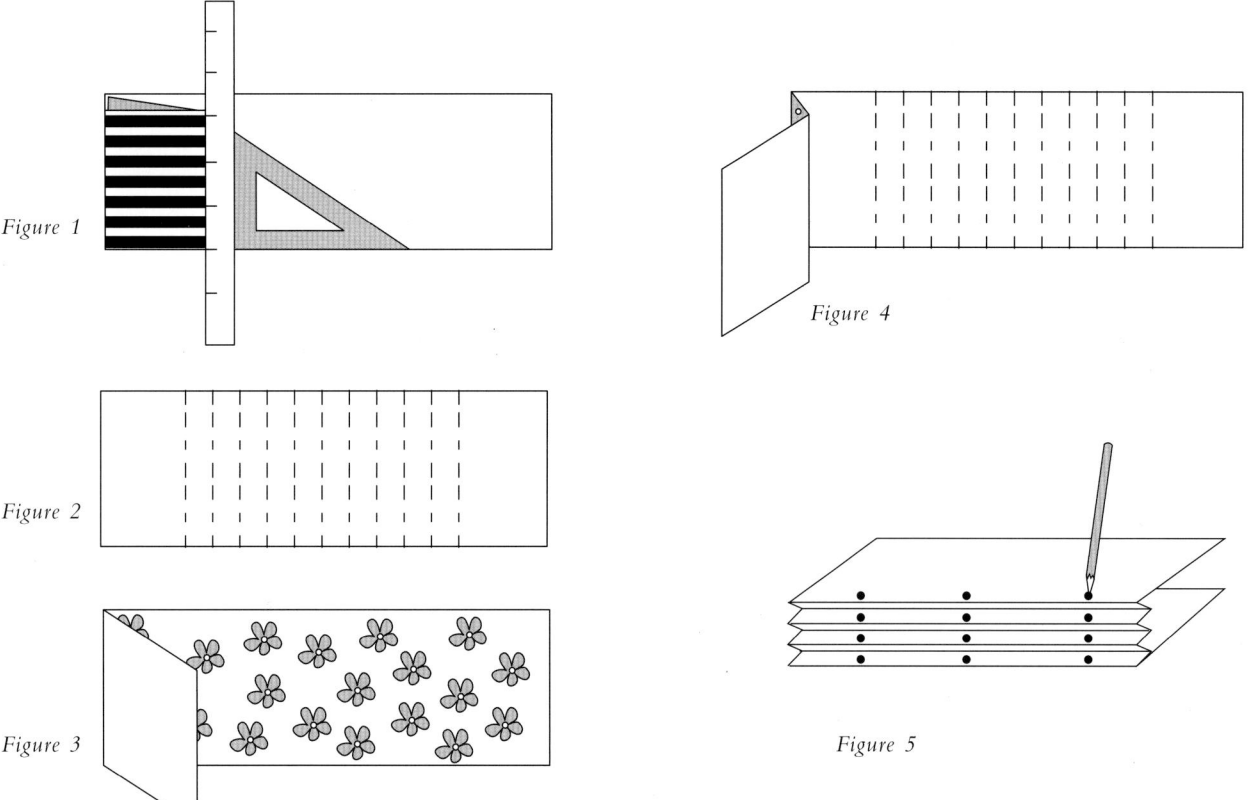

Figure 1

Figure 2

Figure 3

Figure 4

Figure 5

Continue scoring lines until you have scored 2 lines for every signature *minus* 1 line. For example, if there are 6 signatures in your book, you will score 12 minus 1, or 11 lines. There should be a piece of decorative paper left that is the same width as the top page of a signature (figure 2).

Turn the paper over, decorative surface facing up. Fold along the first scored line to the left (figure 3). Turn the paper over and fold the next scored line in the opposite direction (figure 4). Turn the paper over again and fold the next line the opposite way. Continue folding back and forth, accordion style, until all scored lines are folded, making sure to keep the line at the top of the long piece of paper perfectly straight. All the pleats need to be the same size.

3 • To sew the signatures into the concertina and to each other, first fold up the concertina and press it closed. Pencil in lines across all the folds in the four locations shown in figure 5.

Open out the concertina. Place a signature all the way inside the first fold. Open both the signature and the concertina fold and use the awl to punch small holes through the con-

certina paper and all pages of the signature at the same time. Be careful to keep everything perfectly lined up. Place cardboard under the pile to make it easier to punch holes. Remove the signature and pile it back up to make it easier to handle the next concertina and signature combination.

Cut a piece of waxed thread as long as the length of a signature times the number of signatures. Add a couple of feet for good measure. Thread the needle. Do not knot the thread. Pick up the first signature and place it inside the concertina at its first fold. Stick the needle into the first hole at the bottom from the outside (the concertina side) and pull the thread until there is a tail left that is about 4" (10 cm) long (figure 6). You are now on the inside of the signature. Put the needle into the next hole up, and, while holding the tail, pull the thread taut. *Be sure to pull thread parallel to the spine of the signature to avoid tearing the paper.* Now from the outside, put the needle into the third hole and pull the thread taut. Next, from the inside, put the needle into the top hole and pull the thread taut.

Pick up the second signature and

put it inside the second pleat. Put the needle into the top hole of the second signature from the outside and pull the thread taut, thereby joining the first and second signatures and pulling their concertina folds together. You are now on the inside of the second signature. Put the needle into the second hole from the top and come out. Pull the thread taut. Place the needle from the outside into the second hole from the top of the *first* signature, thereby joining the two signatures again. Pull the thread from the inside of the first signature and put the needle into the next hole down. You will come out of the first signature at the third hole down. Put the needle into the third hole down of the second signature from the outside. Pull the thread taut. From the inside of the second signature, put the needle into the last, or bottom, hole. When you come out, pull the thread taut and then tie the thread, *without cutting it,* to the tail that is hanging at the bottom hole of the first signature. This knot ties the two signatures together and completes the joining of the first two concertina folds (figure 7).

Pick up the third signature, put it in place, and put the needle into the

Figure 6   Figure 7

Figure 8

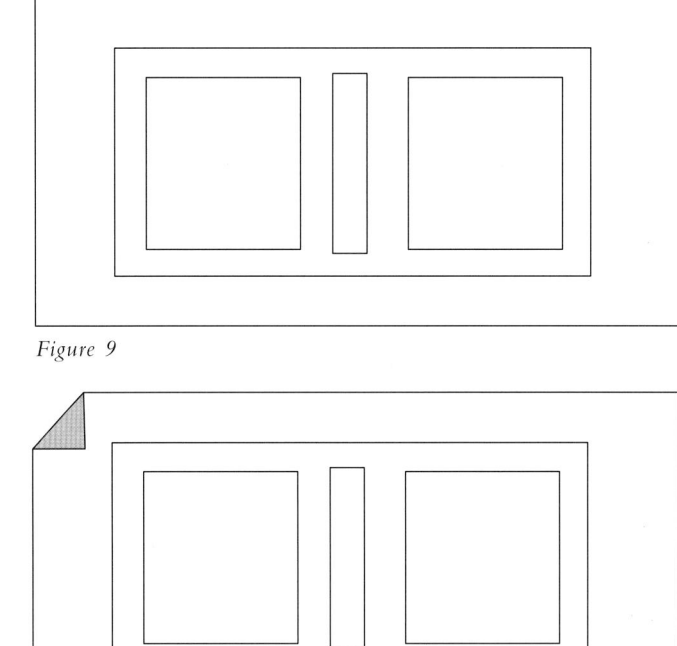

Figure 9

Figure 10

bottom hole, from the outside. Sew this signature to the second signature, just as you sewed the first two together. The only difference is that when you come out of the top (last) hole of the third signature, instead of tying the thread to a tail, you will scoop the needle under the top stitch that is already in place between the first and second signatures, and then reach across and go into the top hole of the fourth signature. Sew all the other signatures and concertina pleats together in this manner. When the last signature is in place, tie off the thread on the outside and trim to ¼" (1 cm). You call the sewn together signatures the *text block*.

4▪ To make the cover, measure and cut front and back covers so that they are ¼" (1 cm) longer and ½" (1 cm) wider than the text block. Use a ruler and triangle to be sure measurements are accurate and lines are perfectly straight and make all cuts with the craft knife. Cut a board for the spine of the book the same length as the front and back cover boards. Gently press down on the closed text block and measure the thickness of the slightly compressed pages. Cut the

spine board ⅛" (3 mm) wider than the compressed text block.

5▪ The cover cloth can be treated to make it stain resistant and to keep it from absorbing too much glue. Take the cloth outside and spray the side that will be on the outside of the cover with fabric-treatment, and let it dry. Place the cloth on a table with the inside of the cloth facing up. Apply acrylic gel medium liberally to the entire surface and let it dry.

6▪ Lay the boards out on the wrong side of the cover cloth as shown in figure 8. The spacing between the front and back covers and the spine is critical: It must be equal to 1½ times the board thicknesses. Draw a pencil line 1" (2.5 cm) from all board edges and cut out the cloth along this line (figure 9).

7▪ Pencil a line 1" (2.5 cm) up from the bottom edge of the cover. Place the cover boards in position along this line. Mark where each board will be glued, being careful to allow 1½ board thicknesses between the cover boards and spine board. Remove the boards and apply glue to the entire piece of

cloth. Lay all three boards in position on the glue.

8▪ Beginning with the upper left corner, fold the cloth down on a diagonal and press it in place (figure 10). Apply extra glue to the unglued surfaces that appear on the folded area. Now fold the upper right corner in the same way and add extra glue. Carefully fold the entire flap of cloth down over the tops of the cover and spine boards and press the folded cloth into place. Be sure to rub every bit of the surface so that the cloth is completely glued to the boards as well as to itself in the spaces between the boards. Repeat this step with the two bottom corners. Then fold and glue the side edges in the same manner (figure 11, page 46). Turn the cover over and rub the entire surface with a dry rag to help the cloth stick.

9▪ To glue the text block and bookmark into the cover, open out the cover so that the inside is facing up. Run a thin line of glue in the middle of the spine board from the top down about 4" (10 cm). Place 4" (10 cm) of one end of the ribbon along this glue (figure 11, page 46).

Figure 11

Figure 12

10• Place a piece of waxed paper inside the concertina cover on the front of the text block. Apply glue to the entire outside of the paper. Quickly, before the glue dries, place the spine of the text block against the spine of the cover, lining it up exactly. Peel the glued paper down and press it inside the cover board (figure 12). Rub all over the page to make sure it is completely adhered. Place a clean piece of waxed paper between the

inside cover and the first page of the text block, and close the book, with the glued side down. Now open the back cover. Place a sheet of waxed paper between the concertina cover and the last page of the text block. Brush glue over the entire concertina cover, just as you did on the front cover. Position the text block and front cover so that the spine is flat on the table. Press the glued paper inside the back cover. Put a clean piece of waxed paper between the cover and the text block. Open and close the book a couple of times to be sure everything is correctly lined up. Then close the book and let it dry (with the waxed paper still in place) under a few heavy books overnight. Trim the bookmark.

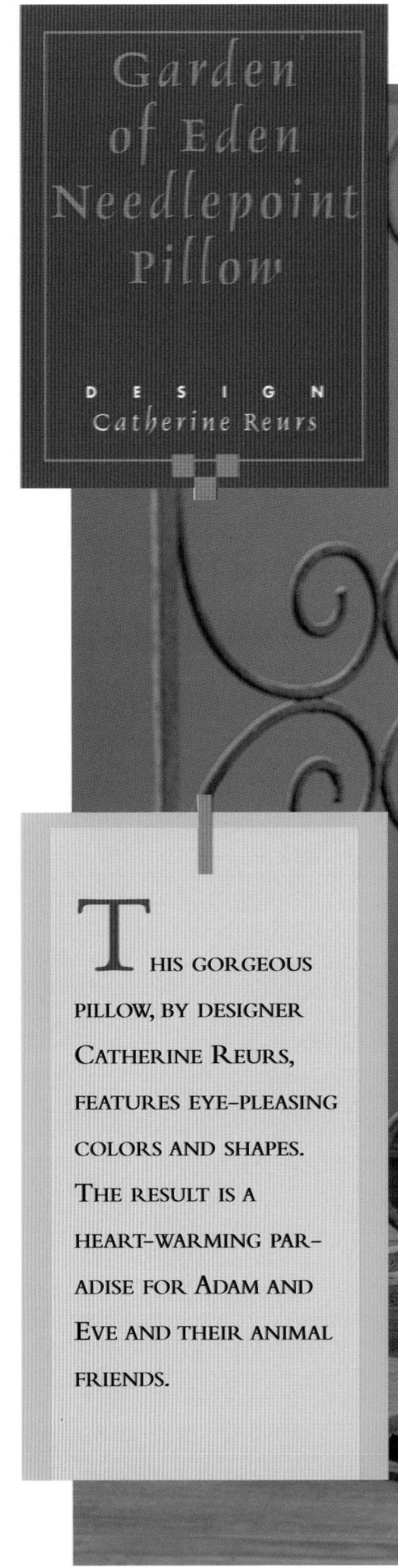

Garden of Eden Needlepoint Pillow

DESIGN
Catherine Reurs

THIS GORGEOUS PILLOW, BY DESIGNER CATHERINE REURS, FEATURES EYE-PLEASING COLORS AND SHAPES. THE RESULT IS A HEART-WARMING PARADISE FOR ADAM AND EVE AND THEIR ANIMAL FRIENDS.

GARDEN OF EDEN NEEDLEPOINT PILLOW (*photo on page 47*)

SIZE
16¾" x 16¾"
(43 x 43 cm)
201 sts wide x
201 sts high

❖ Materials and Tools

10 colors of Paternayan Persian tapestry wool

12-mesh cotton needlepoint canvas 21" x 21" (54 x 54 cm)

size 18 tapestry needle

pillow filling

velveteen backing fabric

twisted cord trim

❖ Instructions

FOLLOWING THE CHART

Follow the charts on pages 129 and 130, using the color key on page 129.

WORKING THE DESIGN

Use continental stitch throughout. Separate and use 2 plies of Paternayan Persian wool in your needle (Persian wool comes as 3 plies twisted together).

FINISHING THE PILLOW

Choose backing fabric that matches one of the background colors in the needlepoint. Trim the edges of the canvas to within 1" (2.5 cm) of the needlepoint stitches. Using a piece of the backing fabric cut to the same size as the trimmed needlepoint, place back and front pieces with the right sides together. Stitch between the first and second row of needlepoint stitches, leaving an opening on the bottom for inserting the pillow filling. Turn the pillow right side out, insert the pillow filling, turn the edges of the opening, and slip stitch together (or put in a zipper). If desired, sew twisted cord trim over the seam that joins the pillow front to the backing fabric.

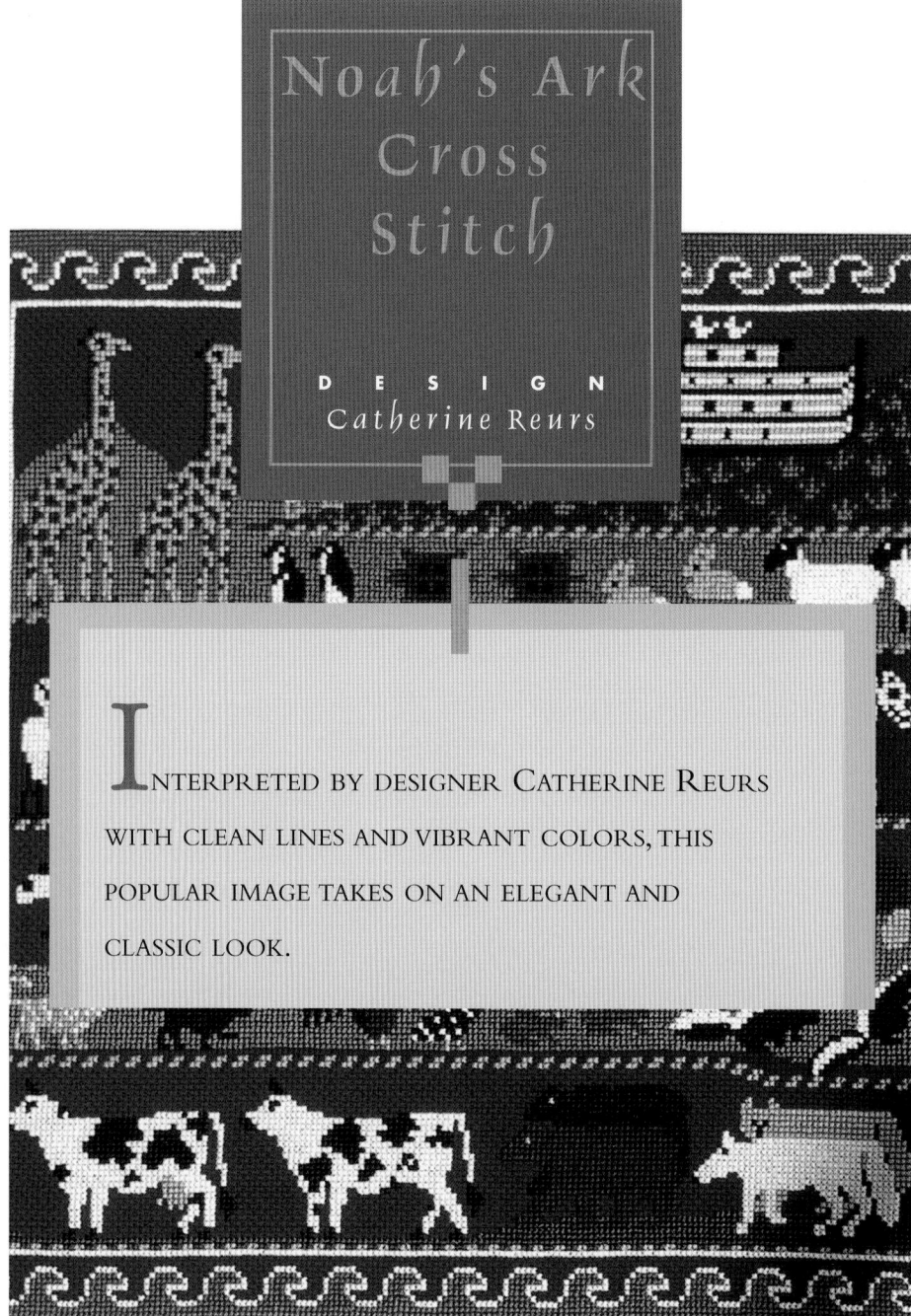

Noah's Ark Cross Stitch

DESIGN
Catherine Reurs

INTERPRETED BY DESIGNER CATHERINE REURS WITH CLEAN LINES AND VIBRANT COLORS, THIS POPULAR IMAGE TAKES ON AN ELEGANT AND CLASSIC LOOK.

❖ Materials and Tools

10 colors of DMC or Anchor embroidery floss

14-count cross stitch fabric 22" x 22" (56.5 x 56.5 cm)★

cross stitch needles

★14-count Zweigart Aida royal blue cloth (3706-567) was used here

❖ Instructions

FOLLOWING THE CHART

Follow the charts on pages 134 and 135, using the color key on page 134.

WORKING THE DESIGN

Separate and use 3 plies of embroidery floss in your needle (floss comes as 6 plies twisted together).

Designer Reflections

I recommend having your finished cross stitch professionally framed using acid-free materials. There is a thrill (well worth the cost!) of sending off a misshapen piece of needlework and, weeks later, receiving a perfectly finished piece.

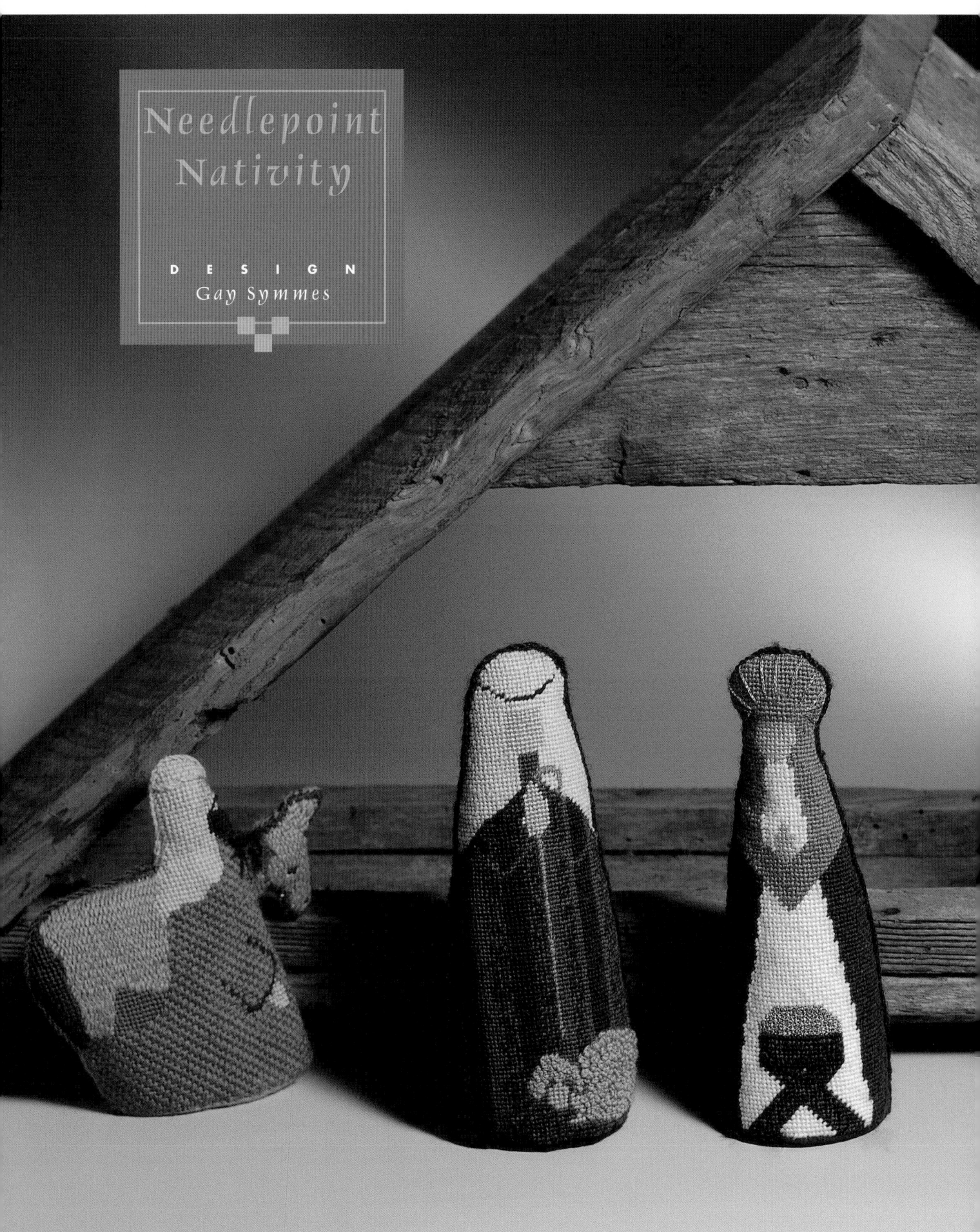

Needlepoint Nativity

DESIGN
Gay Symmes

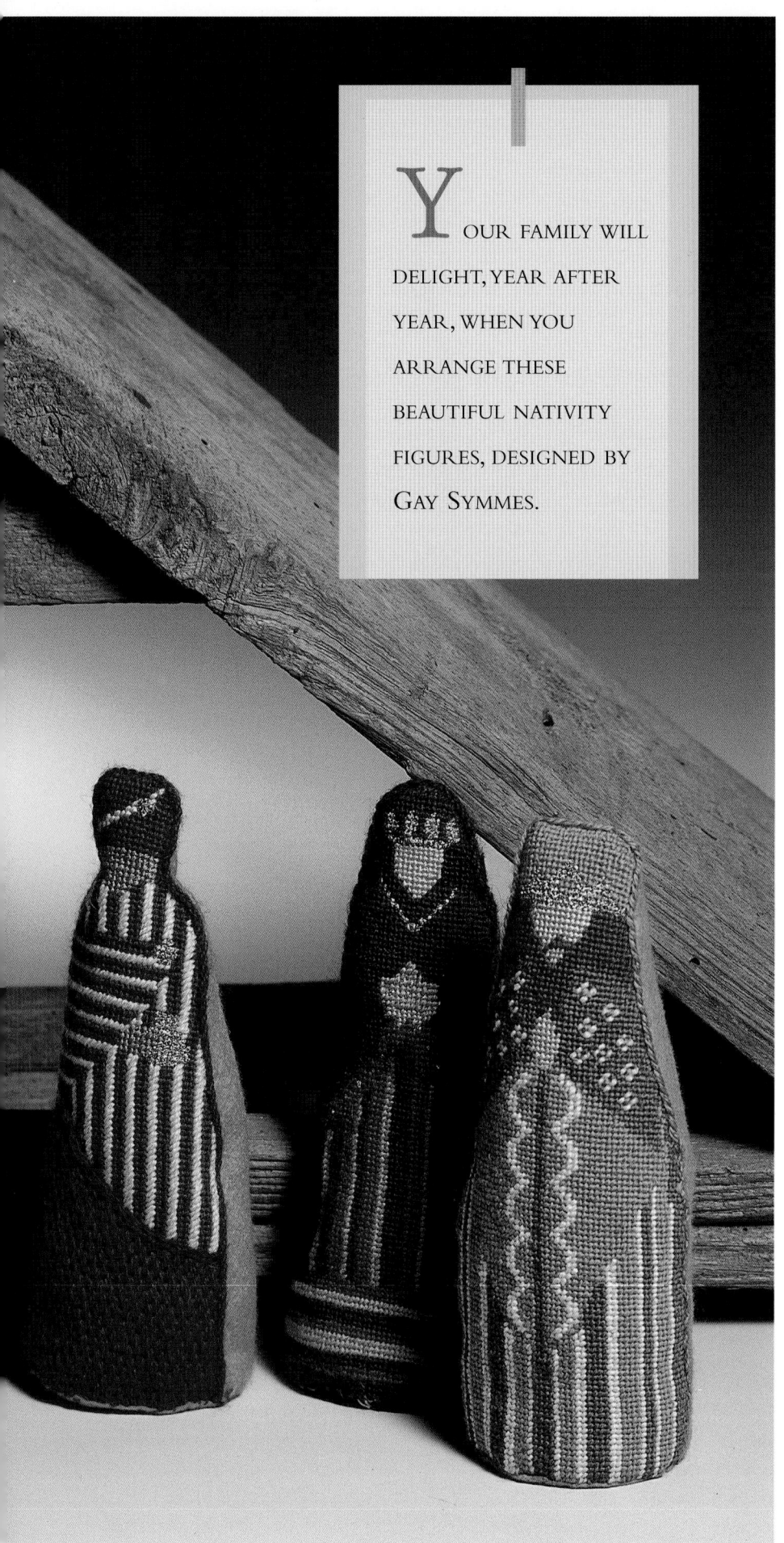

Y OUR FAMILY WILL DELIGHT, YEAR AFTER YEAR, WHEN YOU ARRANGE THESE BEAUTIFUL NATIVITY FIGURES, DESIGNED BY GAY SYMMES.

Materials and Tools

3-ply tapestry wool in the following colors:

light blue, dark blue, white, cream, dark brown, light brown, dark gray, light gray, rust, gold, pink, emerald green, light green, dark purple, and light purple

metallic gold embroidery floss

12-mesh cotton needlepoint canvas 22" x 22" (56.5 x 56.5 cm)

#18 tapestry needle

stuffing material

felt to match each figure

hand-sewing needle

piece of cardboard

scissors

craft glue

Instructions

1 ▪ Trace the six painted figures (page 52) and enlarge them on a copier. Then transfer the patterns to the canvas.

2 ▪ For all stitches, use 2 strands of the 3-ply wool. Specific stitches are suggested for each figure, but you may substitute basketweave throughout. It's best to work all six figures before cutting the canvas. However, if you decide to cut them into separate pieces, be sure to do so evenly, and tape the unfinished edge.

3 ▪ When the needlework is complete, block the canvas. Cut the stitched figures apart, leaving a ½" (1.5 cm) margin of unworked canvas around each figure. Fold this back and steam, tack, and clip as needed.

4 ▪ Use the needlepoint figures as patterns to cut felt in complementary colors. With scraps of matching wool, slip stitch the felt to the figures, sewing wrong sides together. Leave

SHEPHERD

Work in basketweave throughout. For the cloak, work the stripes in varying widths using dark brown for one stripe and a mixture of 1 strand dark gray and 1 strand dark brown for the next. After stitching the lamb, use 1 strand of light gray and add French knots to make the fur look curly.

RUST WISE MAN

Work the cloak in rust and cream stripes with a single stitch over 2 rows of canvas. After the needlework is done, add gold metallic thread to create an ornament on the turban and a button on the cloak. Work the lower half of the cloak in diagonal mosaic stitch or basketweave.

PURPLE WISE MAN

Use basketweave throughout. Use gold metallic thread for the crown and to create the necklace on top of the stitched cloak. Add dots of metallic thread, also, to accent the robe and the gift he holds in his hands.

GREEN WISE MAN

Use basketweave throughout. Use metallic thread for the crown. The design on top of the cloak may be worked in as you go or may be added on top of the completed work.

the bottom of each figure open. Fill the figures with stuffing material. (*Tip:* Shredded nylon stockings work well.) Cut 6 cardboard circles and 6 felt circles to fit the bottoms of the figures. Glue a cardboard circle to a felt circle and then slip stitch the stiffened circle to the bottom of each figure. A final optional step is to cover the side seams with a very finely twisted length of yarn.

MARY

Use basketweave throughout. Outline the Baby's bed with dark brown, then work the boards with a mixture of 1 strand brown and 1 strand dark gray to give the look of weathered wood. Work Mary's halo in gold wool, then add the diagonal lines in metallic gold thread on top of the wool. You may use the same method for the Baby's, halo or you may work it entirely in metallic thread. (This type of thread tends to twist and snag more easily than needlepoint wool and should be worked in shorter lengths.)

JOSEPH

Work his coat in diagonal mosaic stitch to give it a rough look. Outline the sleeve in dark gray. Use basketweave for his beard, mantle, and face. Work the donkey within the outline in encroached Gobelin, then add a bit of dark gray fringe to create the donkey's fringe.

Dove Sweater

DESIGN
Nola Theiss

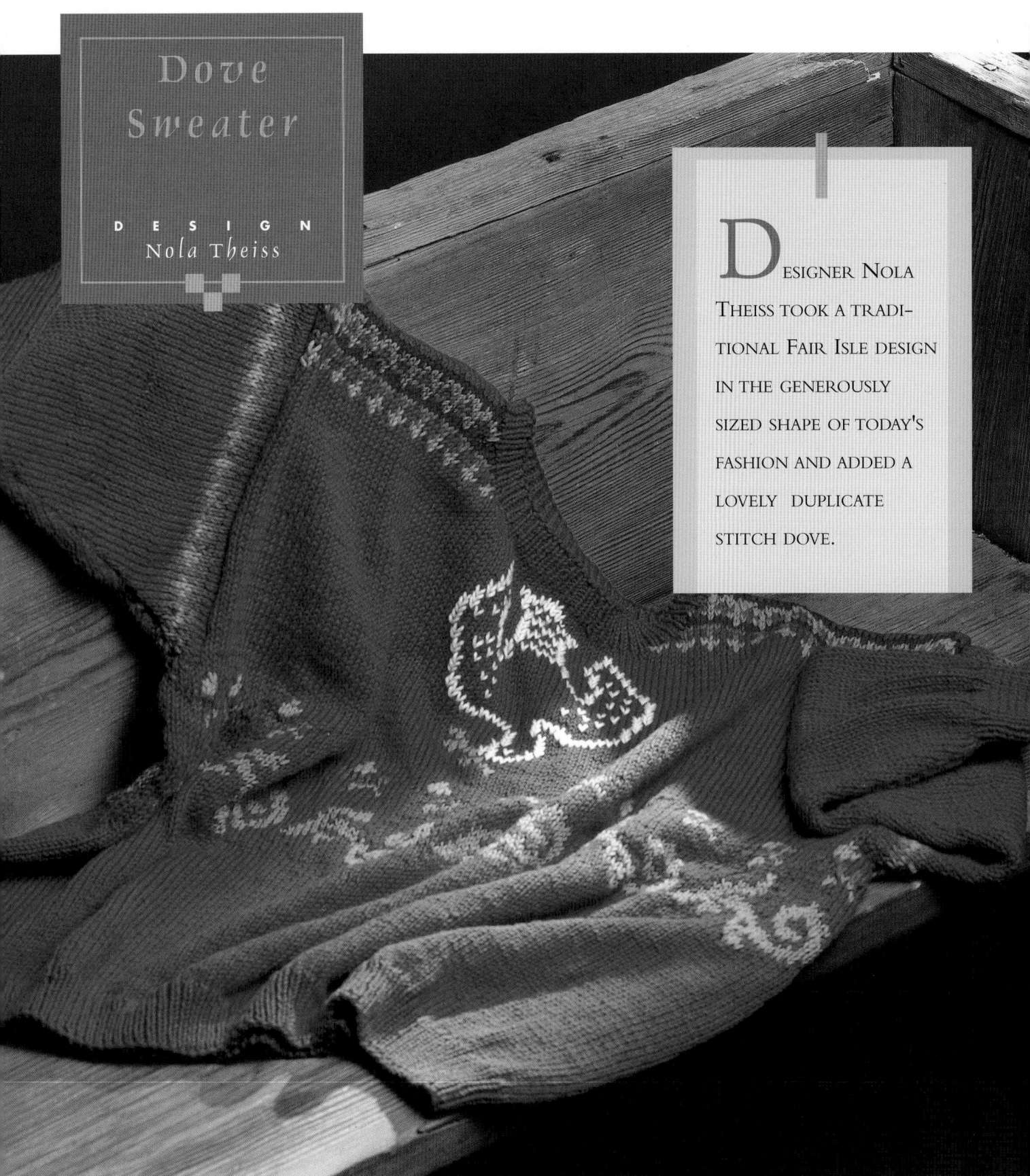

DESIGNER NOLA THEISS TOOK A TRADI-TIONAL FAIR ISLE DESIGN IN THE GENEROUSLY SIZED SHAPE OF TODAY'S FASHION AND ADDED A LOVELY DUPLICATE STITCH DOVE.

SIZE
Medium (Large)
Finished bust measurements:
44" (52"), (113 cm, 133.5 cm)
FINISHED LENGTH
24" (25"), (62 CM, 64 CM)

⚜ Materials and Tools

50 g = approx. 120 yds sport weight cotton:

★11 (13) blue balls - MC

★1 ball each deep red - A, lavender - B, strawberry - C, bright pink - D, green - E, white - F

knitting needles in sizes 3 and 5 U.S. (3.25 mm and 3.75 mm)

circular knitting needles in sizes 3 and 5 U.S. (3.25 mm and 3.75 mm), 36"-39" (92.5-100 cm) long, and 16" (41 cm) long

stitch holders

GAUGE

U.S. size 5 (3.75 mm) needles in St st: 4" (10 cm) = 22 sts x 30 rows

TO SAVE TIME, TAKE TIME TO CHECK YOUR GAUGE!

CHARTS ARE ON PAGES 131 and 132.

⚜ Instructions

BODY

1 ▪ With smaller size circular needle and MC, cast on 220 (268) sts and work 2" (5 cm) in 1/1 ribbing. Work in rounds, being sure not to twist sts. Knit 1 round, inc 20 sts evenly spaced around = 240 (288) sts.

2 ▪ Change to larger size circular needle and work St st. Mark beg of round and mark after the 120th (144th) st. When the piece measures 9" (10") (23 cm, 26 cm) from the beg, work by following chart A. Carry unused yarn loosely across wrong side of work.

3 ▪ When chart A is complete, work 1 round in St st in MC, then divide work at markers. Place half the sts on a holder and continue with MC on remaining sts. Bind off 4 sts at beg of next two rows = 112 (136) sts. Work in St st for 8" (21 cm) [60 rows] from division of front and back, dec 1 st on first row = 111 (135) sts.

4 ▪ Continue by working chart B. On the 10th row of chart B, shape neck. Bind off center 45 (53) sts. Place sts of left half on holder. Work sts of right shoulder continuing chart. At neck edge on 2nd row, dec 1 st. When chart is complete, work 2 rows in MC. Piece will measure 24" (25"), (62 cm, 64 cm) from beg. Bind off rem 32 (40) sts. Pick up sts from left shoulder and work to correspond.

5 ▪ Front: Pick up 120 (144) sts from holder and bind off 4 sts at beg of next 2 rows, dec 1 st on first row = 111 (135) sts. Work back and forth in MC in St st for 60 rows.

6 ▪ Shape neck: bind off center 21 (29) sts. Place sts of left shoulder on holder. Continue by working chart B on sts of right shoulder. At the same time, at each neck edge, every 2nd row, bind off 3 sts twice, bind off 2 sts twice, dec 1 st 3 times. When chart is complete, work 2 rows in MC, then bind off rem 32 (40) sts. Pick up sts of left shoulder and work to correspond.

SLEEVES

7 ▪ With smaller size needles and MC, cast on 46 (50) sts and work 2" (5 cm) in 1/1 ribbing. Inc 14 sts evenly spaced across last row = 60 (64) sts. Change to larger size needles and work in St st. At the same time, at each edge of every 4th row, inc 1 st 20 times. At each edge of every 2nd row, inc 1 st 11 (9) times = 122 sts. At the same time, when sleeve measures 15½" (14½"), (40 cm, 37.5 cm) from beg, work by following chart C. When chart is complete, work 4 rows of St st in MC. Bind off all sts.

FINISHING

8 ▪ With E and F, duplicate stitch dove motif by following chart D, centering on back and front over 60 rows of St st section above chart A, beg top edge of dove 1 row below neckband on front, and 2 rows below chart B on back. (Figures 1, 2, 3, and 4 illustrate the basics of duplicate stitch.) Sew shoulder seams.

Figure 1

Figure 1

Figure 1

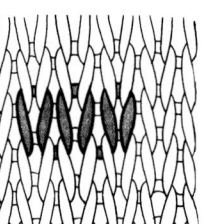

Figure 1

NECKBAND

9 ▪ With smaller size circular needle and MC, pick up and knit 118 (134) sts around neck and work 1" (2.5 cm) in rounds of 1/1 ribbing. Bind off loosely. Sew sleeves to armholes, sewing top 1" (2.5 cm) of sleeve seam to bound off edge of armhole edge. Sew sleeve seams. Press seams lightly.

⚜ Key to Abbreviations

MC = Main Color

1/1 = 1 knit, 1 purl

st or sts = stitch or stitches

St st= stockinette stitch

beg = beginnin

inc = increase

dec = decrease

rem = remaining

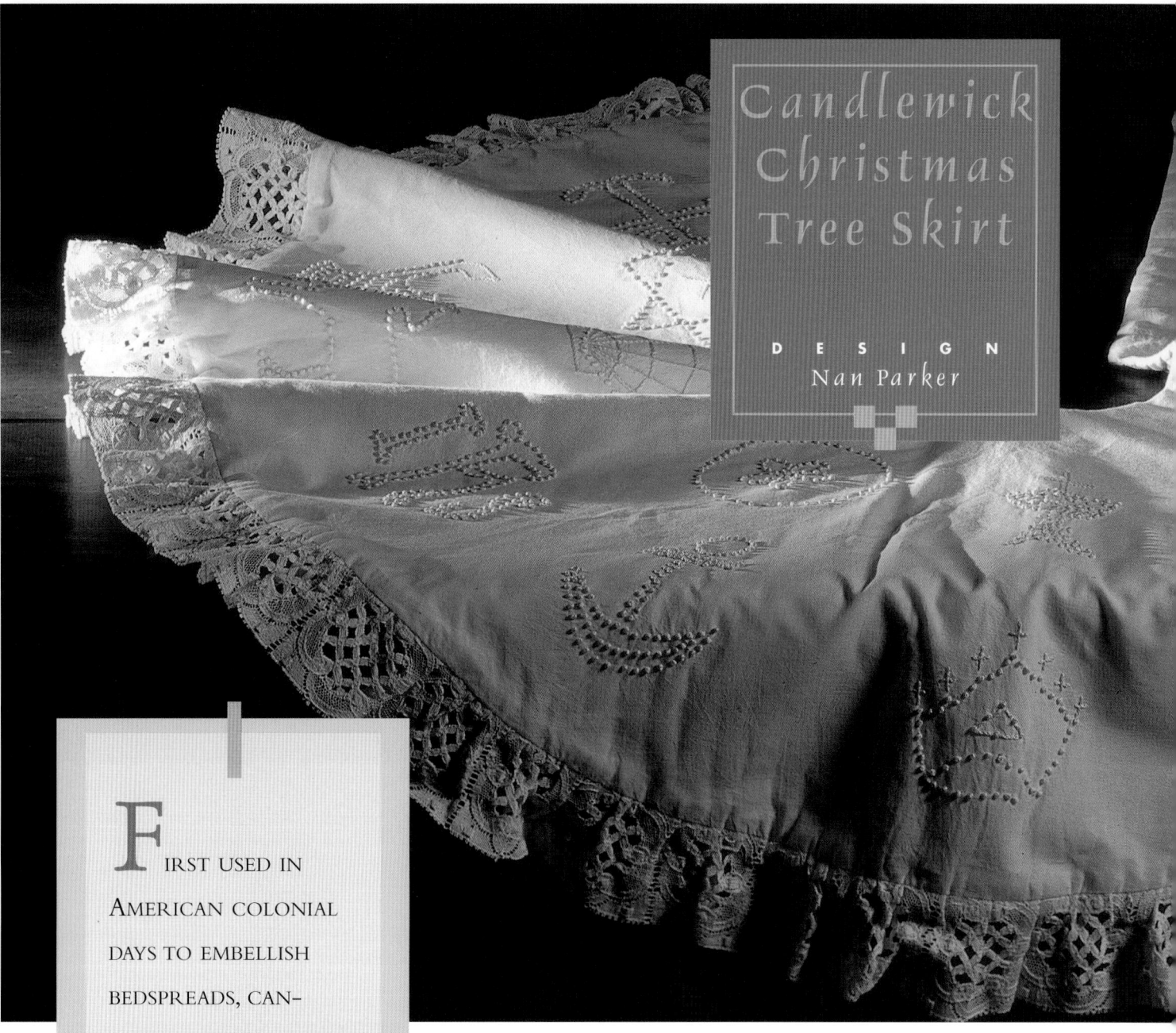

Candlewick Christmas Tree Skirt

DESIGN
Nan Parker

FIRST USED IN AMERICAN COLONIAL DAYS TO EMBELLISH BEDSPREADS, CAN-DLEWICK EMBROIDERY LENDS A DRESSY AND DISTINCTIVE LOOK TO FABRIC, AS DEMON-STRATED IN THIS GOR-GEOUS TREE SKIRT, DESIGNED BY NAN PARKER.

SIZE
60" (1.5 m) in diameter

Materials and Tools

1½ yds. (137 cm) heavy-weight white cotton, 54" (137 cm) wide★

1½ yds. (137 cm) batting, 54" (137 cm) wide

8 yds. (7.35 m) ruffled cluny lace

6 balls (50 yds./46 m) of size 5 pearl cotton thread

large embroidery hoop

#20 chenille needle

blue, water-soluble transfer pen

scissors

heavy towels

iron

★or 1 yd. (91 cm) cotton, 36" (91 cm) wide, for a small tree skirt

✥ Instructions

1 ▪ Cut out two circles from the cotton fabric.

2 ▪ Make a cut to the center of both circles and cut a small circle in the center of both circles.

3 ▪ Enlarge the Christian symbols (pages 132 and 133) on a copier to the desired size. Use the transfer pen to trace the dot patterns onto the right side of one of the fabric circles (see method #1 on page 7).

4 ▪ Embroider all the candlewick knots, using French knots or colonial knots.

5 ▪ Remove the embroidered fabric from the embroidery hoop and immerse it in cold water to remove the blue marks. Roll it in a towel to remove excess moisture. Place the fabric right side down on thick bath towels and iron until dry, being careful not to scorch the fabric.

6 ▪ Trim the thread tails or thread ends.

7 ▪ Cut the batting the same size as the fabric circle. Hand-baste the batting to the wrong side of the embroidered circle.

8 ▪ Pin and baste the ruffled lace, right sides together, to the outer edge of the embroidered skirt.

9 ▪ Pin on the other circle (the skirt backing), right sides together. Leave an opening about 8" (21 cm) long as shown in figure 1.

10 ▪ Machine-stitch, trim, and turn. Hand-baste the opening. Press.

Figure 1

DESIGNER DEE
DEE TRIPLETT
TENDERLY DEPICTS THE
HOLY FAMILY BY
COMBINING FABRIC
PAINT, GENTLY SHADED
YARN, AND SIMPLE
EMBROIDERY
TECHNIQUES.

❖ Materials and Tools

20" x 24" (51 x 62 cm) linen or other textured background fabric

16" x 20" (41 x 51 cm) artist's stretcher strips

thumb tacks or staple gun

fabric paints

paintbrushes

5" x 5" (13 x 13 cm) flesh-colored synthetic suede

ultra-fine permanent brown marker

colored pencils in dark flesh and pink

crewel needles

mixed wool threads—three colors and three values of each color

several bright accent yarns to complement main colors

sewing thread to match

5" x 5" (13 x 13 cm) gold tissue lamé

5" x 5" (13 x 13 cm) lightweight, iron-on interfacing

gold thread

12" (31 cm) of ⅛" (6 mm) gold braid

❖ Instructions

1 ▪ Enlarge and trace the patterns onto the background fabric (method #2, page 7). Attach the fabric to stretcher strips, keeping the grain straight.

2 ▪ With fabric paints, lightly color in the areas for the figures, robes, and straw. (These paints will run if you thin them with too much water.) To suggest fabric folds, aim for uneven coverage. Let dry.

3 ▪ Use the pattern to cut out synthetic suede faces. Draw in the features with brown pen and colored pencils. (Pens take longer to dry on synthetic suede than on more absorbent fabric.) Appliqué the faces in place on the background.

4 ▪ For Mary, lay down strands of blue yarn in lines to suggest folds in her robe. Couch the yarn with matching sewing thread and leave the background unstitched, except in areas of shadow. Fill in the the shadowed areas with split stitches. Stitch her neck area in white yarn using Bokhara couching.

5 ▪ For Joseph, fill in all his clothing with split stitches. Stitch his neck area in white yarn using Bokhara couching. Use French knots for the beard, made with one strand of yarn and three wraps around the needle.

6 ▪ Fill in baby Jesus's garment with split stitches.

7 ▪ For the straw, lay down lines of yarn, and couch or split stitch to hold it in place.

8 ▪ For the halo, fuse lamé to the interfacing. Use a pressing cloth and low heat to avoid melting the lamé. Cut out the halo. Using gold thread, appliqué the halo in place. Cover the lower edge of the halo with additional yarn in adjacent colors, if necessary to cover the bottom edges. Stitch ⅛" (6 mm) braid around the edge of Jesus's head and halo.

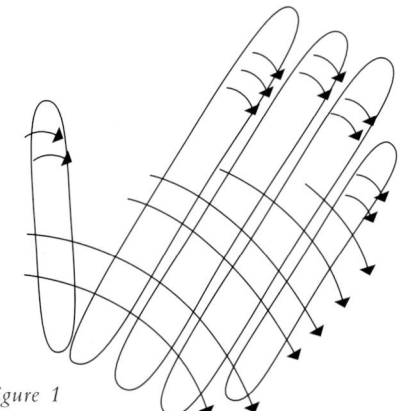

Figure 1

❖ Designer Reflections

I used yarns in straw, soft red, blue, and amethyst, and tiny amounts of bright pink and lavender yarns as accents. I angled the needle in the direction of the stitch when coming up through the background, as well as when going into an existing stitch. Lines of stitching should conform to the shape they describe; generally, this means curving lines rather than straight ones. The direction of stitching lines are suggested in the pattern. I also combined two colors of yarn in the needle to create gentle shading. For the hands and fingers, I stitched a base of thick yarn, then stitched each finger with a flesh color. The palms were stitched diagonally across, as shown in figure 1.

(ENLARGE BY 160%)

59

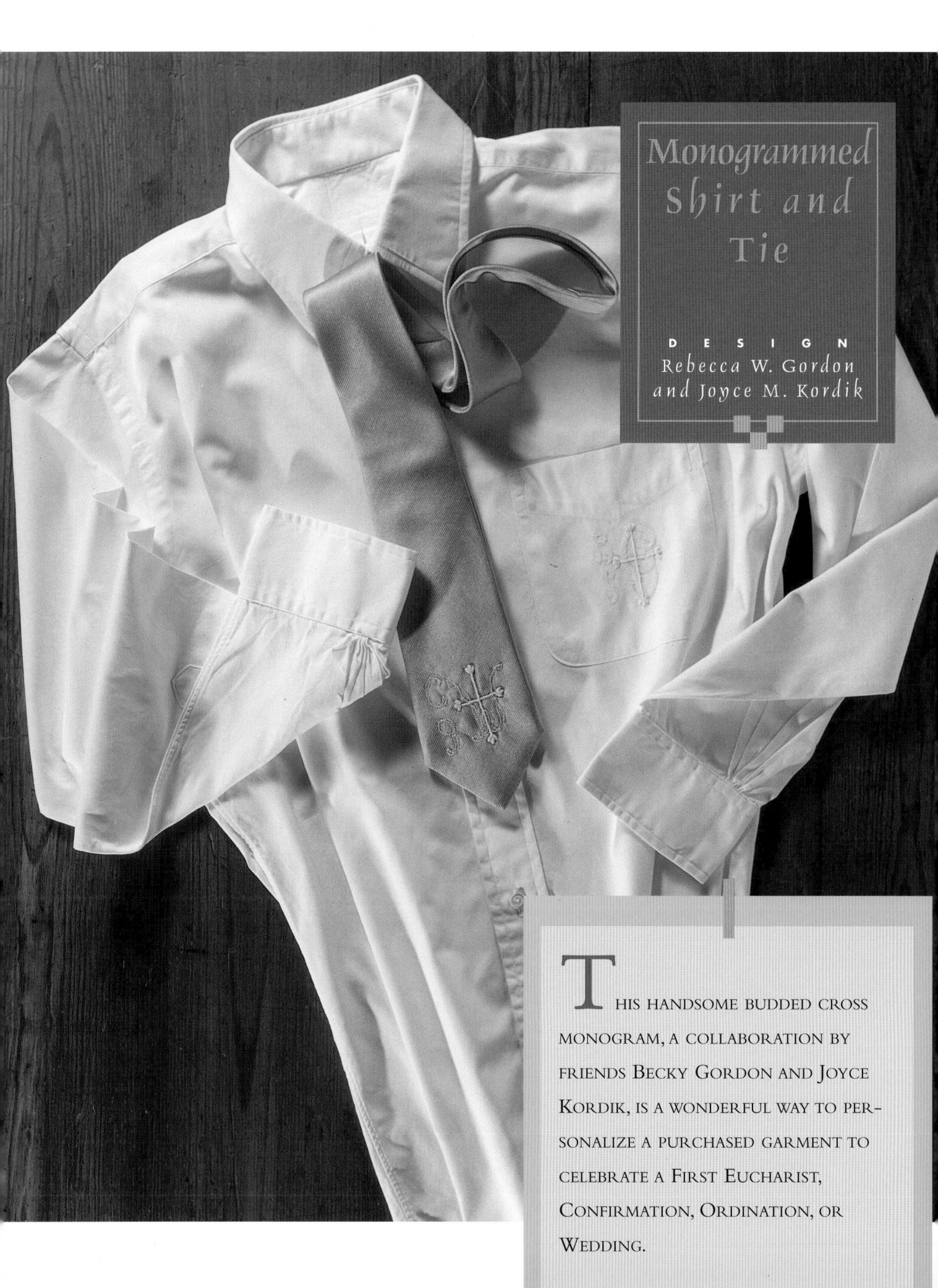

Monogrammed Shirt and Tie

DESIGN

Rebecca W. Gordon
and Joyce M. Kordik

THIS HANDSOME BUDDED CROSS MONOGRAM, A COLLABORATION BY FRIENDS BECKY GORDON AND JOYCE KORDIK, IS A WONDERFUL WAY TO PERSONALIZE A PURCHASED GARMENT TO CELEBRATE A FIRST EUCHARIST, CONFIRMATION, ORDINATION, OR WEDDING.

Materials and Tools

fine-quality white cotton shirt and/or solid color silk tie

fabric stabilizer (for the tie)

embroidery floss

#26 tapestry needle

#7 crewel needle

embroidery hoop, 3" to 3½" (8 to 9 cm) in diameter

embroidery scissors

white paper

craft glue

#2 pencil

straight pins

water-soluble backing

fine-point black marker

Instructions

I ▪ Enlarge the three letters you need and the cross on a copier to the desired sizes (page 127). Cut around the letters and cross and glue them to a piece of paper, arranged to your satisfaction.

2 ▪ For the shirt: Trim the design so that you can place the piece of paper with the design on it inside the pocket. Pin it in place, straight and centered. With the pencil, trace the design onto the fabric. Your stitching will cover these lines. Remove the pins and paper and you are ready to stitch.

3 ▪ For the tie: Because the tie is silk, pencil marks and other forms of transfer medium may be difficult to remove. For this reason, the following method of transfer is recommended. With the black marker, trace the design onto a piece of water-soluble backing and pin in place. Baste the stabilizer in place or leave pinned. Proceed to stitch your design; when you are finished, gently tear away the stabilizer.

4 ▪ The designers used trailing, padded satin buds, shadow work, and backstitch.

Trailing is a tiny, firm satin stitch worked over a core of 1, 2, or 3 strands of thread. Use of an embroidery hoop is optional. Thread your crewel needle with 1 strand of floss. *Do not* tie a knot in this thread. Begin your stitch ½" (1.5 cm) from the end of one arm of the cross. Do a running stitch towards the end of the arm to anchor your thread.

Remove the needle and lay the strand along the arm of the cross—this will cover your running stitch and pencil line, and will become your core thread.

Use a new, single-strand of floss in your crewel needle. Using a waste knot, begin stitching over your core thread, coming up one side of the core thread and down on the other encasing core thread. For a smooth finish, be sure your stitches are closely placed so they completely cover the core thread. To achieve the best results, enter and exit the fabric with the needle at an angle.

To tie off, sink the floss to the back of your work after your last stitch. Weave it under the back side of your stitching and clip it off. Re-thread the core thread, sink it to the back of your work, and clip it off. Don't worry about tying it off because it is secured by the surface stitching. Repeat this process to complete the cross.

5 ▪ *Padded Satin.* The leaf design on the ends of the budded cross were done in padded satin stitch. Use of an embroidery hoop is optional. Thread the crewel needle with 1 strand of floss and knot the end. Start with a waste knot. Make a lazy daisy stitch to outline the center bud. Make one long straight stitch inside the lazy daisy to pad it.

Work a satin stitch to cover the lazy daisy completely. Be careful while stitching to maintain the shape of the bud. Enter and exit with a slanted needle; this should look like a leaf resting on your fabric.

Repeat this process for the two flanking buds. End the stitching by sliding the needle under the stitches in back. Clip your waste knot.

6 ▪ Shadow Work. It is advisable to use an embroidery hoop for this stitch. The success of this stitch (which creates an unbroken line of stitches) depends on the needle re-entering holes made by previous stitches. A tapestry needle is used because it has a blunt tip which creates a hole that is easy to re-enter. The smaller the stitches, the greater the intensity of color that shadows through. An average stitch length is about $\frac{1}{16}$th of an inch or less. When working on a curved area such as these monograms, the stitches on the inside of the curves are shorter than the ones on the outside. Keeping this in mind, you want to have the same number of stitches on each side of the curve.

Thread your tapestry needle with 1 strand of floss. Knot the end and start with a waste knot.

Come up one stitch away from your starting point. The starting point will always be at one of the closed ends of the design.

Follow figure 1 to execute the stitch pattern. Start with A and work A to B, C to B, D to A, E to C, etc. Continue this pattern of stitching to complete the design.

To tie off, weave the needle through the herringbone stitches on the back and clip off the excess.

7 ▪ *Backstitch.* This stitch was used on the tie project to mimic shadow work, which cannot be done on a fabric that is not sheer. Backstitch is worked on one line at a time, starting at one end and working to the other. Maintain a short uniform stitch length. Use of an embroidery hoop is optional.

Figure 1

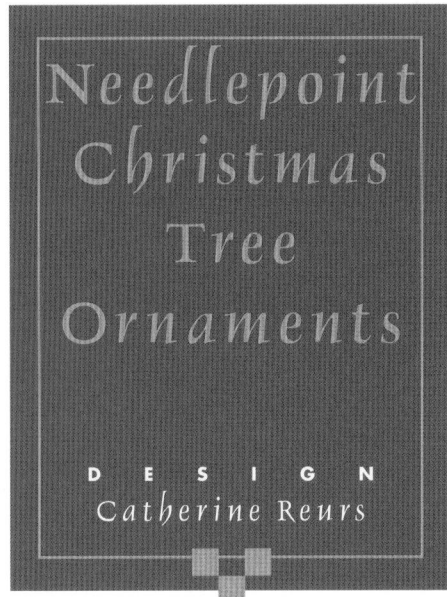

Needlepoint Christmas Tree Ornaments

DESIGN
Catherine Reurs

⊱ Materials and Tools

felt pen or grease pencil

scissors

thin colored ribbon or cord

felt or synthetic suede

hot-glue gun and glue stick

hand-sewing needle and thread

⊱ Instructions

1 ▪ Transfer the pattern onto the plastic canvas before you cut the canvas to size. Mark the outline of each piece on the canvas and count the bars in each piece to check it before cutting. Cut the space between the bars and trim off all the plastic nubs, then clean off the outline marks.

2 ▪ Refer to the charts and color keys (pages 136–137) and to the color photograph as you stitch. Start stitching in the center or in one corner. Stitch the details first, then fill in the background, and finish with the border.

3 ▪ Because the plastic canvas in rigid, your finished needlepoint will not need to be blocked. Create hangers for your ornament by sewing on ribbons. Then glue a piece of felt or synthetic suede to the back to finish them.

THESE GORGEOUS
ORNAMENTS SHIMMER
AND GLEAM THANKS TO
DESIGNER CATHERINE
REURS'S PASSION FOR
COMBINING METALLIC
FIBERS, SEQUINS, SHINY
BUTTONS, AND BEADS
WITH TRADITIONAL
NEEDLEPOINT YARNS.

Ewe with Lamb

SIZE
3¼" x 2¾" (8.5 x 7 cm)
32 sts wide x 28 sts high

ADDITIONAL SUPPLIES

10 colors of various fibers

10-mesh plastic canvas 4" x 4" (10 x 10 cm)

size 18 tapestry needle

WORKING THE DESIGN

Use continental stitch throughout with 1 strand of alpaca, patent leather, and all metallics in your needle. Use all 12 strands of Splendor Silk in your needle.

Christmas Tree

SIZE
3" x 3½" (8 x 9 cm)
41 stitches wide x
49 stitches high (including unstitched border rows)

ADDITIONAL SUPPLIES

3 colors of Madeira metallics and floss

14-mesh plastic canvas 4" x 4½" (10 x 11 cm)

size 22 tapestry needle

1 large gold star sequin, ½" (1.3 cm) wide

13 small round sequins, (6 mm)

12 star sequins (5 mm) in gold, red, blue, and silver

25 gold seed beads

17 white pearls (3 mm)

red sequin trim 20" (51 cm) long

WORKING THE DESIGN

Use continental stitch throughout with 6 strands of Madeira floss and 1 full strand (i.e. all the plies) of Madeira 'Glamour' in your needle.

After the entire design is stitched, sew on white pearl beads in the shape of a garland.Decorate the rest of the tree with round and star sequins, sewing 1 gold seed bead onto the center of each sequin. Baste the red sequin trimming over the unstitched rows on all four sides around the tree. Sew the large gold star sequin to the top of the tree and sew 1 gold seed bead in the center of the large star sequin.

Five-Pointed Star

SIZE
5¼" (13.5 cm)
54 stitches wide x
53 stitches high

⚒ Materials and Tools

2 colors of Kreinik metallics

10-mesh plastic canvas 6" x 6" (15 x 15 cm)

size 18 tapestry needle

1 round green jewel (¾"/2 cm)

5 round red, amber, blue and purple jewels (5"/13 cm)

aqua jewels (½"/1.5 cm)

5 diamond lozenge jewels (¾"/2 cm)

42 white pearls (5 mm)

115 white pearls (3 mm)

25 gold beads (6 mm)

WORKING THE DESIGN

Use continental stitch throughout with 2 full strands (i.e. all the plies) of Kreinik in your needle. After the entire design is stitched, hot-glue the round green jewel to the center of the star. Glue the 5 round jewels around the central green jewel, then glue the clear lozenge-shaped jewels to the five points of the star. Sew the small pearls around the edges of all the jewels, then sew on the gold beads.

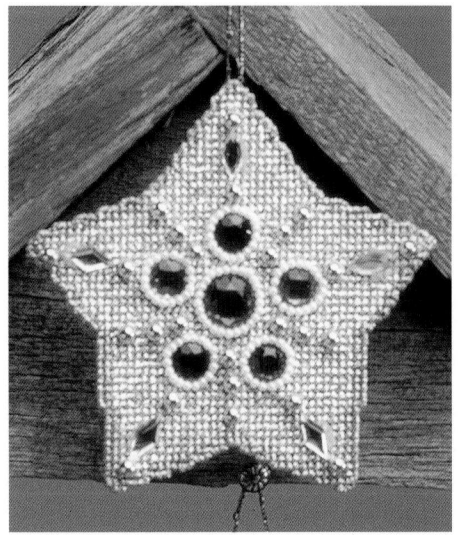

Greek Cross

SIZE
5" x 5" (13 x 13 cm)
49 sts wide x 49 sts high

ADDITIONAL SUPPLIES

2 colors of Kreinik metallics

10-mesh plastic canvas 6" x 6" (15 x 15 cm)

size 18 tapestry needle

1 oval red 'jewel' bead, 1" (2.5 cm) wide

4 oval clear 'jewels,' ¾" (2 cm) long

42 white pearls (5 mm)

40 white pearls (3 mm)

WORKING THE DESIGN

Use continental stitch throughout with 2 full strands (i.e. all the plies) of Kreinik in your needle. After the entire design is stitched, glue the red oval 'jewel' to the center of the cross. Glue the 4 clear 'jewels' to the centers of the four arms of the cross. Sew the large and small pearls around the edge of the red 'jewel' and the edges of the four arms of the cross.

Sheep

SIZE
3" x 3" (8 x 8 cm)
31 stitches wide x
31 stitches high

ADDITIONAL SUPPLIES

6 colors of fibers

10-mesh plastic canvas 4" x 4" (10 x 10 cm)

size 18 tapestry needle

4 miniature gold bells

WORKING THE DESIGN

Use continental stitch throughout with 2 strands (for each fiber) in your needle. After the entire design is stitched, sew 4 miniature bells over the green wreath area.

Painted wood; made in El Salvador

Jewelry & Beads

Crusader's Cross Amulet Pouch

DESIGN
Carole Tripp

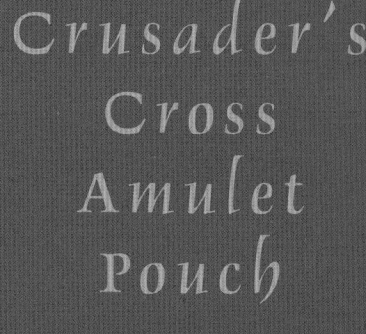

THIS MAGNIFI-
CENT AMULET POUCH,
BEADED WITHOUT A
LOOM, OFFERS YOU THE
CHANCE TO TRY A
CRAFT THAT HAS BEEN
PRACTICED FOR THOU-
SANDS OF YEARS BY
MANY DIVERSE CUL-
TURES. ARMED WITH
CAROLE TRIPP'S
DESIGN, YOU WILL BE
ABLE TO RE-CREATE
THIS STUNNING PIECE
OF BEADWORK.

Materials and Tools

2 grams ivory 11° cylinder seed beads★

4 grams bronze 11° CB

4 grams silver-lined 11° CB

12 grams black 11° CB

(15) 5 x 7 mm black matte faceted drops

(23) 5 x 7 mm light Colorado topaz faceted drops

(22) 4 mm pale yellow faceted beads

(11) 5 mm jet Austrian crystals

(2) 5 mm light Colorado topaz Austrian crystals

(4) 6 mm jet Austrian crystals

(2) 6 mm light Colorado topaz Austrian crystals

(5) 4 mm jet Austrian crystals

(2) 4 mm light Colorado topaz Austrian crystals

(4) 4 mm bronze metallic faceted beads

(5) 8 mm topaz German reproduction beads

(4) 6 mm round black onyx matte beads

(4) 4 mm black onyx rondels

nylon beading thread, sizes "O" and "B"

size 12 English beading needles

cardboard tube, such as an empty paper towel roll

scissors

cellophane tape

★ cylinder seed beads referred to throughout as CB

Instructions

I ▪ *Beading the pouch:* The body of the pouch is done using *even-count tubular Peyote*, worked three-dimensionally on a removable form, such as a cardboard tube (or with no supporting form).

2 ▪ Thread a needle and string with 58 black CB, using size "O" beading thread, doubled (figure 1). Do not loop or knot the first bead. Slide the beads to within 6" (15 cm) of the end of the thread and tie the thread ends together with two square knots; leave a 2- to 3-bead space of bare thread.

3 ▪ Cut the cardboard tube down one side, from one end to the other. Overlap the cut edges to make it smaller. Insert it into the circle of beads, allowing it to expand until it is snug against them. Remove the tube long enough to tape it along the cut edges—keeping it the same size—then reinsert it into the circle of beads. (This initial ring of beads will become rows 1 and 2 when the 3rd row of beads is added, pulling down the ring of beads into the positions shown in figure 2.

4 ▪ Spread the beads so they are evenly spaced around the form. To begin the row, take the needle through the first bead to the left of the knot. Pick up a bead, skip a bead on the ring, and go through the next bead (figure 3 on page 68). Pull the thread down tight enough so that the bead you are adding pushes the bead above it halfway up the neighboring beads. Continue in this manner until you return to the starting place.

5 ▪ When you end row 3, pass the needle through the first bead of row 2 and first bead of row 3. Now you are ready to begin row 4. Every time you end a row, your needle will pass through the first bead of the preceding row and the first bead of the row you are on. (*Tip:* The first bead of every row will move one bead to the left. When following figure 5 (page 69), use the diagonal line as a reference point.)

6 ▪ For the 15 fringes, you will need 2 yard (1.85-m) lengths of size "B" beading thread. Beginning at the left outside edge, follow the pattern to attach the fringe (figure 4 on page 68).

To make each fringe or strand,

Figure 1

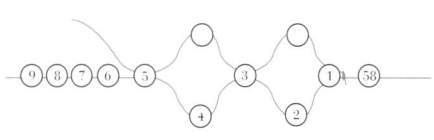

Figure 2

string on the beads in the order given below. To return up the strand, always skip the last black CB bead and go back through the black drop and all the other beads on the strand. Following the thread path illustrated in figure 4, go in the opposite side of

Figure 3

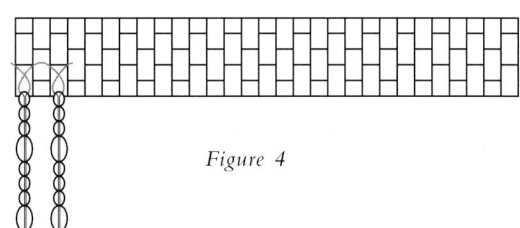

Figure 4

the bead from which each fringe is suspended, and then continue on to the next fringe.

Strand 1: four black CB, one 4 mm pale yellow, two black CB, one 5 x 7 mm light Colorado topaz, two black CB, one gold CB, one black drop, one black CB.

Strand 2: two black CB, two gold CB, one black CB, two bronze CB, one black CB, one 4 mm pale yellow, two black CB, one 5 x 7 mm light Colorado topaz, two black CB, one gold CB, one black drop, one black CB.

Strand 3: three black CBs, one gold CB, one 5 mm jet crystal, one gold CB, one black CB, two bronze CBs, one black CB, one 4 mm pale yellow, two black CB, one 5 x 7 mm light Colorado topaz, two black CB, one gold CB, one black drop, one black CB.

Strand 4: two black CBs, two gold CBs, one black CB, one bronze CB, one black CB, one gold CB, one 5 mm jet crystal, one gold CB, one black CB, two bronze CBs, one black CB, one 4 mm pale yellow, two black CBs, one 5 x 7 mm light Colorado topaz, two black CBs, one gold CB, one black drop, one black CB.

Strand 5: one black CB, one 4 mm light Colorado topaz crystal, two black CB, two bronze CBs, two black CBs, one gold CB, one 5 mm jet crystal, one gold CB, one black CB, two bronze CB, one black CB, one 4 mm pale yellow, two black CB, one 5 x 7 mm light Colorado topaz, two black CB, one gold CB, one black drop, one black CB.

Strand 6: three black CBs, one 4 mm bronze, one ivory CB, one bronze CB, one 4 mm jet crystal, two bronze CBs, one 5 mm jet crystal, one gold CB, one black CB, two bronze CB, one black CB, one 4 mm pale yellow, two black CB, one 5 x 7 mm light Colorado topaz, two black CB, one gold CB, one black drop, one black CB.

Strand 7: two black CBs, two ivory CBs, two bronze CBs, one 4 mm jet crystal, one bronze CB, two black CBs, one gold CB, two black CBs, one bronze CB, one 5 mm jet crystal, one gold CB, one black CB, two bronze CBs, one black CB, one 4 mm pale yellow, two black CBs, one 5 x 7 mm light Colorado topaz, two black CBs, one gold CB, one black drop, one black CB.

Strand 8: one black CB, one bronze CB, one black CB, one 4 mm jet crystal, one bronze CB, one ivory CB, one bronze CB, one 8 mm topaz German bead, one bronze CB, two black CBs, one bronze CB, one 5 mm jet crystal, one gold CB, one black CB, two bronze CBs, one black CB, one 4 mm pale yellow, two black CBs, one 5 x 7 mm light Colorado topaz, two black CB, one gold CB, one black drop, one black CB.

Strand 9: Repeat strand 7

Strand 10: Repeat strand 6

Strand 11: Repeat strand 5

Strand 12: Repeat strand 4

Strand 13: Repeat strand 3

Strand 14: Repeat strand 2

Strand 15: Repeat strand 1

7▪ *For the neck chain:* use "B" beading thread. Cut one piece of thread 4 yards (3.7 m) long and double it. Anchor the thread into the body of the pouch. Wax the thread so it stays together. Come up one bead toward the front of the bag (figure 00). Begin to string beads as follows: three gold CBs, one bronze CB, one black CB, one rondel, one 8 mm German topaz, one rondel, one black CB, three bronze CBs, two gold CBs, five black CB, one gold CB, one 6 mm round black, two bronze CBs, three black CBs, two gold CBs, four black CBs, one bronze CB, one black CB, one 5 x 7 mm oval, one black CB, three bronze CBs, one black CB, two gold CBs, three black CBs, one bronze CB, one 8 mm German topaz, one bronze CB, two black CBs, three gold CBs, five black CBs, three bronze CBs, one 6 mm black crystal, one bronze CB, three black CBs, two gold CBs, four bronze CBs, two black CBs, one 5 x 7 mm oval, two black CBs, three gold CBs, two bronze CBs, five black CBs, two bronze CBs, one 4 mm pale yellow, two bronze CBs, three black CBs, two gold CBs, four black CBs, two bronze CBs, one black CB, one 6 mm light colorado topaz crystal, two black CBs, one gold CB, three bronze CBs, two black CBs, one gold CB, three black CB, one bronze CB, one 6 mm round black, one bronze CB, two black CBs, three gold CBs, four bronze CBs, two black CBs, one 5 x 7 mm oval, two black CBs, one gold CB, two bronze CBs, four black CBs, one gold CB, two bronze CBs, one gold CB, two bronze CBs, one 4 mm pale yellow, one bronze CB, three black CBs, two gold CBs, one bronze CB, two black CBs, one bronze CB, two gold CBs, one 6 mm jet crystal, two gold CBs, one bronze CB, three black CBs, two bronze CBs, one gold

Figure 5

pale yellow, one bronze CB, three black CBs, two gold CBs, one bronze CB, two black CBs, one bronze CB, two gold CBs, one 6 mm jet crystal, two gold CBs, one bronze CB, three black CBs, two bronze CBs, one gold CB, two black CBs, one 5 x 7 mm oval, two black CBs, three bronze CBs, one black CB, two gold CBs, four black CBs, one 4 mm pale yellow, two black CBs, one bronze CB, two gold CBs, two black CBs, three bronze CBs, one black CB, one 4 mm bronze, two black CBs, one bronze CB, two gold CBs, two black CBs, three bronze CBs, two black CBs, one 5 mm light Colorado topaz crystal, one black CB, three gold CBs, two black CBs, three bronze CBs, two black CBs, ★one gold CB, one 4 mm pale yellow. This last 4 mm pale yellow bead is the center back of the neck chain.

Repeat this pattern in reverse from the "★" to complete the second half of the neck chain. This neck chain is

symmetrical, and the second half is a mirror image of the first. When the second half is completed, connect the last gold CB to the opposite side of the pouch again toward the front of the bag. Weave the thread through two to three beads to center the neck chain on this side of the pouch. To complete the second strand of the neck chain, add two gold CBs, one bronze CB, one black CB, and go back through the 4 mm rondel, the 8 mm German topaz, and the 4 mm rondel, add one or two black CBs or as many as needed to equal the CBs between the two larger accent beads. Take the needle and thread and wrap it around the first strand five to six times until the second strand stays twisted around the first. Make sure the CBs stay together at the base of the thread during the twisting to prevent the thread from knotting. Go through the 6 mm black bead. Add black CBs to equal the distance to the next accent bead. Wrap the thread around the

first strand several times. *Remember to always wrap in the same direction.* Go through the 5 x 7 mm oval. Continue adding black CBs, wrapping the thread around the first strand of beads and going through the next accent bead until you have completed the second twisted strand. To end, add one black CB, one bronze CB, and two gold CBs, go through the back side of the pouch, and weave the end in to secure it.

The beauty of the bracelet and necklace designed by Terry Taylor is that no two are alike. Follow his approach and create your own unique and stunning jewelry, accented with special holy medals, crosses, or other Christian items you have collected.

❖ Materials and Tools

beads: glass, metal, or whatever suits your fancy

holy medals, charms, crosses, or other Christian symbols in metal

nylon beading thread

beading needle

clasps★

jump rings

bead glue

round-nose jewelry pliers

wire cutters (optional)

★ A variety of clasps can be purchased in bead-supply stores. The designer chose toggle clasps because he likes the look.

I am a compulsive flea market shopper. I must paw through those tangles of costume jewelry and rescue what appeals to my eye. Lately, I have been drawn to pieces that have some sort of symbolic content removed from their contextual reference.

For both the necklace and the bracelet I was inspired by finding two broken rosaries, one with black glass beads, and the other with pale amber plastic beads, and a crucifix with touches of copper where the metal plate finish had worn off with use.

Instructions

1 • Determine the length you wish for the bracelet or necklace.

2 • Measure a suitable length of bead thread, double it, and add extra for good measure.

3 • On a flat work surface, experiment with the bead arrangement before stringing the beads. (*Tip:* The designer wanted to use beads from the broken rosaries he had collected. Using wire cutters, he simply snipped the wire links and removed the beads.) Working on a towel or beading board can be helpful.

4 • When you are satisfied with your arrangement, thread a beading needle with the length of doubled thread. Thread the beads onto the thread. When all the beads are strung, check the length of the necklace or bracelet. Add or subtract beads as needed.

5 • Loosely knot both ends of the thread. Determine the placement of your accent charms. Attach the charms as desired along the length of the bracelet or necklace with jump rings.

6 • Use a secure knot to attach the thread ends to the clasps you have chosen. When secure, dot the knot with bead glue. Allow to dry and then clip the excess thread.

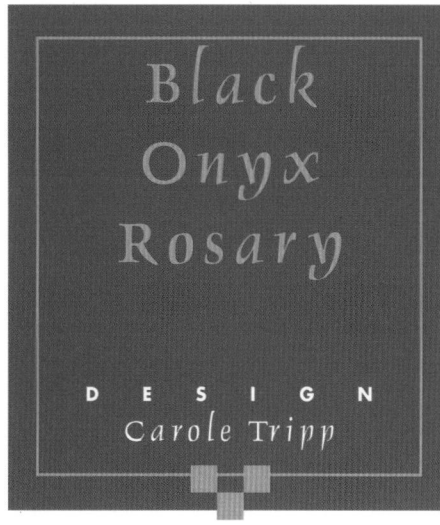

Black Onyx Rosary

DESIGN
Carole Tripp

Simple and stately, this handsome rosary, designed by Carole Tripp, will make a meaningful gift for a special man in your life.

❖ **Materials and Tools**

(59) 6 mm black onyx beads

sterling silver 22-gauge wire, 6½' (2 m)

crucifix charm

Christ/IHS medallion

chain-nose pliers

round-nose pliers

❖ **Instructions**

1 ▪ To make bead links: Cut a piece of wire about 12" (31 cm) in length. Using chain-nose pliers, make a ¼" (1 cm) right angle bend at one end of the wire (figure 1). Using round-nose pliers, make a loop by rolling the bent sections backwards (figure 2). Place one 6 mm bead on the wire and slide it down next to the loop. Using chain-nose pliers, bend the wire just above the bead to form a right angle. Cut the wire ¼" (1 cm) in length. Make sure both loops are in the same plane (figure 3). Make 59 bead links in this manner.

2 ▪ To make wire links: These are made the same as bead links, but without adding the bead.

3 ▪ To connect the bead links: Carefully open one end of the bead link by bending the loop forward or backward but *not* out to the side. Place another closed bead link into the opening and gently close the loop. Make sure the end of the wire touches the place where the wire was originally bent to assure complete closure of the link. Continue in this manner until ten 6 mm onyx beads have been connected. Make four more 10-bead sections and join these together as follows: first 10-bead section, ★two wire links, one 6 mm bead link, two wire links, second 10-bead section. Continue from ★ until the five 10-bead sections have been connected.

4 ▪ To complete rosary: Using the wire links, connect the top section of the medallion to each end of the bead

chain. Connect one wire link to the bottom of the medallion and add one 6 mm bead link. Add two wire links and connect three 6 mm bead links to these wire links. Connect two wire links and the last 6 mm bead link. Using the remaining wire link, connect the crucifix to the rosary.

Figure 1

Figure 2

Figure 3

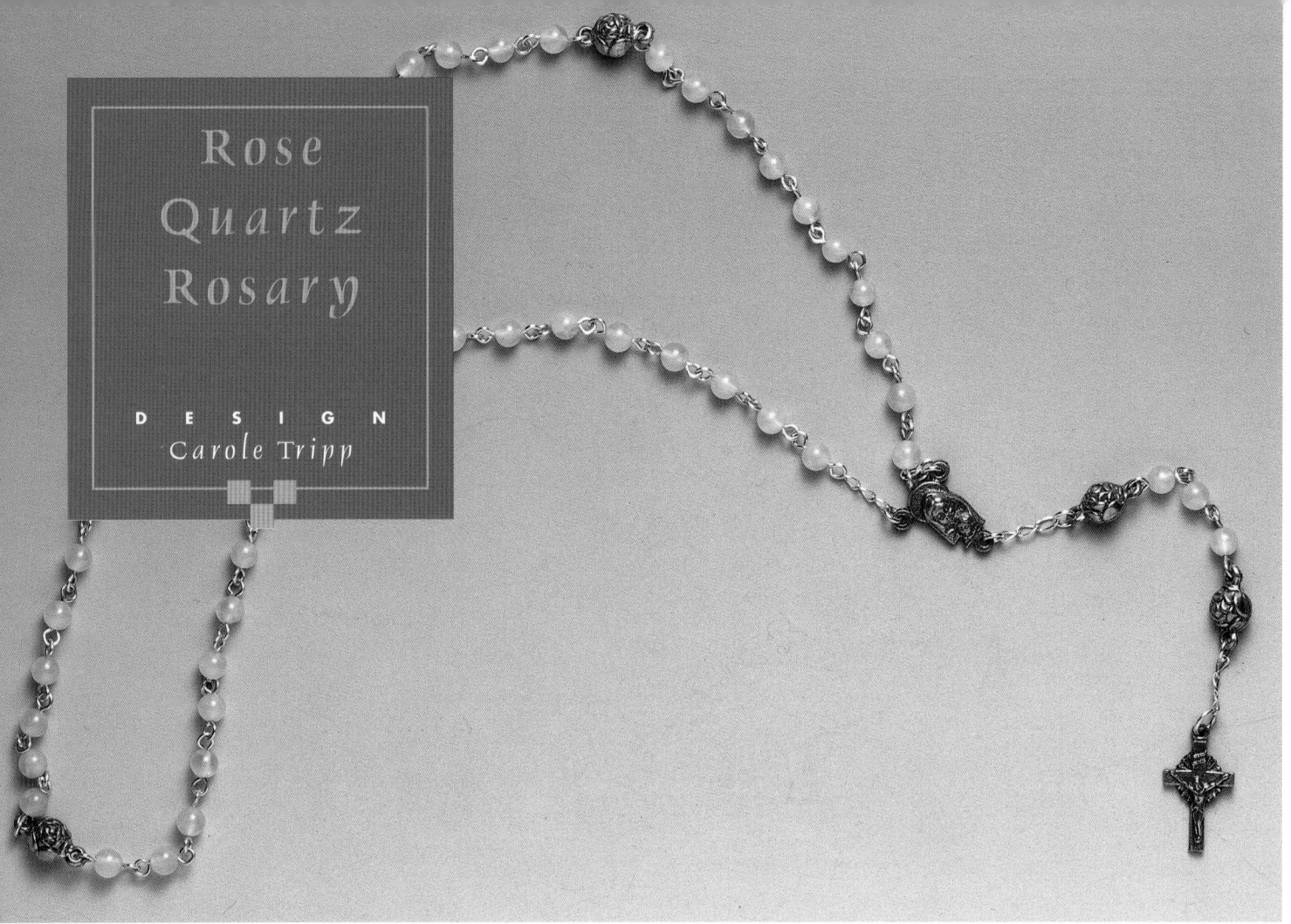

Rose Quartz Rosary

DESIGN
Carole Tripp

T HE DELICATE BEAUTY OF SMALL ROSE QUARTZ BEADS, ARTFULLY ASSEMBLED INTO A ROSARY BY DESIGNER CAROLE TRIPP, LENDS JUST THE RIGHT TOUCH FOR A GIRL'S CONFIRMATION.

❖ Materials and Tools

(53) 4 mm rose quartz beads

(6) 6 mm rosebud connectors

sterling silver 22-gauge wire, 4½' (1.4 m) long

(4) 4 mm sterling silver jump rings

(1) 5 mm sterling silver jump ring

crucifix charm

Madonna and child medallion

chain-nose pliers

round-nose pliers

wire cutters

❖ Instructions

1 ▪ Follow step one on page 72 (substitute the fifty-three 4 mm beads).

2 ▪ Follow step 3 on page 72 (substitute ten 4 mm quartz beads). Make four more 10-bead sections. Join these bead sections together with a rosebud connector.

3 ▪ To complete the rosary: Cut the chain into four sections, each ⅝" long. Connect one section of chain to the beginning of the first bead section and the end of the last bead section. Using a 4 mm jump ring, connect the top of the Madonna medallion to the chain sections. Connect a jump ring to the bottom of the medallion while adding a piece of chain. Connect the chain to a rosebud connector using a 4 mm jump ring. Connect the three remaining 4 mm rose quartz bead links to the rose bud connector, and connect the last rosebud to the last 4 mm bead link. Place the 5 mm jump ring on the crucifix charm. Using a 4 mm ring, connect the remaining section of chain between the last rosebud connector and the crucifix charm.

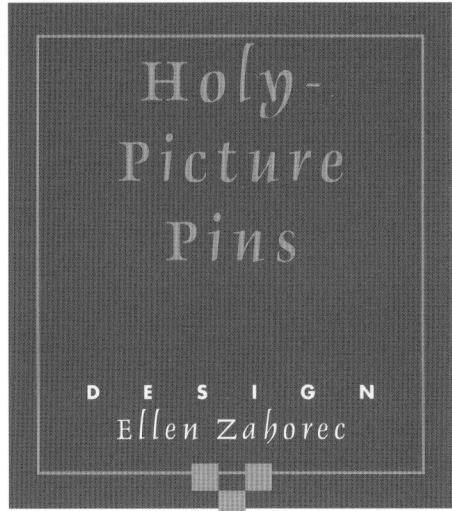

Holy-Picture Pins

DESIGN
Ellen Zahorec

SIZE
3" x 3" (8 x 8 cm)

THESE STUNNING PINS, DESIGNED BY ELLEN ZAHOREC, ARE SIMPLE TO MAKE, AND LOOK GREAT ADORNING A COAT. WITH THE ADDITION OF A RIBBON LOOP, YOU CAN TURN THEM INTO CHRISTMAS TREE ORNAMENTS.

⊹ Materials and Tools

holy cards or religious holiday cards

mat board

acrylic paints in colors that complement the holy card

dimensional paints

glitter glue

assorted small beads of various sizes, colors, and shapes

craft glue

strong sewing thread

hot-glue gun and glue sticks

varnish

craft knife

paintbrushes

pin backing, 1" (2.5 cm) long

⊹ Instructions

1 ▪ From the mat board, cut four or five triangular shapes in several sizes, keeping in mind the size pin you want. Make sure your "holy image" will fit the smallest triangle. Cut out one circle.

2 ▪ Cut the "holy image" ¼" (1 cm) wider than the mat board. Glue it to the board and neatly turn the edges to the back .

3 ▪ Paint the remaining triangles with acrylic paints and let dry.

4 ▪ Hot-glue the triangles and the circle together to form an attractive stack with the holy image triangle on top.

5 ▪ String the beads on a 6" (15 cm) length of thread so that you wind up with a section of beads 2" to 2½" (5 to 6.5 cm) long. Tightly wrap the beaded thread across the lower V of the top triangle. Glue the thread ends between two of the triangles to hold the beads in place.

6 ▪ Decorate the shapes with dimensional paint and glitter glue. Let dry.

7 ▪ Apply a coat of varnish and let dry. Hot-glue the pin backing to the back of the largest triangle.

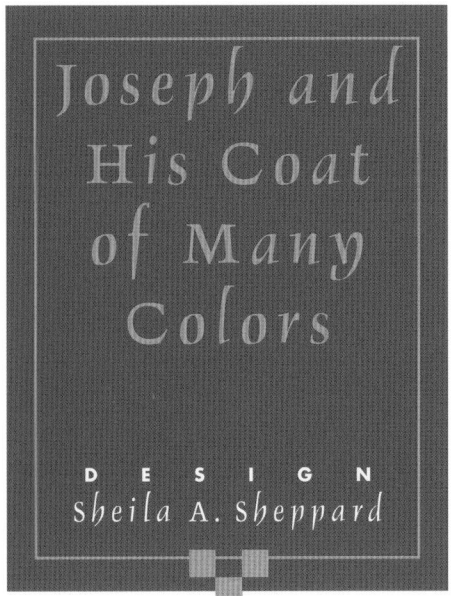

Joseph and His Coat of Many Colors

DESIGN
Sheila A. Sheppard

SIZE
2¼" x 2¾" (6 x 7 cm)

DESIGNER SHEILA SHEPPARD HAS CREATED A DELIGHTFUL JOSEPH, WHO SEEMS READY TO JUMP INTO YOUR LIFE AND ADD A BIT OF MAGIC.

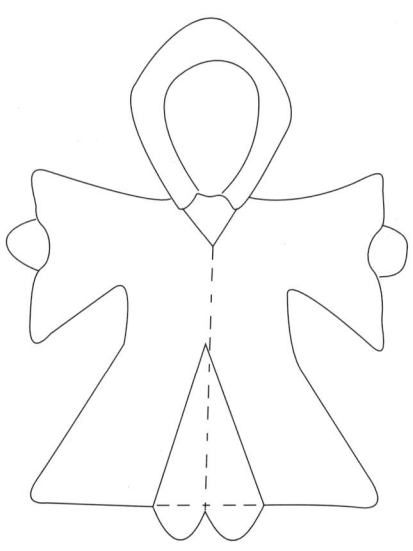

⁑ Materials and Tools

polymer clay:

    1 block of black

    4 to 5 preconstructed round canes and square loaves in a variety of colors and patterns★

    1 black and white jellyroll

    1 preconstructed face cane

    small amount of flesh-colored clay

4 to 5 index cards

tracing paper

pencil

pin back 2" (5 cm) long

wood skewers

toothpicks

parchment paper

rolling pin or pasta machine (do not use for food after)

craft knife

piercing tool

baking sheet

oven, conventional or toaster

★available in craft-supply stores, or you can make them yourself

⁑ Instructions

Note: If you have never worked with polymer clay before, you may want to refer to Leslie Dierks excellent book, *Creative Clay Jewelry* (Lark, 1994).

I ▪ Trace the pattern and transfer it onto an index card. Cut it out and set it aside.

2 ▪ Knead the black clay until it is all the same consistency and roll it out into an ⅛" (3-mm) sheet. (*Tip:* To achieve uniform thickness, place the rolling pin on top of two dowels or wood skewers of the same thickness as you want your clay sheet. Continue rolling the clay until your roller touches the dowels or skewers.)

    This black clay sheet is the base on which you will build up the design. Place the clay on an index card, lay the pattern on top, and cut around the pattern.

3. Cut a very thin slice from the face cane, roll it to a thickness of ⅝" (1.6 cm), and place it on the head area, leaving enough border for the slices of hair cane.

4. Roll the colored canes and loaves to a thickness of about ¼" to ½" (1 to 1.5 cm). Place these thin slices on the black clay, making sure to duplicate the pattern on both sides of the robe so that the design is symmetrical. Apply two slices to create shoes. Blend the slices so that the surface is a uniform thickness. Do not cover the hands.

5. Trim any excess clay from the neck area. Roll the black and white jellyroll to a thickness of ⅛" (3 mm) and cut into very thin slices. Apply these all around the face cane, blending the edges.

6. Flatten a small ball of flesh-colored clay for each hand and press into place. Use the piercing tool to create fingers.

7. Gently peel the whole piece off the index card. Place Joseph, face down, on a clean index card.

8. Roll out another piece of black clay to a thickness of ¹⁄₁₆" (2 mm) and cut into a rectangle ¾" x ½" (2 x 1.5 cm). Set this aside.

9. Position the pin back evenly on the back of Joseph, just below the shoulders, with the latch lock on the left side. Press into the clay very gently with the pin in the open position. Lay the black rectangle over the flat pin bar. Use a toothpick to gently push in around the edges and corners to tack the two clays pieces together. Do not push in too deeply.

10. Preheat the oven, following the manufacturer's directions. Place Joseph, still face down on the index card, onto a baking sheet lined with parchment paper (neither paper will burn). Bake according to the package directions. Allow the pin to cool completely.

▪ Designer Reflections

The pattern for the Joseph pin is actually an angel pattern that I use quite often for other pieces. My sister, Linda Poland, a storyteller in Jonesborough, Tennessee, requested a Joseph pin for her Joseph story. I make many story character pins for her and other storytellers.

Please use all safety precautions when working with polymer clay, and keep in mind that sometimes, when you work with a pattern, the finished polymer clay piece will be a bit larger.

Painted wood; made in Russia

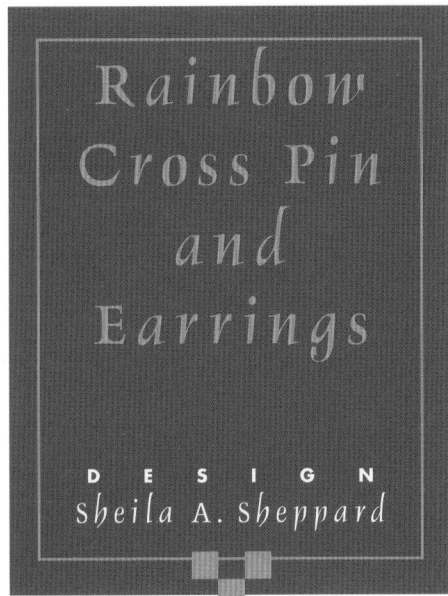

Rainbow Cross Pin and Earrings

DESIGN
Sheila A. Sheppard

SIZE
Pin 1¾" x 2" (4.5 x 5 cm),
Earrings 1" x 1"
(2.5 x 2.5cm)

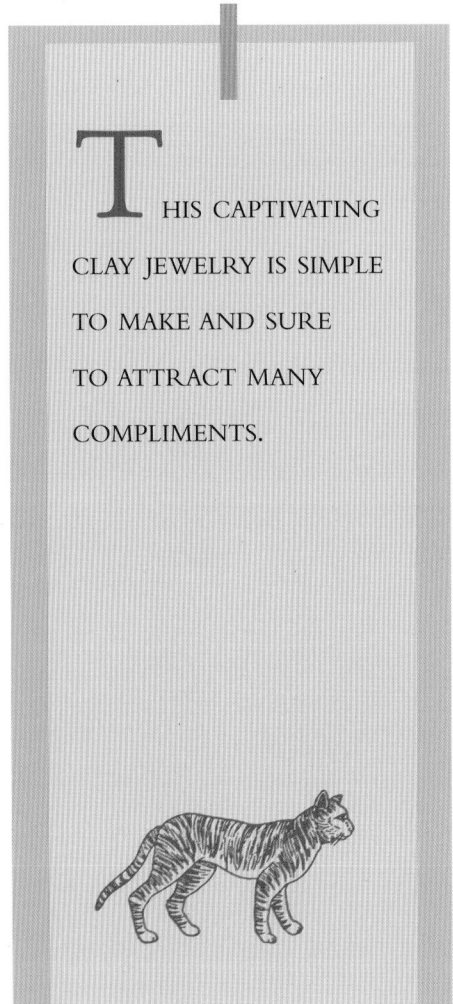

THIS CAPTIVATING CLAY JEWELRY IS SIMPLE TO MAKE AND SURE TO ATTRACT MANY COMPLIMENTS.

❖ Materials and Tools

polymer clay:

> 1 block black

> 3 blocks each of red, yellow, and blue

> 3 blocks each of violet, orange, and green

pencil

tracing paper

3 to 4 index cards

parchment paper

toothpicks

pin back 1" (2.5 cm) long

jewelry wire, 24-gauge, silver or gold

1 pair French hooks, silver, stainless steel, or gold

2 seed beads, 4 mm, in any rainbow color

bamboo skewer

rolling pin or pasta machine (do not use for food after)

craft knife

slicing blade

ruler

piercing tool

round-nose pliers

baking sheet

oven, conventional or toaster

★available in craft-supply stores

❖ Instructions

1 ▪ Trace figures 1 and 2 and transfer them onto index cards. Cut the patterns out and set them aside.

2 ▪ Cut ¼" (1 cm) from each of the seven blocks of clay. Be sure to wipe your blade carefully between colors. Knead each slice of clay to ensure uniform consistency.

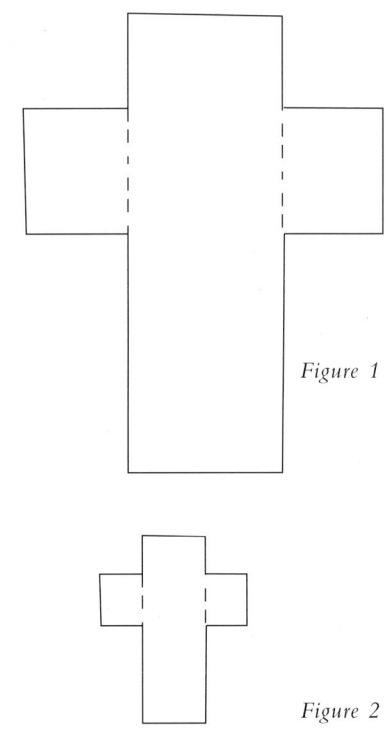

Figure 1

Figure 2

3. Roll out each slice to a thickness of ¼" (1 cm). Stack the colors as follows: red, orange, yellow, black, green, blue, and violet. Trim the edges of the stack squarely. Cut the stack in half and make a new stack by putting one on top of the other. At this point, you may see some blending of colors, and that's fine. Press this stack down evenly with the rolling pin. Slice about ⅜" (1 cm) down the stack, as shown in figure 3.

4. Now you have a ⅜" (1-cm) thick slab of rainbow. Gently roll this out to a thickness of ¼" (1 cm). Place the slabs onto the paper pattern for the pin. Refer to the photograph and notice how the colors wave: that is achieved by using your fingers to gently push the color stripes to be sure they have bonded to each other. This process also spreads the rainbow slab out enough to accommodate the cross pattern and helps to create the rainbow effect. Note the direction of the rainbow stripe pattern—horizontal on the trunk and vertical on the arms. Note, too, that the length of the trunk is about 2" (5 cm) and the width is about 5/8" (1.5 cm). The arm pieces are both ½" x ½" (1.5 x 1.5 cm) and are pushed in toward the trunk (figure 4).

Figure 3

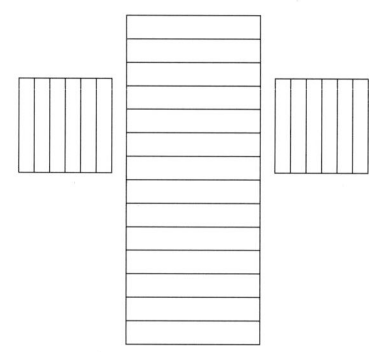

Figure 4

5. Repeat this process with the rainbow slabs for the earrings.

6. Follow steps 7, 8, and 9 on page 77.

7. To make wire eye pins for the earrings: Cut two 1" (2.5 cm) lengths of jewelry wire and wrap them evenly over the flat end of a bamboo skewer (figure 5). Use the pliers to gently twist the two wire ends, with the ends flared (figure 6). Use the craft knife to cut a small pocket in the top of each earring. Insert the flared ends of the eye pins into these pockets and gently press the pockets closed, being sure the wires do not stick out of the clay. Use the pliers to gently bend open the bottom of the French hook, and slip on the seed bead. Repeat with the other French hook and set these aside.

8. Preheat the oven, following the manufacturer's directions. Place the pin and the earrings (still on index cards) onto a baking sheet lined with parchment paper (neither paper will burn). Bake as indicated. Allow the pin and earrings to cool completely.

9. Attach the French hooks to the eye pins, being sure that your favorite side of the earring faces forward. Bend the wire up so that it closes and meets. Do not clamp it too tightly with the pliers, as this will not allow your earring to swing in the loop.

Figure 5

Figure 6

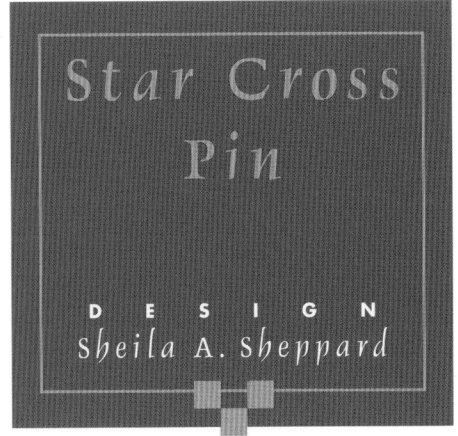

Star Cross Pin

DESIGN
Sheila A. Sheppard

SIZE
2" x 2½" (5 x 6.5 cm)

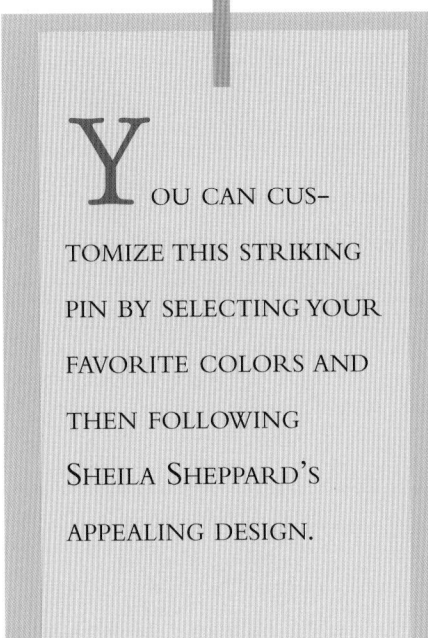

YOU CAN CUSTOMIZE THIS STRIKING PIN BY SELECTING YOUR FAVORITE COLORS AND THEN FOLLOWING SHEILA SHEPPARD'S APPEALING DESIGN.

⊹ Materials and Tools

polymer clay:

    1 block of black

    1 block of white or contrasting color

    preconstructed canes in different colors and patterns★

pencil

tracing paper

3 to 4 index cards

pin back 1" (2.5 cm) long

toothpicks

parchment paper

rolling pin or pasta machine (do not use for food after)

craft knife

baking sheet

tool that extrudes clay into shape of a star★

piercing tool

oven, conventional or toaster

★available in craft-supply stores

⊹ Instructions

1 ▪ Follow steps 1 and 2 on page 76.

2 ▪ Roll the colored canes to a thickness of about ¼" (1 cm) and cut four or five thin slices. Put one at the head of the cross, one at each on the arms, and two at the base.

3 ▪ Use the tool to form a star (or make your own star from canes) from the white (or other color) clay. Place the star in the center of the cross.

4 ▪ Roll two ¼" (1-cm) thick canes of contrasting colors. Hold the two canes together at one end and twist the free ends. Cut some thin slices of the twist and place it around the star. Press and smooth the edges of all the slices of clay so that the surface of the pin is a uniform thickness.

5 ▪ Follow steps 7 through 10 on page 77.

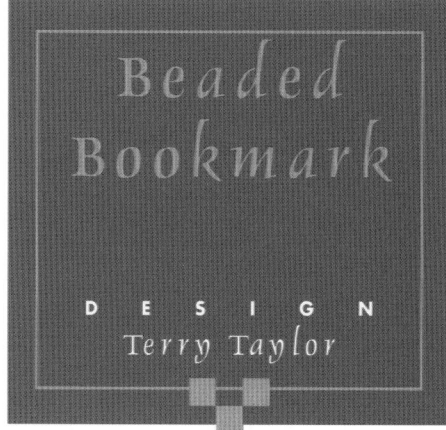

Beaded Bookmark

D E S I G N
Terry Taylor

S I Z E
12" (31 cm) long

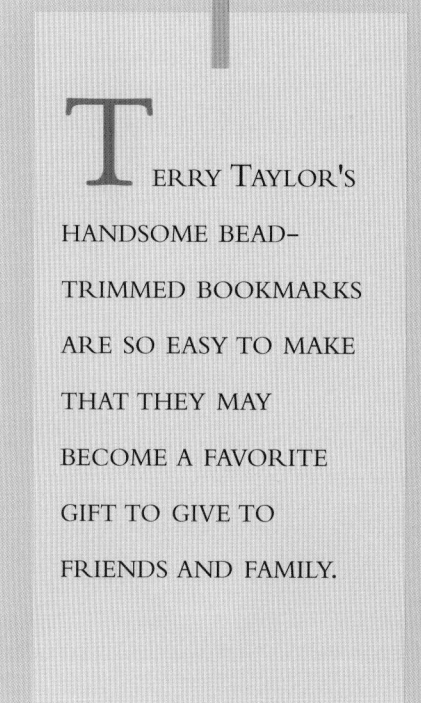

TERRY TAYLOR'S HANDSOME BEAD-TRIMMED BOOKMARKS ARE SO EASY TO MAKE THAT THEY MAY BECOME A FAVORITE GIFT TO GIVE TO FRIENDS AND FAMILY.

❖ Materials and Tools

grosgrain ribbon in color of your choice, 1" x 14" (2.5 x 36 cm)

seed beads in two or three colors to complement ribbon color

small accent beads as desired

metallic braid

holy medals, crosses, or other Christian symbols

matching sewing thread and/or beading thread

fine-sewing needle

beading needle

❖ Instructions

1 ▪ Make a 1" (2.5 cm) fold at each end of the ribbon and finger press or iron a crease in the ribbon. Fold ¼" (1 cm) of this folded edge to the inside to create a neat edge for hemming, as described in step 5.

2 ▪ To make the beaded picot edge, thread a beading needle with either sewing or beading thread. At one end of the ribbon, insert the needle up through the folded crease from the inside. Secure the thread with a tiny backstitch. Thread a number of seed beads onto the thread to create a picot the desired size. When you have determined the size of the picot, bring the needle back down into the crease, secure with a tiny backstitch, and repeat the process to create a picot edge across the edge.

3 ▪ At the opposite edge, you will create a beaded fringe in much the same way as the picot edge. Determine the number of fringe ends you wish to create and how long you want them

to be. You may want a straight fringe or a shaped fringe. Thread a beading needle with beading or sewing thread. Insert the needle up through the folded crease from the inside. Secure the thread with a tiny backstitch. Thread the seed beads and accent beads to create the length of fringe end you desire. When you are satisfied, bring the needle back up through the beads, secure the fringe end with a tiny backstitch, and continue across the end of the ribbon.

4 ▪ Select your accent piece for the upper portion of the bookmark. On the navy blue bookmark shown here, a scrap of jewelry with a fish motif was secured to the ribbon with tiny stitches. On the brown bookmark, a remnant of a scapular was stitched and then outlined with gold braid, and then couched into place to hide the raw edges of the scapular.

5 ▪ Finish the bookmarks by sewing the folded edges with tiny hemstitches.

Mixed Media

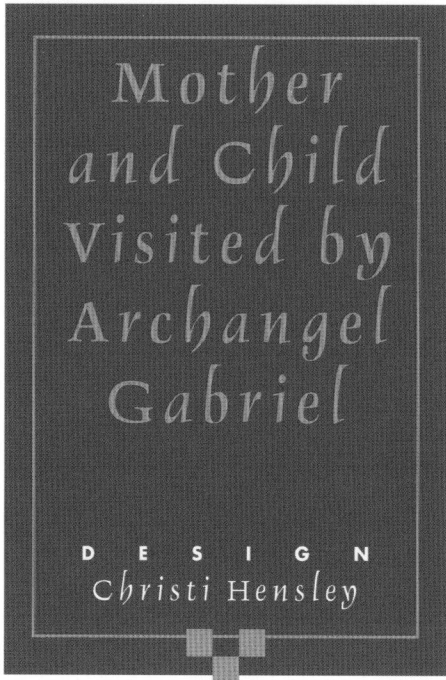

Mother and Child Visited by Archangel Gabriel

DESIGN
Christi Hensley

SIZE
Mother—15" (38.5 cm),
Gabriel—19" (49 cm)

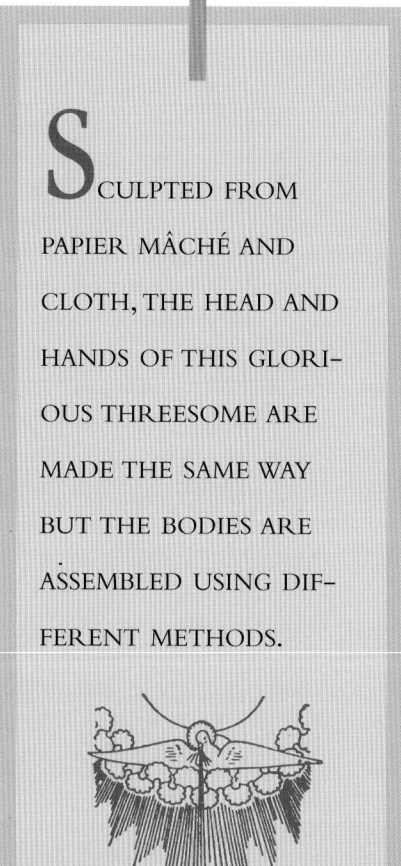

SCULPTED FROM PAPIER MÂCHÉ AND CLOTH, THE HEAD AND HANDS OF THIS GLORIOUS THREESOME ARE MADE THE SAME WAY BUT THE BODIES ARE ASSEMBLED USING DIFFERENT METHODS.

❧ Materials and Tools

HEAD AND HANDS—MOTHER, CHILD, AND ANGEL GABRIEL

aluminum foil

instant papier mâché

fine-grade sandpaper

gesso sealer

acrylic paints: flesh-tone, red, pink, blue, brown, and black

paintbrushes

1 lb. (454 g) paraffin wax

empty coffee can

kitchen knife

mohair or wool for hair

thin gold cord for halos

BODY—MOTHER AND CHILD

wooden dowel, ¼" x 13" (1 x 33 cm)

wooden base

#16 wire, 14" (36 cm) long

standard size pillow case in solid color

½ yd. (46 cm) white cotton gauze fabric

drill with ¼" (1-cm) drill bit

hot-glue gun and glue sticks

scissors

BODY—ANGEL GABRIEL

poster board, 17" x 28" (44 x 72 cm)

2½ yds. (2.3 m) white cotton gauze fabric

#16 wire, 18" (46 cm) long

cellulose wallpaper paste

white glue

plastic sheeting

dish pan

hot-glue gun and glue sticks

rubber band

straight pins

scissors

❧ Instructions

HEADS AND HANDS

1 ▪ Fashion oval-shaped aluminum foil balls for Mary and Gabriel, each approximately 2" (5 cm) round, with a 1" (2.5-cm) neck stem. The baby's head is about ¾" (2 cm) round.

2 ▪ Prepare instant papier mâché according to the manufacturer's directions. Cover the foil heads with about a ¼" (1 cm) layer of this mixture. Build up the cheeks, nose, and chin with additional dabs of papier mâché. When dry, lightly smooth the surfaces with sandpaper. Apply a layer of gesso sealer.

3 ▪ Shape proportionally sized hands out of aluminum foil, flaring them out at the wrist area for easier assembly. Finish them as in step 2.

4 ▪ Paint the head and hands with flesh-colored acrylic paint and let dry. Add simple facial features, using the photograph as a guide.

5 ▪ Create a double-boiler setup with a pot of water and the coffee can. Melt the wax in the coffee can and heat it to about 190° F (88° C). Hold the head by the neck stem and dip it into the wax. Don't worry about coating the bottom of the neck. For the baby's head, attach it to a toothpick and dunk it in the melted wax. Let the heads cool. Dip them two or three times, letting the wax dry between coats.

6 ▪ Scrape the wax off the scalp area and hot-glue the wool or mohair in place.

BODY—MOTHER AND CHILD

7 ▪ To build an armature: Drill a ¼" (1 cm) hole in the wooden base and glue in the wooden dowel. Fold the 14" (36 cm) piece of wire in half; each half will form one of Mary's arms. Twist the wire around the dowel and hot-glue it in place. Attach the hands

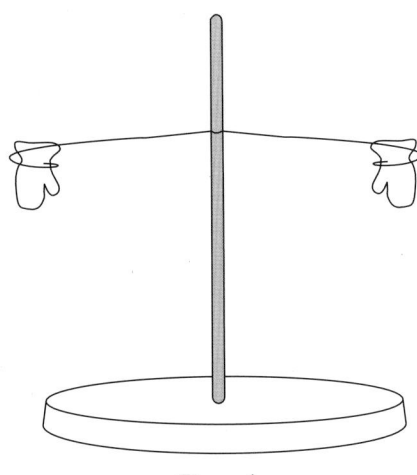

Figure 1

on the ends of the wire by wrapping wire around them; you can also use hot glue (figure 1).

8. To attach Mary's head to the dowel you may have to remove or open up the foil inside the neck cavity. Drip some hot glue inside the bottom of the neck opening and push it down firmly onto the dowel.

9. Cut the pillow case into two sections as shown in figure 2. The section

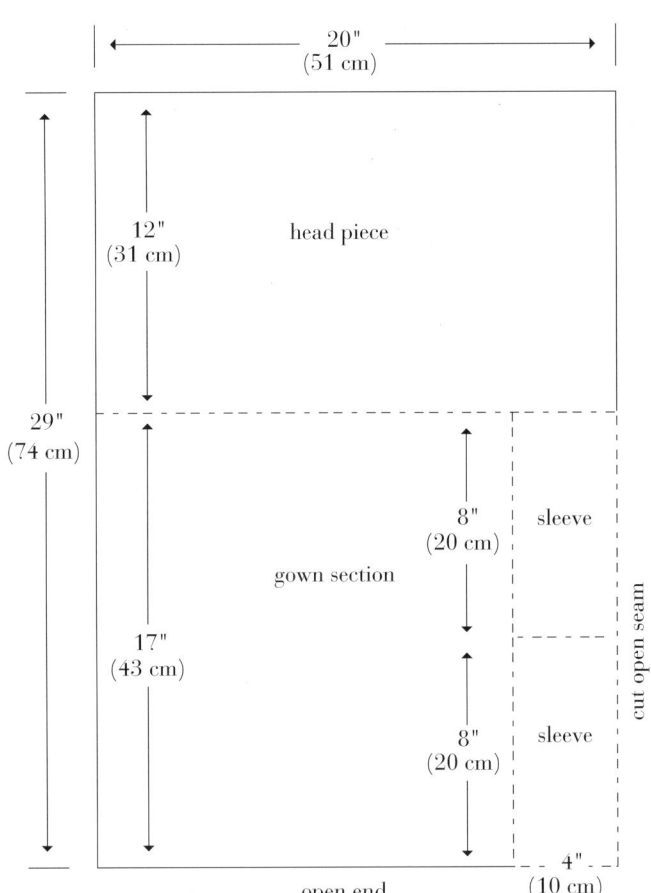

Figure 2

for her gown will open out to about 17" x 40" (44 x 103 cm). From this piece, cut two strips, each 4" x 8½" (10 x 22 cm), and wrap them around the wire arms, using a dab of hot glue to secure them. Wrap the piece for her gown around the wire armature, tucking and wrapping so no raw edges show in the front. When the fabric is arranged to your liking, anchor the gown to the wire with hot glue. The long head piece will cover the back of the gown, so don't worry about using a lot of glue to secure the gown. (*Tip:* Before you glue the gown, practice wrapping the fabric a few times to achieve the drape and shape you want.)

10. Cut a piece of white gauze 12" x 20" (31 x 51 cm). Fold it in half lengthwise. Drape it over Mary's head, with the folded edge facing forward. Tack it to her head and to the sides of the gown with a small dab of hot glue.

Painted clay; made in Mexico

84

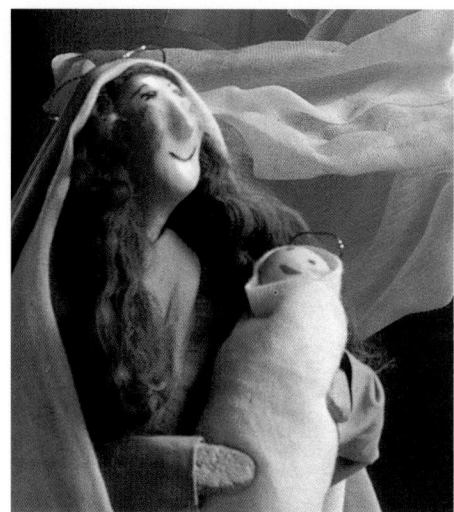

11. Use the remaining piece of pillow case to complete the head piece. Finish the raw edge by folding it inward and hot gluing. Arrange the head piece so it covers Mary's back. Glue it in place.

12. Cut a strip of white gauze 12" x 20" (31 x 51 cm) and wrap it to create swaddling clothes about 6" (15 cm) in length. Leave an opening for the baby's head and hot-glue the head to the white gauze.

13. For the halos, cut two lengths of gold cord to size and glue them to the backs of Mary's and Jesus's heads.

Body-Angel Gabriel

14. Form a cone with the poster board and glue it together. The narrow opening should be about 1" (2.5 cm) and the wide opening about 9" (23 cm). Trim the cone so it will stand (figure 3).

15. To form the Angel's arms, wrap and glue the piece of wire to the outside of the cone as shown in figure 3. Attach the hands to the ends of the cones by wrapping and gluing.

16. Prepare the fabric stiffening paste as follows: Prepare 4 cups (946 ml) of cellulose wallpaper paste according to the package directions. Mix in 1½ cups (355 ml) of white glue. (This mixture will keep a good while if stored in the refrigerator in a sealed container.) Put the paste into a wide shallow container, such as a dish pan.

17. Cut about 1½ yds. (1.4 m) of white gauze and cut this into three pieces—two for the sleeves and a larger one for the robe. Dip these pieces into the paste and squeeze off the excess. (*Tip:* It is a good idea to cover the work surface with plastic sheeting.) Drape and wrap the wet fabric to create a flowing robe. Hide and tuck under any raw edges. Use straight pins to shape and hold the fabric while it dries. Gather and secure the fabric at the top of the cone with a rubber band. Pull enough fabric up past the rubber band so that you can tuck it inside the top of the cone and have a finished looking neckline. The rubber band can be cut off when the robe is dry. Bend the arms to the desired position. The stiffened fabric will take a few days to dry completely.

18. When the robe is dry, trim any strings or raveled edges. Glue the Angel's head onto the top of the cone (figure 3). Make a halo out of a piece of gold cord and glue it to the head.

Figure 3

19. The wings will have to be shaped and left to dry on the plastic sheeting. Cut two pieces of white gauze about 22" x 22" (56.5 x 56.5 cm). Dip the pieces into the paste, then lay them on the plastic, side by side. Scrunch, ripple, and swirl the fabric to create billowing wings. Play with the fabric until you achieve two similarly shaped wings, then let them dry for a few days. Peel the dry wings off the plastic, trim as necessary, and hot-glue them to the back of the Angel Gabriel.

Carved wood; made in Haiti

85

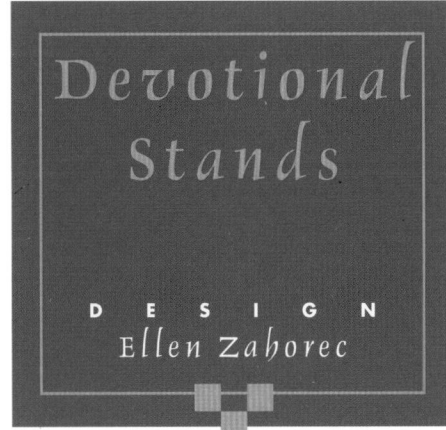

Devotional Stands

D E S I G N
Ellen Zahorec

SIZE
7" x 10" (18 x 26 cm)

THESE DISTINCTIVE STANDS CAN BE USED AS DECORATIVE REMINDERS OF FAVORITE SAINTS AND FEAST DAYS. DESIGNER ELLEN ZAHOREC LIKES TO PLACE HER STANDS ON A BEDSIDE TABLE, ACCOMPANIED BY LIGHTED VOTIVE CANDLES.

❖ Materials and Tools

sign holders for retail store displays★

holy cards or prayer cards★★

poster or mat board

craft knife

good-quality paper glue

spray paint

enamel paint markers

★Can be purchased from retail-store supply catalogues

★★Can be purchased from religious materials stores, church gift shops, and catalogues

❖ Instructions

I ▪ Mount the holy card on poster board or mat board, and cut to fit the size of the opening in the sign holder. Place the mounted card in the frame.

2 ▪ Spray the metal frame the desired color and decorate it with enamel paint markers. You can replace the card with another card to commemorate different occasions. (*Tip:* You can also place the mounted card in a metal or wooden picture frame and decorate the frame.)

▪ Designer Reflections

About seven years ago, I decided to incorporate sacred images into my collages, especially images of the Theotokos, The God Bearer. These images are a reminder of my Byzantine Catholic Slavonic heritage. Catholic ritual had such a vivid visual influence in my life that I felt it necessary to begin to portray my own contemporary version of what I experienced in my early childhood. Eastern Rite Catholic services were mysterious, smelled heavily of incense and flowers, and the elaborate ornamentation was a visual feast for the eye. It is that experience that I hope to capture and express, along with the sacredness of the original iconography that adorns today's churches.

Painted wood; made in Russia

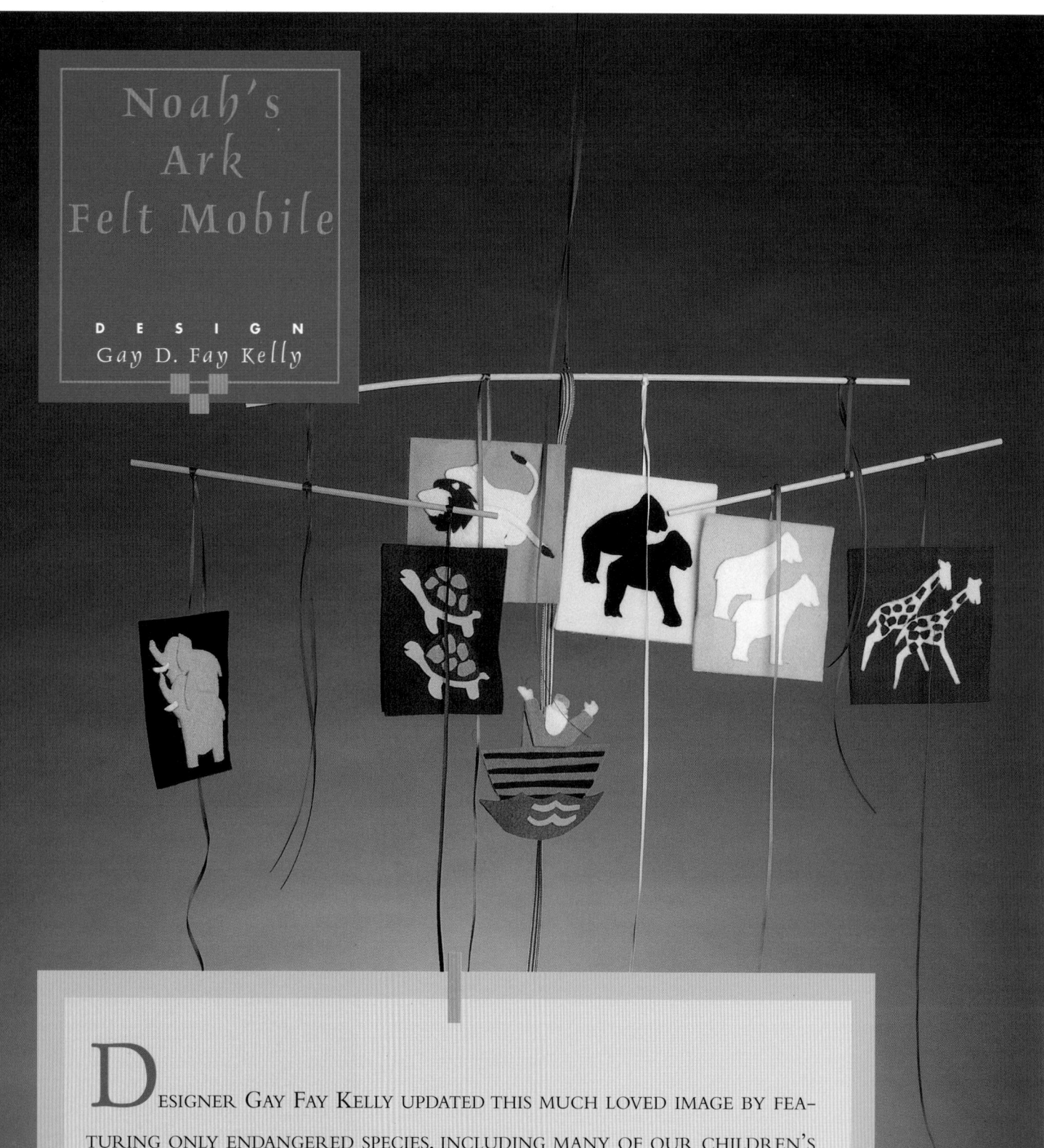

Noah's Ark Felt Mobile

DESIGN
Gay D. Fay Kelly

Designer Gay Fay Kelly updated this much loved image by featuring only endangered species, including many of our children's favorite creatures—elephants, sea turtles, lions, gorillas, giraffes, and polar bears. She symbolized the rainbow by placing the animals on different colored felt squares.

SIZE:
**Each square is 5" x 5"
(13 x 13 cm)**

▸Materials and Tools

12" x 12" (31 x 31 cm) of felt in each of the following colors: orange, yellow, dark purple, red, bright green, russet brown, dark brown, light beige, turquoise, ivory, white, dark blue, light blue, black, and light sea green-gray

3 to 4 yds. (2.7 to 3.7 m) red satin ribbon, ⅛" (3 mm) wide

1 yd. of the following colors of satin ribbon, ⅛" (3 mm) wide: purple, green, navy, and yellow

1 yd. (91.4 cm) of rainbow ribbon, ½" (1.5 cm) wide

piece of wooden dowel, 4' long by ¼" wide (1.2 m x ?cm)

tracing paper

sharp pencil

craft glue for fabric

1 yd. (92.5 cm) iron-on heavy-duty adhesive (optional)

small brass screw eye

sharp, pointed scissors

fine-tooth saw

push pin

▸Instructions

1▪ Cut two 5" (13 cm) squares of felt in red, orange, yellow, bright green, dark blue, and dark purple. These are the backgrounds for the animals.

2▪ Enlarge the patterns (page 138) on a copier as indicated and cut them out. They are your templates for cutting out the felt animals. You can also trace the patterns onto iron-on adhesive. Follow manufacturer's directions for adhering the shapes.

3▪ Glue the animal shapes onto the felt squares, leaving a blank set of each of these squares to be attached later. Refer to the photograph to show you which shapes are glued on top of others and which color square is the correct background for each animal. Let the glue dry thoroughly and then glue any edges that may not have adhered adequately.

★*Special note about Noah, his ark, and the waves:* Noah is composed of a three-layer sandwich—coat, body, coat. The brown lines on the hull are repeated on the back of the ark. The waves are composed of two turquoise pieces that sandwich the front and back of the hull. Before gluing Noah to his ark, insert the rainbow ribbon between him and the ark, placing the ribbon so that it is not far off-center. Glue the ribbon, Noah, and the ark together.

4▪ Cut 1 yard (91.4 cm) of red satin ribbon. Center and glue about 4" (10 cm) of the ribbon on the blank red felt square. Before the glue dries, apply glue to the top of the short piece of ribbon and around the edges of the square. Place the decorated red felt square on top, sandwiching the ribbon. Press with your fingers to evenly distribute the glue. Repeat this process for each of the felt squares, matching the ribbon to the felt color. Let the squares dry. Reglue where necessary.

5▪ Cut a 2' (62 cm) piece of dowel for the middle section. Approximately at its balance point, make a small mark on the dowel.

6▪ Loop the unattached end of the rainbow ribbon around the dowel where you have marked it and let the ark hang about 10" (25 cm) away from the dowel. Screw the screw eye through the ribbon and into the dowel. Glue the loose strand of ribbon to the back of the piece of ribbon coming out of the ark.

7▪ Attach the two middle felt squares to each side of the dowel, using lark's

head knots, so that the knots can be moved for balancing. Let the length of their ribbons trail: they should not hit Noah's head when they hang down.

8▪ Use the remaining red ribbon to hang the mobile from the screw eye at a height convenient for adjusting the balance. Hang the two side dowels from the center dowel. When you are satisfied with the arrangement of the squares, place a dab of glue on each ribbon where it meets the dowel. Rub it in, let it dry thoroughly, and check for adhesion. Trim the trailing ribbons so they are about the same length. It's a good idea to hang the mobile high enough that small children cannot reach up and pull the trailing ribbons.

▸Designer Reflections

When listening to a homily about stewardship and humanity's responsibility for caring for our earth, I realized that the story of Noah's Ark (which was not, alas, the subject of the priest's sermon, but was the test pattern of my thoughts when they strayed) was a story of species preservation. I decided to use only endangered species in my mobile. I found the list of recognizable animals woefully long: Most of the animals usually shown being saved by Noah are now in danger of extinction.

Faux Stained Glass Madonna and Child

DESIGN
Louise Riddle

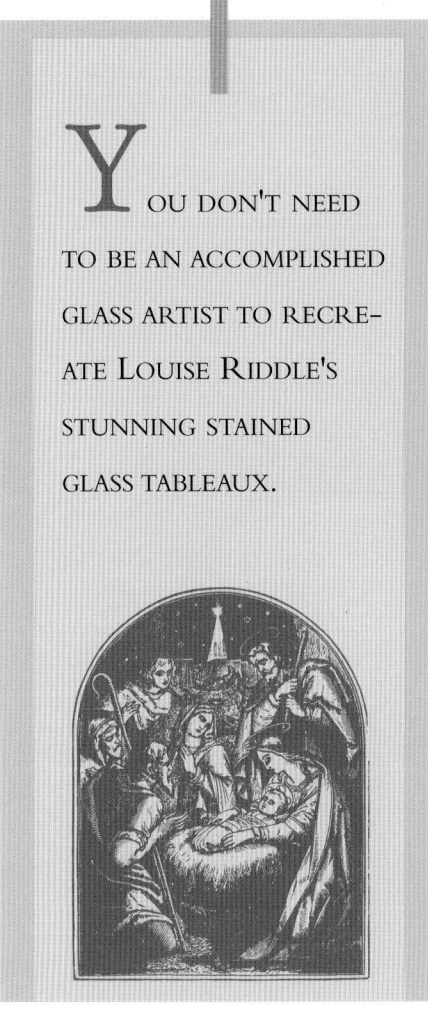

Y OU DON'T NEED TO BE AN ACCOMPLISHED GLASS ARTIST TO RECREATE LOUISE RIDDLE'S STUNNING STAINED GLASS TABLEAUX.

❧ Materials and Tools

clear pane of glass, 14" x 20" (36 x 51 cm)

masking tape

liquid leading

transparent glass stains in colors of your choice

cotton swabs or toothpicks

frame

framer's points

❧ Instructions

1 ▪ Enlarge the pattern on page 139 on a copier, as indicated.

2 ▪ Clean the glass pane. Tape the pattern onto the back of the glass.

3 ▪ Apply liquid leading along all the lines of the pattern, making sure the leading has no gaps where the lines meet. (Gaps will allow paint to run into areas where you may not want it.) Place the glass on a level surface, with the pattern still taped on, and allow the leading to dry.

4 ▪ Fill in all the sections with desired colors of glass stains. Air bubbles will mar the appearance of the completed project and should be avoided or removed with cotton swabs or toothpicks while the paint is still wet.

5 ▪ After the paints are dry, remove the pattern. With the leading side facing front, secure the glass pane in a frame with framer's points.

Carved sandstone; made in Kenya

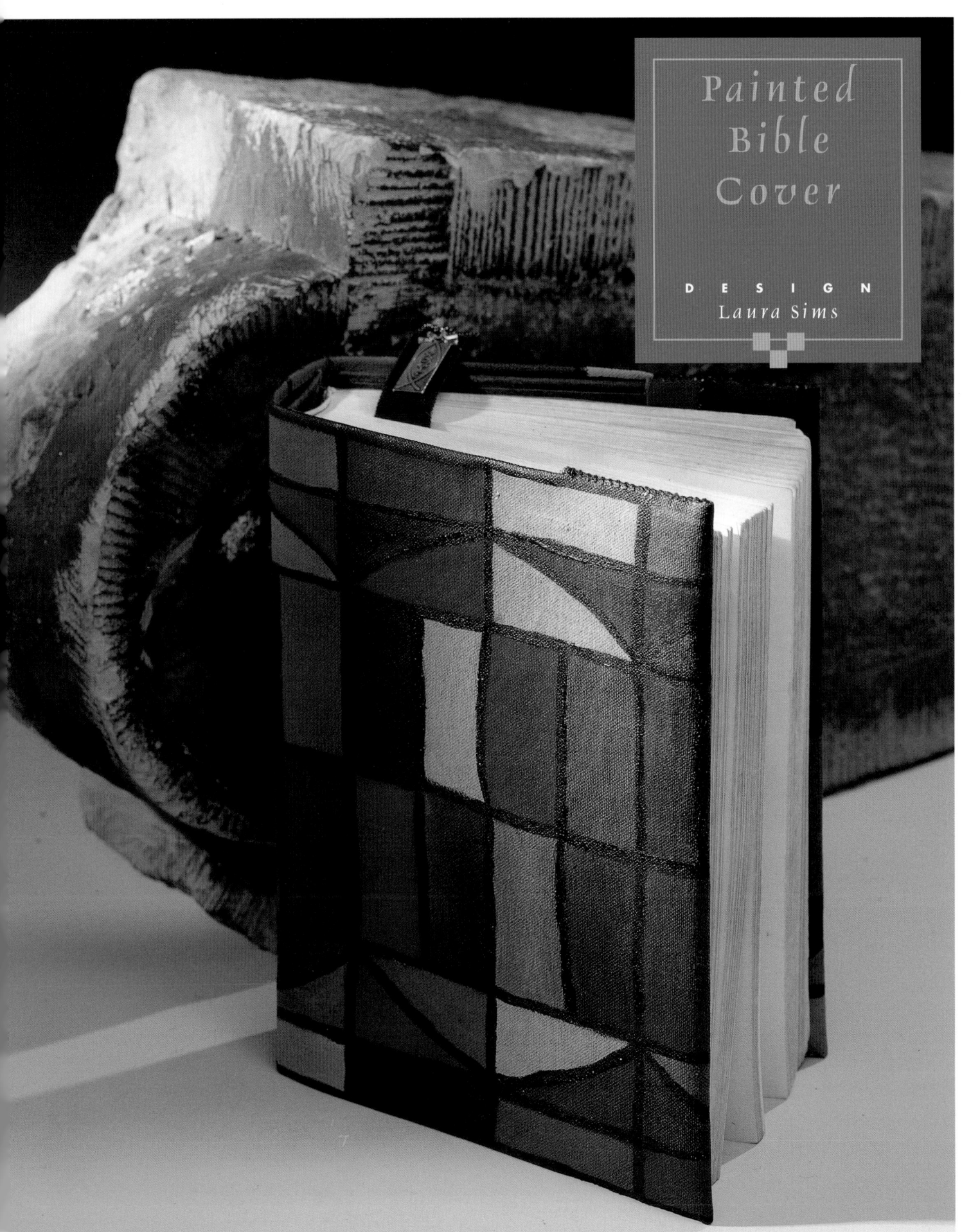

Painted
Bible
Cover

DESIGN
Laura Sims

DESIGNER LAURA SIMS TOOK HER INSPIRATION FOR THIS ATTRACTIVE BIBLE COVER FROM THE STAINED GLASS WINDOWS SHE ADMIRES IN RURAL CHURCHES.

SIZE
14" x 20" (36 x 51 cm)

⁑ Materials and Tools

cotton duck★

scissors

ruler

pencil

textile acrylic paints

paintbrushes

fusible web

sewing needle and heavy thread

★You will need a piece of fabric 2½" (6.5 cm) wider than the north/south dimensions and 8" (21 cm) wider than the east/west dimensions of the bible you plan to cover.

⁑ Instructions

1 ▪ On the right side of the fabric, draw a grid. Draw a center line from north to south that corresponds with the center of the bible's spine. (Remember that the side to the right of the center line will cover the front of the book.) Divide the squares to your liking to create a design (figure 1).

2 ▪ Paint in the design and let it dry.

3 ▪ Lay the fabric painted side down. Fold the four edges of the fabric in 1" (2.5 cm), press in place, and miter the corners. Bond the fabric with fusible web to hold the flaps in place.

4 ▪ Fold the east side in 3" (8 cm) and whipstitch the fabric together at the top to form a pocket. Do the same on the west side. Slip the cover on the book, using these side pockets to hold it securely.

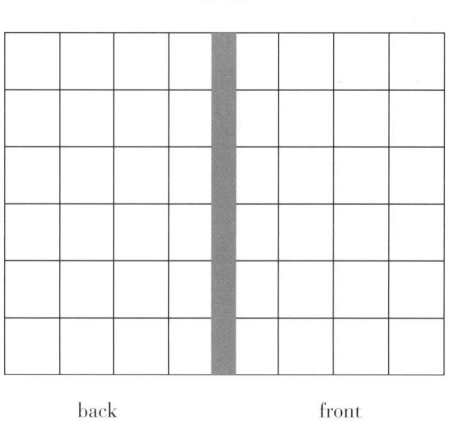

center

back   front

Figure 1

Painted clay; made in China

Painted Tin Nativity

DESIGN
Mary Jane Miller

Making these charming tin figures could be a family affair: After the tin is cut, the children or grandchildren can paint them with their favorite colors.

⋗ Materials and Tools

flashing or thin aluminum sheeting

oil-based paints in bright colors of your choice★

paint thinner

scissors

masking tape

metal scribe or sharp nail

tin snips

hammer

leather embossing tools and/or chisels and screwdrivers

old piece of inner tube or piece of heavy rubber

paintbrushes

★Model airplane and car paint work best.

⋗ Instructions

1 ▪ Draw the figures onto paper, using the photograph as a guide. Cut out the patterns and tape them to the tin.

2 ▪ Trace around the paper with a metal scribe or sharp nail. Remove the paper template and cut out the figures, using tin snips.

3 ▪ Place each tin figure on the piece of rubber and hammer out any curling or crimping so that all the shapes lay flat. Use the leather tools, chisels, or screwdrivers and the hammer to scribe details in their robes, beards, fleece, etc., using the photograph as a guide. (*Tip:* Practice these detail lines on a scrap of tin to make sure the tools will not scratch the tin.)

4 ▪ Dilute the paint with paint thinner and paint the figures. Let them dry for at least one day.

5 ▪ Fold the tab under so that the figures stand upright.

Jesse Tree Ornaments

DESIGN
Gay D. Fay Kelly

In designer Gay Fay Kelly's family, colorful ornaments with these Old Testament symbols were hung on a Jesse Tree during Advent. These simple-to-make circles also make distinctive and meaningful Christmas Tree decorations.

SIZE:
3" (8 cm) in diameter

✤ Materials and Tools

½ yd. (46 cm) felt: white, dark purple

scraps of felt in orange, golden yellow, light purple, rose, red, bright green, russet brown, dark brown, light beige, turquoise, ivory, white, dark blue, light blue, black, and light sea green-gray

3 yds. (2.7 m) purple satin ribbon, ⅛" (3 mm) wide

1 yd. (92.5 cm) satin ribbon, ⅛" (3 mm) wide, in each of the following colors: orange, green, navy, and red

tracing paper

sharp pencil

craft glue for fabric

1 yd. (92.5 cm) iron-on heavy-duty adhesive (optional)

sharp, pointed scissors

✤ Instructions

The ornaments consist of symbols of Old Testament predecessors of Christ, the three exceptions being Joseph (carpenter's tools), Mary (lily) and John the Baptist (shell with water). The other ornaments, displayed in the photograph in chronological order, are: Adam (apple), Noah (ark), Abraham (tent), Isaac (ram), Jacob (ladder), Joseph (coat of many colors), Moses (tablets), Samson (strong arm), Ruth (sheaf of wheat), Samuel (lamp), David (harp), Solomon (crown), Elijah (raven), Isaiah (lantern), Ezekiel (flaming chariot), Daniel (lion), Jonah (whale), Joseph (carpenter's tools), Mary (lily), and John the Baptist (shell with water).

I ▪ From the purple and white felt, cut 20 circles, each 3" (8 cm) wide.

2 ▪ Trace the patterns (page 140) and cut them out—these are your templates for cutting out the felt shapes. Refer to the photograph for color selection and to see how the shapes are assembled. Accent Joseph's coat with strips of colored ribbon. (*Tip*: You can also make these ornaments by tracing the patterns onto iron-on adhesive. Follow manufacturer's directions.)

3 ▪ Glue the shapes onto the purple and white felt circles. Leave a blank set of circles to be attached later.

4 ▪ Cut a 9" (23 cm) piece of purple ribbon for each ornament. Fashion a small loop and glue it to the back side of one of the decorated felt circles, positioned so that the loop is centered above the decoration. Before the glue dries, apply glue around the edges of the circle. Choose a blank circle of a different color and sandwich the ribbon loop between the two felt circles. Press the circles together to evenly distribute the glue. Complete all the ornaments in this way. Let them dry thoroughly.

Christmas Tree Ornaments

DESIGN
Michelle Koepke West

WITH SIMPLE TECHNIQUES AND ORDINARY MATERIALS, DESIGNER MICHELLE WEST CREATED TWO EXTRAORDINARY ORNAMENTS THAT SYMBOLIZE ASPECTS OF HER FAITH.

Star of David

⁑ Materials and Tools

18" (46 cm) gold cord made with wire inside, ¼" (1 cm) wide

1 yd. (92.5 cm) gold ribbon, ⅛" (3 mm) wide

scissors

hot-glue gun and glue sticks

⁑ Instructions

1 ▪ Cut the heavy gold cord into two lengths, each 9" (23 cm) long. Shape one of the lengths into a triangle with 3" (8-cm) long sides. (The wire inside the cord will allow it to keep its shape.) Glue the loose end to the corner of the triangle. Repeat this process with the other piece of cord.

2 ▪ Interlock the two triangles by slipping the point of one triangle under the center and over the top of a flat side of the other triangle. Use a drop of hot glue at all the meeting points to hold the two triangles together.

3 ▪ Cut three 6" (15-cm) pieces of gold ribbon, and glue them to the bottom point of the star. Cut a 4" (10 cm) length of ribbon and glue it to the top of the triangle to make a hanging loop.

Wooden Cross Ornament

⁑ Materials and Tools

2 cinnamon sticks

18" (46 cm) gold ribbon, ⅛" (4 mm) wide

18" (46 cm) purple ribbon, ⅛" (3 mm) wide

30-gauge floral wire, 6" (15 cm) long

tiny purple, red, and white dried flowers

sharp knife

scissors

hot-glue gun

glue sticks

⁑ Instructions

1 ▪ Cut the cinnamon sticks so that you have one piece 5" (13 cm) long and another 3½" (9 cm) long. Wire the two sticks together to form the cross.

2 ▪ Make a many-looped bow with the purple and gold ribbon and let the streamers hang down. Glue the bow to the cross. Glue clusters of dried flowers onto the bow and the cross in a pleasing arrangement.

⁑ Designer Reflections

I feel drawn to this symbol because King David was the beloved King of Israel—"a man after God's own heart." The wooden cross ornament uses colors that are significant to the meaning of the cross: gold for the King, purple for His royalty, white for His righteousness, and red for the blood He shed for us.

Painted clay; made in Peru

Wood

Scandinavian Cross

DESIGN
Mark Strom

SIZE
9½" x 25" (24.5 x 64 cm)

To create this elegant cross, Mark Strom artfully combined dark and light wood, presented in simple, strong lines.

✂ Materials and Tools

walnut, 21" x 5¾" x ¾" (54 x 14.5 x 2 cm)

maple, 25" x 1⅛" x ½" (64 x 3.5 x 1.5 cm)

maple, 9½" x 1⅛" x ⅜" (24.5 x 3.5 x 1 cm)

maple strip, 67½" x ¼" x ⅜" (1.7 m x 1 x 1 cm)

wood glue

#50 & #220 sandpaper

cream-colored lacquer

½" (1.5 cm) brads

wood putty

(3) #8 countersink screws, 1" (2.5 cm) long

sturdy hanger

satin finish lacquer

paintbrushes

router

⅜" (1 cm) round-over bit

½" (1.5 cm) cove bit

radial arm saw

miter box and saw

electric drill

hammer

nail punch

Tip: Unless you are an experienced woodworker, it is advisable to have the walnut and the maple cut to the sizes listed above by the wood supplier. All the wood can be cut on a table saw and radial arm saw, but it is a difficult process and not the safest.

✂ Instructions

1 ▪ Pick the best-looking face of the walnut board. Using the round-over bit, rout the edges around the entire board. Flip the board over and use the cove bit to rout a cove around the whole board. Sand until smooth.

2 ▪ It is advisable to try out steps 2 and 3 first using two scraps of wood. On the 25" (64-cm) long piece of maple, measure down 4½" (11.5 cm) and mark. Measure down 5⅛" (13.5 cm) and mark. Using a radial arm saw, cut a dado or slot exactly halfway (¼"/1 cm) through the piece between the lines marked.

3 ▪ On the 9½" (24.5-cm) long piece of maple, measure down 4¼" (11 cm) and mark, then measure down 5⅜" (13.5 cm) and mark. Cut as described in step 2.

4 ▪ Glue the two pieces together to form the cross body and sand until smooth.

5 ▪ From the long strip of maple, cut 2 strips, each 20" (51 cm) long.

Cut 6 strips, each 5¼" (13.5 cm) long from the same stock. Cut a 45-degree miter cut on one end of each piece. Position them against the cross body with the ¼" (1 cm) side facing up. (In this cross, each strip is ½" (1.5 cm) shorter than the cross body it rests against. The long bottom strips are cut to suit your own tastes.) Sand until smooth, and paint with the cream-colored lacquer.

6 ▪ Attach the painted strips to the cross body using ½" (1.5 cm) brads. Do not nail any closer than 1½" (4 cm) from the end of the strip or the wood will split. This can be avoided by pre-drilling with a drill bit the same size or slightly smaller than the brad. After nailing in place, countersink with the nail punch, fill the holes, sand smooth, and touch up with paint.

7 ▪ Lay the cross face down. Place the walnut board face down on top of the cross. Leave 2½" (6.5 cm) of the cross extending past the walnut back on the bottom. Center the cross on the walnut board by carefully measuring each side. Mount the back to the cross by countersinking the #8 screws, one at the top, middle, and bottom of the cross. Be careful to countersink the screws the least amount possible so they do not protrude from the face of the cross.

8 ▪ Measure down 4" (10 cm) from the top of the walnut board and mark. Find the center of the board at the 4" (10 cm) mark. Mount the hanger exactly on the center or the cross will hang improperly.

9 ▪ Finish the entire cross, front and back, with three coats of clear lacquer.

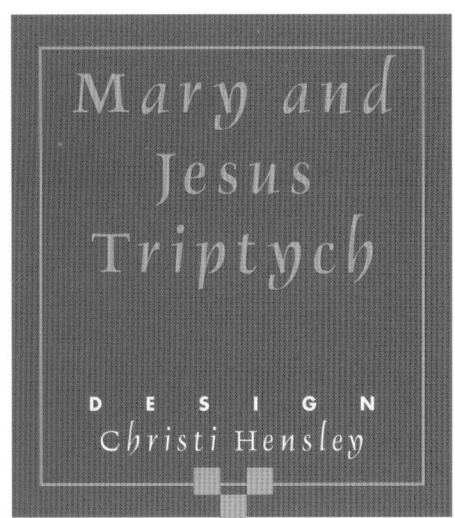

Mary and Jesus Triptych

DESIGN
Christi Hensley

SIZE
(unopened)
7" x 7" (18 x 18 cm)

Transform a favorite Christmas card into what resembles an elegant, 14th century altarpiece, using modest materials and simple techniques.

⁑ Materials and Tools

piece of plywood, ¼" x 10" x 12" (1 x 26 x 31 cm)

Christmas cards

scraps of heavy paper or wallpaper with floral pattern

leather or cloth scraps, 2" x 5" (5 x 13 cm)

white cardboard or card stock, about 5" x 5" (13 x 13 cm)

instant papier mâché

gesso sealer

acrylic paints: gold and black

jigsaw

kitchen knife

fine-grade sandpaper

paintbrushes

damp cloth

scissors

white craft glue

⁑ Instructions

1 ▪ Enlarge figure 1 and figure 2 (page 141) on a copier as indicated. Transfer figure 1 onto the plywood. Use the jigsaw to cut out the three sections.

2 ▪ Prepare the papier mâché according to the package directions. Position the three pieces as shown in figure 1. On the edges, build up a papier mâché frame about ½" (1.5 cm) wide and ¼" (1 cm) thick. Use a knife to help shape and mold the edges; use the knife and/or any interesting shaped objects to make decorative impressions on the wet papier mâché frame. Let the frame dry and sand it lightly.

3 ▪ Paint the frame with gesso sealer and let it dry. Paint the frame and the back of the plywood gold and let dry. To achieve the antique-looking finish, dab a small amount of black paint onto the damp cloth and lightly rub over the gold paint.

4 ▪ Paint the middle panel black and let it dry. Cut and glue the picture and the decorative paper onto the panels.

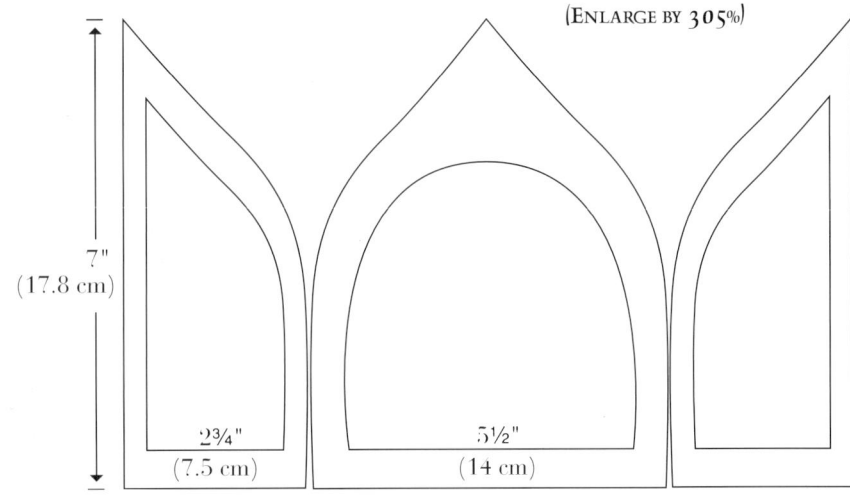

A perfect fit is difficult; try cutting the picture smaller than the opening and letting the black background show around the edges.

5. Turn the two side panels over and fit them together as shown in figure 2. Transfer the dove pattern onto white card stock or thin cardboard. Cut out the dove, position it on the two panels, and glue in place. Outline the dove with black paint.

6. Cut the leather or cloth scraps into two pieces, each 1" x 2½" (2.5 x 6.5 cm). Use them to join the side panels to the center, attaching them to the frame with glue or tacks.

(ENLARGE BY 305%)

7"
(17.8 cm)

2¾"
(7.5 cm)

5½"
(14 cm)

Figure 1

Church Birdhouse

DESIGN
Robin Clark

D ESIGNED BY ROBIN CLARK, THIS CHARMING BIRDHOUSE IS SURE TO MAKE REGULAR CHURCHGOERS OUT OF YOUR FAVORITE BACKYARD WRENS.

❧ Materials and Tools

cedar or pine, ¾" (2 cm) thick:

(1) 5½" x 8¼" (14 x 21.5 cm)— roof

(1) 4¾" x 8¼" (12 x 21.5 cm)— roof

(2) 6¼" x 7" (16 x 18 cm)—sides

(2) 5½" x 9¾" (14 x 25 cm)— front/back

(1) 1½" x 1½" x 2" (4 x 4 x 5 cm)—tower

(1) 7¼x 8½" (18.5 x 22 cm)—base

cedar or pine, ⅜" (1.5 cm) thick:

(5) 1½" x 3¾" (4 x 9.5 cm)— windows

(1) 2¾" x 4½" (7 x 11.5 cm)— door

(1) 2" x 2" (5 x 5 cm)—tower trim

(1) 3" (7.5 cm)—cross

sandpaper

wood glue

wood filler

primer

high-gloss white enamel paint

acrylic paints in red, blue, green, light yellow, dark yellow, brown, gray, and black

decking screws or nails, 1¼" (3.5 cm) wide

½" (1 cm) brad

saw

band saw

paintbrushes

❧ Instructions

1 ▪ Cut all the pieces as indicated. On the front and back pieces, measure 7" (14 cm) up the sides and cut a 45-degree angle to form a peak. Cut the curved tops on the windows and the door. Cut the wood for the cross so that you have one 1½" (4 cm) piece and two ½" (1.5 cm) pieces. Glue the three pieces together to form the cross.

2 ▪ Drill a hole 1½" (4 cm), centered 7" (14 cm) up on the front piece.

3 ▪ Using nails, screws, or glue, attach the sides to the front and back.

4 ▪ Center the box on the base and attach it with nails or screws from underneath.

5 ▪ Lay the narrower roof piece even with the peak and secure it with nails, screws, or glue. Overlap the wider roof piece and secure it with nails, screws, or glue.

6 ▪ Cut the tower piece so it straddles the roof's peak. Glue it on. Secure the cross to the tower with a ½" (1 cm) brad. Glue on the windows and the door (one window goes on the back).

7 ▪ Fill all holes with wood filler and sand all rough surfaces.

8 ▪ Apply a coat of primer to the entire birdhouse and let dry. Apply several coats of white enamel to the entire birdhouse, letting each coat dry thoroughly.

9 ▪ Using a "dry" brush, stipple the front of the five windows, including the half window in the door) with acrylic paints to create a stained glass effect. When the paint is dry, use black paint to outline and cross-hatch the windows. Paint the door brown; when dry, add yellow handles and a single vertical black line to create the two halves of the door.

10 ▪ Streak the roof with wide, rough strokes of gray paint. Paint the cross dark yellow. Last, paint the base green, using swirling strokes to create a grass-like effect.

Carved wood; made in West Bank, Palestine

Noah's Ark Headboard

DESIGN
Mary Jane Miller

DESIGNER MARY JANE MILLER TRANSFORMED AN OLD HEADBOARD AND FOOTBOARD BY TREATING IT AS A MURAL FOR HER DECORATIVE PAINT- ING. USE HER CRE- ATION TO INSPIRE ONE OF YOUR OWN!

‣ Materials and Tools

headboard, old or new

sandpaper

acrylic primer

pencil

acrylic paints in colors of your choice

paintbrushes

oil-based polyurethane

‣ Instructions

I ▪ Sand the headboard well, then prime it and let it dry. Priming seals the wood and prevents old wood stain from bleeding through, and covers any variation in the finish. Sanding smooths rough surfaces or can inten- tionally roughen the surface if it is too smooth or glossy to accept paint well. (*Tip:* The more ornate the headboard is, the more work it will be to ade- quately sand and prime the wood.)

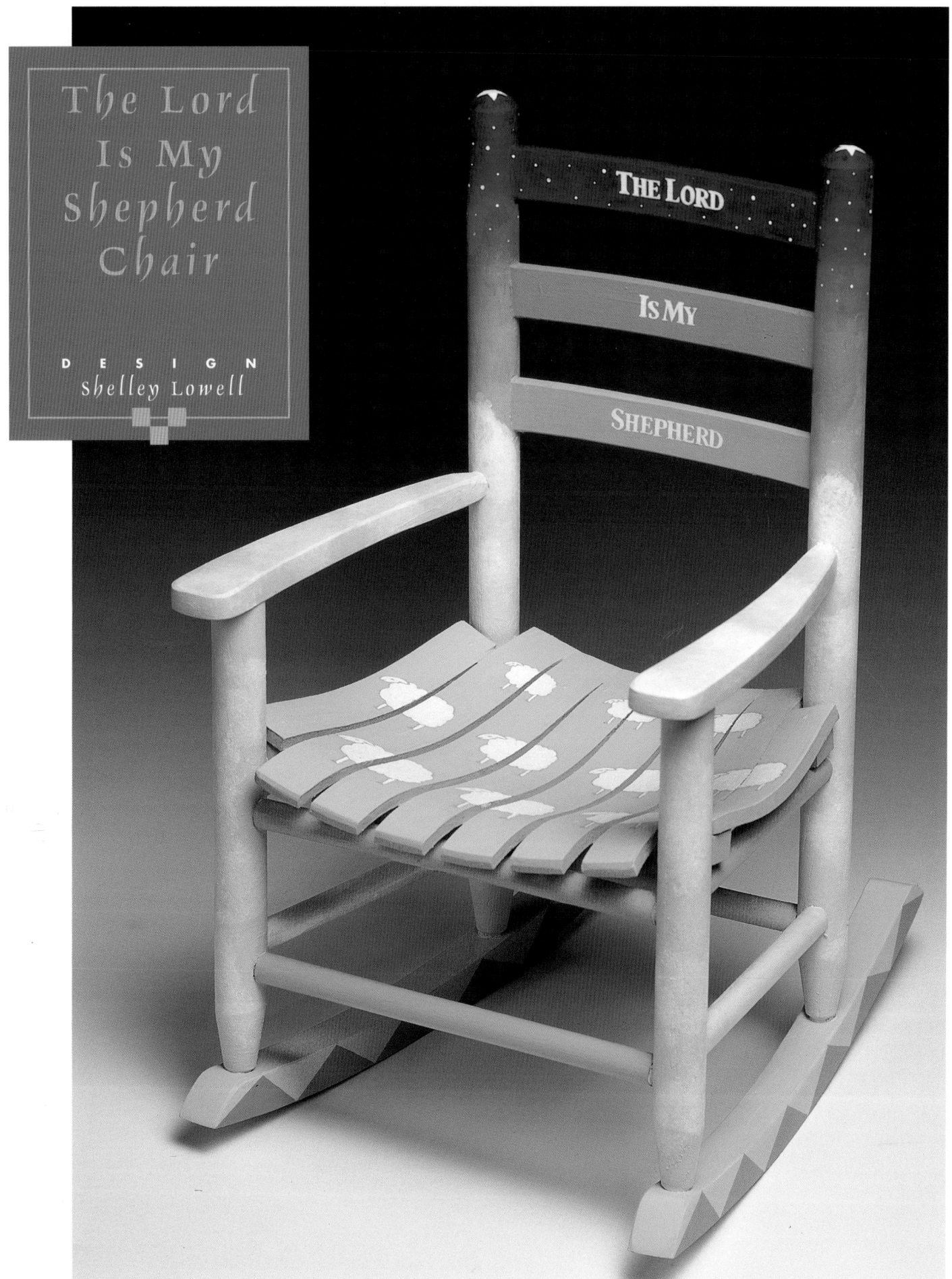

The Lord
Is My
Shepherd
Chair

DESIGN
Shelley Lowell

THE LORD

IS MY

SHEPHERD

2 ▪ Sketch your design on the primed surface. One good source for ideas is a child's color-illustrated book of Bible stories.

3 ▪ Begin to paint the design. Work slowly and carefully until you finish. Let the paint dry for at least two days.

4 ▪ Apply two coats of oil-based polyurethane, letting each coat dry for two days.

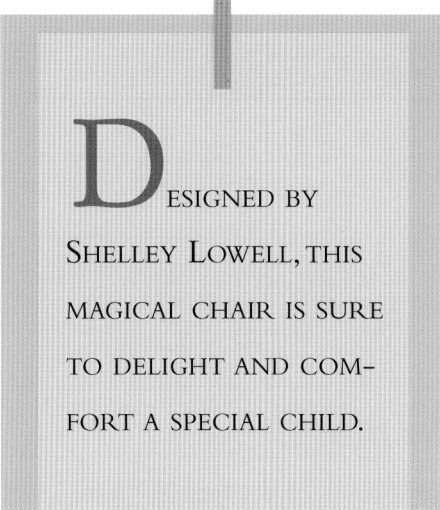

D ESIGNED BY SHELLEY LOWELL, THIS MAGICAL CHAIR IS SURE TO DELIGHT AND COMFORT A SPECIAL CHILD.

⯈ Materials and Tools

child's wooden rocking chair

wood filler

sandpaper, medium and fine grit

gesso

acrylic paint: light green, yellow, dark blue, orange, white, and light violet

paintbrushes in various sizes, flat- and round-tipped, including a #0 brush and a #1 or #2 chisel-point

6 small empty jars

ruler

pencil

masking tape

drawing of a star

white pastel pencil

lettering for words

graphite or charcoal pencil

plastic tray

small sea sponge for clouds

water-based polyurethane

⯈ Instructions

1 ▪ Fill holes, cracks, or uneven areas with wood filler. Remove excess, let dry, and sand.

2 ▪ Go over the entire chair with sandpaper to smooth, first with medium grit sandpaper and then with fine grit. Wipe or vacuum off all the wood dust.

3 ▪ Paint the entire chair with gesso. When dry, sand with fine grit sandpaper. Apply one more coat and let dry. If there are still rough areas, lightly sand again and repaint with gesso if you need to.

4 ▪ Paint the top and the underside of the seat, the front and back rungs, and the tops of the rockers with the green paint. Let dry. In one of the empty jars, mix a batch of lighter green by adding a little yellow to the green paint. Mix enough to cover the top of the seat, the top of each rocker, and to cover any drips from the other colors.

5 ▪ Mix five shades of the dark blue paint with white paint (one in each jar) so that you wind up with a range of blue, from very light blue to a shade slightly lighter than the original dark blue. Make sure you mix enough color for each section. If you feel comfortable, you can apply the blue paints on the chair so that each shade blends into each other. Otherwise, apply the blue paints in graduated bands as shown in figure 1 on page 110. (You may want to measure off and draw lines across the chair back to delineate between shades.) Paint the arms and the spindles that connect to the rocker the lightest shade of blue.

6 ▪ Paint the four sides of the rocker base and the two side rungs yellow. When dry, measure the bottom of each rocker. The rockers on this chair are 18" (46 cm) long, so the designer divided each rocker into six sections of 3" (8 cm) each. Measure the top part of the rocker and locate the middle of each section. With a ruler and pencil, connect the marks to make tri-

angles. Paint the bottom triangles orange. You can use tape to mask off the yellow, or you can paint freehand. You will probably have to apply two or three coats.

7 ▪ You can draw a star freehand on a piece of paper or make a photocopy of a drawing of a star from a book. On the backside of the paper, rub white pastel pencil all around the edges of the star. Trim off any excess paper so you can easily position the star on the top of each side spindle. With a hard pencil or ink pen, trace over the star on top of the chair. When you remove the paper, you should see the outline of the star on the top of the spindle. Paint the stars white with at least two coats.

8 ▪ Use this same technique to trace on the words. You can find alphabet books with many styles of lettering in art- or craft-supply stores. Or you may find letters you like in a book you already own. Simply trace the letters, then photocopy them to the size you want. Using charcoal or graphite pencil on the backside of the photocopy, trace the letters onto the slats. This method makes the piece look more custom than if you used stencils. But, if you prefer, you can use stencils.

9 ▪ Paint the letters white with the chisel-pointed brush. Use the side of the brush rather than the tip, thin the paint with water, and use the paint sparingly. Then go over the letters with a second or third coat. If you go out of the lines, retouch with the base paint when you have completed all the letters.

10 ▪ For the small stars, put some white paint in a cup or bottle cap and thin with a little water. Dip the back end of the brush into the paint and dot the paint onto the chair.

11 ▪ For the sheep, make three photocopies of figure 2 on page 110, each one in a different size. Transfer the patterns onto the chair seat using the method described in step 8. Place the largest sheep up front and the smallest ones in the back, so they appear to be receding into the distance. Paint the sheep white with two coats of paint. Then outline them with a #0 brush using light violet.

12▪ For the clouds, thin some white paint with water in a small tray. Wet the sea sponge and squeeze out as much excess water as possible. Dip it into the white paint, dab off the excess, and then dab the sponge onto the chair, using the photograph to guide you.

13▪ Proudly sign and date your creation.

14▪ Let the chair dry for at least 24 hours to allow the paint to cure properly. Apply three coats of polyurethane and let dry thoroughly.

Figure 1

Figure 2

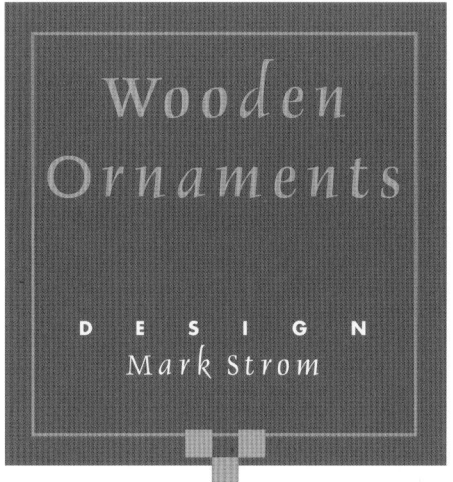

Wooden Ornaments

DESIGN
Mark Strom

SIZE:
Wheat bundle and dove—
3" (8 cm) in diameter

Celtic Cross—
2½"x 5" (6 x13 cm)

DESIGNED BY MARK STROM, THIS TRIO OF HANDSOME SCROLL SAW ORNAMENTS, REPRESENTING A BUNDLE OF WHEAT, A DESCENDING DOVE, AND A CELTIC CROSS, WILL MAKE LOVELY ADDITIONS TO ANY CHRISTMAS TREE.

▪Materials and Tools

12" x 12" (31 x 31 cm) plywood, 1/8" (3 mm) thick★

pencil and compass

#220 sandpaper

wood glue

paintbrushes

acrylic paint in white and ivory

permanent markers in black and gold

clear lacquer

heavy gold thread

scroll saw

drill and 1/4" and 1/32" bits

★enough plywood to make all three ornaments

Wheat/ Descending Dove

▪Instructions

I▪ Use the compass and pencil to draw a circle on the plywood, 3" (8 cm) in diameter. Using the same center, draw another circle, 2-¾" (7 cm) in diameter, inside the circle.

2▪ Drill a ¼" (6-mm) hole in the middle circle and use that as your entry point for the scroll saw blade. Cut the inside circle out first, then cut the outside circle.

3▪ Transfer the wheat or the dove pattern (page 141) onto the uncut plywood.

4▪ Cut 1 wheat piece and 2 dove pieces and sand.

5▪ Stain and paint the wheat bundle and/or the two doves as desired. After the pieces are dry, glue them onto the circle(s) you cut in step 2.

6▪ Drill a ¹⁄₃₂"-hole in the top edge of the circle, insert a length of gold thread, and tie the ends to create a loop.

Celtic Cross

▪Instructions

I▪ Use the compass and pencil to draw a circle on the plywood, 2" (5 cm) in diameter. Using the same center, draw another circle, 1-¾" (4.5 cm) in diameter, inside the circle.

2 ▪ Drill a ¼" (6-mm) hole in the middle circle and use that as your entry point for the scroll saw blade. Cut the inside circle out first, then cut the outside circle.

3 ▪ Transfer the cross pattern (page 141) onto the plywood and cut it out. Sand the wood well.

4 ▪ Outline the cross with gold and black markers, using the photograph as a guide.

5 ▪ Glue the cross onto the circle you cut in step 2. Finish with two coats of clear lacquer and let dry.

6 ▪ Drill a ¹⁄₃₂"-hole in the top edge of the circle, insert a length of gold thread, and tie the ends to create a loop.

Gourds

The remarkable gourd people and animals that appear on pages 112 to 117 were created by Ginger Summit. Let them inspire you to transform humble gourds into truly holy ones.

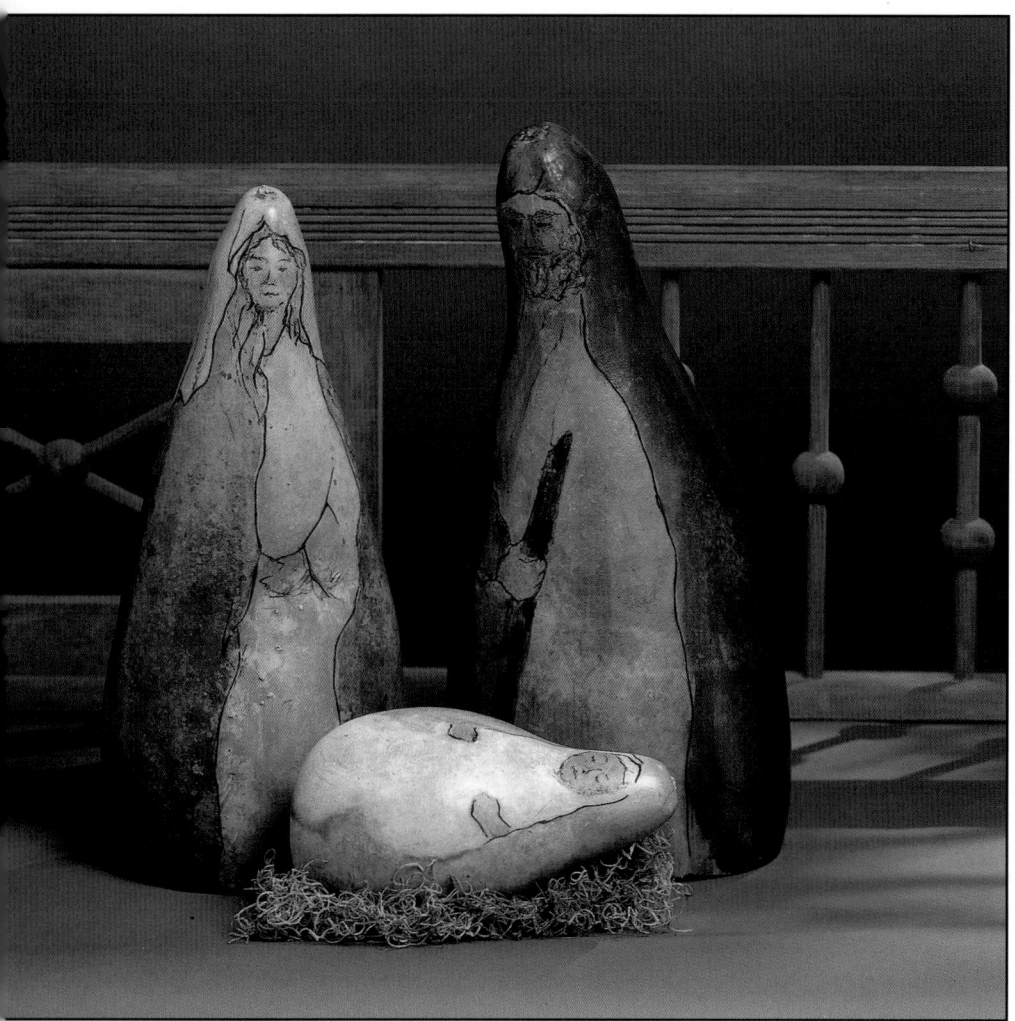

NATIVITY (*photo on page 112*)

Additional Supplies and Tools

smooth ornamental gourds, cured (people)

smooth or warty ornamental gourd, cured (sheep)

bushel gourd with a long stem, cured (manger)

buttons, twigs

gourd scraps

leather scraps

¼" (6 mm) dowels

hinges and screws

blue acrylic paint

gold star

I ▪ For the people, select gourds that have one narrow end (for the head). If the gourds do not sit upright on a flat surface, place them on a small glass and mark a line around the base of the gourd. Cut the bottom off with a hobby knife or saw, and clean out the interior pulp and seeds. Choose the smallest gourd for the baby and leave it uncut.

2 ▪ Draw the features and clothing with a pencil and go over the lines with a wood-burning tool. Use leather dyes and/or acrylic paints to add appropriate colors. When dry, apply varnish.

3 ▪ Add additional embellishment, such as a twig for the shepherd's crook, buttons for the gift containers, and clipped fleece for the beards or hair.

4 ▪ Drill a ⅛" (3 mm) hole in the top of each gourd figure and glue in a loop of ribbon for a hanger.

5 ▪ For the sheep, refer to step 6 of the Shepherd and Sheep project on page 116.

❧ Materials and Tools

pencil

wood-burning tool

acrylic paints

paintbrushes

leather dyes

permanent marking pens

craft glue

wood glue

sandpaper

files

varnish spray

drill and drill bits

bleach

rubber gloves

large plastic dish pan or tub

plastic or metal kitchen scrubbing pad

dull kitchen knife

brush with stiff, natural bristles

pencil

sharp knife

keyhole saw, hobby saw, motorized cutting tool, or small hand-held power jigsaw

old metal kitchen spoon

metal scouring pad

❧ Instructions For All Gourds

Soak the gourd in a tub of water into which you have mixed a small amount of bleach. Cover the gourd with an old towel to weigh it down so that the entire gourd is submerged. Soak the gourd for 30 minutes. Scrub off the mold with a scrubbing pad and brush; scrape of stubborn spots with a dull knife.

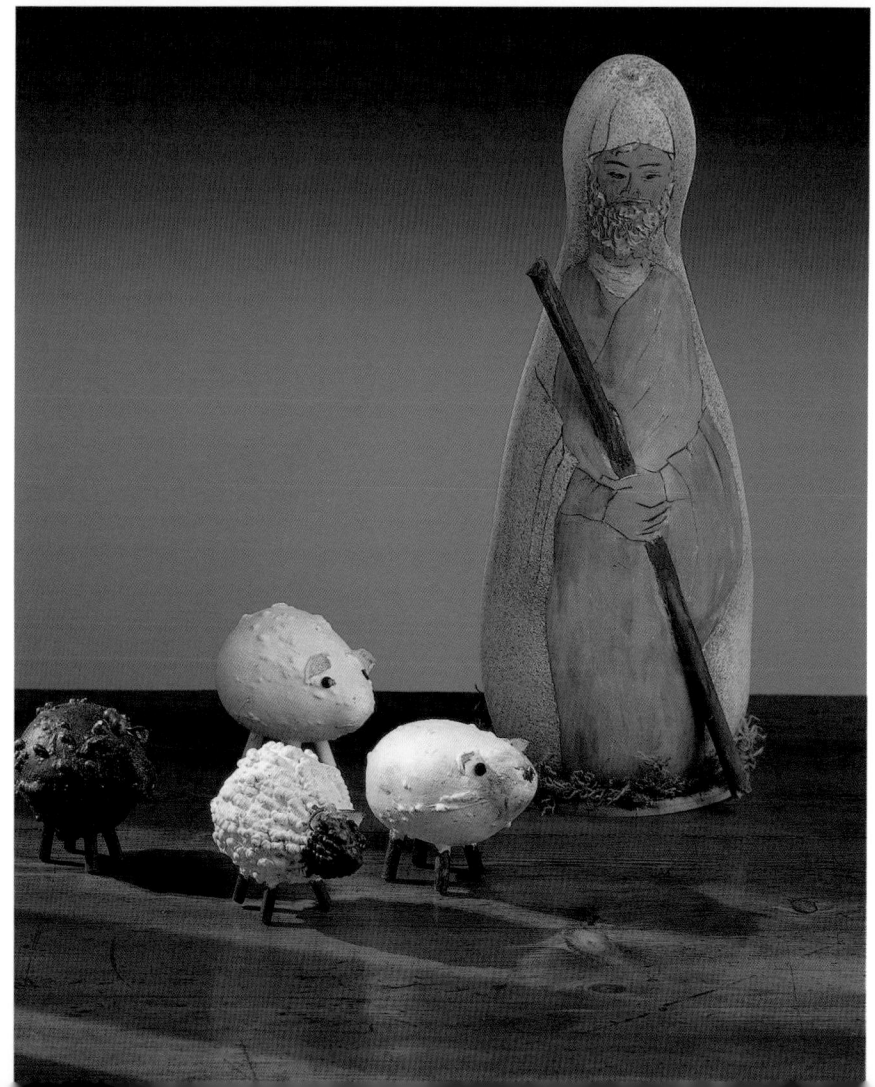

6. For the manger: Mark the doors with a pencil and cut it out using a hobby saw or keyhole saw. Remove the seeds and pulp and smooth the interior with sandpaper. Reattach the door with small hinges. Glue first, then secure with small screws. Add a roof with shingles cut from gourd scraps or from straw or other similar materials. Use diluted leather dyes to shade the exterior of the manger and the gourd shingles. Paint the top of the gourd blue and glue on the star. When dry, varnish.

THREE KINGS

Additional Supplies and Tools

3 penguin or powderhorn gourds, cured

oil pastels

rubber stamps

embossing compounds

2 ▪ Sketch the features and clothing and then wood burn the outlines. Color the gourds with leather dyes. When dry, varnish.

THREE KINGS (*photo on page 115*)

Additional Supplies and Tools

3 penguin or powderhorn gourds, cured

oil pastels

rubber stamps

embossing compounds

gold leaf

gold metallic paint

found objects, such as buttons, wooden finial, beads, seashells

gesso

toothpick

⸭ Instructions

I ▪ If the gourds do not stand upright, complete step 1 of the Nativity project on page 114.

2 ▪ Wood burn the facial features and the outlines of the clothing. Decorate and shade with acrylic paints, leather dyes, and/or oil pastels.

3 ▪ Add texture to the painted on fabric by using stamps and embossing compounds which are available in many colors, including metallics. When dry, varnish.

4 ▪ For gift containers, glue on seashells, buttons, and beads.

5 ▪ Create texture for the beards by mixing acrylic paint with gesso. Apply the mixture to the gourd in a very thick layer, and then create texture by daubing with a toothpick.

SHEPHERD AND SHEEP (*photo on page 115*)

Additional Supplies and Tools

penguin or powderhorn gourd, cured

3 or 4 warty ornamental gourds, cured

narrow stick with slight bow

wood putty

masking tape

off-white textured spray paint

off-white shoe polish

wood stain

¼" 96 mm) dowels

varnish spray

⸭ Instructions

I ▪ If the large gourd does not stand upright, complete step 1 of the Nativity project on page 114.

2 ▪ Draw, then wood burn, the facial features and clothing.

3 ▪ For the staff, soak the stick so that you can bend it slightly. Determine where the shepherd's hands will hold the staff and drill holes above and below the hand. Use a file to shape the holes so that the stick will lie against the body at the correct angle. Use wood putty to fill in the spaces where the gourd shell and holes were adjusted for the stick.

4 ▪ Create texture on the robe with textured spray paint. First, sketch the clothing, then use masking tape to cover all the other gourd surfaces. Spray with at least two coats of paint. When dry, shade the robe with leather dyes or shoe polish. Apply wood stain to staff.

5 ▪ For the beard, see step 5 of the Three Kings project on this page.

6 ▪ For the sheep: Hold the ornamental gourds on their sides and determine the placement of the legs. Drill four holes. Insert one piece of dowel into the gourd as far as it will go. Mark the end of the leg (the foot). Remove the dowel and cut four pieces this length. Glue in the legs. Cut triangles from the leather scraps to make ears. Cut slits in the top of the gourd and glue the ears in place. Paint the sheep, and when dry, apply the varnish.

JONAH AND THE WHALE

Additional Supplies and Tools

2 penguin or powderhorn gourds, cured

ornamental gourd, cured

leather scraps

tiny nails or screws

masking tape

wood filler

scrap of fabric

acrylic paint: light gray, dark gray, white, black, silver, and blublack permanent marking pens

varnish spray

⁑ Instructions

1 ▪ The gourd you select for the whale should be able to lie securely on one side. Sketch a line around the broad end of the gourd for the opening of the mouth, making sure that it goes back at least one-third of the gourd's length. Connect the ends of the mouth line with a line that runs under the whale's belly.

2 ▪ With a sharp knife, make a slit along this line and cut the gourd with a saw. Remove the entire lower jaw section. Clean out the gourd using scraping tools and rough sandpaper.

3 ▪ Attach the lower jaw to the underbody of the whale with a hinge made from a scrap of leather. If the leather is thick, you may want to gouge out a part of the gourd shell so

that the leather will lie even with the surface of the gourd shell. Glue the leather to both the jaw section and the whale's body, and further secure it with tiny nails or wood screws.

4 ▪ On the narrow end of the gourd, mark where the tail will be attached. Experiment with a scrap of a separate gourd to decide the shape and the position of a tail that will best suit your whale. Angle the cut where the tail is to be attached so that the new portion will cover a minimum amount of the opening. Cut the tail section out of the second gourd, being sure to leave plenty of extra gourd that can be sanded or filed down as you fit the two sections together. Work slowly and carefully as you sand and file both the body and the tail until you get a good fit.

5 ▪ Apply a generous coating of wood

glue to both the body of the whale and the tail and secure the pieces with masking tape. Let dry thoroughly. Once the glue is dry, you can remove the tape and use wood putty to fill in any holes or rough spaces in the joint. When the putty is dry, use a file or sandpaper to smooth the entire area.

6 ▪ Paint the whale a light gray, then sponge on the darker gray. Be sure to paint the cut edges of the mouth. When the body is dry, add the eyes. Spray on one or two coats of varnish.

7 ▪ Paint Jonah's robe and shirt. Add his beard, using white, gray, or silver paint. Use permanent marking pens to create the face and outline the hands.

8 ▪ Soak the scrap of fabric in a solution of white glue diluted with water. Mold the fabric over his head and secure with a colored rubber band,

Gourd Ornaments

DESIGN
Ginger Summit

SIZE
4" x 6" (10 x 15 cm)

Representing 11 flowers and plants with Biblical significance, these beautifully decorated gourds, designed by Ginger Summit, are simple to make and will be valued by your family for years to come.

⁑ Materials and Tools

11 or 12 ornamental gourds, cured

pencil

colored pencils

acrylic paints

gold cord

wood-burning tool

clear enamel spray

paintbrushes

hot-glue and glue sticks

⁑ Instructions

1 ▪ Follow step 1, on page 114, for details on how to clean the gourds.

2 ▪ Using the project photograph or other pictures, sketch the flowers and plants onto the surface of the gourd.

3 ▪ Carefully, with light pressure, wood burn along the pencil lines. Paint the gourds to depict the flowers and plants. When the paint dries, spray lightly with enamel to protect the surface of the gourds.

4 ▪ Glue on the gold cord to create a loop for hanging the ornaments.

And when they were come into the house, they saw the young child with Mary his mother, and fell down, and worshipped him: and when they had opened their treasures, they presented unto him gifts; gold, and frankincense, and myrrh.

—St. Matthew 2:11

The righteous shall flourish like the palm tree:
he shall grow like a cedar in Lebanon.
Those that be planted in the house of the Lord shall flourish in the courts of our God.

—Psalm 92:12-13

And he fenced it, and gathered out the stones thereof, and planted it with the choicest vine, and built a tower in the midst of it, and also made a winepress therein: and he looked that it should bring forth grapes, and it brought forth wild grapes.

—Isaiah 5:2

THIS HANDSOME ENGRAVED
AND STAINED GOURD IS A
TESTIMONY TO THE POWER OF
ANCIENT STORIES.

❧ Materials and Tools

penguin or powderhorn gourd, cured, 10" to 16" (26 to 41 cm) tall

assorted shapes and sizes of wood chisels and files

rough sandpaper

soft cloth

leather dye in several shades of brown and dark brown

acrylic paints (optional)

sponge (optional)

❧ Instructions

1 ▪ Clean the gourd as described in step 1 on page 114.

2 ▪ Mark the gourd with horizontal pencil lines that divide it into five or six sections. Make these lines irregular to create the jigsaw puzzle effect and simulate the brickwork of a castle.

3 ▪ Use the sharp knife to make a small slit along one of the lines. Insert your cutting tool into the slit and slowly cut along the irregular line until the gourd is cut into two pieces. (*Tip:* If you use a power tool, make sure the gourd is secure on your work surface. A foam pad will help to keep the gourd from slipping.)

4 ▪ Remove the interior pulp and seeds; most will come out by hand. Use any variety of spoon or scraper to remove the remaining material.

5 ▪ Cut the rest of the gourd along the lines you have marked to create several rings or sections. Smooth the interior of the sections using scraping tools and sandpaper. Lightly sand the edges.

6 ▪ Put the gourd together. Mark where you want the door and windows. Disassemble the gourd and cut out these openings. Sand the edges.

7 ▪ Sketch out a series of irregular rectangles over the entire surface of the gourd to create the effect of stone masonry. Use a motorized power tool or wood chisel to lightly carve these lines.

8 ▪ Rub brown leather dyes on the outside of the gourd sections. By using several shades of brown, you will create the look of weathered stone. You may want to apply acrylic paint with a sponge to increase the aged effect. Apply dark brown leather dye on the insides of the gourd sections and let them dry.

Painting in a style reminiscent of a medieval icon, Mary Jane Miller created this lovely portrait of Jesus.

Patterns

Madonna and Child Banner

(ENLARGE BY 200%)

halo cutting line

halo cutting line

face cutting line

face cutting line

Stitching lines for layers

Figure 2

Ecco Virgo
concipiet...

Bible or Prayer Book Cover

Quilted Wall Hanging

(ENLARGE BY 200%)

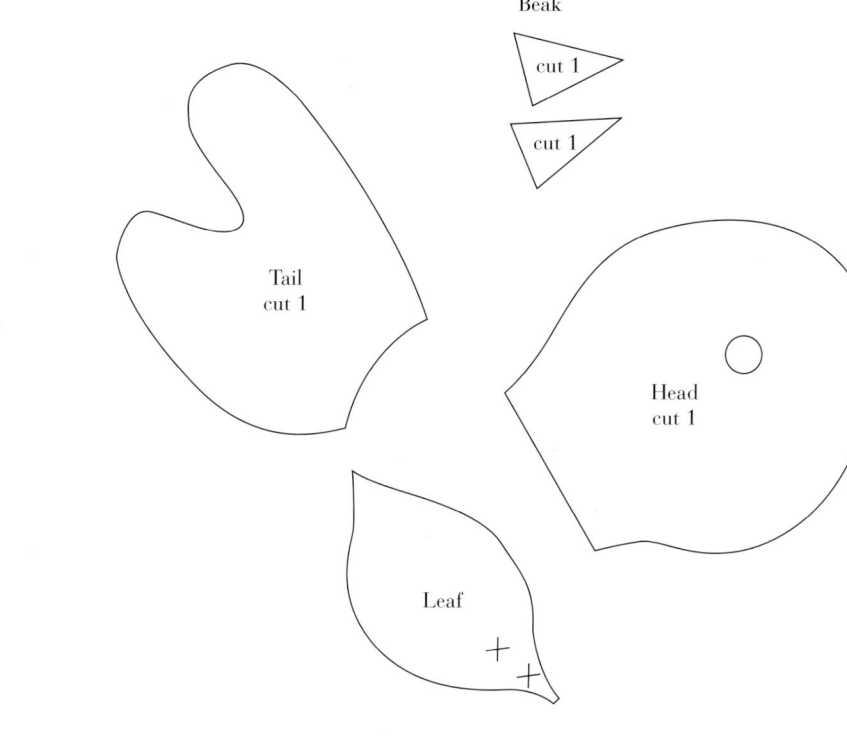

Beak
cut 1

cut 1

Tail
cut 1

Head
cut 1

Leaf

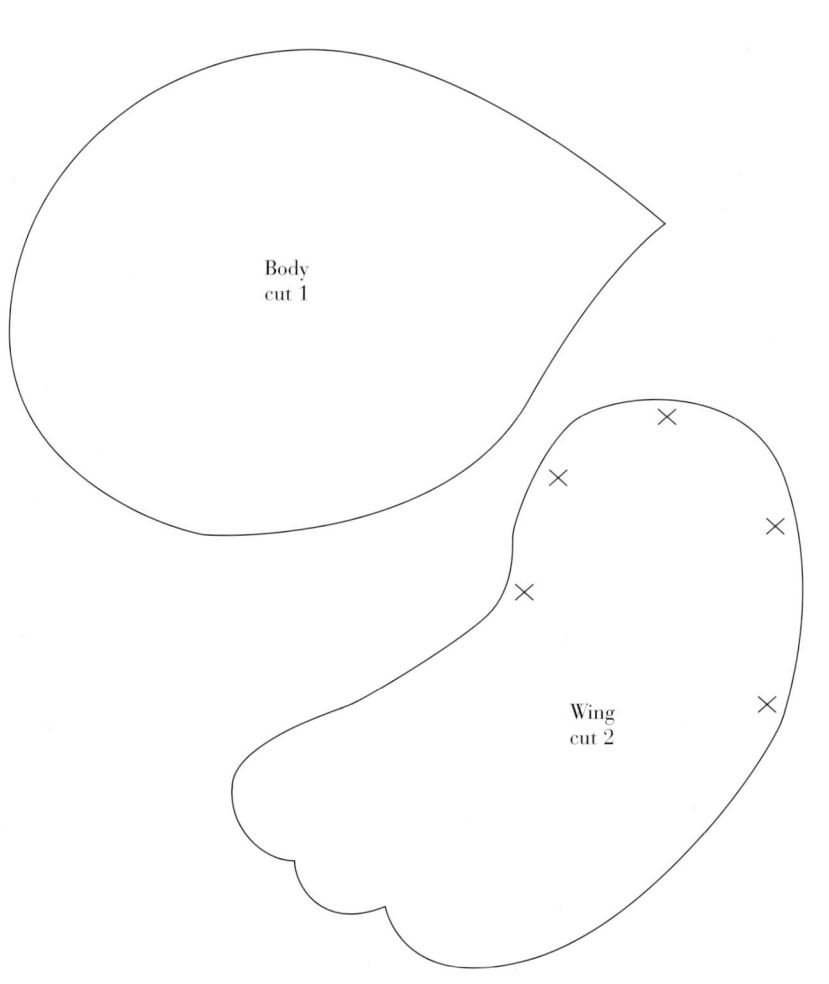

Body
cut 1

Wing
cut 2

Felt Christmas Tree Skirt

Monogrammed Shirt & Tie

Garden of Eden
Needlepoint Pillow

Color Key (all Paternayan Persian Tapestry Wool)

Symbol	Color	Number	Amount
1	Off-White	262	20 yards/18m
■	Dark Coffee Brown	420	10 yards/9m
/	Light Khaki Brown	454	10 yards/9m
＼	Terracotta Brown	480	20 yards/18m
▬	Dark Spruce Green	530	60 yards/55m
G	Grass Green	611	75 yards/69m
T	Cobalt Blue	540	20 yards/18m
•	Sky Blue	542	120 yards/110m
Y	Autumn Yellow	725	40 yards/37m
▲	Christmas Red	969	60 yards/55m

130

Dove Sweater

Key to charts A, B, & C

☐ = MC (blue)

◩ = A (deep red)

◣ = B (lavender)

⌒ = C (strawberry)

⌓ = D (bright pink)

▽ = E (green)

Chart A

Chart B

Chart C

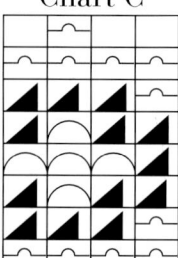

Dove Sweater

Chart D

Candlewick Christmas Tree Skirt

Noah's Ark Cross Stitch

Color Key

Symbol	Color	DMC	Anchor
1	Off-White	Ecru	926
■	Dark Coffee Brown	3371	382
/	Light Khaki Brown	613	899
↘	Terracotta Brown	300	352
▬	Dark Spruce Green	500	879
G	Grass Green	905	258
◁	Cobalt Blue	820	134
o	Sky Blue	798	131
Y	Autumn Yellow	3820	307
⌐	Christmas Red	349	46

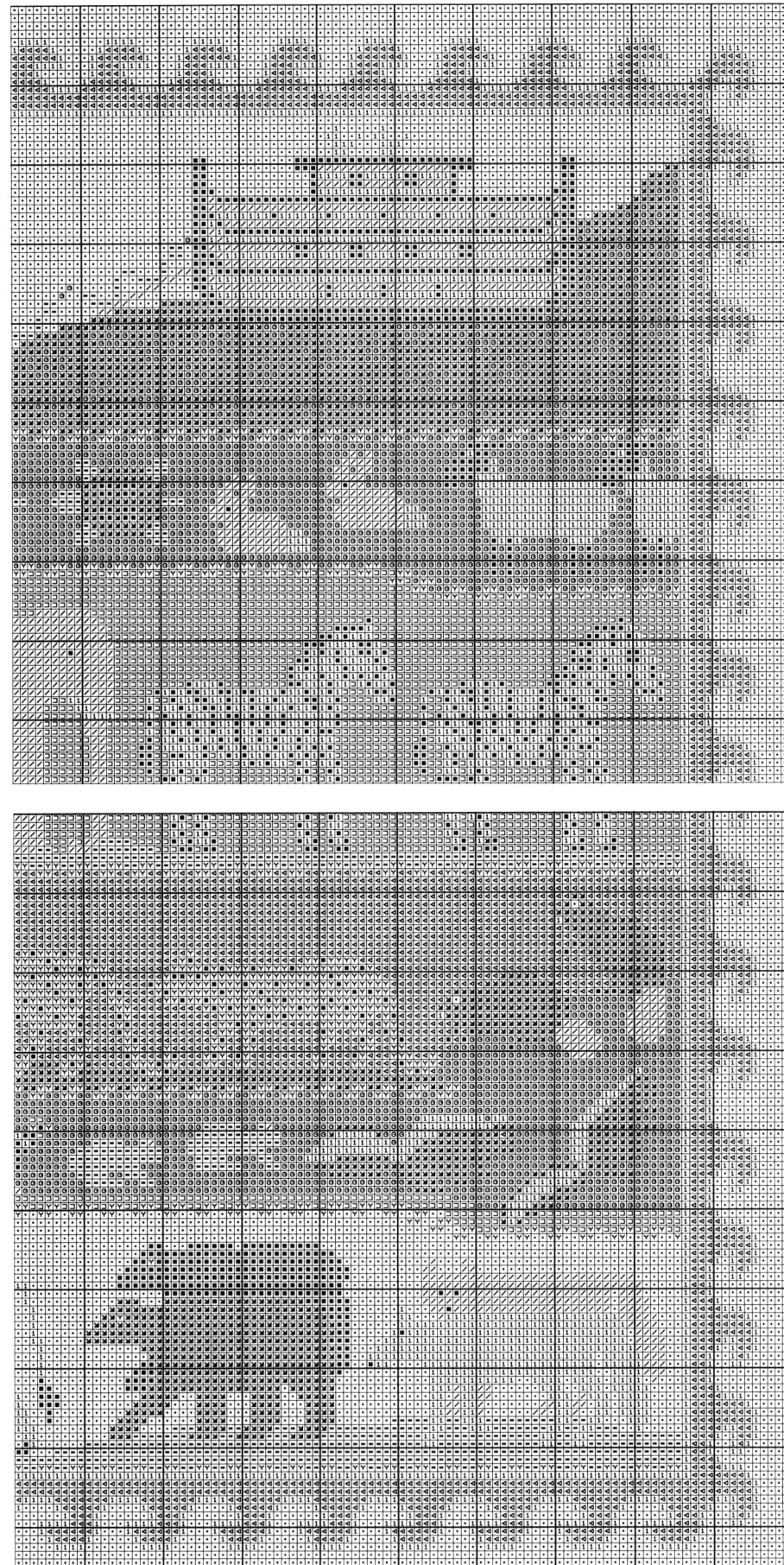

Ewe with Lamb

Color Key

Symbol	Fiber Name	Number	Color	Amount
○	Rainbow Gallery Alpaca 18	AL52	Cream	2 yards/1.8m
╲	Rainbow Gallery Alpaca 18	AL61	Gray	2 yards/1.8m
■	Rainbow Gallery Alpaca 18	AL64	Black	3 yards/2.7m
↖	Rainbow Gallery Patent Leather	PL1	Black	1 yard/.9m
B	Rainbow Gallery Splendor Silk	S868	Blue	1 yard/.9m
G	Rainbow Gallery Splendor Silk	S829	Green	2 yards/1.8m
►	Rainbow Gallery Splendor Silk	S821	Red	1 yard/.9m
+	Rainbow Gallery Gold Rush	DG6C	Gold Metallic	3 yards/2.7m
R	Madiera Carat	270	Red Metallic (bkgd)	4 yards/3.7m
▬	Madiera Carat	258	Green Metallic	3 yards/2.7m

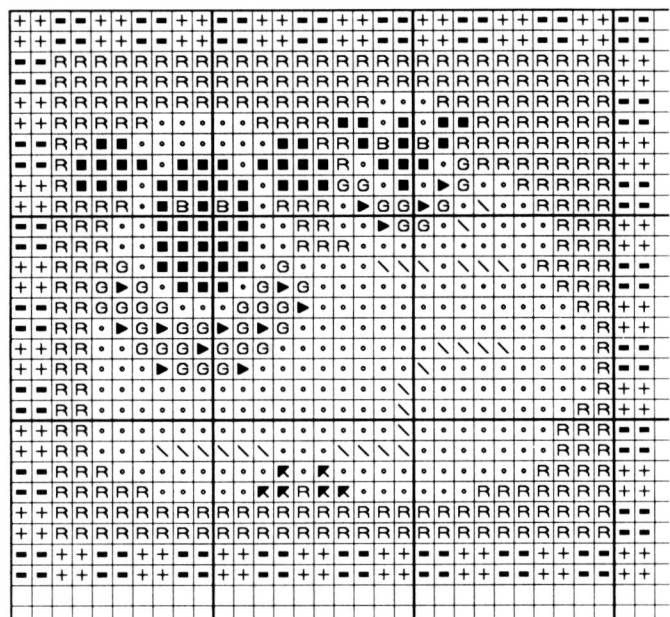

Five Pointed Star

Color Key

Symbol	Fiber Name	Number	Color	Amount
G	Krienik #16 braid	202HL	Gold	1 spool
╲	Krienik #16 braid	001HL	Silver	3 spools

Greek cross

Color Key

Symbol	Fiber Name	Number	Color	Amount
G	Krienik #16 braid	202HL	Gold	4 spools
+	Krienik #16 braid	002HL	Light Gold	1 spool

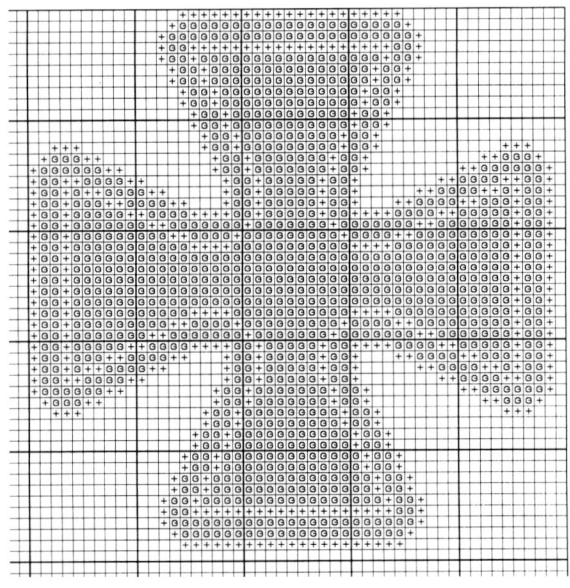

Christmas Tree

Symbol	Fiber Name	Number	Color	Amount
•	Madeira 'Glamour'	2458	Green Metallic	1 spool
■	Madeira 'Glamour'	2425	Gold Metallic	1 spool
○	Madeira Cotton Floss	0101	White	11 yards/10m
U	Leave unstitched			

Sheep

Color Key

Symbol	Fiber Name	Number	Color	Amount
■	DMC #3 Pearl Cotton	310	Black	1 skein
○	Rainbow Gallery Artic Rays Wispy Fringe	AR3	White	2 spools
B	DMC #3 Pearl Cotton	813	Blue	1 skein
R	DMC #3 Pearl Cotton	666	Red	1 skein
▬	Rainbow Gallery Nordic Gold	ND1	Gold	1 spool
G	DMC #3 Pearl Cotton	702	Green	1 skein

Noah's Ark Mobile

Faux Stained Glass Madonna and Child

(ENLARGE BY 200%)

Jesse Tree Ornaments

(ENLARGE BY 140%)

140

Mary and Jesus Triptych

Wooden Ornaments

Figure 2

Contributing Designers

Linda Kaiser-Bonin has played with fabric since her teens, and in subsequent years has experimented with weaving, dyeing, and knitting. These experiences, coupled with a career in fashion merchandising, are the resources she draws from in developing quilt designs. She lives in Jonesborough, Tennessee.

Robin Clark and his wife, Helen, own Robin's Wood Ltd, in Asheville, North Carolina, where they manufacture outdoor products for people and wildlife.

Gwen Diehn teaches in the visual arts department at Warren Wilson College in Swannanoa, North Carolina. She is the author of four activity books for children, including *Geology Crafts for Kids* (Sterling/Lark Books, 1996).

Gay D. Fay Kelly, who lives in Austin, Texas, trained as an artist and art historian (Rice University and the University of Texas), and has exhibited her art nationally. Now she spends most of her time as an older mom (the oldest, but one of the happiest, first-grade moms in school) with young daughters.

Rebecca W. Gordon, an award-winning seamstress, is a full-time mother and wife, and part-time writer and designer. She enjoys smocking, heirloom sewing, and designing embroidery for special occasions. She lives in the Louisville, Kentucky area. She and Joyce Kordik are the authors of *Spiritual Stitching,* a how-to book in search of a publisher.

Christi Hensley lives in Barnardsville, North Carolina, where she is blessed and inspired by her family and the surrounding mountains. Her work is displayed and sold in the region.

Joyce M. Kordik is a full-time mother and wife, and part-time needle arts instructor. An inventive designer, Joyce has won many awards, including the Kentucky State Fair Wearing Apparel Sweepstakes in 1991, and the Best of Show Award in Needlework in 1994 and 1995. She lives in the Louisville, Kentucky area.

Claudia Lee is a full-time studio papermaker and instructor in Kingsport, Tennessee. Her handmade paper figures are sold at shops and galleries.

Kate Mathews is a book editor and writer, who can't resist creating distinctive clothing for herself, using great fabrics and patterns. She lives in Barnardsville, North Carolina.

Shelley Lowell owns Pink Neck Gallery, an art gallery, in Asheville, North Carolina. A painter, sculptor, illustrator, and graphic designer, she received her BFA at Pratt Institute in New York, and now teaches a variety of art classes, including hand-painted furniture, in the Asheville area.

Peggy McClure is a multi-talented sewer who is especially fond of designing Victorian heirloom clothing. She teaches classes in Asheville, North Carolina, in the creation of wearable art.

Mary Jane Miller is a full-time studio artist, who utilizes decorative painting, woodworking, tin work, and a range of other techniques. She lives half the year in Abingdon, Virginia, and the other half in Mexico.

Mary Parker lives in Asheville, North Carolina, where she pursues a career in public service finance in order to indulge her passion for fabric. She teaches classes, particularly in her own machine Sashiko technique, and experiments with every new sewing technique she discovers.

Nan Parker is a retired teacher who moved from Florida to Mountain Rest, South Carolina. She and her husband, Bill, enjoy crafting for friends and shows.

Catherine Reurs, a former career banker in Europe, is an internationally recognized needlepoint and cross stitch designer. Her work has been featured in more than 40 magazines, including *Stitchery* and *House Beautiful*. She is the author of *In Splendid Detail: Needlepoint Art* (Stewart, Tabori, Chang, 1991) and *Splendid Needlepoint* (Lark Books, 1997). She sells needlepoint and cross stitch kits through her mail-order business, Catherine Reurs Needlepoint/In Splendid Detail, in Watertown, Massachusetts.

Louise Riddle lives in Weaverville, North Carolina. She is the manager of Jo-Belles, a craft store in Swannanoa, North Carolina, and has been involved in crafts for more than 30 years. Flowers are her favorite medium for all types of crafts projects.

Karyn Sanders makes one-of-a-kind wedding gowns, christening gowns, and accessories for private clients. Her work has appeared in *Victoria* and *McCalls* magazines. She sells silk ribbon kits through her mail-order business, Sweet Material Things, in Walkill, New York.

Sheila A. Sheppard is a full-time multi-media studio artist who lives in Jonesborough, Tennessee. She strives to maintain the "soul instinct" that fires her creative spirit. She loves working with polymer clay because it is "a hybrid child of earthen clay and a rainbow." She sells her work throughout the Southeast.

Laura Sims marbles fabric professionally in Asheville, North Carolina. Her company, Indigo Stone, produces distinctive marbled clothing and jewelry.

Mark Strom is a professional wood sculptor whose work covers a broad range of applications. During the last three years, he has focused on liturgical sculputure, commissioned by churches throughout the Southeast. He is co-owner of Loth Lorien Woodworking, in Asheville, North Carolina.

Ginger Summit, co-author of *The Complete Book of Gourd Crafts* (Lark Books, 1996) has been fascinated by gourds ever since she retired from teaching seven years ago. She feels passionate about gourds and derives great pleasure from working with them. She lives in Los Altos Hills, California, with her husband, Roger.

Gay Symmes is a Texas native who now lives in Asheville, North Carolina. Her needlework has earned awards from the Houston Contemporary Arts Museum and from state and country fairs. Her avocation grew into a cottage industry during the 1980s, when she supplied needlework to a Dallas mail-order house.

Kim Tibbals is an art director and graphic designer who pours much of her artistic energy into drawing, sewing, herbal crafts, gardening, and broom making. She lives in Waynesville, North Carolina.

Dee Dee Triplett considers dollmaking her primary focus, and teaches her craft at workshops around the country. She started as a designer of cross stitch which led to other types of needlework. She lives in Bryson City, North Carolina.

Carole Tripp, who trained in clothing and textile design, owns and operates Creative Castle, a bead-supply store in Newbury Park, California. She designs beadwork, teaches beading classes, and designs and manufactures jewelry kits.

Terry Taylor is an artist whose work takes many forms, including the pique-assiette technique for making mosaics, beadwork, and one-of-a-kind cards. He lives in Asheville, North Carolina.

Nola Theiss, who had designed knitwear for 16 years, is the author of many needlecraft books, including *Crocheted Gifts in a Weekend* and *Decorating Sweaters with Duplicate Stitch,* both published by Sterling/Lark in 1995. She is a nationally known teacher of knitting and crochet and lives on Sanibel Island, Florida.

Michelle Koepke West has an associate degree in commercial art and advertising, though she finds three-dimensional art more exciting. She has been a floral designer for ten years and is currently employed at Jo-Belles in Swannanoa, North Carolina.

Ellen Zahorec is a mixed-media studio artist, specializing in handmade paper and collage. Her work has been shown internationally and is part of numerous private and corporate collections. She lives in Cincinatti, Ohio.

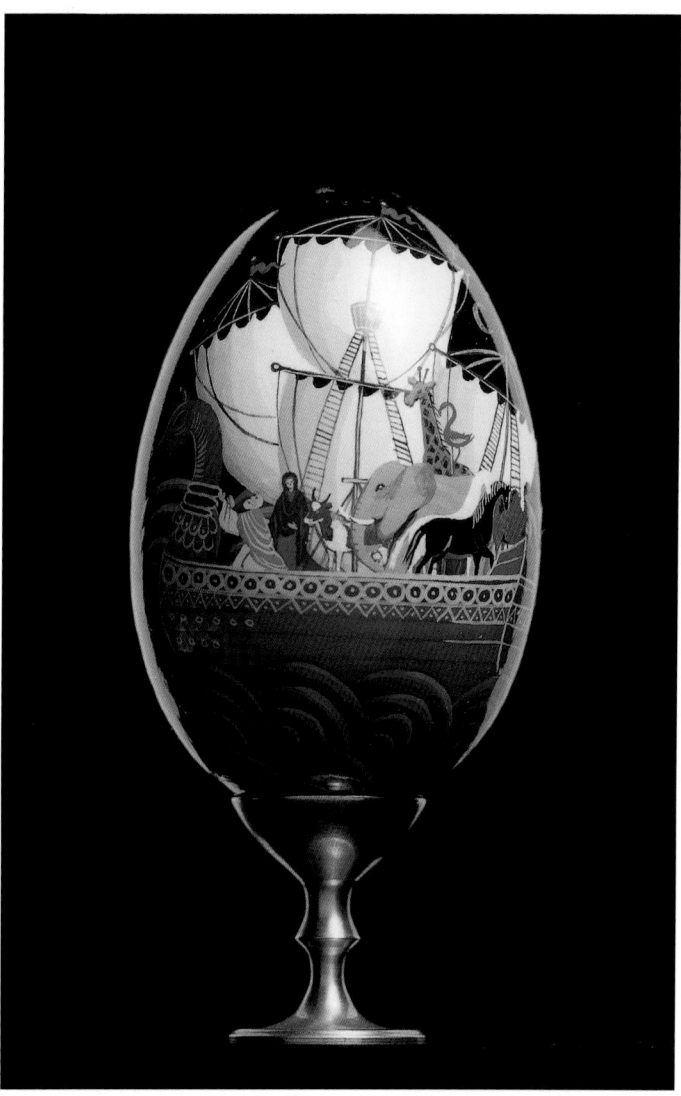

Painted wood; made in Russia

143

Index

Acknowledgments

A number of Asheville, North Carolina, businesses once again let us borrow and photograph their distinctive store merchandise to use as props and incidental art. Thank you, thank you. Diane LaSpada and Ann Inlay, former and current managers of the World Market Place, loaned us the beautiful crafts from around the world. The props were generously loaned to us by Sandi Sutger and Sharon de Young of A Natural Home, Katie Skinner and Vann Boyd of The Loft of Asheville, Brian Hasmuk of Antiques on Broadway, Ronnie Myers of Magnolia Beauregard's Antiques, Ivo Ballentine and Robin Cape of Preservation Hall, and Craig Culbertson and Otto Hauser of Stuf Antiques. Very special thanks go to Rob Pulleyn of Lark Books for letting us use his apartment and for taking such a large leap of faith.

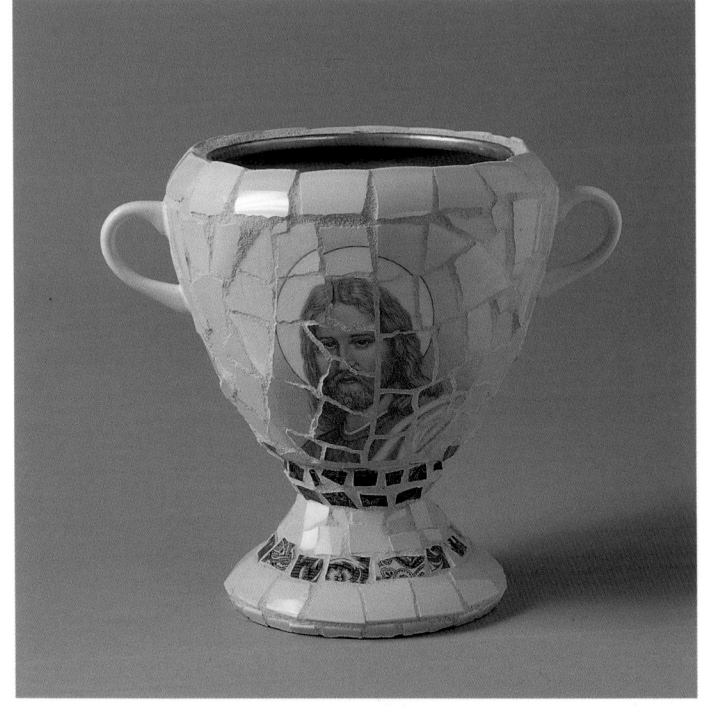

Terry Taylor created this handsome mosaic urn with the face of Jesus.

D0607374

THE Poetry
Dictionary

John Drury

Foreword by Dana Gioia

STORY PRESS
CINCINNATI, OHIO

Other fine Story Press Books are available from your local bookstore or direct from the publisher.

99 98 97 96 95   5 4 3 2 1

Library of Congress Cataloging-in-Publication Data

Drury, John.
  The poetry dictionary / John Drury.
      p.   cm.
  Includes index.
  ISBN 1-884910-04-1 (alk. paper)
  1. Poetry—Dictionaries. I. Title.
PN1021.D78   1995
808.1′03—dc20   95-4816
                                                                                  CIP

Designed by Clare Finney
Cover illustration by Tom Landecker

The permissions on pages 314-318 constitute an extension of this copyright page.

for Laurie and Eric

John Drury was born in 1950 in Cambridge, Maryland. He is the author of *The Stray Ghost*, a collection of poems, and *Creating Poetry*, a book for writers. His poems have appeared in *The Paris Review*, *Poetry*, *Western Humanities Review*, *Shenandoah*, *The New Republic*, and other periodicals. He is an associate professor of English at the University of Cincinnati.

Acknowledgments

A leave from my teaching at the University of Cincinnati gave me time to work on this dictionary. I want to thank Professor Edgar Slotkin of the English Department for helping me with the pronunciations of Welsh terms, and Professor Pearl Chao of Asian Languages for correcting my translation of Li Bai. I also want to thank Dana Gioia, Jack Heffron, Laurie Henry, Heather McHugh, Donna Poehner, and Laura Smith.

FOREWORD

Why would a poet need a poetry dictionary? Conventional wisdom proclaims that poets are spontaneous and emotional creatures who burst forth naturally into song as untutored as birds in a pear tree. General opinion also holds that reference books are impersonal, intellectual compilations utterly at odds with creativity and imagination. Conventional wisdom is, of course, absolutely wrong. A poet's favorite book is nearly always the dictionary. W.H. Auden used his unabridged *Oxford English Dictionary* so frequently that he eventually read its thirteen sturdy volumes to pieces.

I cannot imagine a poet—beginning or established—who would not want *The Poetry Dictionary* on his or her bookshelf. All writers, even those with Ivy League degress, are largely self-taught, and the process of learning goes on a lifetime. When formal education ends, the challenge of continued learning falls on the individual. Most people find the burden too great, but genuine writers flourish under such circumstance: They delight in pursuing knowledge according to their own dictates, but they need reliable guides.

John Drury has designed an invaluable book for poets. He has not only provided concise, clear, accurate, and current definitions of the terms and traditions of poetry; he has also presented judiciously selected examples of each form, genre, movement or period. One can read *The Poetry Dictionary* with equal satisfaction either as an informed guide to the practice and history of verse or as an annotated anthology of model poems. Students learn different things from abstract definitions and specific poems, and they need to see both.

Education fosters self-discovery. By learning about the past, we enhance our understanding of the present; by studying others, we gain better perspective on ourselves. A young writer who explores *The Poetry Dictionary* will—consciously or unawares—be investigating his or her own possibilities as an artist. Reading about *the Movement* among British poets of the 1950s may strike a sympathetic chord of skeptical anti-romanticism. Or coming upon *deep image poetry*, a poet may suddenly recognize the imaginative direction his or her future

work needs to take. An ambitious writer will instinctively want to try out many possibilities from the sonnet to surrealism before settling into a personal style. And, as the poet gradually discovers an individual voice, he or she will realize that it grew not merely out of some single source but from the still ongoing process of understanding and assimilating each object of study.

Sometimes what we learn by accident proves more important than what we study by plan. The wonderful thing about dictionaries is the arbitrary juxtapositions the alphabet creates. No surrealist poet excelled *Webster's* unintentionally inspired sequence of neighboring words: *chime in, chimera, chimney, chimp*! In *The Poetry Dictionary* we might diligently look up *kenning* only to discover *kyrielle*. Suddenly we learn something intriguing we had not realized we needed to know. An idea, a departure point, or even a poem might unexpectedly appear.

Learning should mix instruction with delight, accessibility with surprise. *The Poetry Dictionary* opens its subject to the reader with exemplary pride and enjoyment. No lover of poetry will find this book less than a pleasure.

Dana Gioia

HOW TO USE THIS BOOK

One of the principles of this dictionary is the grouping of related terms, whenever possible, into major entries. For example, *figures of classical rhetoric* contains a list of rhetorical devices, with definitions and examples. The most important of these devices, such as *alliteration*, also appear in individual entries. Subordinate terms are also placed within larger entries. The term *sestet*, for example, appears in the entry *sonnet*. In lieu of a welter of tiny entries, there is an index containing all of the terms used in the dictionary. If you need to find a specific term, check the index first.

Many of the entries contain one or more "model poems": examples that show the uses of a poetic form or device, starting with the first instance, if possible, and then proceeding to more recent examples, innovations, and perhaps departures from the tradition. Most of the examples are whole poems, but when excerpts from longer works have been unavoidable, I have tried to select enough material to give a good sense of how a poet uses the particular form or device.

Throughout the dictionary, terms that appear elsewhere as individual entries are preceded by asterisks (*). The reader is also referred to related terms through notes in parentheses. For example, in the entry *georgic* a note reads "(*See: idyll, pastoral*)." In *pastoral* there is a poem that is spoken by two characters, a shepherd and the girl he pursues, so that it also exemplifies *dialogue*. One goal of the book is to present a web of connections, to show how the elements of poetry are intertwined.

A note in the *sonnet* entry lists several related terms (*curtal sonnet, Eugene Onegin stanza, sonnet sequence*, and *tailed sonnet*). But there are numerous sonnets throughout the dictionary. In addition to nine examples in *sonnet*, and variations in *curtal sonnet* and *Eugene Onegin stanza*, there are twelve sonnets elsewhere, one in each of the following entries: *animal poem, city poem, dialogue, end-stop, found poem, fugitives, new formalism, Pre-Raphaelite Brotherhood, rhetoric, sprung rhythm, symbolist poetry*, and *prose, free verse*, and *metrical verse*. There are also fourteen-line poems that may or may not be sonnets in *abstract poetry* and *object poem*.

The pronunciation guides avoid linguistic symbols and use simple equivalents from normal American usage, as in the term *rondeau* (*ron-dóe*). Accents appear above the accented syllables. The idea is to make it easier for the reader. The disadvantage is that there are often various ways to pronounce different sound combinations in English (such as *ough*). But an array of symbols requiring a key and constant reference by the puzzled reader, who is unlikely to specialize in phonetics, would violate the spirit of this book. I have, in any case, tried to avoid ambiguities in the pronunciation guides. One possible confusion, however, is the vowel sound *ay*, which is pronounced here as in "say" or "day."

I have aimed to include the most necessary poetic terms, along with a helpful selection of poems, in this dictionary. Inevitably, choices must be made and material omitted, however reluctantly.

Some of the omissions involve subject matter, such as political poetry and religious poetry. However, both of these kinds, as well as many others, are represented within various categories: political poetry by Langston Hughes's "I, Too" in *harlem renaissance* and Adrienne Rich's "The Ninth Symphony of Beethoven Understood at Last as a Sexual Message" in *line break*; religious poetry by the poems of Basho and Issa in *haiku* (representing Zen Buddhism), Hafiz's "Where Can I Hear the News" in *ghazal* (representing Sufism, or Islamic mysticism), passages from the Bible in *biblical verse* and *psalm* (representing Judaism), and poems by George Herbert in *echo verse* and *emblematic verse* and Gerard Manley Hopkins in *curtal sonnet* and *sprung rhythm* (representing Christianity).

For whatever kind of poetry the reader may prefer, this dictionary is a way station—a place of maps, fuel, refreshment, first aid—whose purpose is to lead the reader back to reading and to encourage the writer to venture forth. It represents not a last word but directions along the way, signposts for the journey.

Abstract Language   Words that represent ideas, intangibles, and concepts such as "beauty" and "truth."

When John Keats uses those two words at the end of his "Ode on a Grecian Urn," they follow four-and-a-half stanzas that describe the scenes depicted on the urn, images fixed in time, unchanging—and the urn itself utters the abstractions:

> "Beauty is truth, truth beauty,"—that is all
> Ye know on earth, and all ye need to know.

Most contemporary poets prefer *concrete language (words that represent particular, tangible things, such as "woodchuck" or "telescope" or "bungalow") to abstractions—or at least use a larger proportion of concrete to abstract words. In many poems, the abstraction may be what all the concrete details add up to, although there is usually no existing word that can sum them up. (If there is, the poem will be a kind of *allegory.)

Abstract Poetry   Poetry that aims to use its sounds, textures, rhythms, and rhymes to convey an emotion, instead of relying on the meanings of words.

Edith Sitwell coined the term, and poems in her *Facade* exemplify it. Abstract poetry does not represent any particular object, or focus on any definite subject. Instead, it proceeds the way an abstract painter paints—not portraits or landscapes but arrangements of pigments,

blocks of color, slashes and swirls of paint. Abstract poetry aspires to be similarly nonrepresentational.

NURSERY RHYME (from *FACADE*)
Edith Sitwell (1887-1964)

Said King Pompey, the emperor's ape,
Shuddering black in his temporal cape
Of dust, 'The dust is everything—
The heart to love and the voice to sing,
Indianapolis,
And the Acropolis,
Also the hairy sky that we
Take for a coverlet comfortably.'
Said the Bishop,
Eating his ketchup:
'There still remains Eternity
Swelling the diocese,
That elephantiasis,
The flunkeyed and trumpeting sea.'

NOTE: A later version, reacting against the way the poem "deliberately guttered down into nothingness, meaninglessness," appears in Sitwell's *The Canticle of the Rose: Poems: 1917-1949*.

Academic Verse   Poetry that adheres to the accepted standards and requirements of some kind of "school." Poetry approved, officially or unofficially, by a literary establishment.

Plato's academy is the source of the word, meaning a school for advanced education. The Greek critics in Alexandria, Egypt, codified the terms of poetry and commented on the works of ancient poets such as Sappho. The French Academy formulated rules for neoclassical poetry. Today, universities serve as headquarters for poetry workshops, where students have their poems critiqued by a teacher (who is usually a published poet) and other student poets. Although there is really no central "authority" that stipulates what kinds of poems are acceptable, the workshop poem is a recognizably homogenized product of the system: low-key, conversational, imagistic, autobiographical, written in a free verse of medium-length lines. Of course, many fine poems fit that description, but some readers object to the

proliferation of poems that seem safe and formulaic. In the early twentieth century, Ezra Pound called for "breaking the pentameter" of what was the academic verse of its time: rhymed *iambic pentameter.

Another sense of academic verse seizes upon the bookish nature of such poems. We may properly call poems that display learning (from John Milton's *Paradise Lost* to Ezra Pound's *The Cantos*) academic. Anthony Hecht's early poems, which are elaborately formal, exemplify how impressive such a professorial style can be. The use of difficult forms (such as the double sonnet), elevated diction, and strict meter may be the poetic equivalents of cap and gown.

Usually, however, the term *academic* is pejorative. We dismiss a poem by saying it is academic, suggesting that it slavishly follows a current fashion or smacks of the schoolroom.

Accent *(also called stress)* A syllable that is emphasized (marked by ´ when scanning a poem).

In a polysyllabic word, accent is inherent in the pronunciation of a word—and can be verified in a dictionary: *pattern*, for example, has an accent on the first syllable (*pat*); *conglomeration* has accents on the second and fourth of its five syllables (*glom* and *ra*); *altitude* has a strong accent on its first syllable (*al*) and perhaps a weak accent, or secondary stress, on its third (*tude*). The accenting of monosyllabic words, however, depends on the context and position in a line. Nouns and verbs are more likely to be accented than articles and prepositions, but any word that falls on a metrical stress can be emphasized, however slightly. The actual effect of an accent is often a rise in pitch and volume, more of a push or a punch than an unstressed syllable will have; a peak as opposed to a dip; a burst as opposed to a lull.

Accentual Meter A rhythmic pattern based on a recurring number of accents (or stresses) in each line of a poem or section of a poem.

Whereas in *accentual-syllabic meter, weak syllables can be accented, however slightly, because they are surrounded by even weaker syllables, a stress in accentual verse must have a definite thump. It must be heard and felt. The number of unstressed syllables is not counted, but it should be varied from line to line. (Similarly, in syllabic verse, the number of syllables is constant but the number of accents should change from line to line.)

The earliest English poetry was accentual. (See *alliterative meter*.) Robert Graves, in his essay "Harp, Anvil, Oar," suggests that the rhythm of accentual meter comes from the strokes of rowing over rough seas. It may also come from the prevalence of burly, monosyllabic words in Anglo-Saxon, from which we now draw much of our basic vocabulary of physical words such as *rock, boat, thrash, burst*.

The following accentual poem by Donald Justice is written in two-stress lines. The syllable count varies from line to line, ranging from three ("End of piers") to six ("And offers to show you"). But some of the lines seem at first to have more than two stresses:

> The cózy shíp's-bar
> I héar a great spláshing

The word "bar" might seem accented, except that the phrase "ship's-bar" works as a single unit (like "wet-bar"). If we don't accent "ship's," it falls under the influence of the adjective "cozy," making the ship, rather than the bar, a small, intimate space. In the other line, "great" might be accented, but "splash" is even more emphatic, and the swing of the two-stress meter, already well established, forces us to hear two primary stresses. However, the near accent of "great" does have a pleasingly ambiguous sound effect; it makes the line stand out, weighted more heavily than the others, and leads to the climax, an image of grandfathers lolling in tubs.

DREAMS OF WATER
Donald Justice (b. 1925)

1.

An odd silence
Falls as we enter
The cozy ship's-bar.

The captain, smiling,
Unfolds his spyglass
And offers to show you

The obscene shapes
Of certain islands,
Low in the offing.

I sit by in silence.

2.

People in raincoats
Stand looking out from
Ends of piers.

A fog gathers;
And little tugs,
Growing uncertain

Of their position,
Start to complain
With the deep and bearded

Voices of fathers.

3.

The season is ending.
White verandas
Curve away.

The hotel seems empty
But, once inside,
I hear a great splashing.

Behind doors
Grandfathers loll
In steaming tubs,

Huge, unblushing.

Accentual-Syllabic Meter *(also called syllable-stress meter)*   A rhythmic pattern based on a regular count of both the syllables and the accents (or stresses) in a line.

English poetry combines the accentual meter of Anglo-Saxon with the syllabic meter of French, as in these lines by Geoffrey Chaucer from *The Canterbury Tales*:

A Knyght ther was, and that a worthy man,
That fro the tyme that he first bigan
To riden out, he loved chivalrie.

(When reading Chaucer's Middle English—which doesn't get much easier than this—the reader should pronounce any final "-e" not followed by a vowel or "h" in the next word; "-ed," as in "lovèd," is

also pronounced.) Both the syllables and the accents are counted. In iambic pentameter, the pattern stipulates ten syllables (or eleven if the last one is unstressed) and five accents:

> Ă Knýght | thĕr wás, | aňd thát | ă woŕth- | y̆ mán,
> Thăt fró | thĕ tým- | ĕ thăt | hĕ fiŕst | bĭgán
> Tŏ rí- | dĕn oút, | hĕ lóv- | ĕd chív- | ălríĕ.

The poet can vary the strict iambic pattern in many ways (by substituting different feet for some of the iambs, for example), but all such changes really involve playing off the expected number of syllables against the position and relative strength of the accents.

Specific varieties of accentual-syllabic meter depend upon two factors: the kind of *foot (arrangement of stressed and unstressed syllables) and the number of feet per *line. Here are lists of (1) the most common feet used in English verse, and (2) the terms identifying the number of feet in a line:

Pattern of syllables	*Foot*	*Example*	*Feet per line*
˘ ˘ ´	anapest, anapestic	(ascertaín)	1 monometer
´ ˘ ˘	dactyl, dactylic	(párasol)	2 dimeter
˘ ´	iamb, iambic	(debáte)	3 trimeter
˘ ˘	pyrrhic	(of a)	4 tetrameter
´ ´	spondee, spondaic	(fást fóod)	5 pentameter
´ ˘	trochee, trochaic	(crócus)	6 hexameter
			7 heptameter
´	monosyllabic foot	(hít)	8 octameter
˘	extra unstressed syllable in a *feminine ending	(the last syllable in demánding)	

Not all of these feet, however, can work as a metrical basis for a line. Since the pyrrhic foot consists of two unstressed syllables, any noun, verb, adjective or polysyllabic word will require an accent, which will leap up and overwhelm the lowly pyrrhic foot. Spondaic meter might occur on occasion, in a particular line, but it would not work as

the basis for a poem, since minor words (such as articles, conjunctions, and most prepositions) will be unstressed, and polysyllabic words will usually contain unstressed syllables. Meter based upon two-syllable feet (iambic and trochaic) is called duple meter, while meter based upon three-syllable feet (anapestic and dactylic) is called triple meter. Pyrrhic and spondaic feet are useful as *substitutions to vary the rhythm of a particular meter, so that it doesn't sound mechanical.

The most common accentual-syllabic meter in English verse is iambic. Pentameter is the most common line length, followed by tetrameter, then trimeter and hexameter (used in the *alexandrine).

Trochaic meter is most often tetrameter, as in William Blake's "The Tyger." The first line of Edgar Allan Poe's "The Raven" is trochaic octameter, but it *sounds* like two trochaic lines: "Once upon a midnight dreary, ‖ while I pondered, weak and weary." The internal rhyme reinforces the sense of two separate parts.

Triple meter (such as anapestic or dactylic) tends to sound overly light or overly powerful. The rhythmic swing makes it hard to be subtle or to reproduce the natural rise and fall of speech, unless the poet introduces enough substitutions (iambs, trochees, spondees, monosyllabic feet) to let the melody overcome the metronome.

(*See: anapest, dactyl, foot, iamb, meter, minor ionic, pyrrhic, spondee, trochee.*)

Acrostic *(uh-crós-tic; Greek, "tip, point" + "line, verse, stich")* Poem in which the initial letters of the lines, read downward, spell out a name or message. Other possibilities exist for hiding the acrostic, such as moving the letter one space over in each succeeding line. Acrostics are usually used for *light verse, *riddles or puzzles, and *occasional verse. The following poem commemorates a "golden afternoon" of boating and storytelling. The first letters spell out a girl's name.

> from *THROUGH THE LOOKING GLASS*
> Lewis Carroll (1832-1898)
>
> A boat, beneath a sunny sky
> Lingering onward dreamily
> In an evening of July—

Children three that nestle near,
Eager eye and willing ear,
Pleased a simple tale to hear—

Long has paled that sunny sky:
Echoes fade and memories die:
Autumn frosts have slain July.

Still she haunts me, phantomwise,
Alice moving under skies
Never seen by waking eyes.

Children yet, the tale to hear,
Eager eye and willing ear,
Lovingly shall nestle near.

In a Wonderland they lie,
Dreaming as the days go by,
Dreaming as the summers die:

Ever drifting down the stream—
Lingering in the golden gleam—
Life, what is it but a dream?

NOTE: On July 4, 1862, Rev. Charles Dodgson and Rev. Robinson Duckworth took the three young Liddell sisters on a boat ride up the Thames River, one of many rowing expeditions with the girls. Alice Pleasance Liddell, whose name is encoded in this acrostic, was then ten years old. During this afternoon, as Dodgson (whose pseudonym was Lewis Carroll) later wrote, "I told them the fairy-tale of Alice's adventures underground. . . ."

Alcaics, Alcaic Stanza *(al-káy-ic)* A stanza form named after the Greek poet Alcaeus, a contemporary of Sappho in the late seventh to early sixth century B.C. Its metrical pattern (with the symbols for long and short syllables used in Greek *quantitative meter) is:

	Short syllables that can be long
˘ – ˘ – ˘ – ˘ – ˘ –	1 or 5
˘ – ˘ – ˘ – ˘ – ˘ –	1 or 5
˘ – ˘ – ˘ – ˘ – ˘	1, 5, or 9
– ˘ ˘ – ˘ ˘ – ˘ – ˘	10

A poet writing in English accentual-syllabic meter can change the long syllables to accents (or stresses) and the short ones to unstressed syllables. If a poet counts only the number of syllables, the pattern is 11-11-9-10. In Greek the stanza is unrhymed. Horace uses alcaics in many of his odes, which were originally in Latin. Alfred, Lord Tennyson's "Milton" is also in alcaics. (*See: ode, Sapphics*.)

> STORM IN THE STATE
> Alcaeus (7th-6th century B.C.; tr. Richmond Lattimore)
>
> I cannot understand how the winds are set
> against each other. Now from this side and now
>   from that the waves roll. We between them
>   run with the wind in our black ship driven,
>
> hard pressed and laboring under the giant storm.
> All round the mast-step washes the sea we shipped.
>   You can see through the sail already
>   where there are opening rents within it.
>
> The forestays slacken. . . .

Alexandrine *(al-ec-zán-drin; deriving perhaps from the name of Alexandre Paris, a French poet, or from Alexander the Great, the subject of heroic poems in this form)* A line in iambic hexameter, or six iambic feet (˘ ´ ˘ ´ ˘ ´ ˘ ´ ˘ ´ ˘ ´); a line consisting of twelve syllables.

In its syllabic form, the alexandrine is the most important kind of line in French poetry, which requires a *caesura (or pause) in the middle, after the sixth syllable. Sometimes, in English verse, it is inserted in an otherwise pentameter poem, as in the final line of the *Spenserian stanza. Here is an example from Edmund Spenser's *The Faerie Queen*:

> And Shame his ugly face did hide from living eye.

English poems entirely in alexandrines are relatively uncommon, probably because the line tends to split into two distinct parts, usually containing three feet each.

Allegory *(Greek, combining the words for "other" and "speak," meaning to speak of one thing in terms of something else)*

1. Figurative language in which characters, images, and events stand for something abstract. Themis, the courtroom's representation of a blindfolded woman holding a sword and a set of scales, is an allegory for Justice. Allegory differs from *symbolism in that it represents more of a one-to-one correspondence and is used systematically and extensively. A true symbol is often hard to define in words other than the poem's. The image resonates so powerfully that it suggests other meanings, as with William Blake's "tyger," which represents a kind of intense force in the unconscious, or an electric power from the underworld, or a creative fire in the murky cosmos. If the tiger were merely an allegory, one might reduce it to a kind of equation: tiger = evil. In current popular usage, *allegory* is often used as a synonym for *symbol*.

2. A poem or other literary work that uses allegories. Edmund Spenser's *The Faerie Queen* is perhaps the best-known allegory in English poetry. In Book III, for example, Sir Guyon (Temperance) charges a knight who knocks him off his horse; the knight turns out to be Britomart, a lady, who represents Chastity. (Her lance is enchanted.) Characters in an allegory serve more as chess pieces than as human beings. Or perhaps they are concepts masquerading as people.

Alliteration *(uh-lít-uh-ráy-shun; Latin, "to letter")* Generally, the repetition of consonant sounds (also called *consonance). More precisely, the repetition of initial consonant sounds, as in this song from William Shakespeare's *As You Like It*:

> It was a lover and his lass—
> With a hey, and a ho, and a hey nonino—

In this song "l" is alliterated in the first line, "h" in the second. Alliteration is essential in *alliterative meter (also called Anglo-Saxon strong-stress meter), but it occurs frequently in much later English poetry. It is usually a prominent aural effect and can sound ridiculous if used carelessly or indiscriminately. In *Love's Labour's Lost*, Shakespeare parodies it when Holofernes "affects the letter" (or practices alliterating) in Act IV, Scene II: "The preyful princess pierc'd and prick'd a pretty pleasing pricket." Over-alliterating may lead to similar

tongue-twisters: "Peter Piper picked a peck of pickled peppers" or "She sells seashells by the seashore."

Here are the particular terms for various kinds of "letter" repetition:

Kind of Alliteration	Repeats
alliteration (also beginning, head, or initial rhyme)	initial consonants (roof/righteous: *r*) (brain/brush: *br*)
consonance (final alliteration)	consonants at the end of words (thick/creek: *k*)
parallel (or cross) alliteration	interwoven consonants (big time/bus trip: *b, r*)
polyptoton (poh-lip-tów-tun)	consonants in the middle of words (runner/flannel: *n*)
submerged (or thesis) alliteration	unstressed syllables of words (mailbox/carob: *b*)
suspended alliteration	reversal of a consonant-vowel combination found in one word in another word that follows (tawny/aeronautics: *t, aw, n*)

The repetition of vowel sounds is usually called *assonance, although it too is sometimes considered a kind of alliteration. Although *alliteration* and *consonance* are both used loosely to encompass various kinds of consonant repetition, it is perhaps useful to distinguish between them.

Alliteration differs from rhyme in several respects: alliteration (like assonance) repeats one isolated sound at several points within one or more lines and does not usually appear at any particular point; rhyme, however, usually repeats at least *two* sounds together, a vowel and consonant (or consonants) and usually appears at the end of a line or (in the case of internal rhyme) at rhythmic points within a line, perhaps at the second and fourth stresses of a four-stress line. Although it is common enough to find *slant rhyme that repeats only the final consonants of its rhyme words, it is unusual (and unconvincing) to find true alliteration passed off as rhyme.

Alliteration depends for its success or failure on the poet's ear. Since, except in Anglo-Saxon meter, there are no rules dictating where and when (or even if) to alliterate, the poet must pace these repetitions carefully. Alliteration can be especially striking in adjacent words, but it can also rise like a series of wave crests if nonalliterating words intervene. After a certain amount of time, a consonant ceases to resonate. Even though it may be repeated, it will not sound like a repetition. Exactly what that interval may be is hard to determine, except by trial and error, but rhyme sounds persist much longer in the ear than does alliteration. (Assonance seems to last somewhere between the two.) We can wait several lines for a rhyme to recur, but the gap of a single pentameter line without an echoing consonant pretty much muffles the effect of alliteration. Often, instead of sticking to a single alliterating sound, the poet will braid or interweave two or more consonants, alternating them and making the effect richer, more colorful, not so monochromatically emphatic.

Alliteration is used primarily as a sound effect, either euphonious or cacophonous or onomatopoeic, something pleasant or plangent for its own sake, but it also serves to link associated words, to tighten the structure of a poem, and to formalize the language, making it more highly wrought (which may or may not be desirable).

INVERSNAID
Gerard Manley Hopkins (1844-1889)

This darksome burn, horseback brown,
His rollrock highroad roaring down,
In coop and in comb the fleece of his foam
Flutes and low to the lake falls home.

A windpuff-bonnet of fáwn-fróth
Turns and twindles over the broth
Of a pool so pitchblack, féll-fröwning,
It rounds and rounds Despair to drowning.

Degged with dew, dappled with dew
Are the groins of the braes that the brook treads through,
Wiry heathpacks, flitches of fern,
And the beadbonny ash that sits over the burn.

What would the world be, once bereft
Of wet and of wildness? Let them be left,
O let them be left, wildness and wet;
Long live the weeds and the wilderness yet.

NOTE: *coop*: water cooped up; *comb*: water moving over stones; *twindle*: a portmanteau word combining "twists," "twitches," and "dwindles" (possibly taken from an obsolete word meaning "twin"); *degged*: sprinkled; *heathpacks*: heather; *flitches*: ragged, russet tufts.

Alliterative Meter *(also called Anglo-Saxon meter, Old English meter, and strong-stress meter)*   The accentual, alliterative meter of Anglo-Saxon England before the effects of the Norman Conquest—in particular the assimilation of French vocabulary and poetics—finally took hold in the work of Geoffrey Chaucer.

A line of alliterative meter contains four stresses, with a noticeable pause or *caesura in the middle of the line. Three of the four stresses are usually alliterated (but sometimes two, sometimes two different pairs, and sometimes all four). Each half-line to the left and right of the caesura is called a hemistich. Alliteration usually occurs from one hemistich to the other, across the caesura. In Anglo-Saxon practice, alliteration includes not just repeated consonants, but also vowels (any vowel or diphthong with any other).

Alliterative verse often uses parallelism and *kennings, figurative expressions used repetitively, such as "whale road" instead of "sea"—much like the epithets of Homeric epics ("Earth-shaker" instead of "Poseidon").

Beowulf is the best known example of strong-stress meter, but Chaucer's contemporary William Langland was still using it in *Piers Plowman*. Chaucer could draw on the alliterative tradition when he chose, even in lines that adhere to the prevailing pattern of rhymed *iambic pentameter couplets:

The **helm**es *they* to**hew**en and to**shred**e;
Out **brest** the **blood** with **stierne** **strem**es *red*e;
With **myghty mac**es the **bon**es they to**brest**e.
He **thurgh** the **thikk**este of the **throng** gan **threst**e;
Ther **stomblen steed**es **strong**e, and *doun* **gooth** *al*;
He *roll*eth under *foot* as *dooth* a *ball*

> He **foyn**eth on his **feet** with *his* tron*choun*,
> And **he** hym **hurt**leth with his **hors** a*doun* . . .
> *(The Knight's Tale*, lines 2609-16)

NOTE: *tohewen*: hew into pieces; *toshrede*: cut into shreds; *brest*: burst; *stierne*: violent; *tobreste*: break into pieces; *threste*: thrust; *foyneth*: thrust and parry; *tronchoun*: truncheon.

Most of these lines alliterate and have four strong stresses, as in alliterative meter: alliterated stresses are printed in boldface, while unalliterated stresses are italicized. Yet each line also rhymes in pairs or couplets (*toshrede/rede*) and scans, with acceptable variations, as iambic pentameter:

> Thĕr stómb- | lĕn stéed- | ĕs strónge, | añd dóun | gŏoth ál

It isn't hard to see why accentual-syllabic meter, such as iambic pentameter, won out over alliterative meter: one is flexible enough to contain the other. From the example, however, it is clear that alliterative meter is strong and aggressive. It conveys physical force, such as fighting, powerfully and memorably.

Although Gerard Manley Hopkins used alliteration with great frequency and force in his poems in the nineteenth century, alliterative meter was not revived until Ezra Pound imitated it loosely in his translation of an Anglo-Saxon poem, *The Seafarer*, and in "Canto I." Other twentieth-century poets also have used alliterative meter on occasion: W.H. Auden (*The Age of Anxiety*), Richard Wilbur ("Junk" and "Lilacs"), C. Day Lewis ("As One Who Wanders Into Old Workings"), James Dickey ("Mary Sheffield"), Richard Eberhart ("Brotherhood of Men"), and Fred Chappell ("My Grandfather's Church Goes Up"). (*See: accentual meter, bob and wheel.*)

> *from PIERS PLOWMAN*
> *William Langland (14th century)*
>
> In a somer seson,   whan soft was the sonne,
> I shope me into shroudes,   as I a shepe were;
> In habite as an heremite   unholy of workes

Went wide in this world,   wondres to here.
Ac on a May morninge   on Malverne hulles
Me bifel a ferly,   of fairy me thoughte:
I was wery forwandred   and went me to reste
Under a brode banke   by a bornes side,
And as I lay and lened   and loked on the wateres,
I slombred in a sleping,   it sweyed so merye.
Thanne gan I to meten   a merveilouse swevene,
That I was in a wildernesse,   wist I never where.

(lines 1-12)

NOTE: The space in each line indicates the caesura. These are the first twelve lines of a long visionary poem in Middle English. Pronounce each final "e"; also pronounce the "gh" in "thoughte" like "ch" in the Scottish *loch*.

shope: dressed; *shepe*: shepherd; *here*: hear; *ac*: but; *bifel*: befell; *ferly*: marvel; *wery*: weary; *forwandred*: from wandering; *bornes*: brook's; *lened*: rested; *sweyed*: sounded; *gan*: began; *meten*: to dream; *swevene*: dream; *wist*: knew.

THE LILACS / Richard Wilbur (b. 1921)

Those laden lilacs
                    at the lawn's end
Came stark, spindly,
                    and in staggered file,
Like walking wounded
                    from the dead of winter.
We watched them waken
                    in the brusque weather
To rot and rootbreak,
                    to ripped branches,
And saw them shiver
                    as the memory swept them
Of night and numbness
                    and the taste of nothing.
Out of present pain
                    and from past terror
Their bullet-shaped buds
                    came quick and bursting,
As if they aimed
                    to be open with us!

But the sun suddenly
> settled about them,
And green and grateful
> the lilacs grew,
Healed in that hush,
> that hospital quiet.
These lacquered leaves
> where the light paddles
And the big blooms
> buzzing among them
Have kept their counsel,
> conveying nothing
Of their mortal message,
> unless one should measure
The depth and dumbness
> of death's kingdom
By the pure power
> of this perfume.

NOTE: One line of "The Lilacs" is not alliterated but uses initial assonance (vowel repetition) in its place.

Allusion *(Latin, "playing with, touching upon")*   Reference to a literary work, a myth, a Biblical story, a historical event, or some other cultural artifact.

Although excessive allusion can seem pedantic and may perplex and dishearten some readers, allusion is still one of the great means of compression (and therefore power) in poetry. The mere mention of certain names, places, and events can shoot an electric current through a poem, linking the distant past to the present. A *symbol is, perhaps, another kind of allusion, not a reference to names but to images or details that go back in human history and deep in the human psyche: garden, cross, ship, labyrinth.

The following poem is spoken in the voice of Sidney Lanier, nineteenth-century American poet and Confederate veteran. The speaker alludes to the Greek myth of Danae.

THE YELLOW STEEPLE
Andrew Hudgins (b. 1951)

On my way home from work, I jumped the fence
and cut across the Baptist cemetery.
As I walked over Sarah Pratt,
I saw a workman standing on a scaffold
and swatting a coat of yellow paint
over the peeling whitewash on the steeple.
He dropped a can of paint, and as it fell
the paint dispersed into a mist
and spread a rain of yellow dots
across a corner of the cemetery—
the bushes, trees, headstones, and me.
It ruined my coat. I didn't care:
I felt like Danae when she
was loved by Zeus in the golden rain.
Then, looking up, I saw a hawk.
It didn't move at all—not once—
but hung arrested in the air
till I released the breath I held
in awe of its pinpoint, predatory grace.
Still watching it as I walked home,
I barked my shins on a marble angel,
slid down a bank of slick white mud,
fell in the creek, and came up laughing.

It was one of those sustaining days
when you're absolutely sure you have a soul.

NOTE: Here is Arthur Golding's 1567 translation of the passage about Danae in Ovid's
Metamorphoses (Book IV):

That Persey was the sonne of Jove; or that he was conceyved
By Danae of golden shower through which shee was deceived.

Alphabet Poem *(also abecedarius)* A poem arranged according to
the alphabet, so that the first line is devoted to A and perhaps uses
words that begin with A. In *The White Goddess*, Robert Graves discusses the "tree alphabets" of Welsh poetry. David Young's poem
"A Lowercase Alphabet" is an exercise in metaphor, commenting on
how the letters look.

17

A LOWERCASE ALPHABET
David Young (b. 1936)

a   snail going up the wall
b   hang up the little dipper
c   mouth, moon, riverbend
d   the dipper in the mirror
e   tiny eye of the whale
f   oil well, skate, old pistol
g   what did you do to your glasses?
h   a chimney for every hut
i   the levitation of the spot
j   landscape with fishhook and planet
k   where three roads almost meet
l   romance of the periscope
m   comb from the iron age
n   the hut that lost its chimney
o   simplification of the blood
p   the dipper dead and buried
q   its mirror buried with it
r   geyser that goes off crooked
s   little black love seat
t   the portable cross
u   cross section of a trough
v   the hawk above the valley
w   a graph for winter, pigsfoot
x   dancer, hourglass, black suspenders
y   the root begins to sprout
z   path of the rabbit

Ambiguity *(Latin, "driving both ways")* A word, phrase, image, or idea whose meaning is unclear or which signifies more than one thing, like a pun or a double entendre.

"Dark leaves," for example, could signify a tree's leaves that are dark in color, or shady, or mysterious, or sinister; it could also mean that darkness is departing and might suggest nighttime, or a room without lamps, or a period of ignorance (like the so-called Dark Ages).

In *Seven Types of Ambiguity*, William Empson describes ambiguity

as "any verbal nuance, however slight, which gives room for alternative reactions to the same piece of language." The basic type of ambiguity involves "a word or a grammatical structure [that] is effective in several ways at once." Empson discusses the ambiguity of a line from William Shakespeare's Sonnet 73 (which begins "That time of year thou mayst in me behold"):

> To take a famous example, there is no pun, double syntax, or dubiety of feeling, in
>
> *Bare ruined choirs, where late the sweet birds sang,*
>
> but the comparison holds for many reasons; because ruined monastery choirs are places in which to sing, because they involve sitting in a row, because they are made of wood, are carved into knots and so forth, because they used to be surrounded by a sheltering building crystallised out of the likeness of a forest, and coloured with stained glass and painting like flowers and leaves, because they are now abandoned by all but the grey walls coloured like the skies of winter, because the cold and Narcissistic charm suggested by choir-boys suits well with Shakespeare's feeling for the object of the Sonnets, and for various sociological and historical reasons (the protestant destruction of monasteries; fear of puritanism), which it would be hard now to trace out in their proportions; these reasons, and many more relating the simile to its place in the Sonnet, must all combine to give the line its beauty, and there is a sort of ambiguity in not knowing which of them to hold most clearly in mind.

Empson also asserts that "the machinations of ambiguity are among the very roots of poetry."

In poetry, ambiguity can be like a "forking" move in chess: a player can move one piece (a knight, for example) to a position from which it threatens two or more enemy pieces at once. Ambiguous language can suggest doubleness, opposites merging, paths branching out. It can be a way of speaking with the proverbial "forked tongue" or with "tongue in cheek." It is also a way to compress the language of poetry, to make it richer, denser, more resonant.

On the other hand, ambiguity can be a serious fault in writing that requires clarity. In logical prose (such as a legal document), this kind of ambiguity ruins the text. In poetry, however, the poet may want to use words that perform several tasks concurrently, like a one-man band playing kazoo, banjo, and kick drum, with cymbals between his knees. And the language may lead beyond the poet's original intent into less conscious, more mysterious associations. Ambiguity that muddles is bad; ambiguity that magnifies is good.

Amphibrach *(ám-fi-brack; Greek, "short at each end")* A foot consisting of a stressed syllable surrounded by two unstressed syllables (˘ ´ ˘). Words that are amphibrachic include "alluring," "deliver," and "commotion." In a sense, it is very common in English verse, as the last foot in an iambic line with a feminine ending (for example, Emily Dickinson's "The auc- | tioneer | of parting"), but that extra unstressed syllable is usually considered a coda to the iambic line, not really part of its final foot. The amphibrach, however, is sometimes found in the *limerick. Along with the *anapest and the *dactyl, it occurs in lines written in triple meter, as in Robert Browning's "I sprang to | the stirrup. . . ."

Anacrusis *(an-a-cróo-sis; Greek, "striking up a tune")* Unstressed syllable or syllables prefixed to a line, but not part of its metrical pattern.

For example, there is anacrusis in the second of the following trochaic lines from William Butler Yeats' "Under Ben Bulben":

> Under bare Ben Bulben's head
> In Drumcliff churchyard Yeats is laid.

The meter throughout the poem is trochaic tetrameter, but many lines begin with an unstressed syllable. Out of its metrical context, such a line would be iambic tetrameter. However, the anacrusis follows a trochaic line, one that itself lacks a final unstressed syllable (making it catalectic or truncated). That initial unstressed syllable serves merely as a bridge, a repositioning of the syllable omitted from the trochaic line above. To test this practice, which sounds complicated but is in fact simple, imagine moving "In" from the start of Yeats'

second line to the end of his first. Instead of adding an extra un-stressed syllable, anacrusis really restores one. (Ben Bulben, inciden-tally, is a mountain in Ireland.)

The term *anacrusis* was borrowed from music, for which it indicates a note just before the melody's first bar. (*See: catalexis.*)

Anapest, Anapestic (*án-a-pest, an-a-pés-tic; Greek, "beaten back"*) A foot consisting of two unstressed syllables followed by a stress (˘ ˘ ′).

Single words can be anapestic ("unaware," "imprecise," "sere-nade"), but secondary stress in the first syllable often plays tricks in actual lines, seizing more accent than it would command outside of the context of a poetic line. Phrases can also be anapestic ("in the house," "if a book") but the same tendency, in English, to impose a relative stress on an otherwise unstressed syllable bordered by other weak syllables ("and *in* the *house*," "but *if* a *book*") makes a series of anapests hard to continue in any natural way.

Anapestic meter, like dactylic, is called triple meter (because each foot contains three syllables). Here is an anapestic line from Herman Melville's "The Maldive Shark":

> Frŏm hĭs sáw-pĭt ŏf moúth, frŏm hĭs chárnĕl ŏf máw,

In English, anapestic meter often starts galloping and becomes hard to restrain, as in Lord Byron's "The Destruction of Sennacherib," whose first stanza is perfectly regular (if the "-ian" of "Assyrian" is elided into one syllable):

> The Assyrian came down like a wolf on the fold,
> And his cohorts were gleaming in purple and gold;
> And the sheen of their spears was like stars on the sea,
> When the blue wave rolls nightly on deep Galilee.

Byron's lines are powerful, but their expressive range is limited by the anapestic onrush. Making the feet less predictably anapestic can help, either by omitting an occasional unstressed syllable or replacing an unstressed syllable with a stress (as Browning does in the poem that follows). In fact, it's unusual to find a poem entirely in anapestic feet. The first foot will frequently be iambic, but a mere preponderance

of anapests will make a line sound anapestic—or at least like some sort of triple meter. Often amphibrachic, anapestic, and dactylic meter are hard to distinguish in English. A dactylic line can end on a catalectic foot (one that is "incomplete," missing its last one or two syllables). And if the line begins with an unaccented syllable, the line could still be predominantly dactylic, that extra syllable acting as a kind of prefix. (*See: amphibrach, anacrusis, dactyl, catalexis.*)

The speaker of the following poem in anapestic pentameter is David, the future King of Israel and supposed author of the Psalms.

SAUL (Part V) / Robert Browning (1812-1889)

> Then I tuned my harp,—took off the lilies we twine round
>   its chords
> Lest they snap 'neath the stress of the noontide—those
>   sunbeams like swords!
> And I first played the tune all our sheep know, as, one
>   after one,
> So docile they come to the pen-door, till folding be done.
> They are white and untorn by the bushes, for lo, they have
>   fed
> Where the long grasses stifle the water within the
>   stream's bed;
> And now one after one seeks its lodgings, as star follows
>   star
> Into eve and the blue far above us,—so blue and so far!

Anaphora *(uh-náf-or-a; Greek, "carrying back")* A rhetorical device in which several successive lines, phrases, clauses, or sentences begin with the same word or phrase.

For example, in Part 42 of "Song of Myself," Walt Whitman repeats the word "ever" at the start of each line:

> Ever the hard unsunk ground,
> Ever the eaters and drinkers, ever the upward and downward
>   sun, ever the air and the ceaseless tides,
> Ever myself and my neighbors, refreshing, wicked, real,

> Ever the old inexplicable query, ever that thorn'd thumb,
>   that breath of itches and thirsts,
> Ever the vexer's *hoot! hoot!* till we find where the sly one
>   hides and bring him forth,
> Ever love, ever the sobbing liquid of life,
> Ever the bandage under the chin, ever the trestles of death.

Although anaphora can sound monotonous, mechanical, and artificial, it can also bind a group of lines powerfully and memorably. The device is especially well suited to giving a sense of definite, obvious structure to long-lined free verse. But it is also an important device in metrical verse, as in the first six of these lines from Alexander Pope's *The Rape of the Lock* (Canto IV):

> Not youthful Kings in Battel seiz'd alive,
> Not scornful Virgins who their Charms survive,
> Not ardent Lovers robb'd of all their Bliss,
> Not ancient Ladies when refus'd a Kiss,
> Not Tyrants fierce that unrepenting die,
> Not *Cynthia* when her *Manteau's* pinn'd awry,
> E'er felt such Rage, Resentment, and despair,
> As Thou, sad Virgin! for thy ravish'd Hair.

(*See: biblical verse, figures of classical rhetoric, free verse.*)

Animal Poem   A poem that observes, describes, contemplates, or speaks from the viewpoint of a creature that is not human.

An astonishing number of fine, freshly observed poems have been written about animals. Something about other species seems to coax the best out of poets. In mythology, Orpheus charmed the beasts by his singing, yet he was torn to pieces by human beings. Although Robinson Jeffers' view may be extreme ("I'd sooner, except the penalties, kill a man than a hawk," from "Hurt Hawks"), many poets look empathetically at other creatures, "All things innocent, hapless, forsaken" (Theodore Roethke, "The Meadow Mouse").

Poets who start writing about animals tend to write a great many poems about them. John Clare, whose sonnet "The Vixen" appears below, also wrote "Badger," "The Fox," "Marten," "The Hedgehog," "The Partridge," "The Yellow-Hammer," and many others. At a time

when animals mattered more to poets as symbols than as creatures (for example, William Blake's lamb and tiger), Clare observed the natural world closely and reported back with affection. Marianne Moore, another close observer, wrote "The Fish" (included in *syllabics), "The Jerboa," "The Frigate Pelican," "The Buffalo," "The Monkeys," "The Paper Nautilus," "The Wood-Weasel," "Elephants," and "The Arctic Ox (or Goat)." Ted Hughes has written "The Thought Fox," "The Jaguar," "View of a Pig," "Hawk Roosting," "An Otter," "Pike," and "A March Calf." Mary Oliver has written "Moles," "The Bobcat," "The Kitten," "Egrets," "A Poem for the Blue Heron," "Vultures," and "The Snakes." (*See: plant poem.*)

THE VIXEN / John Clare (1793-1864)

Among the taller wood with ivy hung,
The old fox plays and dances round her young.
She snuffs and barks if any passes by
And swings her tail and turns prepared to fly.
The horseman hurries by, she bolts to see,
And turns agen, from danger never free.
If any stands she runs among the poles
And barks and snaps and drives them in the holes.
The shepherd sees them and the boy goes by
And gets a stick and progs the hole to try.
They get all still and lie in safety sure,
And out again when everything's secure,
And start and snap at blackbirds bouncing by
To fight and catch the great white butterfly.

Anthology *(Greek, "bouquet of flowers")* A collection of poems or stories by various authors.

Early examples include the *Greek Anthology*, a collection of *epigrams compiled in the tenth century A.D. but reaching back to the seventh century B.C., and the *Shih Ching* (*Classic Anthology of Songs*, also called the *Confucian Odes*), a collection of Chinese poems compiled before the fifth century B.C.

There are several kinds of poetry anthologies:

1. historical, either comprehensive (*The Norton Anthology of Poetry*)

or specific (twentieth-century French poetry, Imagist poetry, Surrealist poetry);

2. thematic, dealing with topics such as the Old Testament, paintings, dogs, love, jazz, work, and sports;

3. celebratory, including the "best" work from a magazine (such as *Shenandoah* and *The Georgia Review*) or an institution (such as the Iowa Writers' Workshop);

4. regional, such as Southern poetry;

5. demographic, organized according to gender, race, ethnic background, or sexual preference;

6. argumentative, offering a range of poems that represent how the editor thinks poets should write (such as Robert Bly's *News of the Universe* and Donald Allen's *The New American Poetry, 1945-1960*). Argumentative anthologies can serve as the publicity vehicles for *movements and schools of poetry.

Some anthologies, such as Richard Howard's *Preferences*, include favorite poems chosen by the poets, their own or those written by other poets. And this dictionary contains what might be called a terminological anthology.

Anti-Poem A text that rebels against the conventions, pretensions, formality, diction, imagery, rhythms, and/or traditions of poetry; a poem in spite of itself (since it can't very well be a non-poem, like a rock or a rutabaga or a jackhammer); a protest or a prank; a parody or send-up of what we think of as a poem; a new kind of poem stripped of fakery, phoniness, and elevated language.

In her poem "Poetry," Marianne Moore remarks, "I too dislike it." Nicanor Parra, the Chilean poet and physicist, author of a book called *Anti-Poems*, asserts "The time has come to bring this ritual up-to-date." He also says "You can do anything in poetry."

> ROLLER COASTER
> Nicanor Parra (b. 1914; tr. Miller Williams)
>
> For half a century
> Poetry was the paradise
> Of the solemn fool.
> Until I came along
> And built my roller coaster.

> Go up, if you feel like it.
> It's not my fault if you come down
> Bleeding from your nose and mouth.

Apostrophe *(a-pós-tro-fee; Greek, "turning away")*   An address, exclamation, or question posed to someone or something, perhaps an absent person (as in a Wordsworth sonnet, "Milton! thou shouldst be living at this hour") or an abstraction (as in a Wordsworth ode, "O Duty!"). In grammar it is called the vocative, as in "O Rose, thou art sick" (William Blake) and "Bright star, would I were steadfast as thou art" (John Keats).

Argument *(Latin, from the verb "to make clear")*

1. A prose summary of the plot in a poem, or a section of a poem, that it precedes. Each book of John Milton's *Paradise Lost*, for example, begins with a one-paragraph argument. It is similar to a headnote but is generally longer and more of a synopsis.

2. The logical sequence of events in a poem. In poetry rooted in rationalism, cause and effect will usually determine the structure of the poem. Argument encompasses narrative (in which it may be the same as the plot), exposition, description, and persuasion. Reacting against the strictures and structures of logic, *Symbolist poets such as Stéphane Mallarmé jettisoned argument from the requirements of poetry. Images became more important in themselves, their connections intuitive and suggested rather than determined by rational connections. Later poets, such as the *Surrealists, sought to explore the unconscious, rejecting logic in the name of psychology.

Ars Poetica *(arz po-ét-i-ca; Latin, "the art of poetry")*   A poem that explores or presents the poet's view of what poetry is and how one should write it. Horace's "The Art of Poetry" is in fact a verse letter that discusses how to write poems and how to conduct oneself as a poet.

In the twentieth century, an *ars poetica* can appear in the guise of prose criticism, like Paul Valéry's *The Art of Poetry*. But poets still use the form in verse, often speaking through metaphor, as in Norman Dubie's "Ars Poetica." In a poem called "Ars Poetica," Archibald

MacLeish presents his views in a series of similes, asserting, for example, that a poem should be "palpable and mute/ As a globed fruit." Czeslaw Milosz has written, in more questioning terms, a poem called "Ars Poetica?"

Assonance *(áss-uh-nunce; Latin, "sounding or responding to with the same sound")*
1. The repetition of vowel sounds, like the short "i" repeated in Sylvia Plath's "Strips of tinfoil winking like people" (from "The Bee Meeting," in whose title the long "e" is also assonated). The repetition of consonants is called *alliteration or *consonance.
2. A kind of approximate rhyme or *slant rhyme that repeats vowels but changes the consonants (grape/shave, pine/ripe); also called vowel rhyme. Old French and Spanish have used assonance regularly in place of rhyme, as in the *Song of Roland* and the *Poem of the Cid. (See: rhyme.)*

Aubade *(oh-báhd; French, "dawn poem")* A poem set at sunrise, usually about the parting of lovers, like the "Parting is such sweet sorrow" scene in Shakespeare's *Romeo and Juliet.*

Audience Those who read the poems of a given poet; also those for whom that poet may write. (The two audiences are not necessarily the same.) Walt Whitman asserted, "To have great poets there must be great audiences too."

Automatic Writing A process of writing in which the writer does not pause but writes as quickly and unhesitatingly as possible.
Pioneered by the *Surrealists, such as André Breton, it was primarily a means of drawing forth unconscious thoughts, of scaring up mental odds and ends not sorted into rational compartments, of conjuring the disturbing materials of dream and nightmare. In James Merrill's long poem *The Changing Light at Sandover*, the words communicated by the Ouija board (transcribed in capital letters by "DJ," the poet's companion) represent a kind of automatic writing like the words received at a séance—a flow of knowledge from the beyond.

B

Ballad *(bá-lud, the a as in ask; Latin "dance")* A song that tells a story; often a narrative poem in the *ballad stanza. (In popular music, a ballad is a love song played at a slow tempo.)

From 1500 to the early twentieth century, hawkers sold printed broadside ballads at county fairs. But more commonly they have been sung and passed down by oral tradition. Consequently, ballads turn up in widely differing versions when copied out or recorded by folk-song collectors. Many Scottish ballads crossed the ocean with settlers who made their homes in the Appalachian mountains. In an American version of "Barbara Allan," for example, Sir John Graeme underwent a name-change to "Sweet William" and Michaelmas (November 11) became "the merry month of May."

Many poets, imitating the folk tradition, have written literary ballads. Examples include Samuel Taylor Coleridge's *The Rime of the Ancient Mariner*, John Keats' "La Belle Dame Sans Merci," Federico Garcia Lorca's *Gypsy Ballads*, Elizabeth Bishop's "The Burglar of Babylon," and Robert Hayden's "The Ballad of Nat Turner."

Although many ballads are written in the ballad stanza, others (such as "The Three Ravens") appear in different stanzaic forms, perhaps with refrains or a chorus.

THE THREE RAVENS / Anonymous

There were three Ravens sat on a tree,
  Down a downe, hay down, hay downe,
There were three Ravens sat on a tree,
  With a downe;

There were three Ravens sat on a tree,
They were as blacke as they might be,
   With a downe derrie, derrie, derrie, downe, downe.

The one of them said to his make,
Where shall we our breakefast take?

Downe in yonder greene field
There lies a Knight slain under his shield.

His hounds they lie downe at his feete,
So well they can their Master keepe.

His Haukes they flie so eagerly
There's no fowle dare him come nie.

Downe there comes a fallow Doe
As great with yong as she might goe.

She lift up his bloudy hed
And kist his wounds that were so red.

She got him up upon her backe
And carried him to earthen lake.

She buried him before the prime,
She was dead her selfe ere even-song time.

God send every gentleman
Such haukes, such hounds, and such a Leman.

NOTE: *make*: mate; *nie*: near; *prime*: sunrise; *even-song*: sunset; *Leman*: lover.

Ballad Stanza   A four-line stanza in which the first and third lines contain four stresses each and the second and fourth lines contain three stresses each (a pattern of 4-3-4-3) and in which only the even-numbered lines rhyme (*XaXa*).

If the first and third lines rhyme as well, this stanza is called the hymn stanza, common meter, or common measure (*abab*). Another difference is that the hymn stanza is more regularly iambic, while the ballad stanza is looser. In practice, however, ballads can be written in the hymn stanza and hymns in the ballad stanza.

There are several common variations permitted in the ballad stanza. The poet can (1) drop the fourth stress from lines 1 and/or 3, so that

the line ends on an unstressed syllable (˘ ´ ˘ ´ ˘ ´ ˘); (2) add a fourth stress to lines 2 and/or 4 (˘ ´ ˘ ´ ˘ ´ ˘ ´); (3) add internal rhyme to lines 1 and/or 3, so that the second and fourth stresses in the line rhyme as in this stanza from Samuel Taylor Coleridge's "The Rime of the Ancient Mariner":

In mist or *cloud*, on mast or *shroud*,	*a a*
It perched for vespers *nine*;	*b*
Whiles all the *night*, through fog-smoke *white*	*c c*
Glimmered the white Moon-*shine*.	*b*

Although the stanza above is in regular iambics, ballads often tend toward *accentual meter, with varying numbers of unstressed syllables.

There are two other common variations of the ballad stanza. Long meter consists of four tetrameter lines (4-4-4-4). Short meter is primarily trimeter, except for line three, which is tetrameter (3-3-4-3).

Ballad Stanza		*Hymn Stanza*	
Stresses	Rhyme	Stresses	Rhyme
4	none	4	a
3	a	3	b
4	none	4	a
3	a	3	b
(loose iambics)		(strict iambics)	

SIR PATRICK SPENCE / Anonymous

The king sits in Dumferling town,
    Drinking the blood-red wine:
O where will I get a good sailor
    To sail this ship of mine?

Up and spake an elder knight,
    Sat at the king's right knee:
Sir Patrick Spence is the best sailor
    That sails upon the sea.

The king has written a braid letter
    And sign'd it wi' his hand;
And sent it to Sir Patrick Spence,
    Was walking on the sand.

The first line that Sir Patrick read,
  A loud laugh laughèd he:
The next line that Sir Patrick read,
  The tear blinded his e'e.

O who is this has done this deed,
  This ill deed done to me;
To send me out this time o' the year,
  To sail upon the sea?

Make haste, make haste, my merry men all,
  Our good ship sails the morn.
O say not so, my master dear,
  For I fear a deadly storm.

Late, late yest're'en I saw the new moon
  Wi' the old moon in her arm;
And I fear, I fear, my dear master,
  That we will come to harm.

O our Scots nobles were right loath
  To wet their cork-heel'd shoon;
But lang o'er a' the play were play'd,
  Their hats they swam aboon.

O lang, lang may their ladies sit
  Wi' their fans into their hand,
O ere they see Sir Patrick Spence
  Come sailing to the land.

O lang, lang may their ladies stand
  Wi' their gold combs in their hair,
Waiting for their own dear lords,
  For they'll see them no mair.

Half o'er, half o'er to Aberdour,
  It's fifty fadom deep:
And there lies good Sir Patrick Spence,
  Wi' the Scots lords at his feet.

NOTE: *braid*: long, broad; *e'e*: eye; *shoon*: shoes; *aboon*: above; *Aberdour*: Aberdeen, Scotland; *fadom*: fathoms.

Ballade *(buh-láhd; Latin "dance")*   A French fixed form, first popular in the fourteenth to fifteenth centuries in Europe, consisting of three stanzas rhymed *ababbcbC* and an envoi ("send-off," a kind of coda or postscript) rhymed *bcbC* (the capital letter indicating a refrain).

Through an entire ballade, there are only three different rhyme sounds. The French poet and thief, François Villon, is a master of the ballade, as is the English poet Geoffrey Chaucer. Because of its intricate rhyming and refrains, the form is now often considered most suitable for light verse, but Villon's ballades demonstrate the great potential for intensity and passion. In our time Marilyn Hacker has excelled in the form.

Although titled a "ballad" by the translator, who takes liberties with the rhyming, the poem below is really a ballade. (*See: ubi sunt.*)

THE BALLAD OF DEAD LADIES
François Villon (1431-?; tr. Dante Gabriel Rossetti)

Tell me now in what hidden way is
  Lady Flora the lovely Roman?
Where's Hipparchia, and where is Thais,
  Neither of them the fairer woman?
  Where is Echo, beheld of no man,
Only heard on river and mere,—
  She whose beauty was more than human? . . .
But where are the snows of yester-year?

Where's Héloise, the learned nun,
  For whose sake Abeillard, I ween,
Lost manhood and put priesthood on?
  (From Love he won such dule and teen!)
  And where, I pray you, is the Queen
Who willed that Buridan should steer
  Sewed in a sack's mouth down the Seine? . . .
But where are the snows of yester-year?

What Queen Blanche, like a queen of lilies,
  With a voice like any mermaiden,—
Bertha Broadfoot, Beatrice, Alice,
  And Ermengarde the lady of Maine,—
  And that good Joan whom Englishmen
At Rouen doomed and burned her there,—

Mother of God, where are they then? . . .
But where are the snows of yester-year?

Nay, never ask this week, fair lord,
  Where they are gone, nor yet this year,
Save with thus much for an overword,—
  But where are the snows of yester-year?

Beat Emphasis on a particular syllable.

The term is used more for music than for poetry, in which it is more often called *accent or stress. It is occasionally misused to mean syllable, but the musical analogy applies, as in a drum beat. A three-beat line would contain three accents or stresses.

Beat Poetry An anti-academic school of poetry that sprang up in the fifties in San Francisco; characterized by fast-paced, associative free verse, a resemblance to jazz, a debt to Walt Whitman, a free-spirited attitude, and language that is irreverent and slangy.

Beat poetry is best known in the poems of Allen Ginsberg, Gregory Corso, Lawrence Ferlinghetti, and Gary Snyder, and in the fiction and poetry of Jack Kerouac. Ferlinghetti's City Lights Press and James Laughlin's New Directions Press have been the movement's chief publishers. The word *beat* (popularized as the cartoonish "beatnik") may mean "worn-out" or "beatific," or it may refer to a rhythmic beat, as in the pulse and improvisations of jazz.

The following poem by Allen Ginsberg pays homage to poets Walt Whitman and Federico Garcia Lorca. Although it's presented as a series of prose paragraphs, those paragraphs are cadenced like the long lines of Whitman, with their "enumerations," and like Ginsberg's other oratorical poems, such as *Howl* and *Sunflower Sutra*.

A SUPERMARKET IN CALIFORNIA
Allen Ginsberg (b. 1926)

What thoughts I have of you tonight, Walt Whitman, for I walked down the sidestreets under the trees with a headache self-conscious looking at the full moon.

In my hungry fatigue, and shopping for images, I went into the neon fruit supermarket, dreaming of your enumerations!

What peaches and what penumbras! Whole families shopping at night! Aisles full of husbands! Wives in the avocados, babies in the tomatoes!—and you, Garcia Lorca, what were you doing down by the watermelons?

I saw you, Walt Whitman, childless, lonely old grubber, poking among the meats in the refrigerator and eyeing the grocery boys.

I heard you asking questions of each: Who killed the pork chops? What price bananas? Are you my Angel?

I wandered in and out of the brilliant stacks of cans following you, and followed in my imagination by the store detective.

We strode down the open corridors together in our solitary fancy tasting artichokes, possessing every frozen delicacy, and never passing the cashier.

Where are we going, Walt Whitman? The doors close in an hour. Which way does your beard point tonight?

(I touch your book and dream of our odyssey in the supermarket and feel absurd.)

Will we walk all night through solitary streets? The trees add shade to shade, lights out in the houses, we'll both be lonely.

Will we stroll dreaming of the lost America of love past blue automobiles in driveways, home to our silent cottage?

Ah, dear father, graybeard, lonely old courage-teacher, what America did you have when Charon quit poling his ferry and you got out on a smoking bank and stood watching the boat disappear on the black waters of Lethe?

Berkeley 1955

Biblical Verse *(also called Hebraic verse)* Long-lined, unmetrical verse whose prosody is governed by rhetorical devices, such as the repetition and variation of words and phrases, and by the use of synonyms and antonyms, likenesses and opposites, parallels and antitheses.

It is found in the Hebrew Bible and in translations of the Old Testament. Repetition gives the verse power and cohesiveness, while the departure from metrical regularity lets the lines ebb and flow.

Walt Whitman depends upon Biblical verse throughout *Leaves of*

Grass. Christopher Smart (1722-1771) imitates it in "For I will consider my Cat Jeoffry" (from *Jubilate Agno*):

> For he is of the tribe of Tiger.
> For the Cherub Cat is a term of the Angel Tiger.
> For he has the subtlety and hissing of a serpent, which in goodness he suppresses.
> For he will not do destruction if he is well-fed, neither will he spit without provocation.
> For he purrs in thankfulness when God tells him he's a good Cat.
> For he is an instrument for the children to learn benevolence upon.
> For every house is incomplete without him, and a blessing is lacking in the spirit.
>
> (lines 724-730)

(*See: free verse, psalm.*)

THE SONG OF SOLOMON (II, King James Version of The Bible)

I am the rose of Sharon, and the lily of the valleys.
As the lily among thorns, so is my love among the daughters.
As the apple-tree among the trees of the wood, so is my beloved among the sons. I sat down under his shadow with great delight, and his fruit was sweet to my taste.
He brought me to the banqueting house, and his banner over me was love.
Stay me with flagons, comfort me with apples: for I am sick of love.
His left hand is under my head, and his right hand doth embrace me.
I charge you, O ye daughters of Jerusalem, by the roes, and by the hinds of the field, that ye stir not up, nor awake my love, till he please.
The voice of my beloved! behold, he cometh leaping upon the mountains, skipping upon the hills.
My beloved is like a roe, or a young hart: behold, he standeth behind our wall, he looketh forth at the windows, shewing himself through the lattice.
My beloved spake, and said unto me, Rise up, my love, my fair one, and come away.
For lo, the winter is past, the rain is over and gone;
The flowers appear on the earth; the time of the singing of birds is come, and the voice of the turtle is heard in our land;

The fig-tree putteth forth her green figs, and the vines with the tender
grape give a good smell. Arise, my love, my fair one, and come away.
O my dove, that art in the clefts of the rock, in the secret places of the
stairs, let me see thy countenance, let me hear thy voice; for sweet
is thy voice, and thy countenance is comely.
Take us the foxes, the little foxes, that spoil the vines: for our vines
have tender grapes.
My beloved is mine, and I am his: he feedeth among the lilies.
Until the day break, and the shadows flee away, turn, my beloved, and
be thou like a roe or a young hart upon the mountains of Bether.

NOTE: *roe*: the male of a small species of deer; *hind*: a female red deer; *sick*: deeply
affected by longing; *hart*: a male red deer, usually over five years old; *turtle*:
turtle-dove.

Black Mountain School A group of poets associated with Black
Mountain College, an experimental school in North Carolina, in the
1950s. Much of their early work appeared in *Origin* and *The Black
Mountain Review*.

Although the poems of Robert Creeley, Denise Levertov, Charles
Olson, and Robert Duncan are very different, they share a belief in
what Levertov calls "organic form" (a "sense of seeking out inherent,
though not immediately apparent, form," as opposed to the use of
"prescribed forms") and a preference for free verse. They were influenced by William Carlos Wiliams, Ezra Pound, and Objectivist poets
such as Louis Zukofsky. Charles Olson formulated the group's central
poetic theory in an essay, "Projective Verse," which insisted that the
poet's breath determined the rhythms of a poem, and that the page
was an open space in which the poet could transcribe those breath
rhythms, a process called "composition by field" or "open composition." Projective verse aims to be a process of registering perception
directly on the page, during composition, rather than drawing on
previous observations and established forms.

I KNOW A MAN
Robert Creeley (b. 1926)

As I sd to my
friend, because I am
always talking,—John, I

sd, which was not his
name, the darkness sur-
rounds us, what

can we do against
it, or else, shall we &
why not, buy a goddamn big car,

drive, he sd, for
christ's sake, look
out where yr going.

ONE A.M. / Denise Levertov (b. 1923)

The kitchen patio in snowy
moonlight.   That
snowsilence, that
abandon to stillness.
The sawhorse, the concrete
washtub, snowblue. The washline
bowed under its snowfur!
Moon has silenced
the crickets, the summer frogs
hold their breath.
Summer night, summer night, standing
one-legged, a crane
in the snowmarsh, staring
at snowmoon!

LA CHUTE / Charles Olson (1910-1970)

my drum, hollowed out thru the thin slit,
carved from the cedar wood, the base I took
when the tree was felled

o my lute, wrought from the tree's crown

my drum, whose lustiness
was not to be resisted

                    my lute,
from whose pulsations
not one could turn away

                                                        They
        are where the dead are, my drum fell
        where the dead are, who
        will bring it up, my lute
        who will bring it up where it fell in the face of them
        where they are, where my lute and drum have fallen?

NOTE: *la chute*: fall.

Blank Verse   Unrhymed *iambic pentameter, invented in sixteenth-century England by the Earl of Surrey for his translation of two books of Virgil's epic *The Aeneid*.

Instead of trying to translate Virgil's Latin into unrhymed dactylic hexameter lines, like the original's, Surrey shortened the line from six to five feet, a more natural length for English, and used iambs instead of dactyls. So much was not new. Gavin Douglas had already translated the entire epic into heroic couplets. Surrey, who owes much to Douglas's version, kept the iambic pentameter but omitted the rhymes. The result was blank verse. William Shakespeare and Christopher Marlowe made it great in their plays, establishing Surrey's invention as one of the most important forms in English poetry.

Blank verse is flexible, not bound by the recurring sound effects and structural webbing of rhyme. It is an effective form for talk (the monologues of Robert Browning) and storytelling (the narratives of Robert Frost), the human voice conversing. It started with a translation of a foreign epic but made possible a native version of the real thing, John Milton's *Paradise Lost*. And, perhaps because of the importance of blank-verse soliloquy in Elizabethan drama, it underlies some of the best meditative poetry by William Wordsworth and Wallace Stevens.

        from *THE AENEID*, BOOK TWO / Virgil
        (tr. Henry Howard, Earl of Surrey, ca. 1517-1547)

        The Grekes chieftains, all irked with the war
        Wherein they wasted had so many years
        And oft repulst by fatal destinie,
        A huge hors made, hye raised like a hill,
        By the divine science of Minerva;

Of cloven firre compacted were his ribbs;
For their return a fained sacrifice,
The fame whereof so wandred it at point.
In the dark bulk they closde bodies of men
Chosen by lot, and did enstuff by stealth
The hollow womb with armed soldiars.
   There stands in sight an isle hight Tenedon,
Rich and of fame while Priams kingdom stood:
Now but a bay, and rode unsure for ship.
Hether them secretly the Grekes withdrew,
Shrouding themselves under the desert shore.
And, wening we they had ben fled and gone,
And with that winde had fet the land of Grece,
Troye discharged her long continue dole.
The gates cast up, we issued out to play,
The Grekish camp desirous to behold,
The places void and the forsaken costes.
Here Pyrrhus band, there ferce Achilles pight,
Here rode their shippes, there did their battels joyne.
Astonnied some the scathefull gift beheld,
Behight by vow unto the chaste Minerve,
All wondring at the hugenesse of the horse.

(lines 18-44)

NOTE: Aeneas is telling the story of the Trojan horse. The final -*ed* of verbs should be pronounced. "Soldiars" consists of three syllables here: sól-di-ars.

Minerva: Roman goddess of wisdom (Athena to the Greeks); *firre*: fir; *fained*: feigned; *enstuff*: furnish with soldiers; *hight*: named, called; *rode*: harbor; *hether*: hither; *wening*: thinking; *fet*: arrived at; *dole*: sorrow, grief; *Pyrrhus and Achilles*: Greek heroes; *pight*: pitched camp; *scathefull*: harmful, injurious; *behight*: promised.

from THE TEMPEST
William Shakespeare (1564-1616)

Be not afeard. The isle is full of noises,
Sounds and sweet airs, that give delight and hurt not.
Sometimes a thousand twangling instruments
Will hum about mine ears, and sometime voices
That, if I then had wak'd after long sleep,
Will make me sleep again; and then, in dreaming,
The clouds methought would open and show riches

> Ready to drop upon me, that, when I wak'd,
> I cried to dream again.
> > (Act III, Scene II, lines 144-152)

NOTE: Caliban, "a savage and deformed Slave," speaks here to Stephano, "a drunken Butler," and Trinculo, "a Jester." A trimeter line, like the last one here, may occasionally be used in a passage otherwise in pentameter, whether rhymed or not. John Milton uses the variation effectively in "Lycidas."

from *THE PRELUDE* / William Wordsworth (1770-1850)

> Nor less when spring had warmed the cultured Vale,
> Moved we as plunderers where the mother-bird
> Had in high places built her lodge; though mean
> Our object and inglorious, yet the end
> Was not ignoble. Oh! when I have hung
> Above the raven's nest, by knots of grass
> And half-inch fissures in the slippery rock
> But ill sustained, and almost—so it seemed—
> Suspended by the blast that blew amain,
> Shouldering the naked crag, oh, at that time
> While on the perilous ridge I hung alone,
> With what strange utterance did the loud, dry wind
> Blow through my ear! the sky seemed not a sky
> Of earth—and with what motion moved the clouds!
> > (from "Introduction—Childhood and School-Time")

Blason *(also blazon; German, "shield")* A poem composed in lines of eight to ten syllables, concluding with an epigram, on a theme of praise or blame, usually about a single part of a woman's body. The term comes from 1536, when the French poet Clément Marot wrote his *Blason de Beau Tétin* (Blason of a Beautiful Nipple).

Blues An African-American song form, derived from the field hollers of slaves in the South. It can refer either loosely to a song about being blue, about loss and hard times, or more specially to a song in three-line blues form, in which the first two lines are roughly identical and the third line rhymes with them.

W.C. Handy, who popularized the form, discovered the blues while touring with his Knights of Pythias Band in the Mississippi Delta around 1903. His "St. Louis Blues" (1914) begins:

> I hate to see de evenin' sun go down,
> Hate to see de evenin' sun go down,
> 'Cause ma baby, he done lef dis town.

In "New St. Louis Blues," the poet Sterling A. Brown updates the story, writing about a "Market Street woman noted fuh to have dark days."

Langston Hughes was a pioneer in adapting the musical form to poetry, dividing each blues line into two shorter lines, so that his blues stanza contains six lines instead of three. His rhymes come at the end of even-numbered lines.

Sherley Anne Williams varies this way of writing out the blues, staggering her lines in "Any Woman's Blues," so that a single line breaks into halves:

> Soft lamp shinin
>   and me alone in the night.

Her stanzas contain three of these two-part lines.

In his "Con/tin/u/way/shun Blues," Etheridge Knight quotes Mary Helen Washington, who says, "blues are more than cries of oppression." He then continues:

> They say the blues is just a slave song
> But I say that's just a lie
> Cause even when we be free, baby—
> Lord knows we still have got to die
>   lovers will still lie
>   babies will still cry

One way to vary the blues form is to make the second line rhyme differently from the first (as in the third stanza of Sandra McPherson's "Bad Mother Blues," which is included below). Another is to omit the repeated line, which is essentially what Knight does in the example above. (Like Hughes, he splits the blues line into two shorter ones.) Knight also adds two indented, even shorter lines, a kind of coda, to the stanza, the way a blues singer might improvise extra phrases and rhymes before continuing to the next verse.

MORNING AFTER
Langston Hughes (1902-1967)

I was so sick last night I
Didn't hardly know my mind.
So sick last night I
Didn't hardly know my mind.
I drunk some bad licker that
Almost made me blind.

Had a dream last night I
Thought I was in hell.
I drempt last night I
Thought I was in hell.
Woke up and looked around me—
Baby, your mouth was open like a well.

I said, Baby! Baby!
Please don't snore so loud.
Baby! Please!
Please don't snore so loud.
You jest like a little bit o' woman but you
Sound like a great big crowd.

BAD MOTHER BLUES / Sandra McPherson (b. 1943))

When you were arrested, child, and I had to take your pocketknife
When you were booked and I had to confiscate your pocketknife
It had blood on it from where you'd tried to take your life

It was the night before Thanksgiving, all the family coming over
The night before Thanksgiving, all the family coming over
We had to hide your porno magazine and put your handcuffs undercover

Each naked man looked at you, said, Baby who do you think you are
Each man looked straight down on you, like a waiting astronomer's star
Solely, disgustedly, each wagged his luster

I've decided to throw horror down the well and wish on it
Decided I'll throw horror down the well and wish on it
And up from the water will shine my sweet girl in her baby bonnet

A thief will blind you with his flashlight
                        but a daughter be your bouquet
A thief will blind you with his flashlight
                        but a daughter be your bouquet
When the thief's your daughter you turn your eyes the other way

I'm going into the sunflower field where all of them are facing me
I'm going into the sunflower field so all of them are facing me
Going to go behind the sunflowers, feel all the sun that I can't see

Bob and Wheel A five-line stanza, rhymed *ababa*, in which the first line (the "bob") contains one or two metrical stresses and each of the next four lines (the "wheel") contains three. A bob may also occur by itself as a refrain—what George Saintsbury calls a "short-line pivot."

The stanza occurs in Middle English poetry, most notably in the anonymous *Sir Gawain and the Green Knight*. In each section of this long narrative poem, the bob and wheel serves as the "tail" at the end of a series of unrhymed lines written in Anglo-Saxon *alliterative meter. The last alliterative line is enjambed into the bob, which rhymes with the second and fourth lines of the wheel that follows. Each line of the wheel contains alliteration. Here is John Gardner's translation of the eighth section of Part Two of *Sir Gawain and the Green Knight* (Anonymous, 14th century). The last five lines form the bob and wheel:

He struck the steed with his spurs and sprang on his way
So swiftly that Gringolet's shoes struck fire on the stone;
And all who saw that sweet knight sighed in their hearts,
And each man there said the same to every other,
Grieving for that knight: "By Christ, it's sad
That you, lad, must be lost, so noble in life!
It would not be easy to find this man's equal on earth.
It would have been wiser to work more warily;
We might one day have made him a mighty duke,
A glowing lord of the people in his land;
Far better that than broken like this into nothing,
Beheaded by an elf for undue pride.
Who ever heard of a king who'd hear the counsel
Of addle-pated knights during Christmas games?"
Many were the warm tears that watered their eyes
When that handsome hero rode from the high hall
                    that day.   ◄——— *bob*
    He paused at no abode
    But swiftly went his way   } *wheel*

    Down many a devious road,
    As all the old books say.

Burns Stanza *(also called habbie stanza, Scottish stanza)* A six-line stanza rhyming *aaabab*, with a metrical count of 4-4-4-2-4-2 feet (or accents) for the six lines.

The stanza was a favorite of the Scottish poet Robert Burns. The four *a* rhymes in each stanza require some virtuosity and the two shorter lines give each stanza a neat musical flip, a quickening, at its end.

TO A MOUSE, ON TURNING HER UP
IN HER NEST, WITH THE PLOUGH,
NOVEMBER, 1785 / Robert Burns (1759-1796)

Wee, sleeket, cowran, tim'rous *beastie*,
O, what a panic's in thy *breastie*!
Thou need na start awa sae hasty,
 Wi' bickering brattle!
I wad be laith to rin an' chase thee,
 Wi' murd'ring *pattle*!

I'm truly sorry man's dominion
Has broken Nature's social union,
An' justifies that ill opinion,
 Which makes thee startle,
At me, thy poor, earth-born companion,
 An' *fellow-mortal*!

I doubt na, whyles, but thou may *thieve*;
What then? poor beastie, thou maun live!
A *daimen-icker* in a *thrave*
 'S a sma' request:
I'll get a blessin wi' the lave,
 An' never miss't!

Thy wee-bit *housie*, too, in ruin!
It's silly wa's the win's are strewin!
An' naething, now, to big a new ane,
 O' foggage green!
An' bleak *December's winds* ensuin,
 Baith snell an' keen!

Thou saw the fields laid bare an' wast,
An' weary *Winter* comin fast,

An' cozie here, beneath the blast,
  Thou thought to dwell,
Till crash! the cruel *coulter* past
  Out thro' thy cell.

That wee-bit heap o' leaves an' stibble,
Hast cost thee monie a weary nibble!
Now thou's turn'd out, for a' thy trouble,
  But house or hald,
To thole the Winter's *sleety dribble*,
  An' *cranreuch* cauld!

But Mousie, thou art no thy-lane,
In proving *foresight* may be vain:
The best laid schemes o' *Mice* an' *Men*,
  Gang aft agley,
An' lea'e us nought but grief an' pain,
  For promis'd joy!

Still, thou art blest, compar'd wi' *me*!
The *present* only toucheth thee:
But Och! I *backward* cast my e'e,
  On prospects drear!
An' *forward*, tho' I canna *see*,
  I *guess* an' *fear*!

NOTE: *sleeket*: sleek; *cowran*: cringing; *na*: not; *brattle*: clatter, hurry; *wad*: would; *rin*: run; *pattle*: spade used to clean a plough; *whyles*: sometimes; *maun*: must; *daimen*: occasional; *icker*: ear of corn (in the British sense, meaning a grain such as wheat); *thrave*: two shocks of grain; *lave*: remainder; *wa's*: walls; *win's*: wind, breath; *foggage*: rank grass; *baith*: both; *snell*: bitter; *coulter*: iron blade which is fixed in front of a ploughshare to make a vertical cut in the soil; *stibble*: stubble; *monie*: many; *hald*: refuge; *thole*: endure; *dribble*: a trickling stream; *cranreuch*: hoar-frost; *cauld*: cold; *thy-lane*: thyself; *gang aft agley*: go oft awry.

Cadence *(Latin, "falling")* The rising and falling of spoken language, the rhythmic shape made by a flow of words.

Cadence may consist of either the alternation of stressed and unstressed syllables or the swelling and subsiding of phrases. *Rhythm is the pattern made by these cadences. When Ezra Pound discusses composing "in the sequence of the musical phrase, not in sequence of a metronome," he is arguing for the rhythmic primacy of cadence. Interestingly, though the term has musical associations, it also applies to conversation. Although cadence is necessarily present in metrical verse (as it is in prose and speech), it is crucial to free verse, especially in long lines like those of Walt Whitman's poetry, which is sometimes called cadenced verse. Here is a stanza from his "Out of the Cradle Endlessly Rocking":

> The aria sinking,
> All else continuing, the stars shining,
> The winds blowing, the notes of the bird continuous echoing,
> With angry moans the fierce old mother incessantly moaning,
> On the sands of Paumanok's shore gray and rustling,
> The yellow half-moon enlarged, sagging down, drooping, the face of
>   the sea almost touching,
> The boy ecstatic, with his bare feet the waves, with his hair the
>   atmosphere dallying,
> The love in the heart long pent, now loose, now at last tumultuously
>   bursting,
> The aria's meaning, the ears, the soul, swiftly depositing,

The strange tears down the cheeks coursing,
The colloquy there, the trio, each uttering,
The undertone, the savage old mother incessantly crying,
To the boy's soul's questions sullenly timing, some drown'd secret
    hissing,
To the outsetting bard.

The cadences vary, depending on the phrase lengths, from a single isolated word ("drooping") to a whole uninterrupted line ("On the sands of Paumanok's shore gray and rustling"). In this passage, as in much of Whitman's verse, the commas neatly delineate many of the cadences. In short-lined free verse, however, a cadence may be interrupted by a line break (an effect called *enjambment, or "run-on line"). In metrical verse, cadence will be joined and perhaps controlled by *meter (a regular pattern of stressed and unstressed syllables). Here is the opening stanza of William Wordsworth's "Resolution and Independence":

> There was a roaring in the wind all night;
> The rain came heavily and fell in floods;
> But now the sun is rising calm and bright;
> The birds are singing in the distant woods;
> Over his own sweet voice the Stock-dove broods;
> The Jay makes answer as the Magpie chatters;
> And all the air is filled with pleasant noise of waters.

The first six lines are *iambic pentameter (a pattern of five feet, each consisting of an unstressed and a stressed syllable); the last line is hexameter (one extra foot); the rhyme scheme is *ababbcc*. There is considerable rhythmic variety from line to line (because the heavier stresses fall in different places and because the natural cadences vary), but the iambic meter is powerful and controlling in itself; cadence serves at the meter's pleasure.

In the absence of rhyme and meter, cadence simply becomes more noticeable. Cadence and line breaks are the chief compositional tools of the free verse poet—along with rhetorical devices such as *anaphora (repetition of the first word or phrase in successive lines).

Caesura *(si-zhóor-uh or si-zóor-uh; Latin, "cut")*   A pause or break in the middle of a line, marked with || when scanning a poem. The caesura in each of these lines from Shakespeare's Sonnet 18 is indicated by a comma:

> So long as men can breathe, or eyes can see,
> So long lives this, and this gives life to thee.

Poets composing in *iambic pentameter usually try to vary the place where the caesura occurs from line to line. There can be, of course, more than one in a line, and some lines seem to rush along without much of a pause at all. But the absence of punctuation does not necessarily mean that there is no caesura. In the first line of the same sonnet—"Shall I compare thee to a summer's day?"—there is a slight pause after "thee."

Canto *(cán-toe; Italian, "song"; the Italian plural is "canti" but in English "cantos" is acceptable)*   A section or chapter in a larger poem, like the 100 cantos of Dante's *Divine Comedy*.

Edmund Spenser's allegorical epic, *The Faerie Queen*, consists of six books, each divided into twelve cantos. Alexander Pope's *The Rape of the Lock* and Lord Byron's *Don Juan* are also divided into cantos. Ezra Pound's major work, an epic in search of its form, never found a title beyond the provisional one, *The Cantos*.

Canzone *(can-zóh-nee or cahn-tsoh-nay; Italian, "song")*   An Italian lyric form of varying length, metrical patterns, and rhyme schemes, intended to be set to music and appropriate for serious subjects like beauty, valor, love, and virtue.

Dante, who called the canzone "a composition of words set to music," divided the canzone into two parts, the "head" and the "tail," but he further divided the head into two formally identical parts, making the form both two- and three-part. Stanza length varies from seven to twenty lines. Lines usually contain seven or eleven syllables. It often concludes with a *commiato* (valediction). According to Dana Gioia, the canzone "tends to be lyric and obsessive."

One early canzone, "Within the Gentle Heart" by Guido Guinizelli (c. 1235-1276), exerted a powerful influence on the Italian poets such

as Dante who followed him. Here, in D.G. Rossetti's translation, is the first of Guido's six stanzas, each one rhymed *ababcdcede*, with a stress pattern of 5-5-5-5-3-5-3-5-3-5 (imitating the Italian pattern of syllables):

> Within the gentle heart Love shelters him
> As birds within the green shade of the grove.
> Before the gentle heart, in nature's scheme,
> Love was not, nor the gentle heart ere Love.
> For with the sun, at once,
> So sprang the light immediately; nor was
> Its birth before the sun's.
> And Love hath his effect in gentleness
> Of very self; even as
> Within the middle fire the heat's excess.

Although the form of a canzone can vary widely, two particular patterns deserve mention. One taken from a canzone by Dante ("Amor, tu vedi ben che questa donna," or "Love, very well you notice how this woman"), is now considered the fixed form of the canzone in English. It resembles the *sestina, in that end-words, not rhymes, are repeated in a circular pattern; it also adds a shorter stanza called the tornada at the end, using all the end-words. There are five twelve-line stanzas, using five end-words in a fixed pattern, with a six-line tornada. Later poets (such as W.H. Auden and John Ashbery in poems called "Canzone") have used a tornada of five lines—one for each end-word. In Dante's first stanza, translated here by Joseph Tusiani, the word "Love" refers to Cupid or Eros:

> Love, very well you notice how this woman
> scorns and ignores your power all the time,
> deeming herself the only lovely woman.
> Oh, since she saw she was my only woman,
> for this your ray that fills my face with light,
> she was more cruelty than she was woman,
> so that her heart, no more a heart of woman,
> is that of some wild beast, hateful and cold;
> for, though the weather be quite warm or cold,
> with these my eyes I only see a woman
> carved not of flesh but of a lovely stone
> by the most skillful artisan of stone.

Here is the pattern of end-words that Dante uses (the Italian originals are *donna, tempo, luce, freddo,* and *petra*):

	Stanza 1	*Stanza 2*	*Stanza 3*	*Stanza 4*	*Stanza 5*	*Tornada*
1	woman	stone	cold	light	time	woman
2	time	woman	stone	cold	light	stone
3	woman	stone	cold	light	time	cold
4	woman	stone	cold	light	time	cold
5	light	time	woman	stone	cold	light
6	woman	stone	cold	light	time	time
7	woman	stone	cold	light	time	
8	cold	light	time	woman	stone	
9	cold	light	time	woman	stone	
10	woman	stone	cold	light	time	
11	stone	cold	light	time	woman	
12	stone	cold	light	time	woman	

Another variation appears in a *canzon* form invented by the twelfth-century Provençal poet Arnaut Daniel. He uses isolated rhyme (or *rimas dissolutas*), so that a rhyme word does not recur within a stanza but appears in succeeding stanzas. All the first lines of different stanzas, for example, use the same rhyme. Ezra Pound's translation of the first two stanzas of Arnaut's "Canzon: Of the Trades and Love" shows the pattern:

Though this measure quaint confine me,	*a*
And I chip out words and plane them,	*b*
They shall yet be true and clear	*c*
When I finally have filed them.	*d*
Love glosses and gilds them knowing	*e*
That my song has for its start	*f*
One who is worth's hold and warrant.	*g*
Each day finer I refine me	*a*
And my cult and service strain them	*b*
Toward the world's best, as ye hear,	*c*
"Hers" my root and tip have styled them.	*d*
And though bitter winds come blowing,	*e*
The love that rains down in my heart	*f*
Warmeth me when frost's abhorrent.	*g*

The next four stanzas continue the pattern (the first lines, for example, rhyming "resign me," "entwine me," "assign me," and "malign me"). The tornada uses the rhymes of the last three lines of the stanza: "doing," "ox-cart," and "torrent."

Canzone 1	*Canzone 2*
Each letter represents the same word repeated:	Each letter represents a rhyme (which repeats from stanza to stanza):
Stanza 1: *ABAACAADDAEE*	Stanza 1: *abcdefg*
Stanza 2: *EAEEBEECCEDD*	Stanza 2: *abcdefg*
Stanza 3: *DEDDADDBBDCC*	Stanza 3: *abcdefg*
Stanza 4: *CDCCECCAACBB*	Stanza 4: *abcdefg*
Stanza 5: *BCBBDBBEEBAA*	Stanza 5: *abcdefg*
Tornada: *AEDCB*	Stanza 6: *abcdefg*
	Tornada: *efg*
(used by Dante, who adds a line in the tornada: *AEDDCB*)	(used by Arnaut Daniel)

Carmen *(cár-men; Latin, song; plural carmina)* A lyric poem or song in Latin, such as the *carmina* of Catullus. (*See: translation for several versions of his Carmen 85.*)

Carol *(Greek, "choral dance")* Generally, a song of joy or praise, such as a Christmas carol.

More specifically, it is a form in which early English carols were composed. It consists of four-line stanzas rhymed *aaab*. Usually the rhymes of the first three lines change from stanza to stanza, while the *b* rhyme remains the same throughout the carol, so that several stanzas will rhyme aaab cccb dddb, etc. Furthermore, these recurring *b* rhymes can be alternating *refrains, and those refrains can precede the carol as a rhymed couplet. However, in the following three stanzas taken from an anonymous carol, the *a* lines rhyme together from stanza to stanza and the *b* lines are not refrains:

> Now is Yole comen wyth gentil chere—
> Of myrthe and gamen he hath no pere;
> In every lond wher he cometh nere
>   Is myrthe and gamen, I dar wel seye.

Now is comen a messager
Of thy lord, Sir Newe Yeer;
Biddeth us alle ben myrie heer
   And make as myrie as we may.

Ther-fore every man that is heer
Synge a carole on his manere;
If he can non we shullen him lere,
   So that we ben myrie alwey.

NOTE: *lere*: teach.

Catalexis, Catalectic *(cat-uh-léx-us or -léc-tik; Greek, "left off")* The omission of one or more unstressed syllables at the end or at the beginning of a metrical line; also called truncation.

In William Blake's "The Tyger," the last foot of each trochaic tetrameter line is catalectic:

Týgĕr, | týgĕr, | búrnĭng | bríght

By contrast, Henry Wadsworth Longfellow's *Hiawatha* retains the final unstressed syllable in its *trochaic tetrameter and is called acatalectic (metrically complete, with no syllables omitted from the pattern):

Bý thĕ | shíniňg | bíg sĕa | wátĕr

If two unstressed syllables are omitted from a final foot in dactylic meter, the foot is more properly called brachycatalectic (the prefix *brachy-* meaning "short").

In iambic meter, catalexis would occur in the first foot, cutting off the initial unstressed syllable; such a line is also called headless.

If a syllable is added to a metrical line, the line is hypermetric, as in the *feminine ending in iambic meter:

Tŏ bé | ŏr nót | tŏ bé: | thát ĭs | thĕ qués- | tĭon.

The extra syllable is not counted as a separate foot, nor is it part of the fifth foot.

If an unstressed syllable is prefixed to a line of trochaic meter (whether catalectic or not), the addition is called *anacrusis, as in the second of the following catalectic lines (also from Blake's "The Tyger"):

> Whát ĭm- | mórtăl | hánd ŏr | éye
> Coŭld | fráme thў̆ | féarfŭl | sýmmĕ- | trý?

(*See: anacrusis, trochee.*)

Cento (*chén-toe or sén-toe; Latin, "patchwork"*)   A poem made up of passages from poems by one or more authors; a patchwork of quotations; a literary collage; a pastiche (in its sense as a mixture of poetic excerpts).

Originally a cento was composed entirely of quotations from a single source, such as the Roman poet Virgil. Although it began as a game for scholars, it has become an allusive, postmodernist, intertextual form, as in John Ashbery's "To a Waterfowl" and Charles Tomlinson's "A Biography of the Author: A Cento." The end of T.S. Eliot's *The Waste Land*, with its barrage of quoted fragments, becomes a cento. Marianne Moore's liberal interpolation of quotations in her poems is similar in method. (*See: found poem, Oulipo, parody.*)

Chance Poetry (*also called aleatory poetry*)   Poetry written using chance methods, such as words written on cards and drawn at random to furnish an order for a poem's vocabulary. The leading American proponents of chance poetry have been Jackson MacLow and John Cage (an important avant-garde composer who also experimented with chance methods, or indeterminacy, in music).

Surrealists invented a game called *cadavre exquis* (French, "exquisite corpse") in which a player fills in an assigned grammatical blank in a sentence without knowing what words others have contributed— similar to the American game Mad-Libs.

One of the easiest ways to use chance as a stimulus for writing poems is to open a dictionary—or any book—at random and put your finger on a word, and then incorporate that word, along with other strokes of luck, into a poem.

To write the following poem on the assassination of Robert F.

Kennedy, Donald Justice chose words and grammatical indicators, wrote them on cards, and drew them randomly as he composed his lines. To write a series of poems on several Presidents of the United States, Jackson MacLow assigned the Phoenician meanings of the alphabet to letters of the Presidents' names and developed the poems from what came up. Here is the alphabetical key: A (ox), B (house), C (camel), D (door), E (window or Look!), F (hook), H (fence), I (hand), K (palm of the hand), L (ox-goad), M (water), N (fish), O (eye), P (mouth), Q (knot), R (head), S (tooth), T (mark), V (hook), X (prop), Y (hook), Z (weapon). Letters developed after the Phoenicians include G (camel), J (hand), U (hook), and W (hooks).

THE ASSASSINATION / Donald Justice (b. 1925)

It begins again, the nocturnal pulse.
It courses through the cables laid for it.
It mounts to the chandeliers and beats there, hotly.
We are too close. Too late, we would move back.
We are involved with the surge.

Now it bursts. Now it has been announced.
Now it is being soaked up by newspapers.
Now it is running through the streets.
The crowd has it. The woman selling carnations
And the man in the straw hat stand with it in their shoes.

Here is the red marquee it sheltered under,
Here is the ballroom, here
The sadly various orchestra led
By a single gesture. My arms open.
It enters. Look, we are dancing.

from THE PRESIDENTS OF THE UNITED STATES OF AMERICA / Jackson MacLow (b. 1922)

1789

George Washington never owned a camel
but he looked thru the eyes in his head
with a camel's calm and wary look.

Hooks that wd irritate an ox
held his teeth together

and he cd build a fence with his own hands
tho he preferred to go fishing
as anyone else wd
while others did the work *for* him
for tho he had no camels he had slaves enough
and probably made them toe the mark by keeping an eye on them
for *he* wd never have stood for anything fishy.

1801

Marked by no fence
farther than an eye cd see
beyond the big waters
Thomas Jefferson saw grass enough for myriads of oxen
to grind between their teeth.

His farmer hands itched
when he thought of all that vacant land and looked about for a way to
    hook it in for us
until something unhooked a window in his head
where the greedy needy teeth & eyes of Napoleon shone
eager for the money which
was Jefferson's bait to catch the Louisiana fish.

Chant Royal A French form, consisting of five eleven-line stanzas (rhymed *ababccddedE*) and a five-line envoi, or "send-off" (rhymed *ddedE*). The *E* line is a refrain (and in this form rhymes with the ninth line of each stanza).

Originally, no rhyme word could appear twice, the subject had to be heroic, the audience had to be royal, and the language had to be suitable for regal ears. It is similar to the *ballade.

Character Sketch *(also people poem, portrait)* A poem or story about a person. Sketch, however, suggests something incomplete, a draft rather than a finished work. Robert Lowell's "Commander Lowell" qualifies as a character sketch but is also a complete portrait and a memorable poem. The choice of terms may be more a matter of preference and tone than anything else. "Character sketch" sounds more modest, less formal, than "portrait." It need not be less finished or less accomplished.

Character sketches range from the satirical squibs by the Roman poet Catullus to Elizabeth Bishop's fond, wry poem about "Manuelzinho."

THE LAST WOMAN WITH LOTUS FEET
Marilyn Chin (b. 1955)
LOCKE, CA 1983

She hobbled down to tell us about the widows
of gold-diggers no taller than you and me, women

who dragged their men out from under oxcarts and wheelbarrows
while she, still virgin, sat and brewed

Chrysanthemum tea that squealed in a copper kettle.
Its steam was blue—as lorries passed . . .

I saw the bandage darkening around her ankles.
There was more to tell now, less to show.

Childhood Poem   A poem about a child or the memories of being a child; a description, narration, dramatic monologue, or meditation set during the time of youth, first discoveries, and early explorations of self and the world.

Childhood does not appear often as a subject for serious poetry until the Romantic period, around the turn of the nineteenth century. William Wordsworth, who was keenly interested in the growth of consciousness, declared, "The Child is Father of the Man." He devotes his major work, *The Prelude* (1805, 1850), to an exploration of his own childhood. (An example appears in *blank verse.) Childhood seemed like a time uncorrupted by learning, experience, and responsibility. In "The School Boy" (which appears below), William Blake speaks out for a boy who hates the regimentation of the classroom, a distaste similar to what the children feel in Rainer Maria Rilke's "Childhood" (a twentieth-century poem translated by Randall Jarrell):

> The time of school drags by with waiting
> And dread, with nothing but dreary things.

In the view of the Romantics, the natural world serves the child better as a field of study than any imposed curriculum.

The freshness of a child's encounters with the world continues to supply subjects and imagery and even methods for poetry (as in the wild, playful associations of Theodore Roethke's "Lost Son" poems). One might say that each child is inherently a poet, but that adolescence and adulthood stifle the gift in most of us. Concentrating on childhood returns the poet to a sense of experiencing the world in all its newness, yet accompanied by the language to capture that experience.

THE SCHOOL BOY
William Blake (1757-1827)

I love to rise in a summer morn,
When the birds sing on every tree;
The distant huntsman winds his horn,
And the sky-lark sings with me.
O! what sweet company.

But to go to school in a summer morn
O! it drives all joy away;
Under a cruel eye outworn,
The little ones spend the day,
In sighing and dismay.

Ah! then at times I drooping sit,
And spend many an anxious hour.
Nor in my book can I take delight,
Nor sit in lernings bower,
Worn thro' with the dreary shower

How can the bird that is born for joy,
Sit in a cage and sing.
How can a child when fears annoy,
But droop his tender wing,
And forget his youthful spring.

O! father & mother, if buds are nip'd,
And blossoms blown away,
And if the tender plants are strip'd
Of their joys in the springing day,
By sorrow and cares dismay,

How shall the summer arise in joy
Or the summer fruits appear
Or how shall we gather what griefs destroy
Or bless the mellowing year,
When the blasts of winter appear.

Children's Poetry

1. Poetry written for children, usually by adults. *Nursery rhymes are the most familiar kind of children's poetry, but Robert Louis Stevenson's *A Child's Garden of Verses* contains poems written by a professional poet and intended for children. The writer of children's poems will usually simplify the language and ideas and highlight the rhythms and sound effects. In these particulars, the same process applies to songs (and many nursery rhymes are, in fact, singable). William Blake's *Songs of Innocence and of Experience*, while symbolic and profound, are at the same time simple and musical, full of what might be called "primary images" (on the analogy of primary colors): archetypes such as "lamb," "tiger," "rose." Nancy Willard invokes Blake's songs in her recent book for children, *William Blake's Inn*.

2. Poetry written by children. The explosion of Poetry-in-the-Schools programs has encouraged children and teenagers to become involved in poetry in the most compelling way: by writing it. Kenneth Koch, a poet and one of the earliest, most energetic teachers in the schools, has written and edited *Wishes, Lies, and Dreams* and *Rose, Where Did You Get That Red?* to discuss how to teach children to read and write poems and to present generous samples of their work.

W.H. Auden remarks that there are often prodigies in music and mathematics, seldom in poetry. The greatest teenage poets include Arthur Rimbaud and Dylan Thomas. Usually it takes experience—in language, literature, and life—to make a poet. The child's fresh view of the world is a start, but not enough in itself. (Even as teenagers, Rimbaud and Thomas had read widely.)

Chinese Poetic Forms The rhymed song forms in which most Chinese poetry has been composed. In English, we know Chinese poems mainly through the free-verse translations of Ezra Pound, Arthur Waley, and others. But most Chinese poems have been rhymed, their meter governed by the number of characters in each line. The meter is syllabic, each character equalling a single syllable

(as it does not in Japanese poetry), but it is governed by arrangements of two categories of tones: level (long and keeping the same pitch) and deflected (relatively short, in which the pitch moves upward or downward). There are three kinds of deflected tone: rising, falling, and entering. The tone pattern, free in early Chinese poetry, was later fixed in several forms.

There are several major poetic forms in Chinese:

• Four-syllable verse: four (occasionally five) characters per line, rhymed *aaXa bbcc cdcd*.

• Ancient verse: five- or seven-syllable lines, in which even-numbered lines rhyme, using either a single rhyme throughout or changing it at will; no fixed tone pattern.

• Regulated verse: eight lines, all five syllables or seven syllables, rhyming even lines (and sometimes line one) on the same rhyme sound, with two acceptable tone patterns for each syllable length. In addition, the four lines in the middle form two couplets, each pair antithetical; for example, if one line says, "In the morning, she lifts the curtain," the other might say, "In the evening, she loosens her hair."

• Lyric meters (or Tz'u): poem written to existing music, in lines of unequal length (as opposed to equal lines, or *shih*, as in the forms listed above).

SONGS IN THE OLD STYLE: 52
Li Bai (700-762; tr. John Drury)

I started at the rush of spring torrents.
By summer, the streams grew thin.
I can't bear seeing the autumn tumbleweeds
lifting up. At the end, what can I lean on?

A faint breeze extinguishes the orchids,
dew sprinkled on beans and sunflowers.
A fine man—not me—hopes for something.
Day by day, the green world scatters.

Chorus *(Greek, "dance, group of dancers")*

1. A group of performers, sometimes represented by a leader, who comment on the action in the plays of ancient Greece, singing and

moving in a stylized dance. The choral *ode (also called the Pindaric ode) is structured in three parts that represent those movements: the turn, counter-turn, and stand (or strophe, antistrophe, and epode).

2. The stanza of a *song that is repeated, usually after the *verse, which is different each time. (In song, a verse is a stanza; in poems that are not songs, a verse is a single line.) The pattern can go on indefinitely, but it begins like this:

> Verse 1
> CHORUS
> Verse 2
> CHORUS
> Verse 3
> CHORUS

For example, the little-known first verse of a well-known song begins, "Katie Casey was baseball-mad,/ Had the fever and had it bad." The chorus begins, "Take me out to the ballgame." It is a chorus because it is repeated and because everyone may sing along.

The chorus is sometimes called a *refrain, although a refrain usually consists of one line, perhaps two, while a chorus may contain several. The chief difference, however, lies in where the terms are currently used: chorus in songs, refrain in poems. Burden is another synonym, an older one that applies to the refrain or chorus in, say, an Elizabethan lute-song. (*See: verse, song.*)

Cinquain *(sing-káne; French, "group of five")*
1. A five-line stanza, sometimes called a quintain (although the term is obsolete), a quintet (although the term suggests a musical ensemble), or a pentastich (especially if the stanza is unrhymed).

Various rhyme schemes are possible. Thomas Wyatt's "My Lute, Awake" (whose stanzas rhyme *aabab*) begins:

> My lute, awake! Perform the last
> Labor that thou and I shall waste,
> And end that I have now begun;
> For when this song is sung and past,
> My lute, be still, for I have done.

George Herbert's "The Pulley" uses a rhyme scheme of *ababa* for each of its four stanzas:

> When God at first made man,
> Having a glass of blessings standing by,
> "Let us," said he, "pour on him all we can.
> Let the world's riches, which dispersèd lie,
> Contract into a span."

The five-line stanzas of Edmund Waller's "Song" rhyme *ababb*. The poem begins:

> Go, lovely rose!
> Tell her who wastes her time and me
> That now she knows,
> When I resemble her to thee,
> How sweet and fair she seems to be.

William Wordsworth's "Peter Bell," a long narrative in five-line stanzas, rhymes *Xabba*. (The first line is unrhymed.) Here is the poem's last stanza:

> And Peter Bell, who, till that night,
> Had been the wildest of his clan,
> Forsook his crimes, renounced his folly,
> And, after ten month's melancholy,
> Became a good and honest man.

Lord Byron, who was never one to renounce his own follies, parodies Wordsworth's poem in "Epilogue," using the same rhyme scheme:

> And now I've seen so great a fool
> As William Wordsworth is for once;
> I really wish that Peter Bell
> And he who wrote it were in hell
> For writing nonsense for the Nonce.

Other cinquains include the *limerick, *mad song stanza, *tanka, *quintilla,—and cinquain (as described below, a five-line poem with

a fixed syllabic arrangement). Because of this particular use of "cinquain," it might be a good idea to revive the obsolete term "quintain" to refer more generally to any five-line stanza.

2. A poetic form, inspired by Japanese *tanka, invented by Adelaide Crapsey (who wrote twenty-eight of them), with a syllabic arrangement of 2-4-6-8-2 in its five lines. In her own cinquains, Crapsey allows herself to add or subtract a syllable from any given line.

NIAGARA
Adelaide Crapsey (1878-1914)

Seen on a Night in November

How frail
Above the bulk
Of crashing water hangs,
Autumnal, evanescent, wan,
The moon.

City Poem   A poem about life in a city, or about the city itself; a modern counterpart to poems about rural life variously known as bucolics, *eclogues, *georgics, *idylls, and *pastorals.

A city poem might be called an "urban pastoral" (or perhaps an "urbanic"), usually in an ironic sense. The rise of such poems coincides with the Industrial Revolution just before the turn of the nineteenth century.

LONDON / William Blake (1757-1827)

I wander thro' each charter'd street,
Near where the charter'd Thames does flow,
And mark in every face I meet
Marks of weakness, marks of woe.

In every cry of every man,
In every Infant's cry of fear,
In every voice, in every ban,
The mind-forg'd manacles I hear.

How the Chimney-sweeper-s cry
Every blackning Church appalls;
And the hapless Soldier's sigh
Runs in blood down Palace walls.

But most thro' midnight streets I hear
How the youthful Harlot's curse
Blasts the new-born Infant's tear,
And blights with plagues the Marriage hearse.

COMPOSED UPON WESTMINSTER BRIDGE, SEPTEMBER 3, 1802
William Wordsworth (1770-1850)

Earth has not anything to show more fair:
Dull would he be of soul who could pass by
A sight so touching in its majesty;
This City now doth, like a garment, wear
The beauty of the morning; silent, bare,
Ships, towers, domes, theaters, and temples lie
Open unto the fields, and to the sky;
All bright and glittering in the smokeless air.
Never did sun more beautifully steep
In his first splendor, valley, rock, or hill;
Ne'er saw I, never felt, a calm so deep!
The river glideth at his own sweet will:
Dear God! the very houses seem asleep;
And all that mighty heart is lying still!

A STEP AWAY FROM THEM
Frank O'Hara (1926-1966)

It's my lunch hour, so I go
for a walk among the hum-colored
cabs. First, down the sidewalk
where laborers feed their dirty
glistening torsos sandwiches
and Coca-Cola, with yellow helmets
on. They protect them from falling
bricks, I guess. Then onto the
avenue where skirts are flipping
above heels and blow up over
grates. The sun is hot, but the
cabs stir up the air. I look
at bargains in wristwatches. There
are cats playing in sawdust.

On
to Times Square, where the sign
blows smoke over my head, and higher
the waterfall pours lightly. A
Negro stands in a doorway with a
toothpick, languorously agitating.
A blonde chorus girl clicks: he
smiles and rubs his chin. Everything
suddenly honks: it is 12:40 of
a Thursday.
Neon in daylight is a
great pleasure, as Edwin Denby would
write, as are light bulbs in daylight.
I stop for a cheeseburger at JULIET'S
CORNER. Giulietta Masina, wife of
Federico Fellini, è bell' attrice.
And chocolate malted. A lady in
foxes on such a day puts her poodle
in a cab.
There are several Puerto
Ricans on the avenue today, which
makes it beautiful and warm. First
Bunny died, then John Latouche,
then Jackson Pollock. But is the
earth as full as life was full, of them?
And one has eaten and one walks,
past the magazines with nudes
and posters for BULLFIGHT and
the Manhattan Storage Warehouse,
which they'll soon tear down. I
used to think they had the Armory
Show there.
A glass of papaya juice
and back to work. My heart is in my
pocket, it is Poems by Pierre Reverdy.

NOTE: Pierre Reverdy: French Surrealist poet (1889-1960).

Clerihew *(from Edmund Clerihew Bentley, 1875-1956, who invented the form)* A light verse form, rhymed *aabb*; its first line is the name

of a famous person and its second forms a comic predicate; lines three and four comment further, comically, on some biographical fact or absurd fancy related to that person.

The meter in a clerihew tends to be intentionally rough and irregular, shortening or lengthening according to the author's whim. Bentley invented the form in 1890 when he was sixteen, a student at St. Paul's boys' school in London. His first clerihew follows. (He later changed "Abominated" to "Detested" in line two):

> Sir Humphry Davy
> Abominated gravy.
> He lived in the odium
> Of having discovered sodium.

Closure The way a poem ends.

In Barbara Herrnstein Smith's *Poetic Closure* (1968), the term is reserved for metrical verse, but we can apply it to all poems. Endings can range from the quiet (an easing out or what the Elizabethans called a "dying fall") to the emphatic and dramatic, the orchestra's final thump. Often the last line will, in fact, be the poem's climax, but it could also be a refrain, strong because repeated but not exactly unexpected. Poems can also end on a question, an exclamation, or an ellipsis—like a movie or song fading out . . . The ending can be a single word, or a phrase, or a sentence, or a long sentence covering many lines. A whole poem can consist of a single sentence (a useful exercise to try out). The ending can be detached, preceded by a stanza break, or connected to the rest of the poem so that there's a continual buildup like a wave cresting. Any of these possibilities—and others as well (should the poem end with an image? an aphorism? somebody talking?)—can determine a poem's closure.

Cobla *(French)* Any poem that is one stanza long. It was the troubadours' equivalent of the *epigram, as well as their usual word for *stanza. The current sense of the word comes from *cobla esparsa*, a single isolated stanza.

Concrete Language Words that denote particular, palpable things (such as "boat," "persimmon," "flip," and "jump"), as opposed to

*abstract language (such as *truth, infinity,* and *perseverance*). Most poets prefer concrete language, words that appeal to the senses and provide *images.

Confessional Poetry Work by some American poets of the mid-twentieth-century that uses personal and private details from their own lives, material once considered too embarrassing to discuss publically.

M.L. Rosenthal coined the term in his book *The New Poets,* which deals with poets such as Robert Lowell, Sylvia Plath, Anne Sexton, and John Berryman. These poets may be variously "confessional" in the religious sense of a penitent declaring sins to a priest, in the psychological sense of a patient revealing secrets to an analyst, or in the judicial sense of an accused person admitting to a crime. At best, this poetry explores previously forbidden subjects with an honesty and directness that electrifies the language; at worst, it indulges in personal gossip, wallows in emotional excess, and confines its vision to egocentric musings, self-pity, and megalomania. Confessional poetry may expose family secrets, sexual affairs, physical abuse (either given or received, or both), cowardice and cruelty, and usually does so in the guise of autobiography. Rosenthal points out, however, that "the private life of the poet himself, especially under stress of psychological crisis . . . is felt at the same time as a symbolic embodiment of national and cultural crisis."

MAN AND WIFE / Robert Lowell (1917-1977)

Tamed by *Miltown,* we lie on Mother's bed;
the rising sun in war paint dyes us red;
in broad daylight her gilded bed-posts shine,
abandoned, almost Dionysian.
At last the trees are green on Marlborough Street,
blossoms on our magnolia ignite
the morning with their murderous five days' white.
All night I've held your hand,
as if you had
a fourth time faced the kingdom of the mad—
its hackneyed speech, its homicidal eye—
and dragged me home alive. . . . Oh my *Petite,*
clearest of all God's creatures, still all air and nerve:

you were in your twenties, and I,
one hand on glass
and heart in mouth,
outdrank the Rahvs in the heat
of Greenwich Village, fainting at your feet—
too boiled and shy
and poker-faced to make a pass,
while the shrill verve
of your invective scorched the traditional South.

Now twelve years later, you turn your back.
Sleepless, you hold
your pillow to your hollows like a child;
your old-fashioned tirade—
loving, rapid, merciless—
breaks like the Atlantic Ocean on my head.

NOTE: *Miltown*: a tranquilizer.

Connotation   The suggested meaning of a word, as opposed to its denotation, or dictionary meaning.

Consider the differences among synonyms: *physician, doctor, sawbones, surgeon, quack*. Each has a different level of respect (or disrespect), an emotional charge. Connotations are the overtones of words, their vibrations—good or bad. One might argue that connotation is to denotation as the figurative is to the literal. Connotation is the complex of things we associate with a word; it is like an aura or a resonance or an electric field around that word. Poets in search of *le mot juste* (the exact word) must weigh these associations that both complicate and enrich.

Consonance   1. The repetition of consonant sounds. The term is often used synonymously with *alliteration (which is, however, usually confined to the repetition of initial consonants).

2. *Slant rhyme that repeats consonants but changes the vowels, such as *book/rack*.

(*See: Welsh poetic forms for a different kind of consonance, common in Celtic poetry but perhaps untransferable to English.*)

Corrupted Form Intentional flouting, breaking, disregard, or sabotage of a poetic form's rules or conventions.

A corrupted form crosses the line beyond acceptable variations, but such a departure is not necessarily bad. For example, the *villanelle ordinarily contains nineteen lines. Acceptable variations include reversing the order of the final two *refrain lines, omitting two of the middle *tercets (as Leconte de Lisle does), or adding two tercets (as Marilyn Hacker does)—usually in pairs so that both refrains can recur. Donald Justice's "Variations for Two Pianos," included below, is a corrupted villanelle. It contains the two refrains that make it a villanelle but transforms the first tercet into a *couplet (the two refrain lines), omitting the inner rhymes of the remaining tercets, and changing the concluding *quatrain to a single line, a repetition of the first refrain.

Corrupted form is effective because it surprises us with the contortions of a familiar pattern; it grabs our attention because we recognize what's there but realize it's been transformed; it makes an old form new. Since it is really a quirk of criticism that one particular rhyme scheme and refrain pattern became the so-called fixed form of the villanelle, there is much to be said for such corrupting. (And it drives the sticklers crazy.) It may be better to honor the spirit of a poetic form than the letter (which, as scripture tells us, "killeth").

> VARIATIONS FOR TWO PIANOS
> Donald Justice (b. 1925)
>
> There is no music now in all Arkansas.
> Higgins is gone, taking both his pianos.
>
> Movers dismantled the instruments, away
> Sped the vans. The first detour untuned the strings.
> There is no music now in all Arkansas.
>
> Up Main Street, past the cold shopfronts of Conway,
> The brash, self-important brick of the college,
> Higgins is gone, taking both his pianos.
>
> Warm evenings, the windows open, he would play
> Something of Mozart's for his pupils, the birds.
> There is no music now in all Arkansas.

How shall the mockingbird mend her trill, the jay
His eccentric attack, lacking a teacher?
Higgins is gone, taking both his pianos.

There is no music now in all Arkansas.
for Thomas Higgins, pianist

Couplet *(cúp-let)* A pair of rhymed lines; a two-line stanza.

The couplet is also called a *distich, especially if unrhymed. The *heroic couplet (rhymed couplets in *iambic pentameter) began with Geoffrey Chaucer but reached its peak of influence in the early eighteenth century, especially in the work of Alexander Pope. The couplet also figures prominently in the Shakespearean *sonnet, whose last two lines rhyme, as in sonnet 116 ("Let me not to the marriage of true minds"):

If this be error, and upon me prov'd,
I never writ, nor no man ever lov'd.

Couplets are essential to a Middle Eastern form, the *ghazal, and turn up in a great deal of free verse, as a semi-metrical way to introduce a sense of regularity and balance.

THE TUFT OF FLOWERS
Robert Frost (1874-1963)

I went to turn the grass once after one
Who mowed it in the dew before the sun.

The dew was gone that made his blade so keen
Before I came to view the leveled scene.

I looked for him behind an isle of trees;
I listened for his whetstone on the breeze.

But he had gone his way, the grass all mown,
And I must be, as he had been—alone,

"As all must be," I said within my heart,
"Whether they work together or apart."

But as I said it, swift there passed me by
On noiseless wing a bewildered butterfly,

Seeking with memories grown dim o'er night
Some resting flower of yesterday's delight.

And once I marked his flight go round and round,
As where some flower lay withering on the ground.

And then he flew as far as eye could see,
And then on tremulous wing came back to me.

I thought of questions that have no reply,
And would have turned to toss the grass to dry;

But he turned first, and led my eye to look
At a tall tuft of flowers beside a brook,

A leaping tongue of bloom the scythe had spared
Beside a reedy brook the scythe had bared.

The mower in the dew had loved them thus,
By leaving them to flourish, not for us,

Nor yet to draw one thought of ours to him,
But from sheer morning gladness at the brim.

The butterfly and I had lit upon,
Nevertheless, a message from the dawn,

That made me hear the wakening birds around,
And hear his long scythe whispering to the ground,

And feel a spirit kindred to my own;
So that henceforth I worked no more alone;

But glad with him, I worked as with his aid,
And weary, sought at noon with him the shade;

And dreaming, as it were, held brotherly speech
With one whose thought I had not hoped to reach.

"Men work together," I told him from the heart,
"Whether they work together or apart."

Cretic *(krée-tik; Greek, "Cretan"; also called amphimacer or amphimac, Greek, "long at each end")* A *foot consisting of two stressed syllables with an unstressed syllable in between them (´ ˘ ´). The following phrases are cretic: "breakfast bar," "here and there," "what I want."

However, in the context of a line in English, a cretic foot is rare. The stresses tend to break off into separate feet: "The break- I fast bar I is closed"; "Here and I there the I peo-ple I gath-er"; "What I I want now I is peace."

Curse   An imprecation or damnation in verse, the act of what Robert Graves calls the "left hand" of poetry (while the right hand praises). In a poem by Graves, "Traveller's Curse after Misdirection," the lost speaker rails against those who have misled him, imploring "May they stumble, stage by stage,/ On an endless pilgrimage" and hoping that they fall with each step, each time breaking their necks.

Curtal Sonnet   An abridged *sonnet, containing eleven lines arranged in two stanzas, the first rhymed *abcabc* and the second either *dbcdc* or *dcbdc*, the last line indented and shorter than the others.
   Gerard Manley Hopkins invented the curtal sonnet and used it for two poems, "Pied Beauty" in 1877 and "Peace" two years later.

PIED BEAUTY / Gerard Manley Hopkins (1844-1889)

Glory be to God for dappled things—
   For skies of couple-colour as a brinded cow;
     For rose-moles all in stipple upon trout that swim;
Fresh-firecoal chestnut-falls; finches' wings;
   Landscape plotted and pierced—fold, fallow, and plough;
     And all trades, their gear and tackle and trim.

All things counter, original, spare, strange;
   Whatever is fickle, freckled (who knows how?)
     With swift, slow; sweet, sour; adazzle, dim;
He fathers-forth whose beauty is past change:
         Praise him.

NOTE: *brinded*: brindled

D

Dactyl, Dactylic *(dák-tul, dak-tíl-ik; Greek, "finger")*   A foot consisting of a stress followed by two unstressed syllables (´ ˘ ˘).

Dactylic words include "harmony," "bigamist," and "precipice." In many cases, however, the third syllable of a dactylic word receives secondary stress. The impulse to alternate stressed and unstressed syllables in English is so powerful, those secondary stresses actually favor iambic meter, especially when the dactylic word is followed by an unstressed syllable: "harmony and bliss," "bigamist who flees," "precipice of doom."

Dactylic meter, like *anapestic, is called triple meter because each foot contains three syllables. In the original Greek, Homer's *Iliad* and *Odyssey* are written in dactylic hexameter (six feet, most of them dactyls); so is the Latin verse of Virgil's *Aeneid*. The pattern of long and short syllables is arranged as follows:

$$\text{-- ˘ ˘ | -- ˘ ˘ | -- ˘ ˘ | -- ˘ ˘ | -- ˘ ˘ | -- --}$$

NOTE: Foot 5 can be a spondee (-- --) and foot six can be a trochee (-- ˘).

Henry Wadsworth Longfellow imitates dactylic hexameter in a long narrative poem, *Evangeline*, whose first line is:

This is the forest primeval. The murmuring pines and the hemlocks

Rolfe Humphries, who translated Latin poets such as Virgil, Ovid, and Juvenal, says of dactylic hexameter, "This meter, in our usage, tends to gallop if not run away, Buckety, Buckety, Buckety, Buckety, Buckety, Bump down."

In English, dactylic meter can sound too rigid, too rhythmically headstrong, too uniformly propulsive if not varied a good deal. Tennyson's "The Charge of the Light Brigade" exemplifies this dactylic onrush:

> Half a league, half a league,
> Half a league onward,
> All in the valley of Death
>   Rode the six hundred.
> 'Forward the Light Brigade!
> Charge for the guns!' he said.
> Into the valley of Death
>   Rode the six hundred.

The dactylic impetus becomes so powerful that ordinarily strong words like "league" and "said" grow weak, rushed over, and the usually minor "In-" of "Into" receives a kind of field promotion to the commanding status of "vall[ey]" and "Death" in the same line. It would seem false to the poem not to follow this bumpity-bumpity ride of dactyls as they charge.

To harness the galloping of the meter, the poet can (1) substitute trochees or spondees for dactyls, (2) omit both unstressed syllables from the last foot (*catalexis) or change it to a trochee, (3) begin an occasional line with an extra unstressed syllable (*anacrusis), or (4) change one of the unstressed syllables in a dactyl to a stress. Of course subject, manner, and tone can help too, as can pauses and colloquial speech patterns. The first stanza of Paul Laurence Dunbar's "Little Brown Baby," which is written in African-American dialect of the nineteenth century, ends:

> Look at dat mouf—dat's merlasses, I bet;
>   Come hyeah, Maria, an' wipe off his han's.
> Bees gwine to ketch you an' eat you up yit,
>   Bein' so sticky an' sweet—goodness lan's!

In the poem a father is speaking to his child. Although Dunbar's lines here are metrically strict (allowing for the truncation of the last two unstressed syllables), they sound spoken, not bombastic.

William Carlos Williams asserted that "American speech tends toward dactylic," and poets such as Allen Ginsberg and James Dickey have agreed both in critical remarks and in their own practice. All three of those poets allow themselves great rhythmic leeway in their poems, which are not consistently dactylic at all—nor metrical, in most cases. What they mean by "dactylic" may actually be close to what Robert Frost means by "loose iambics," whose extra unstressed syllables do make the verse sound more conversational, more natural, more easygoing—perhaps more American.

Deep Image Poetry Work by poets such as Robert Bly and James Wright, who published, during the 1960s, free-verse poems about mysterious images drawn largely from rural life and the natural world.

This imagery draws the reader into depths of consciousness, as in the following lines by Wright: "Mother of roots, you have not seeded/ The tall ashes of loneliness." Bly also emphasizes darkness as part of this deepening: "Now I want to go back among the dark roots;/ Now I want to see the day pulling its long wing." These deep images are like Yeatsian symbols, or talismans strange in their simplicity, or links that connect the physical world to the unconscious or to the spiritual.

Bly edited an influential magazine called *The Fifties*, then *The Sixties*, and then (for one issue on "Leaping Poetry") *The Seventies*. The magazine featured translations of Spanish, German, and Norwegian poetry that brought something new—associative, visionary, and passionate—into American poetry. As certain words became connected with this poetry ("dark" and "stone," for example), imitators changed what was striking into something formulaic and stale. By the late seventies, a reaction had set in against the fashion of "deep images," although such images, whatever one calls them, are the roots of poetry.

DRIVING TOWARD THE LAC QUI PARLE RIVER
Robert Bly (b. 1926)

I

I am driving; it is dusk; Minnesota.
The stubble field catches the last growth of sun.
The soybeans are breathing on all sides.

Old men are sitting before their houses on carseats
In the small towns. I am happy,
The moon is rising above the turkey sheds.

II

The small world of the car
Plunges through the deep fields of the night,
On the road from Willmar to Milan.
This solitude covered with iron
Moves through the fields of night
Penetrated by the noise of crickets.

III

Nearly to Milan, suddenly a small bridge,
And water kneeling in the moonlight.
In small towns the houses are built right on the ground;
The lamplight falls on all fours in the grass.
When I reach the river, the full moon covers it;
A few people are talking low in a boat.

Denotation   The dictionary definition of a word, as opposed to its *connotation or suggested meanings.

While the connotation is like the figurative sense of a word, the denotation is the literal sense. For example, *stallion* means "male horse" (its denotation), but it suggests something powerful, sexually aggressive, and conceitedly beautiful (its connotation). A poet should be exact about the denotations of words and sensitive to their connotations.

Dialogue, Dialog *(dié-uh-log; Greek, "conversation")*   A poem in which two voices alternate, or in which different speakers take turns.

Usually a dialogue involves characters conversing, the back-and-forth of voices, verbal sparring, as in the following *sonnet from Shakespeare's *Romeo and Juliet*. But in Andrew Marvell's "A Dialogue Between the Soul and Body" (1681), the voices represent the spirit and the flesh.

In the twentieth century, Richard Howard has written "two-part inventions," borrowing the title of J.S. Bach's compositions for two musical voices. In these verbal inventions, voices may alternate, as in

"Wildflowers" (whose speakers are Walt Whitman and Oscar Wilde), or one character's entire speech or monologue may be answered by another's, as in "After the Facts" (which presents a letter and its response). (*See: dramatic monologue, dramatic poetry, letter poem, pastoral.*)

from ACT I, SCENE V of *ROMEO AND JULIET*
William Shakespeare (1564-1616)

Romeo.	If I profane with my unworthiest hand
	This holy shrine, the gentle fine is this:
	My lips, two blushing pilgrims, ready stand
	To smooth that rough touch with a tender kiss.
Juliet.	Good pilgrim, you do wrong your hand too much,
	Which mannerly devotion shows in this;
	For saints have hands that pilgrims' hands do touch,
	And palm to palm is holy palmer's kiss.
Romeo.	Have not saints lips, and holy palmers too?
Juliet.	Ay, pilgrim, lips that they must use in pray'r.
Romeo.	O, then, dear saint, let lips do what hands do!
	They pray; grant thou, lest faith turn to despair.
Juliet.	Saints do not move, though grant for prayers' sake.
Romeo.	Then move not while my prayer's effect I take.

Didactic Poetry *(die-dák-tik; Greek, "skilled in teaching")* Poetry that teaches something; more specifically, poetry whose primary purpose is to instruct.

In "The Art of Poetry," the Roman poet Horace declares that poetry should both delight and instruct; Robert Frost says that a poem "begins in delight and ends in wisdom." When that instruction is paramount, rather than an outgrowth of imaginative pleasure, the poem may become moral propaganda or something merely handy, such as "Thirty days hath September,/ April, June, and November." But some explicitly didactic poems teach practical lessons without sacrificing the poetry. The *Georgics* of Virgil, for example, give instructions in farming and are a pleasure to read. The pejorative sense of didactic poetry derives primarily from the "Art for Art's Sake" movement of the 1890s. But a poem that teaches nothing is worth little. A reader

wants at least a sense of encountering something new, of discovering a fresh way to consider human nature and the world.

Dipodics, Dipodic Verse   Originally, in Greek and Latin, meter that counts two *feet as a single unit. In English, however, dipodics are really a kind of *accentual meter. Folk poems such as *ballads and *nursery rhymes tend to give stronger emphasis to every other accent, starting with the first one in a line. Thus, in the ballad, "Lamkin," lines that might be scanned as iambic tetrameter and iambic trimeter emerge as dipodics, with two strong beats in each line: "It's LAMkin was a MASon good/ as EVer built wi' STANE." It is, perhaps, not the doubling up of feet so much as the two-stress line that characterizes dipodics in English, as in the nursery rhyme "RING around a ROSy,/ POCKet full of POSies."

Distich *(dís-tik; Greek, "two" + "line, verse")*   A two-line stanza; sometimes used synonymously with *couplet. Some critics, however, would confine couplet to rhymed pairs of lines but allow distich to encompass unrhymed pairs as well.

Dithyramb, Dithyrambic *(díth-ih-ram, dith-ih-rám-bic)*   Originally a Greek choral hymn for Dionysus, god of wine. Later, any poem that is wild and rhapsodic.

Double Dactyl   An eight-line light-verse form, invented by Anthony Hecht, consisting of two quatrains of dactylic dimeter (′ ˘ ˘ ′ ˘ ˘).

The first line is made up of nonsense words (usually "Higgledy-piggledy"); the second line is the name of a famous person (like the first line in a related form, the *clerihew); at least one line in the second quatrain consists of a single six-syllable word (such as "valedictorian"); the fourth and eighth lines rhyme; the final two unstressed syllables are omitted at the end of each quatrain.

The definitive collection of double dactyls is *Jiggery-Pokery: A Compendium of Double Dactyls* (1966), edited by Anthony Hecht and John Hollander. Here is a double dactyl based on Part IV of Jonathan Swift's *Gulliver's Travels*:

> Higgledy-piggledy
> Lemuel Gulliver
> Wasn't a visitor
> Houyhnhnms would seek.
>
> Horse sense would tell them his
> Anthropomorphical
> Form was the same as a
> Yahoo physique.

Double Foot   Two metrical feet in combination. In English, the only common double foot is the *minor ionic or double iamb ($\smallsmile \smallsmile \, ' \, '$), a pyrrhic foot and a spondee. The rhythm is endemic to the English language, occurring in many phrases: "the absurd fact," "with a blank look," "an obscure nerd." (*See: classical feet.*)

Dramatic Monologue   Poem spoken by a character or through a *persona* (Greek for "mask"), rather than by the poet or an unidentified speaker.

In a dramatic monologue, the speaker must be identified, although he or she need not be named. The character who speaks the monologue will usually be human, but it can be an animal (like the pig in Philip Levine's "Animals Are Passing from Our Lives") or a plant (like the redwoods in Louis Simpson's "The Redwoods") or perhaps an inanimate object. The speaker can be a real person, an imaginary character, a historical or literary figure—anyone except the poet or some neutral voice. Robert Browning's dramatic monologues essentially lifted the Shakespearean soliloquy out of the play, and presented it without the larger context of a whole drama, without the actual interaction of characters on a stage. All of the action is compressed into the monologue, which may either be spoken or written to another character or spoken in isolation, the speaker talking to himself. Events before the monologue must be suggested or mentioned. When the speaker is unaware of the implications of what he says, but the implied listener or the reader understands them, the monologue contains dramatic irony. (*See: letter poem.*)

MY LAST DUCHESS / Robert Browning (1812-1889)

FERRARA

That's my last Duchess painted on the wall,
Looking as if she were alive. I call
That piece a wonder, now: Frà Pandolf's hands
Worked busily a day, and there she stands.
Will't please you sit and look at her? I said
"Frà Pandolf" by design, for never read
Strangers like you that pictured countenance,
The depth and passion of its earnest glance,
But to myself they turned (since none puts by
The curtain I have drawn for you, but I)
And seemed as they would ask me, if they durst,
How such a glance came there; so, not the first
Are you to turn and ask thus. Sir, 'twas not
Her husband's presence only, called that spot
Of joy into the Duchess' cheek: perhaps
Frà Pandolf chanced to say "Her mantle laps
"Over my Lady's wrist too much," or "Paint
"Must never hope to reproduce the faint
"Half-flush that dies along her throat": such stuff
Was courtesy, she thought, and cause enough
For calling up that spot of joy. She had
A heart—how shall I say?—too soon made glad,
Too easily impressed; she liked whate'er
She looked on, and her looks went everywhere.
Sir, 'twas all one! My favour at her breast,
The dropping of the daylight in the West,
The bough of cherries some officious fool
Broke in the orchard for her, the white mule
She rode with round the terrace—all and each
Would draw from her alike the approving speech,
Or blush, at least. She thanked men,—good! but thanked
Somehow—I know not how—as if she ranked
My gift of a nine hundred years old name
With anybody's gift. Who'd stoop to blame
This sort of trifling? Even had you skill
In speech—(which I have not)—to make your will
Quite clear to such an one, and say "Just this
"Or that in you disgusts me; here you miss,

"Or there exceed the mark"—and if she let
Herself be lessoned so, nor plainly set
Her wits to yours, forsooth, and made excuse,
—E'en then would be some stooping, and I choose
Never to stoop. Oh, Sir, she smiled, no doubt,
Whene'er I passed her; but who passed without
Much the same smile? This grew; I gave commands;
Then all smiles stopped together. There she stands
As if alive. Will't please you rise? We'll meet
The company below, then. I repeat,
The Count your Master's known munificence
Is ample warrant that no just pretence
Of mine for dowry will be disallowed;
Though his fair daughter's self, as I avowed
At starting, is my object. Nay, we'll go
Together down, Sir! Notice Neptune, tho',
Taming a sea-horse, thought a rarity,
Which Claus of Innsbruck cast in bronze for me.

Dramatic Poetry   Poetry written for performance as a play. It is one of the three main genres of poetry (the others being *lyric poetry and *narrative poetry).

In ancient Greece, plays began as part of Dionysian festivals, during which poets entered their tragedies and comedies in contests and were awarded prizes (or not). Aristotle differentiates the two dramatic forms by saying that tragedy portrays men and women as better than they are, comedy as worse. Tragedy must present the story of a noble man's downfall because of a flaw in his character; it should evoke fear and pity in the audience and have a cathartic effect. Sophocles' *Oedipus the King* (the first part of a trilogy) serves as a model tragedy. The tragedies of Shakespeare are looser, careless of the tradition's "unities" (of time and space), and include explicit portrayals of violence on stage.

The comedies of Aristophanes are satiric, attacking warfare in *Lysistrata* and lampooning the tragic playwright Euripides and Dionysus himself. Comedy admits all sorts of buffoonery—slapstick, puns, mix-ups, malapropisms, battles of wit. The title of Shakespeare's *All's Well That Ends Well* pretty much sums up the point of comedy.

Verse drama (and hence dramatic poetry) has had a hard time in

the twentieth century, although William Butler Yeats, T.S. Eliot, and Federico Garcia Lorca have written serious plays in verse. Musical comedies have provided more room for poetry—but usually in the guise of comic verse and song, not dramatic poetry.

Drott-Kvaett   Old Norse stanzaic form, consisting of eight lines with six syllables in each, three of them accented; each two lines are linked by *alliteration, which must occur in the first syllable of the second line and twice in the line before it; full rhyme appears in even lines, half rhyme in odd lines, and internal rhyme within lines. *Kennings, multi-noun substitutes for nouns, appear frequently. The form was used by *skalds*, Old Norse court poets, but it survives in Iceland to the present day.

Duende   Federico Garcia Lorca's term for "the roots that probe through the mire that we all know of and do not understand, but which furnishes us with whatever is sustaining in art." It is like "soul" in African-American music. In his essay "Duende: Theory and Divertissement," Lorca says that duende is what Goethe recognizes in the violin playing of Paganini: "A mysterious power that all may feel and no philosophy can explain."

Echo Verse A poem in which the last syllable or two of a main line is repeated, perhaps with different spelling or meaning, as if an echo; usually this echo will be indented to a point under or beyond the syllable it mimics, and will function as an independent line of one or two syllables.

Sometimes the word *Echo* will precede the repetition, like the indication of a speaker in a play. Aside from the sheer pleasure of repetition, echo verse often serves the purposes of irony, the meaning of the echo conflicting with what the original sound means ("know" echoed by "No," for example). This incongruity can be especially powerful because the repetition is immediate yet skewed. On the other hand, doubt or uncertainty suggested in a main line can be answered ringingly with an affirmation, a reversal appropriate not for cynical but for religious uses. Any poem in echo verse is bound to be a dialogue, perhaps a play of questions and answers. Finally, echo can be used simply as another kind of rhyme.

HEAVEN / George Herbert (1593-1633)

O who will show me those delights on high!
                             Echo.   *I.*
Thou Echo, thou art mortall, all men know.
                             Echo.   *No.*
Wert thou not born among the trees and leaves?
                             Echo.   *Leaves.*
And are there any leaves, that still abide?
                             Echo.   *Bide.*

What leaves are they? impart the matter wholly.
> *Echo.*   *Holy.*

Are holy leaves the Echo then of blisse?
> *Echo.*   *Yes.*

Then tell me, what is that supreme delight?
> *Echo.*   *Light.*

Light to the minde: what shall the will enjoy?
> *Echo.*   *Joy.*

But are there cares and businesse with the pleasure?
> *Echo.*   *Leisure.*

Light, joy, and leisure; but shall they persever?
> *Echo.*   *Ever.*

Eclogue *(ék-log; Greek, "selection")* A pastoral poem, or one dealing with rural life, especially a dialogue; a singing contest between two shepherds. Sir Philip Sidney (1554-1586) includes an eclogue, "A Double Sestina," spoken by two shepherds named Strephon and Klaius, in his *Arcadia*. *(See: georgic, idyll, pastoral.)*

Elegiac Distich *(él-uh-jié-uk or eh-lée-jee-ák dís-tik)* A couplet with a line of dactylic hexameter followed by a line of dactylic pentameter; used in Greek for elegies and threnodies (laments for the dead).

Some English poets, such as Edmund Spenser, Sir Philip Sidney, and A.C. Swinburne, have experimented with the form. Here is a couplet from Sir Philip Sidney's "Musidorus's Elegiacs" (from *Old Arcadia*):

> Fortune thus gan say: 'Misery and misfortune is all one,
>   And of misfortune, fortune hath only the gift . . .

Sidney is trying to imitate the quantities (long and short syllables) of the original Greek meter, which he gives in a headnote to the poem:

      (15 syllables)
      (13 syllables)

But *accent is so powerful in English, what we really hear is a pattern of six accents in the first line (hexameter) and five in the second (pentameter).

Elegy *(él-uh-gee; Greek "mournful song")* A poem for someone who has died; also called lament and threnody.

The person commemorated in an elegy can be a friend or family member (Ben Jonson's elegy for his son appears below) or a public figure (Walt Whitman's "When Lilacs Last in the Dooryard Bloom'd" mourns the death of Abraham Lincoln). Many poets have written elegies to other poets, such as W.H. Auden's "In Memory of W.B. Yeats."

John Milton's "Lycidas" is a pastoral elegy, a lament for his school friend, Edward King, as if in the voice of one shepherd mourning the death of another:

> For we were nurst upon the self-same hill,
> Fed the same flock, by fountain, shade, and rill.
>   Together both, ere the high Lawns appear'd
> Under the opening eye-lids of the morn,
> We drove a field, and both together heard
> What time the Gray-Fly winds her sultry horn,
> Batt'ning our flocks with the fresh dews of night,
> Oft till the Star that rose, at Ev'ning, bright
> Toward Heav'ns descent had slop'd his westering wheel.
> Mean while the Rural ditties were not mute,
> Temper'd to th'Oaten Flute,
> Rough *Satyrs* danc'd, and *Fauns* with clov'n heel,
> From the glad sound would not be absent long,
> And old *Damaetas* lov'd to hear our song.
>   But O the heavy change, now thou art gon,
> Now thou art gon, and never must return!
> Thee Shepherd, thee the Woods and desert Caves,
> With wilde Thyme and the gadding Vine o'ergrown,
> And all their echoes mourn.
> The Willows, and the Hazle Copses green,
> Shall now no more be seen,
> Fanning their joyous Leaves to thy soft layes.
> As killing as the Canker to the Rose,
> Or Taint-worm to the weanling Herds that graze,
> Or Frost to Flowers, that their gay wardrop wear,
> When first the White-thorn blows;
> Such, *Lycidas*, thy loss to Shepherds ear.
>
> (lines 23-49)

The *pastoral tradition goes back to antiquity—and was from the start a matter of artifice, the specialty of academic poets, not of real shepherds. Nevertheless, the pose need not ruin the poetry; it might simply make it easier to speak of grief.

Elegies are love poems for the dead, tributes and offerings to loss.

ON MY FIRST SON / Ben Jonson (1573-1637)

Farewell, thou child of my right hand, and joy;
My sin was too much hope of thee, loved boy:
Seven years thou'wert lent to me, and I thee pay,
Exacted by the fate, on the just day.
O could I lose all father now! for why
Will man lament the state he should envý,
To have so soon 'scaped world's and flesh's rage,
And, if no other misery, yet age?
Rest in soft peace, and asked, say, "Here doth lie
Ben Jonson his best piece of poetry."
For whose sake henceforth all his vows be such
As what he loves may never like too much.

Elision *(uh-lízh-un; Latin, "to strike out")*   The slurring together of vowels in adjacent words, so that a syllable is effectively deleted. Elision may be marked with an apostrophe, as in John Donne's "Thou'art slave to fate, chance, kings, and desperate men" (from Holy Sonnet 10, "Death Be Not Proud"). It is a way of squeezing two unstressed syllables into one in order to maintain the meter.

Emblematic Verse *(also called calligramme, carmen figuratum, concrete poem, figured poem, pattern poem, shaped poem, visual poem)*   A poem in which the words or letters form a typographical picture, either imitating how something looks or suggesting what the subject does.

Emblematic verse appeared in ancient Greek (depicting ax and egg) and in several poems by the seventeenth-century poet George Herbert (depicting an altar and a pair of wings). In *Alice in Wonderland*, Lewis Carroll presents a mouse's tale in the typographical shape of a mouse tail. Guillaume Apollinaire coined the term calligramme *(cah-lee-gráhm)*, a word similar to "calligraphy," in the title of his 1918 volume, *Calligrammes* (depicting, among other things, the

Eiffel Tower and rainfall). The many typographical experiments by e e cummings (1894-1962) resulted in shapes like a leaf falling and other visual arrangements that simply used the page as a kind of canvas (cummings was a painter as well as a poet). John Hollander's *Types of Shape* consists entirely of emblematic poems; its shapes include a key, a lightbulb, a harpsichord, a bell, a sundial, a lazy susan, a kitty, a kitty with bug, a tie, the state of New York, a double helix, and a swan with its reflection. These poems, however, can still be read aloud.

In the twentieth century, some poets began experimenting with concrete poetry, which often departs entirely from a readable text and presents something closer to graphic art. One sign of this shift is that such a poem can be reduced to an explanation of how it looks (such as a poem in the shape of an apple, using the word *apple* over and over, but replaced in one spot by the word *worm*). Giving the explanation rather than the picture-poem itself is an example of conceptual poetry.

Richard Kostelanetz, a leading experimenter with Concrete Poetry, suggests a new term for emblematic verse: "word-imagery, which encompasses the two major genres of the form—imaged words and worded images." May Swenson has written some of the finest emblematic poems. Her shapes are sometimes abstract, sometimes specific, but tend to look expressively askew, often more suggestive than literal.

EASTER WINGS / George Herbert (1593-1633)

Lord, who createdst man in wealth and store,
    Though foolish he lost the same,
        Decaying more and more
            Till be became
                Most poore;
                With thee
            O let me rise
        As larks, harmoniously,
    And sing this day thy victories;
Then shall the fall further the flight in me.

My tender age in sorrow did beginne;
    And still with sicknesses and shame
        Thou didst so punish sinne,
            That I became
                Most thinne.
                With thee
            Let me combine,
        And feel this day thy victorie;
    For if I imp my wing on thine,
Affliction shall advance the flight in me.

OUT OF THE SEA, EARLY / May Swenson (1919-1989)

A bloody
egg yolk. A burnt hole
spreading in a sheet. An en-
raged rose threatening to bloom.
A furnace hatchway opening, roaring.
A globular bladder filling with immense
juice. I start to scream. A red hydrocepha-
lic head is born, teetering on the stump of
its neck. When it separates, it leaks rasp-
berry from the horizon down the wide esca-
lator. The cold blue boiling waves cannot
scour out that band, that broadens, sliding toward me up the wet sand slope. The
fox-hair grows, grows thicker on the
upfloating head. By six o'clock,
diffused to ordinary gold,
it exposes each silk thread and rumple in the carpet.

End-Stop   A definite halt or strong pause at the end of a line.

Sometimes an end-stop is marked by punctuation such as a period (the "full stop" in British usage), question mark, colon, semicolon, or comma; sometimes there may be no punctuation even though the line is end-stopped, as long as a thought or a phrase is completed and doesn't run over to the next line (in which case the line would be *enjambed). End-stopping tends to slow down the movement of a poem because of the emphasis or pause or hesitation at the end of the line.

The following sonnet by Shakespeare is entirely end-stopped, even though it contains just one period, at the very end. But each line ends with a grammatical break and definite pause (reinforced by the list structure).

SONNET 66 / William Shakespeare (1564-1616)

Tir'd with all these, for restful death I cry:
As to behold desert a beggar born,
And needy nothing trimm'd in jollity,
And purest faith unhappily forsworn,

> And gilded honour shamefully misplac'd,
> And maiden virtue rudely strumpeted,
> And right perfection wrongfully disgrac'd,
> And strength by limping sway disabled,
> And art made tongue-tied by authority,
> And folly, doctor-like, controlling skill,
> And simple truth miscall'd simplicity,
> And captive good attending captain ill:
> > Tir'd with all these, from these would I be gone,
> > Save that to die, I leave my love alone.

NOTE: *desert*: one who who is deserving; *nothing*: one who is undeserving; *strumpeted*: prostituted; *disgrac'd*: defaced; *simplicity*: stupidity.

Enjambment *(en-jám-ment)*   The use of a line whose sense and rhythmic movement continues to the next line. An enjambed line is also called a "run-on" line. It is the opposite of an *end-stop.

Enjambment is one of the essential techniques of *free verse (non-metrical lined poetry). In lieu of meter, the end of a line is an important way to mark the rhythmic flow of a poem (as are *cadence and the repetition of words and phrases, *anaphora, for example). Enjambment is like musical syncopation; instead of pausing, the musical phrase pushes ahead. Enjambment speeds up the movement, quickens the pace (because the sense, interrupted by a line break, demands that the reader rush ahead to complete the phrase or idea).

In the following poem, Mark Irwin uses enjambment to interrupt grammatical connections: "is/ a form," "You knew/ then," "all// in an apple," "paradise/ was," "the present's// perfect drift," "to have/ said," "shepherds/ dying," "spaces/ you would leave," "her awkward sister,// time," "we as humans/ were meant to survive." Some of this enjambment occurs between stanzas (marked //); one enjambed line ends with a comma but forces the reader to push ahead to complete the sense. There are also some end-stops, for while a poet may choose to let enjambment predominate, it is usually desirable to let the cadences come to rest at line's end once in a while. And every poem that is not part of a sequence must necessarily end with an end-stop.

EVE / Mark Irwin (b. 1953)

Such perfect intuition is
a form to worship. You knew
then, the hell of unending, all

in an apple, so that paradise
was a kind of autumn;
yourselves, one with the present's

perfect drift. Better not to have
said a word to Adam
whose lips touched names upon the animals

while you dreamed of zoos, shepherds
dying. Not the green spaces
you would leave, but her awkward sister,

time. You knew that we as humans
were meant to swerve, to wake from sleep
and carry the knowledge of seasons on our tongues.

Epic *(ép-ik; Greek, "song, narrative")*   A long narrative poem that tells a story central to the myths and beliefs of a people.

Traditional epics belong to the oral tradition, in which poets or performers memorize, improvise, add and delete lines, shaping the story that may one day make its way into writing (and even then may be lost, like most of the cycle of Trojan War epics).

Ezra Pound described the epic as a "poem containing history." More specifically, that history belongs to a society, a nation, such as Homer's ancient Greeks or Nazim Hikmet's twentieth-century Turks.

Traditional epics, transmitted orally, include Homer's *The Iliad* and *The Odyssey* (ancient Greek), *Gilgamesh* (Sumerian), and *Mahabharata* (Sanskrit). Literary epics, imitating the subjects and methods of traditional epics, include Virgil's *The Aeneid* and John Milton's *Paradise Lost*. Modern and contemporary epics, exploring ways of magnifying and tying together twentieth-century experience, include Nazim Hikmet's *Human Landscapes* (Turkish) and Pablo Neruda's *Canto General* (Spanish). Some twentieth-century American poets have searched especially hard for epic frameworks that could contain fragments and unite them in something whole, *e pluribus*

unum: Ezra Pound's *The Cantos*, William Carlos Williams' *Paterson* (and perhaps his prose work, *In the American Grain*), H.D.'s *Trilogy* and *Helen in Egypt*, and Hart Crane's *The Bridge*. Charles Olson's *The Maximus Poems* and James Merrill's *The Changing Light at Sandover* may also count as epics. Perhaps Whitman's *Song of Myself* is an epic as well: the story of America through the perceptions of a "representative man" named Walt Whitman.

Epic Simile *(also called Homeric simile)* An extended comparison used in epics such as Homer's *Iliad*. For example, the poet may liken actions on the battlefield to natural phenomena (such as a star disappearing behind clouds) or scenes of country life (such as reapers cutting grain in a field), as in these lines from George Chapman's 1611 translation of *The Iliad* (Book XI, lines 55-66):

> And as amids the skie
> We sometimes see an ominous starre blaze cleare and dreadfully,
> Then run his golden head in clouds and straight appeare again:
> Then in the rere-guard hid himselfe and labour'd every where
> To order and encourage all: his armor was so cleare
> And he applide each place so fast that, like a lightning throwne
> Out of the shield of Jupiter, in every eye he shone.
> And as upon a rich man's crop of barley or of wheate
> (Opposde for swiftnesse at their worke) a sort of reapers seate,
> Beare downe the furrowes speedily, and thicke their handfuls fall:
> So at the joyning of the hoasts ran Slaughter through them all.

The two epic similes in the lines above follow the pattern "And as . . . So . . ." while the simile beginning "like a lightning" is not epic (because it is not extended and does not follow the rhetorical pattern—which can, however, use different words to introduce the two halves of a comparison).

Epigram *(ép-uh-gram; Greek, "inscription")* A short, pithy comic or satirical poem.

In English, an epigram is usually in rhyme and meter, but in the Greek Anthology some of the earliest epigrams are unrhymed and not necessarily comic. Even prose can be described as epigrammatic,

as in Oscar Wilde's *The Importance of Being Earnest*. An epigram will often contain, or itself embody, an aphorism: a memorable remark that encapsulates an insight into some aspect of human nature or the world at large (such as "If treason prosper, none dare call it treason").

EPIGRAM / Alexander Pope (1688-1744)

When other Ladies to the Shades go down,
Still *Flavia, Chloris, Celia* stay in town;
Those Ghosts of Beauty ling'ring there abide,
And haunt the places where their Honour dy'd.

Epigraph *(ép-uh-graf; Greek, "inscription")* A note or quotation that precedes the body of some poems; also called a headnote. At worst, epigraphs can seem academic and stuffy, mere showing off, but they can also acknowledge sources of material, present something that the poem will respond to, or convey important background information for which the poem itself has no room. H.D.'s "Fragment 113" uses an epigraph from Sappho. (*See: fragment.*)

Epitaph *(ép-ih-taf; Greek, "upon a tomb")* Verses that commemorate a person or group of people who have died.
Epitaphs are often inscribed upon tombs or gravestones. They are like elegies squeezed into the limited space of an *epigram. They must be brief and pithy. The following epitaph is spoken in the voices of Spartan soldiers who died fighting while defending the pass at Thermopylae.

EPITAPH / attributed to Simonides of Ceos
(about 556-468 B.C.; tr. Richmond Lattimore)

Traveler, take this word to the men of Lakedaímon:
We who lie buried here did what they told us to do.

Epithalamion, Epithalamium *(ép-uh-thuh-lám-ee-un or -um; Greek, "upon a bridal chamber")* Wedding poem; poem to celebrate a marriage; ode to a bride and groom.
The Song of Solomon is an epithalamion:

Behold, thou art fair, my beloved, yea, pleasant: also our bed is green.
The beams of our house are cedar, and our rafters of fir.

Edmund Spenser's "Epithalamion" and "Prothalamion" both use
elaborately rhymed stanzas, each ending in a refrain, to commemorate
weddings. In the following epithalamion, which contains *refrains that
a chorus might sing, the Ancient Greek poet Sappho refers to Hymen
(the god of marriage) and Ares (the god of war).

FRAGMENT 102 / Sappho
(circa 620-550 B.C.; tr. Guy Davenport)

I

Raise the ridge-pole higher, higher,
O marriage night O binding god
Carpenters! Make the roof-tree taller,
O marriage night O binding god
He comes, the husband, and walks like Ares,
O marriage night O binding god
He's taller by far than a tall man,
O marriage night O binding god

II

Pitch the roof-beam higher, builders.
O hymn Hymen, high men, O!
Joiners! The roof is far too low.
O hymn Hymen, high men, O!
He stands, the husband, as long as Ares,
O hymn Hymen, high men, O!
And he can't get it through the door.

Eugene Onegin Stanza *(also called Pushkin's stanza)* A fourteen-line
stanza (sonnet-length), rhymed *ababccddeffegg* and written in iambic
tetrameter. Its rhyme scheme consists of three kinds of quatrain—
alternating (*abab*), couplet (*ccdd*), and envelope (*effe*)—before the final
rhymed couplet (*gg*).

Aleksandr Pushkin, a nineteenth-century Russian poet, used the
form in a verse novel, *Eugene Onegin* (whose first stanza appears
below). The stanza works well for narrative poetry and comic verse,

somewhat like the *ottava rima stanza of Lord Byron's *Don Juan.* Vikram Seth's recent novel, *The Golden Gate* (1986), is written entirely in Eugene Onegin stanzas—even the dedication and author's biographical note.

EUGENE ONEGIN: A NOVEL IN VERSE,
Aleksandr Pushkin (1799-1837; tr. Babette Deutsch)

"My uncle's shown his good intentions
By falling desperately ill;
His worth is proved; of all inventions
Where will you find one better still?
He's an example, I'm averring;
But, God, what boredom—there, unstirring,
By day, by night, thus to be bid
To sit beside an invalid!
Low cunning must assist devotion
To one who is but half-alive:
You puff his pillow and contrive
Amusement while you mix his potion;
You sigh, and think with furrowed brow—
'Why can't the devil take you now?' "

Chapter One, Stanza I

Fable *(Latin, "to speak")*   A story, in verse or prose, whose characters are animals and which points out a moral.

Aesop's fables, from the ancient Greek, tell stories such as the dog in the manger and the race between the tortoise and the hare. La Fontaine uses rhymed verse to tell his fables. The Br'er Rabbit stories, which derive from West Africa and were told originally by slaves in America, are also fables, though without the tacked-on morals.

> THE FOX AND THE GRAPES
> Jean de La Fontaine (1621-1695; tr. Elizur Wright)
>
> A fox, almost with hunger dying,
> Some grapes upon a trellis spying,
> To all appearance ripe, clad in
>   Their tempting russet skin,
> Most gladly would have eat them;
> But since he could not get them,
>   So far above his reach the vine—
> "They're sour," he said; "such grapes as these,
> The dogs may eat them if they please!"
>
>   Did he not better than to whine?

Fairy Tale   A story immersed in a magic dream world in which frightening, marvelous things happen.

The Grimm brothers collected folktales from the Black Forest in Germany, tales full of violence and difficult journeys and impossible

odds and the visits of supernatural creatures: witches, goblins, trolls, fairy godmothers. Today these stories are often reserved for children. They may be softened, diluted, corrected to remove the violence, presented in cartoons. But their true, inherent power is immense. Bruno Bettelheim, in *The Uses of Enchantment*, argues that real fairy tales, in all their terrifying glory, help children work their way through the thickets of the psyche, much like Hansel and Gretel. These stories exert their power like dreams, like myths (except that Cinderella seems closer to us than Helen of Troy, more like an ordinary person confronting the extraordinary).

For the poet, fairy tales are close to the symbolic source of most true poetry, the dream state of clear but mysterious images and actions. Many poets, including Anne Sexton in the poem below, use fairy tales as source material, either explicitly or unconsciously, like the tunes upon which a composer might write variations. A poet might also invent new tales, as Charles Simic does, suggesting the ones a child listens to and learns from.

CINDERELLA / Anne Sexton (1928-1974)

You always read about it:
the plumber with twelve children
who wins the Irish Sweepstakes.
From toilets to riches.
That story.

Or the nursemaid,
some luscious sweet from Denmark
who captures the oldest son's heart.
From diapers to Dior.
That story.

Or a milkman who serves the wealthy,
eggs, cream, butter, yogurt, milk,
the white truck like an ambulance
who goes into real estate
and makes a pile.
From homogenized to martinis at lunch.

Or the charwoman
who is on the bus when it cracks up

and collects enough from the insurance.
From mops to Bonwit Teller.
That story.

Once
the wife of a rich man was on her deathbed
and she said to her daughter Cinderella:
Be devout. Be good. Then I will smile
down from heaven in the seam of a cloud.
The man took another wife who had
two daughters, pretty enough
but with hearts like blackjacks.
Cinderella was their maid.
She slept on the sooty earth each night
and walked around looking like Al Jolson.
Her father brought presents home from town,
jewels and gowns for the other women
but the twig of a tree for Cinderella.
She planted that twig on her mother's grave
and it grew to a tree where a white dove sat.
Whenever she wished for anything the dove
would drop it like an egg upon the ground.
The bird is important, my dears, so heed him.

Next came the ball, as you all know.
It was a marriage market.
The prince was looking for a wife.
All but Cinderella were preparing
and gussying up for the big event.
Cinderella begged to go too.
Her stepmother threw a dish of lentils
into the cinders and said: Pick them
up in an hour and you shall go.
The white dove brought all his friends;
all the warm wings of the fatherland came,
and picked up the lentils in a jiffy.
No, Cinderella, said the stepmother,
you have no clothes and cannot dance.
That's the way with stepmothers.

Cinderella went to the tree at the grave
and cried forth like a gospel singer:

Mama! Mama! My turtledove,
send me to the prince's ball!
The bird dropped down a golden dress
and delicate little gold slippers.
Rather a large package for a simple bird.
So she went. Which is no surprise.
Her stepmother and sisters didn't
recognize her without her cinder face
and the prince took her hand on the spot
and danced with no other the whole day.

As nightfall came she thought she'd better
get home. The prince walked her home
and she disappeared into the pigeon house
and although the prince took an axe and broke
it open she was gone. Back to her cinders.
These events repeated themselves for three days.
However on the third day the prince
covered the palace steps with cobbler's wax
and Cinderella's gold shoe stuck upon it.
Now he would find whom the shoe fit
and find his strange dancing girl for keeps.
He went to their house and the two sisters
were delighted because they had lovely feet.
The eldest went into a room to try the slipper on
but her big toe got in the way so she simply
sliced it off and put on the slipper.
The prince rode away with her until the white dove
told him to look at the blood pouring forth.
That is the way with amputations.
They don't just heal up like a wish.
The other sister cut off her heel
but the blood told as blood will.
The prince was getting tired.
He began to feel like a shoe salesman.
But he gave it one last try.
This time Cinderella fit into the shoe
like a love letter into its envelope.

At the wedding ceremony
the two sisters came to curry favor

and the white dove pecked their eyes out.
Two hollow spots were left
like soup spoons.

Cinderella and the prince
lived, they say, happily ever after,
like two dolls in a museum case
never bothered by diapers or dust,
never arguing over the timing of an egg,
never telling the same story twice,
never getting a middle-aged spread,
their darling smiles pasted on for eternity.
Regular Bobbsey Twins.
That story.

Feminine Ending *(sometimes called light or falling ending)* A line that ends with an unstressed syllable, such as "O wild West Wind, thou breath of Autumn's being" (Percy Bysshe Shelley).

The extra unstressed syllable is usually considered a metrical appendage, not part of the final foot:

Lǐke tǒ | thě lárk | ǎt bréak | ǒf dáy | ǎ- rís- | iňg
(Shakespeare, Sonnet 29)

The term derives from grammatical gender and is merely a poetic convention; a masculine line ends on a stressed syllable, as in Elizabeth Bishop's line "A blue-white sky, a simple web" (from her poem "Brazil, January 1, 1502").

Figurative Language Language that uses figures of speech, such as *metaphor and *simile, to present something in the guise of something else, or to compare one thing to another. It superimposes a "figure" upon the surface of what's really there, the literal.

Figurative language is a way of saying one thing and suggesting another, so that the words have significance beyond the literal meaning. In Seamus Heaney's sonnet "The Forge," the literal scene is a blacksmith's shop in contemporary Ireland. The figurative scene is the mind or imagination of any craftsman or maker—such as a poet (who also knows "a door into the dark")—whose craft, like smithing

or poetry, seems like a vestige of the past. (*See: metaphor, simile.*)

Sylvia Plath wrote the following poem in January and February of 1960. On April 1 of the same year, she gave birth to her daughter Frieda. In this poem, Plath addresses a fetus in the womb. Almost every line contains a metaphor or simile.

> YOU'RE
>
> Clownlike, happiest on your hands,
> Feet to the stars, and moon-skulled,
> Gilled like a fish. A common-sense
> Thumbs-down on the dodo's mode.
> Wrapped up in yourself like a spool,
> Trawling your dark as owls do.
> Mute as a turnip from the Fourth
> Of July to All Fool's Day,
> O high-riser, my little loaf.
>
> Vague as fog and looked for like mail.
> Farther off than Australia.
> Bent-backed Atlas, our traveled prawn.
> Snug as a bud and at home
> Like a sprat in a pickle jug.
> A creel of eels, all ripples.
> Jumpy as a Mexican bean.
> Right, like a well-done sum.
> A clean slate, with your own face on.
> —Sylvia Plath (1932-1963)

Figures of Classical Rhetoric (*also called rhetorical devices and figures of speech*) Ways of transforming the natural order or literal meaning of words, in order to make a text more inventive, emphatic, rhythmic, impressive, or memorable. There are two main kinds: schemes (changes in word order) and tropes (changes in word sense).

Schemes involve a transformation in the order or arrangement of a word, phrase, clause, sentence, or line. Here are some of the most common schemes:

- *alliteration: repetition of consonants (such as the repeated *w* in e e cummings' "what if a much of a which of a wind");

- anadiplo′sis: repetition of the last word or phrase at the beginning of the next line, phrase, clause, or sentence, as in these lines from an anonymous nursery rhyme, "This Is the Key":

> Flowers in a basket;
> Basket on the bed;
> Bed in the chamber;
> Chamber in the house;
> House in the weedy yard;
> Yard in the winding lane;
> Lane in the broad street;
> Street in the high town;
> Town in the city;
> City in the Kingdom . . .

- *anaph′ora: repetition of the first word or phrase at the beginning of successive lines, as in the opening lines of John Donne's "On His Mistris":

> By our first strange and fatall interview,
> By all desires which thereof did ensue,
> By our long starving hopes, by that remorse . . .

In these lines, the repeated word "By" begins successive lines, but it also begins successive phrases (the fourth instance, not capitalized, appears in the middle of line three).

- anas′trophe: inversion of natural word order, as in George Peele's "His Golden lockes, Time hath to Silver turn'd," which begins with the direct object; the natural word order would be "Time hath turn'd his Golden lockes to Silver," which would change the meter and lose the rhyme—serious defects in a poem written to be set to music (as it was by the Elizabethan lutenist John Dowland);
- antimetab′ole (*an-tih-muh-tab′-uh-lee*): repetition of the words in a phrase in reverse order, as in Molière's "One should eat to live, not live to eat";
- antith′esis: the juxtaposition of conflicting ideas or images, usually arranged in parallel structure, as in Alexander Pope's "What oft was thought, but ne'er so well express'd," contrasting *often* and *never*,

or in John Dryden's "But what we gain'd in Skill we lost in Strength";

- aposiope'sis: a breaking-off or trailing-off of a sentence, leaving something unsaid, usually indicated by an ellipsis (. . .);
- apposi'tion: word or phrase that follows another and identifies it, as in Ralph Waldo Emerson's "Daughters of Time, the hypocritic Days" or Walt Whitman's "Walt Whitman, a kosmos, of Manhattan the son";
- *ass'onance: repetition of vowels, like the long *o* sounds in Lord Byron's "So, we'll go no more a roving";
- asyn'deton: omission of conjunction between series of clauses, as when Walt Whitman says

> All this I swallow, it tastes good, I like it well,
>   it becomes mine,
> I am the man, I suffered, I was there.

The last line could be a pacifist's version of Julius Caesar's "I came, I saw, I conquered" (another example of asyndeton);

- chias'mus (*key-áz-mus*): reversal of grammatical structures in successive phrases or clauses, as in Alexander Pope's "Each strengthens Reason, and Self-Love restrains"; also called criss-cross;
- ellip'sis: omission of word or phrase that is implicit, as in the opening lines of a lute-song by John Dowland (words attributed to Sir Edward Dyer):

> The lowest trees have tops, the Ant her gall,
> The flie her spleene, the little sparke his heate . . .

The verb *has* is implicit after "Ant," "flie," and "sparke."

- epanalep'sis: repetition at the end of a line, phrase, clause, or sentence of the word that began it, as when Shakespeare's King Lear says "Nothing will come of nothing";
- epanortho'sis: the recalling of a word or phrase to substitute something more exact; a revision or second thought displayed in the writing, as when Elizabeth Bishop qualifies her initial placement of the flowers in "Brazil, January 1, 1502":

> and flowers, too, like giant water lilies
> up in the air—up, rather, in the leaves—;

- epis'trophe (*uh-pís-truh-fee*): repetition of a word or phrase at the end of successive lines or clauses, as in the repetition of "nothing" in T.S. Eliot's " 'Do/ 'You know nothing? Do you see nothing? Do you remember/ 'Nothing?' " (from *The Waste Land*);
- epizeux'is (*eh-pih-zoók-sis*): the repetition of a word for emphasis, as in John Keats' "more happy happy love!" (from "Ode on a Grecian Urn");
- isoco'lon: parallel structure between clauses (and this parallel, or parison, must be exact), as in these lines from Shakespeare's *A Midsummer Night's Dream*:

> *Demetrius.* Well roar'd, Lion.
> *Theseus.* Well run, Thisbe.
> *Hippolyta.* Well shone, Moon.

- paren'thesis: insertion of words that interrupt the sentence flow, as when "who knows?" interrupts Elizabeth Bishop's line "impractically shaped and—who knows?—self-pitying mountains";
- par'ison (or parallelism): use of matching structures in related words, phrases, clauses, or lines, as in John Dowland's "to see, to heare, to touch, to kisse, to die" (from "Come Again"), in which the parallel unit is the infinitive; in Alexander Pope's "It stopt, I stopt; it mov'd, I mov'd again" (from *The Dunciad*), a structure of pronoun-verb, different pronoun-same verb is repeated.
- polypto'ton: repetition of words derived from the same root, a kind of play on words or pun, as when Shakespeare's Hamlet says to Polonius "Conception is a blessing, but not as your daughter may conceive";
- polysyn'deton: repetition of conjunctions, such as "and," as in these verses from *Genesis*:

> And the earth was without form, and void; and darkness was upon the face of the deep: and the Spirit of God moved upon the face of the waters.
> And God said, Let there be light: and there was light.
> And God saw the light, that it was good: and God divided the light from the darkness.

Polysyndeton is what Elizabeth Bishop refers to as "Everything only connected by 'and' and 'and.' "

One stanza in Walt Whitman's "Out of the Cradle Endlessly Rocking" uses several of these schemes within six lines:

> *Shake out carols!*
> *Solitary here, the night's carols!*
> *Carols of lonesome love! death's carols!*
> *Carols under that lagging, yellow, waning moon!*
> *O under that moon where she droops almost down into the sea!*
> *O reckless despairing carols!*

The repeated word "carols" appears at the end of the first three lines (epistrophe), at both the beginning and end of line three (epanalepsis), and at the beginning of lines three and four (anaphora). The omission of "carols" in line five is also rhetorical, a kind of ellipsis, as if to suggest "O [carols] under the moon . . ." The word returns at the end of line six, continuing the epistrophe of the opening lines, as if rhyming on the same word, "carols."

Tropes (literally "turns," as in "turns of phrase") involve transformations of meaning. Here are some of the most common tropes:
- *all'egory: story in which characters stand for concepts, as in Edmund Spenser's *The Faerie Queen*;
- anthimer'ia: substitution of one part of speech for another, as when the noun *impact* is used as a verb ("News leaks impact upon the trial") or an adjective is used as an adverb ("Be sure to act proper" instead of "properly");
- *apos'trophe: direct address to someone absent or to something abstract, as in "O Spring!" (the Whitman stanza quoted above is an apostrophe addressed to "carols");
- auxe'sis: use of a more impressive word to exaggerate the importance of something, perhaps ironically, such as calling a shouting match a "brawl" or "riot"; the opposite of meiosis;
- hyper'bole: overstatement or exaggeration, such as "Paying the fine killed me";
- *i'rony: a discrepancy between what is said and what is meant or understood, or between appearance and reality; the use of a word to convey the opposite of its usual meaning, such as "That was fun cleaning the oven";

- li'totes (*lie-tuh-tees or lie-tóe-tees*): understatement, a deliberate way of seeming to make less of something in order to make more, such as "the plan was not uninteresting";
- meio'sis: a "lessening," the use of a less impressive word to minimize the importance of something, such as calling a fistfight a "misunderstanding"; the opposite of auxesis;
- *met'aphor: comparison between two things, such as the "yellow fog" that is a cat (which "rubs its muzzle," Licked its tongue," and "Curled once about the house") in T.S. Eliot's "Love Song of J. Alfred Prufrock";
- *meton'ymy: use of an associated word for what is really meant, such as "hired gun" for "gunslinger";
- onomatopoe'ia (*áh-nuh-máh-tuh-pée-uh*): word or phrase whose sound imitates the sense, such as "plop" or "screech";
- oxymor'on: word combination that seems like a contradiction, such as "happy sorrow";
- paralip'sis: the trick of pretending to avoid discussing something while nevertheless revealing it, of seeming to keep something in while actually letting it out; a kind of irony, as in Marc Antony's "Friends, Romans, countrymen" speech in Shakespeare's *Julius Caesar;*
- periph'rasis (or antonomasia): substitution of a nickname or descriptive phrase, or of a proper name in place of a thing or concept, as in "Jim Crow" for "racial segregation";
- prosopoe'ia (or personification): attachment of human qualities to something nonhuman, like the pig speaking in Philip Levine's "Animals Are Passing from Our Lives" (*See: syllabic verse*);
- pun: play on words, of which there are three kinds:

> antanac' lasis: repetition of a word in different senses, as in Ben Franklin's "If we don't hang together, we'll hang separately";
> paronomas'ia: word alike in sound but different in meaning, as in the riddle "What's black and white and *red* all over?" (a newspaper, because it is *read*);
> syllep'sis: word with different meanings in relation to two other words, for example a verb with two objects (as in "I'll strike the first blow and a match"); called zeugma (*zoóg-muh*) when one of those two "yoked" elements is grammatically incom-

patible with the word that governs them, as in "I struck the first blow, and may you too" (meaning "may strike you too");

• rhetorical question: a question asked without the expectation of a reply, as in Percy Bysshe Shelley's "If Winter comes, can Spring be far behind?";
   • *sim'ile: comparison using a connecting word such as "like," as in W.B. Yeats' "ancient faces like rain-beaten stones";
   • *synec'doche: a part standing for the whole, as in "hired hand" for "farm worker."

George Puttenham, an Elizabethan rhetorician, tried to replace the Greek rhetorical terms with English equivalents, such as "the trespasser" (hyperbaton), "the loud liar" (hyperbole), and the "cuckoo's call" (epizeuxis). They didn't take hold, possibly because the teachers who pounded Greek terms into the heads of their students saw no need to relearn a terminology that served perfectly well.

Foot, Feet A unit of measure in a metrical line; syllables included in a kind of musical bar or measure.

In *accentual-syllabic verse, there are six common feet: the iamb or iambic (˘ ´), the trochee or trochaic (´ ˘), the anapest or anapestic (˘ ˘ ´), the dactyl or dactylic (´ ˘ ˘), the pyrrhic (˘ ˘), and the spondee or spondaic (´ ´). Most lines in English accentual-syllabic verse can be scanned (metrically analyzed) using just these feet, with the addition of the monosyllabic foot (a stressed syllable by itself: ´) and the feminine ending (an unstressed syllable by itself at the end of a line: ˘).

These terms come from Greek prosody (which counts the length of syllables, not their accentuation) and fit uncomfortably into English metrics. However, they do work and are useful in investigating how the rhythm follows or diverges from the *meter (which is a metronomic pattern).

Greek quantitative meter was based on the length of syllables (or quantities): long (–) and short (˘). Robert Graves suggests that the meter derived from dance steps, and that is certainly true in the Greek choral ode, as in the plays of Sophocles, in which the choruses were choreographed: For every group of three stanzas the members of the

chorus would dance first left, then right, and then would stand still. (*See: ode.*)

Alexandrian scholars classified the feet (or metrical units, groups of rhythmically related syllables) by names we still, perhaps mistakenly, use for English verse:

Two-syllable	*Three-syllable*		*Four-syllable*	
˘ – iamb	˘ ˘ – anapest		˘ ˘ ˘ ˘	proceleusmatic
– ˘ trochee	– ˘ ˘ dactyl		– – – –	dispondee
˘ ˘ pyrrhic	˘ – ˘ amphibrach		˘ – – ˘	antipast
– – spondee	– ˘ – cretic or		– ˘ ˘ –	choriamb (us)
	amphimac (er)		– ˘ ˘ ˘	1st paeon
	˘ ˘ ˘ tribrach		˘ – ˘ ˘	2nd paeon
	– – – molossus		˘ ˘ – ˘	3rd paeon
	˘ – – bacchic		˘ ˘ ˘ –	4th paeon
	– – ˘ antibacchic		˘ – – –	1st epitrite
			– ˘ – –	2nd epitrite
			– – ˘ –	3rd epitrite
			– – – ˘	4th epitrite
			– ˘ – ˘	ditrochee
			˘ – ˘ –	di-iamb
			– – ˘ ˘	major ionic
			˘ ˘ – –	minor ionic

For accentual-syllabic verse, change the long-short signs (– ˘) to stressed-unstressed (– ˘). Four-syllable feet tend to break into two two-syllable feet; the minor ionic is very common in English, and is called a *double foot (a pyrrhic and a spondee) and sometimes a double iamb. In accentual-syllabic verse, it is unusual to find three unstressed syllables in a row, unless one or more is elided. The middle of the three tends to assert itself slightly and become accented: a *relative stress. (*See: anapest, amphibrach, cretic, dactyl, iamb, minor ionic, pyrrhic, spondee, trochee.*)

Form (*Latin, "shape"*) 1. An established pattern to which a poem conforms. The typical *sonnet, for example, consists of fourteen iambic pentameter lines written to a set rhyme scheme. By this

definition, the form is a receptacle which holds the words (or content) of a poem.

2. The shape made by the words of an individual poem, whether it follows a traditional pattern or not, whether it is metrical or not, whether it is in verse or in prose. Robert Creeley's remark that "form is just an extension of content" applies to this definition. The form arises from the words (the content) of the poem.

Ezra Pound says "I think there is a 'fluid' as well as a 'solid' content, that some poems may have form as a tree has form, some as water poured into a vase." Robert Hass has asserted that no two sonnets have the same form, obviously true given the second definition, obviously false given the first. It depends upon whether "form" is a physical shape or a platonic ideal. Is it like a mold into which a cook pours various ingredients? Or is it like the shape a person or a tree or a mineral deposit might grow into? Generally, the first definition (form preceding content) applies more to metrical verse, the second definition (form deriving from content) more to free verse.

In any case, metrical poetry is often called formal, and poets who write in rhyme and meter are called formalist. Denise Levertov calls poetry that discovers its form as it proceeds organic. Perhaps the clearest way to distinguish these two definitions of form is to call the first "traditional form" and the second "organic form."

Found Poem Text discovered in some nonpoetic setting (an advertisement, for example), removed from its context, and presented as a poem.

In the following example, Maxine Kumin apparently arranged the found passage into the first twelve lines, and then added her own comment in the concluding couplet of what turned out to be a sonnet. (It rhymes *abbacddceffe gg*.)

POEM FOUND IN *THE NEW HAMPSHIRE DEPARTMENT OF AGRICULTURE WEEKLY MARKET BULLETIN*
Maxine Kumin (b. 1925)

Ground saturated with water. Some
thunderstorms and wind have lodged

> lots of hayland. Frost damage
> in isolated pockets. From
> Strafford, word of leaf miner
> on beets and swiss chard. Timothy
> just out of the boot and ready
> to cut. Corn planting 80 per-
> cent in, needs sun to green up well.
> Rose chafer sighted widely, but
> little sign of chewing yet.
> The next few days are critical.
>
> Thus heavily infested, June
> lurches harvestward again.

Fourteener A line consisting of seven iambic feet; iambic heptameter.

This meter, typically in rhymed couplets, was common in the sixteenth century. The greater flexibility of *iambic pentameter led to
the demise of the fourteener. Fourteeners can easily sound singsong
and monotonous. However, poets who translated from Greek and
Latin, such as George Chapman and Arthur Golding, found in the
fourteener a useful parallel for the classical hexameter line. There was
room to swell and thunder and narrate in the long fourteeners. Here
is Arthur Golding's translation of a passage about Daedalus, the designer of the labyrinth and of wings for himself and his son Icarus,
from Ovid's *Metamorphoses* (Book VIII, 245-51):

> Now in this while gan *Daedalus* a wearinesse to take
> Of living like a banisht man and prisoner such a time
> In *Crete*, and longèd in his heart to see his native Clime.
> But Seas enclosèd him as if he had in prison be.
> Then thought he: though both Sea and land King *Minos* stop fro me,
> I am assurde he cannot stop the Aire and open Skie:
> To make my passage that way then my cunning will I trie.

Fourteeners tend to roll on. In fact, the line is so long, it often seems
to split into two halves, with a *caesura (pause) somewhere near the
middle. Instead of seven stresses together, we often hear them broken
into 4-3, so that a line might sound like:

> I am assurde he cannot stop
> the Aire and open Skie

Rhymed fourteeners are in fact very similar to the *ballad stanza, as in these lines from "The Wife of Usher's Well":

> I wish the wind may never cease,
>   Nor fishes in the flood,
> Till my three sons come home to me
>   In earthly flesh and blood.

The chief difference is that a ballad stanza indicates exactly where the pause appears (a line break after the fourth stress in odd-numbered lines) while a fourteener may or may not have a pause in the middle. A ballad stanza also permits extra unstressed syllables. (Fourteeners from George Chapman's translation of Homer's *Iliad* appear in *epic simile.)

Fragment   A piece or scrap from a larger whole that is either lost or unfinished.

Most of Sappho's poetry has been lost; what survives has come down to us either because ancient scholars quoted parts of it or bits turned up on strips of papyrus used to wrap mummies. A stray line or two may exist, or perhaps only a word here and there, utterances broken off abruptly. Unfinished fragments might include Samuel Taylor Coleridge's "Kubla Khan" (although it may seem complete) and some of Ezra Pound's late Cantos.

Those kinds of fragments are unintentional, but poets also do it on purpose, writing fragments meant to suggest a brokenness in the world, shards that are meant to be expressive as wholes in themselves. William Carlos Williams uses fragments—scraps of imagery, quick glimpses that give way to other views—in some sections of his suite "January Morning." Here is part VI:

> —and a semicircle of dirt-colored men
> about a fire bursting from an old
> ash can,

The section ends with a comma, then part VII shifts to an image of trolley rails in cobblestones.

Another kind of fragment found in poetry, especially the contemporary, is the sentence fragment, a word or phrase or subordinate clause (lacking a main verb) punctuated as if a complete sentence, as in these lines from Weldon Kees' "Aspects of Robinson":

> Robinson afraid, drunk, sobbing Robinson
> In bed with a Mrs. Morse. Robinson at home;
> Decisions: Toynbee or luminol?

The lack of verbs here, and elsewhere in this poem, suggests a static, empty life cluttered up with objects but heading nowhere.

> FRAGMENT 123 / Sappho
> (circa 620-550 B.C.; tr. Guy Davenport)
>
> Black dreams of such virulence[
> That sleep's sweetness[
> And terrible grief[
> The place is religious[
> Happiness, no, and hope neither[
> And I indeed am so[
> Delightful the games[
> And I[
> This[

NOTE: The open bracket ([ ) indicates a gap in the remainder of the line.

> FRAGMENT 113 / H.D.
> (Hilda Doolittle, 1884-1961)
> *"Neither honey nor bee for me."*—Sappho.
>
> Not honey,
> not the plunder of the bee
> from meadow or sand-flower
> or mountain bush;
> from winter-flower or shoot
> born of the later heat:
> not honey, not the sweet
> stain on the lips and teeth:

not honey, not the deep
plunge of soft belly
and the clinging of the gold-edged
pollen-dusted feet;

not so—
though rapture blind my eyes,
and hunger crisp
dark and inert my mouth,
not honey, not the south,
not the tall stalk
of red twin-lilies,
nor light branch of fruit tree
caught in flexible light branch;

not honey, not the south;
ah flower of purple iris,
flower of white,
or of the iris, withering the grass—
for fleck of the sun's fire,
gathers such heat and power,
that shadow-print is light,
cast through the petals
of the yellow iris flower;

not iris—old desire—old passion—
old forgetfulness—old pain—
not this, nor any flower,
but if you turn again,
seek strength of arm and throat,
touch as the god;
neglect the lyre-note;
knowing that you shall feel,
about the frame,
no trembling of the string
but heat, more passionate
of bone and the white shell
and fiery tempered steel.

Free Verse Unmetrical verse; lines that are not measured or counted for number of accents, number of syllables, or length of syllables; lines that are free of meter; also called *vers libre*.

Free verse is as old as the Bible, whose long verses are not metrical, although they are structured according to repetition and variation of words and phrases. Despite the use of occasional free verse by otherwise metrical poets like the eighteenth century's Christopher Smart ("For I Will Consider My Cat Jeoffrey" from *Jubilate Agno*) and Johann Wolfgang von Goethe ("Prometheus"), modern free verse begins in English with Walt Whitman (who modeled his long lines on the Bible and on grand opera) and in French with Arthur Rimbaud (who did not). Rimbaud simply rebelled against everything, both social and poetic conventions.

There are no particular rules for free verse, but there are many precedents. And although free verse cannot be classified numerically, like iambic pentameter, it can nevertheless be described in a general way. There are several distinct types of free verse, dependent on the relative length of the lines, the preponderance of end-stopping or enjambment (run-on lines), the preservation or breaking of phrase units, and the visual or typographical arrangement on the page. A free-verse poet can, of course, combine any or all of these if a poem is long enough (as Ezra Pound does in *The Cantos* and William Carlos Williams in *Paterson*).

Several kinds of free verse are listed below. Model poems follow at the end of the entry.

1. Short-lined free verse: the lines might range between one syllable and several words, about an inch or two of type, between one and three stresses, but these are just estimates—after all, if the lines begin to look and sound like each other, their freedom from meter might be in jeopardy. Early twentieth-century free verse, by the Imagists, for example, tended to retain phrase units as distinct lines; later poetic descendents, such as the Objectivists and the Black Mountain poets, began to enjamb more, breaking phrase units between lines, ending lines with minor words such as prepositions or articles.

2. Long-lined free verse: The lines might stretch between left and right margins, or they might tumble over the right-hand edge; if they do, they are "tucked under," indented a few letters to indicate that they belong to the line above, the two (or three or more) constituting a single, discrete line. The Bible's long lines inspired Walt Whitman, who inspired Robinson Jeffers and Allen Ginsberg and many others. Shorter lines can occasionally be interspersed among the long ones

for rhythmic variation or emphasis, as they are in Walt Whitman's "A Noiseless Patient Spider." (Short-lined free verse is not so tolerant of long lines, although medium lengths are OK; generally long-lined free verse seems more raggedy, while short-lined seems neater.) Whitman's poem also shows how free verse can mimic metrical verse in an approximate way: The poem consists of two stanzas equal in lines (five each) and the first lines of both stanzas are relatively short; the poem, however, does not scan according to either number of syllables or number of accents (although it comes fairly close). Long-lined free verse is more often end-stopped than enjambed.

3. Variable-length free verse: Much free verse mixes short lines with medium-length and long lines. The constant variety can be pleasing in itself, an almost regular irregularity, a nimble shifting, a closing and opening, as in Galway Kinnell's poems in *Body Rags* and *The Book of Nightmares*. This kind of free verse can also be based on an average line that is medium in length, shortening or lengthening for rhythmic or expressive purposes. As such, it is the commonest kind of free verse.

4. Spatial or typographical arrangement: The typewriter or computer keyboard is often used to "score" the music of poetry visually upon the page. Although poets have written *emblematic verse (words arranged into an actual picture, such as a pillar or an altar) since antiquity, technology and the rise of the avant-garde led to experiments by Stéphane Mallarmé, Ezra Pound, William Carlos Williams, e e cummings, and others, using the page as a kind of canvas for the spatial arrangement of words, phrases, and lines, which can be scattered widely or blocked together, using white space for mental pauses.

T.S. Eliot writes, "No *vers* is *libre* for the man who wants to do a good job." At its best, free verse can surge in waves or pull back, inventing itself as it goes. At its worst, it can be (as Ezra Pound, one of its early practitioners, points out) "prose chopped up into lines."

Novices often imagine that short-lined free verse must be speedier than long lines, but that's not usually the case. Short lines invite pauses at the ends of the lines, and the fewer words in each line necessarily receive more prominence than the many words in long lines. Enjambment may quicken the pace over end-stopping—but not always.

Robert Creeley's poems often have lines broken after an article, which imposes at least a slight pause, a musical effect that slows down the movement. Poets who write long-lined free verse, such as Allen Ginsberg and Gerald Stern, tend to read aloud quickly; poets such as Gary Snyder and Creeley read short lines slowly, carefully, punctuating almost every word. It is like the difference between flow and trickle, express and local. At root, there may be a kind of equivalence in lines, so that long lines have to move quickly in the given space, while short lines can prolong the moment.

In the twentieth century, theories have propelled the spread of free verse. The Imagists generally isolated their images in short-lined, phrasal free verse. Ezra Pound, the movement's founder, writes, "To break the pentameter, that was the first heave." He also speaks of composing according to "the musical phrase" instead of the metronome. Following directly upon the theory and the practice of Pound, Charles Olson's projective verse calls for open, organic, inclusive form and flexible rhythms based upon breath units. Robert Duncan's open field composition also seeks open form, deriving "melody and story from impulse not from plan." (*See: beat poetry, biblical verse, Black Mountain School, deep image poetry, imagism, psalm, triadic line.*)

Short-Lined Free Verse

GIRAFFE
Stanley Plumly (b. 1939)

The only head in the sky.
Buoyed like a bird's,
on bird legs too.
Moves in the slowmotion
of a ride
across the longlegged miles
of the same place.
Grazes in trees.
Bends like a bow
over water
in a shy sort of
spreadeagle.
Embarrassed by

such vulnerability,
often trembles, gathering
together
in a single moment
the whole loose
fragment of body
before the run downwind.
Will stand still
in a camouflage of kind
in a rare daylight
for hours,
the leaves spilling
one break of sun
into another,
listening to the lions.
Will, when dark comes
and the fields open
until there are
no fields,
turn in the length
of light
toward some calm
still part of a tree's
new shadow, part of the moon.
Will stand all night
so tall
the sun will rise.

Long-Lined Free Verse

I HEAR AMERICA SINGING / Walt Whitman (1819-1892)

I hear America singing, the varied carols I hear,
Those of mechanics, each one singing his as it should be blithe and
    strong,
The carpenter singing his as he measures his plank or beam,
The mason singing his as he makes ready for work, or leaves off work,
The boatman singing what belongs to him in his boat, the deckhand
    singing on the steamboat deck,

The shoemaker singing as he sits on the bench, the hatter singing as he
    stands,
The wood-cutter's song, the ploughboy's on his way in the morning, or
    at noon intermission or at sundown,
The delicious singing of the mother, or of the young wife at work, or of
    the girl sewing or washing,
Each singing what belongs to him or her and to none else,
The day what belongs to the day—at night the party of young fellows,
    robust, friendly,
Singing with open mouths their strong melodious songs.

Variable-Length Free Verse

GOING HOME BY LAST LIGHT
Galway Kinnell (b. 1927)

1

Redheaded by last light,
with high-stepped, illusionist amble
I walk toward the white room
where she is waiting,
past
pimentos,
red cabbages,
tomatoes flickering in their bins,
past melons, past mushrooms and onions.

2

Those swarms
of Mayflies that used to rise
at the Vermont threshold, "imagos"
thrown up for a day,
their mouths shriveling closed,
their wings,
their sexual parts, newborn and perfect . . .

3

For several minutes
two mosquitoes have been making love
on top of this poem,

changing positions, swooning, even they,
their thighs
fragile as a baby's hairs, knowing
the ecstasy.

4

A day!
The wings of the earth
lift and fall
to the groans, the cold, savage thumpings of a heart.

Typographical Arrangement of Free-Verse Lines

EVERYBODY LYING
ON THEIR STOMACHS,
HEAD TOWARD THE CANDLE,
READING, SLEEPING, DRAWING
Gary Snyder (b. 1930)

The corrugated roof
Booms and fades night-long to

        million-darted rain
    squalls   and

       outside

       lightning

Photographs in the brain
Wind-bent bamboo.
        through

    the plank shutter
     set

Half-open   on eternity

Fugitives A poetic group whose members met at Vanderbilt University in Nashville, Tennessee, in the 1920s and founded a literary periodical, *The Fugitive*, devoted to verse that was generally formalist, ironic, and regional (meaning Southern). They considered themselves

fugitives from the disorder of contemporary poetry, from Victorian sentimentality, and from "the high-caste Brahmins of the Old South." The magazine ran from 1922-25 and was summed up in a 1928 anthology. Some of the most prominent Fugitives were John Crowe Ransom, Allen Tate, and Robert Penn Warren. The social, cultural, and political views of the group developed into Agrarianism, presented in *I'll Take My Stand* (1930), which championed the traditional values of the rural South as a corrective to industrialization. The critical views of the Fugitives developed into an important part of the New Criticism (a term coined by Ransom in a book about the criticism of William Empson, T.S. Eliot, I.A. Richards, and Yvor Winters), which championed the close reading of poems, a minute attention to the actual words and a shunning of what might be behind the words—biographical facts or the poet's intentions.

The following poem by John Crowe Ransom is a dialogue in sonnet form; each stanza begins and ends with a refrain; there is an intentionally old-fashioned—and ironic—sound to what the two figures (Death and the Maiden) say. "Dustcoat" is an especially apt word here; it denotes the long coat worn by a motorist in the early days of automobiles, but it also suggests "dust to dust," an image of death.

PIAZZA PIECE / John Crowe Ransom (1888-1974)

—I am a gentleman in a dustcoat trying
To make you hear. Your ears are soft and small
And listen to an old man not at all,
They want the young men's whispering and sighing.
But see the roses on your trellis dying
And hear the spectral singing of the moon;
For I must have my lovely lady soon,
I am a gentleman in a dustcoat trying.

—I am a lady young in beauty waiting
Until my truelove comes, and then we kiss.
But what grey man among the vines is this
Whose words are dry and faint as in a dream?
Back from my trellis, Sir, before I scream!
I am a lady young in beauty waiting.

G

Georgic *(Greek, "farmer," from "earth" + "work")*   A poem about life in the country, in particular the work of farmers.

The earliest known georgic is Hesiod's *Works and Days*, written around 750 B.C. Virgil (70-19 B.C.) wrote his *Georgics*, or poems about farm life, between 37 and 30 B.C., while he was living on the estate of Maecenas, a Roman statesman and patron of the arts. These poems are *didactic, offering instruction and advice on cultivating fields, planting groves, raising livestock, and keeping bees:

> What makes the valleys laugh and sing, what star
> Should speed the plough and marry vine to elm,
> The care of kine and how to rear a flock,
> What skill shall keep the parsimonious bee,
> Hence is my song . . .
>
> (tr. T.F. Royds)

More recently, the Kentucky poet Wendell Berry has written many poems about the work and life of farming. (*See*: *idyll, pastoral.*)

ENRICHING THE EARTH / Wendell Berry (b. 1934)

> To enrich the earth I have sowed clover and grass
> to grow and die. I have plowed in the seeds
> of winter grains and of various legumes,
> their growth to be plowed in to enrich the earth.
> I have stirred into the ground the offal
> and the decay of the growth of past seasons

and so mended the earth and made its yield increase.
All this serves the dark. I am slowly falling
into the fund of things. And yet to serve the earth,
not knowing what I serve, gives a wideness
and a delight to the air, and my days
do not wholly pass. It is the mind's service,
for when the will fails so do the hands
and one lives at the expense of life.
After death, willing or not, the body serves,
entering the earth. And so what was heaviest
and most mute is at last raised up into song.

Ghazal (*gúh-zul; or gáh-zul; Arabic, "the cry of a gazelle when it is hunted down and trapped" or "to make love; lovers' exchange"*) A poem of five to fifteen couplets, originally in Persian, Arabic, Turkish, and Urdu poetry. The couplets are not connected but are independent units within the poem; the poet is free to make associative jumps from one couplet (or sh'er) to the next. In the original languages, only the first couplet rhymes (*aa*), but the second line of every succeeding couplet rhymes with it (*Xa*). In the last couplet the poet inserts his name or a pseudonym, although this too is usually omitted now.

Some ghazals have short refrains at the end of each couplet, seemingly in lieu of rhyme. In fact, the rhyme word (or radif) comes just before the refrain (or qafia). In the ghazal below by the Persian poet Hafiz, the refrain is "I rise" and the rhyme words (including a *slant rhyme in line one) are "desire," "snare," "where," "air," "there," "share," "air," and "everywhere."

The ghazal may have originated in the erotic prologue of an earlier form, the qasida, which like the ghazal is written in couplets and rhymed *aa Xa Xa Xa*, etc., but which consists of more than fifteen couplets, up to about one hundred, and is used for occasional verse and public declamation. The ghazal is sung and usually about erotic or mystical love.

Federico Garcia Lorca (1898-1936) wrote a number of ghazals, such as his "Ghazal of the Terrifying Presence." Contemporary ghazals generally dispense with rhyme and emphasize the shifts between couplets. Some poets have written impressive sequences using this form: Adrienne Rich (*Ghazals: Homage to Ghalib* and *The Blue Ghazals*), Jim

Harrison (*Ghazals*), and Galway Kinnell ("Sheffield Ghazals," in which long lines ending in periods are used in lieu of couplets).

WHERE CAN I HEAR THE NEWS
Hafiz of Shiraz (14th century; tr. John Drury)
(inscribed on the poet's tomb in Shiraz, Iran)

Where can I hear the news, so that out of desire I rise?
So that, like a homing pigeon from a snare, I rise?

If you command me to your service, I'll renounce
the world and its worldliness, though it's where I rise.

O Lord, loosen the rain from your thunderhead of mercy—
as long as, like dust that floats in the air, I rise.

Bring a singer and some excellent wine to my tomb,
wafting your fragrance, dancing, so that out of there I rise.

Climb to your full height and sway like a cypress to raise me.
Clapping my hands, applauding the world we share, I rise.

Although I'm old, embrace me for a solitary night
so that with the dawn, aroused in the fresh air, I rise.

On the day I die, bless Hafiz with one last look at you
before, leaving desire behind me everywhere, I rise.

GHAZALS (I) / Jim Harrison (b. 1937)

Unbind my hair, she says. The night is white and warm,
the snow on the mountains absorbing the moon.

We have to get there before the music begins, scattered,
elliptical, needing to be drawn together and sung.

They have dark green voices and listening, there are birds,
coal shovels, the glazed hysteria of the soon-to-be-dead.

I suspect Jesus *will* return and the surprise will be
fatal. I'll ride the equator on a whale, a giraffe on land.

Even stone when inscribed bears the ecstatic. Pressed to
some new wall, ungiving, the screams become thinner.

Let us have the tambourine and guitars and forests, fruit,
and a new sun to guide us, a holy book, tracked in new blood.

THE BLUE GHAZALS (9/21/68) / Adrienne Rich (b. 1929)

Violently asleep in the old house.
A clock stays awake all night ticking.

Turning, turning their bruised leaves
the trees stay awake all night in the wood.

Talk to me with your body through my dreams.
Tell me what we are going through.

The walls of the room are muttering,
old trees, old Utopians, arguing with the wind.

To float like a dead man in a sea of dreams
and half those dreams being dreamed by someone else.

Fifteen years of sleepwalking with you,
wading against the tide, and with the tide.

NOTE: This ghazal, like the one by Jim Harrison, is the first in a sequence.

Glosa, Glose *(Spanish, "gloss")*   A Spanish verse form, introduced by
court poets around the turn of the fifteenth century, beginning with
a short stanza or *texte* that states the theme of the poem; succeeding
stanzas explain or gloss each of those lines, repeating them freely as
*refrains. Lewis Turco's "Simon Judson," from *Bordello*, is an example
in English.

H

Haibun   A Japanese form in which prose is interspersed with verse, specifically *haiku—each containing a total of seventeen syllables arranged in three lines. Haibun often takes the form of a diary or travel journal. (*See: verse mixed with prose.*)

ARRIVAL IN TOKYO / James Merrill (1926-1995)

Our section of town is Roppongi, where thirty years ago I dined in W's gloomy wooden farmhouse. The lanes and gardens of his neighborhood have given way to glitzy skyscrapers like this hotel—all crystal and brass, a piano and life-size ceramic Saint Bernard in the carpeted lobby. It is late when the revolving door whisks us forth, later yet when our two lengthening shadows leave the noodle shop to wander before bed through the Aoyama cemetery. Mishima is buried down one of its paths bordered by cherry trees in full, amazing bloom. Underneath, sitting on the ground—no, on outspread plastic or paper, shoes left in pairs alongside these instant "rooms"— a few ghostly parties are still eating and drinking, lit by small flames. One group has a transistor, another makes its own music, clapping hands and singing. Their lantern faces glow in the half-dark's black-beamed, blossom-tented

> dusk within the night.
> The high street lamp through snowy
> branches burns moon-bright.

Haiku *(or hokku, meaning "starting verse")* A Japanese poetic form, three lines containing seventeen syllables, usually arranged 5-7-5.

In English, many haiku simply follow that syllabic pattern. Sometimes a poet will rhyme lines one and three, perhaps using the form as a haiku stanza in a longer poem, as in Richard Wilbur's "Alatus" and "Thyme Flowering Among Rocks." But it could also consist of two or four lines (and a different count of syllables, or no count at all) and still be called a haiku. The spirit of haiku often identifies it more than the meter: a reference to a season (R.H. Blyth calls haiku "the poetry of the seasons"), an image or two of something particular in the natural world, the juxtaposition of surprising images, and a flash of awareness or recognition. Haiku is, after all, an important way of insight in Zen Buddhism. (If a poem has the three-line form but lacks any suggestion of a season, it is technically a senryu.)

Haiku grew out of two earlier Japanese forms, the *tanka (or waka),* a five-line stanza arranged 5-7-5-7-7, and the *renga ("linked verse"),* a collaborative form in which two or more poets would take turns, the first using the first three lines of a tanka, the second using the last two lines, and then continuing for some time. That opening was called a *haiku,* or "starting verse." Basho is credited with pioneering the haiku as an independent form.

In "A Month in Summer," her version of a Japanese poetic diary (or *utanikki),* Carolyn Kizer writes:

> Several years ago, I wrote *haiku* in this way:
>
>> The frost was late this year:
>> Crystal nips the petals
>> As my lover grows impatient.
>
> I have come to prefer the four-line form which Nobuyuki Yuasa has used in translating Issa because, as he says, it comes closer to approximating the natural rhythm of English speech:
>
>> Let down the curtain!
>> Hamlet dies each night
>> But is always revived.
>> Love, too, requires genius.

The poet in English may also write haiku in fewer than three or four lines, as in Allen Ginsberg's rendition of Basho's *Furuike ya*, the best known of all haiku:

Old pond—frog jumps in—kerplunk!

The essential elements of haiku are brevity, immediacy, spontaneity, imagery, the natural world, a season, and sudden illumination.

FOUR HAIKU
Matsuo Basho (1644-94)

sweeping the garden
but letting the temple keep
the willows' droppings
(tr. Cid Corman)

the autumn coolness
hand and hand paring away
eggplants cucumbers
(tr. Cid Corman)

what with fleas and lice
the horse having a good piss
right at the pillow
(tr. Cid Corman)

The temple bell stops—
but the sound keeps coming
out of the flowers.
(tr. Robert Bly)

FOUR HAIKU
Kobayashi Issa (1763-1827; tr. Robert Bly)

This line of black ants—
maybe it goes all the way back
to that white cloud!

I look into a dragonfly's eye
and see
the mountains over my shoulder.

Cricket, be
careful! I'm rolling
over!

Now listen, you watermelons—
if any thieves come—
turn into frogs!

HAIKU
Etheridge Knight (1933-1991)

1

Eastern guard tower
glints in sunset; convicts rest
like lizards on rocks.

2

The piano man
is stingy at 3 A.M.
his songs drop like plum.

3

Morning sun slants cell.
Drunks stagger like cripple flies
On Jailhouse floor.

4

To write a blues song
is to regiment riots
and pluck gems from graves.

5

A bare pecan tree
slips a pencil shadow down
a moonlit snow slope.

6

The falling snow flakes
Cannot blunt the hard aches nor
Match the steel stillness.

7

Under moon shadows
A tall boy flashes knife and
Slices star bright ice.

8

In the August grass
Struck by the last rays of sun
The cracked teacup screams.

9

Making jazz swing in
Seventeen syllables AIN'T
No square poet's job.

Harlem Renaissance   An African-American literary movement centered in Harlem in the 1920s.

Influenced by jazz and blues, continuing the poetic tradition that was presented in James Weldon Johnson's *The Book of American Negro Poetry* (1922), the poets of the Harlem Renaissance celebrated black culture, contemplated the movement of blacks from the rural South to the urban North, and attacked the forces that oppressed blacks in America.

Poets of the Harlem Renaissance include Langston Hughes, Jean Toomer, Claude McKay, and Countee Cullen.

I, TOO / Langston Hughes (1902-1967)

I, too, sing America.

I am the darker brother.
They send me to eat in the kitchen
When company comes,
But I laugh,
And eat well,
And grow strong.

Tomorrow,
I'll sit at the table
When company comes.
Nobody'll dare
Say to me,
"Eat in the kitchen,"
Then.

Besides,
They'll see how beautiful I am
And be ashamed,—

I, too, am America.

Heroic Couplet   Two adjacent lines of *iambic pentameter that rhyme together. Defined more strictly, the lines in a heroic couplet form a discrete unit, a complete sentence, and often use phrases that are parallel, antithetical, or otherwise balanced, as in John Dryden's *Absalom and Achitophel*:

In Friendship false, implacable in Hate:
Resolv'd to Ruine or to Rule the State.

Iambic pentameter couplets first appeared in English in *The Canterbury Tales* of Geoffrey Chaucer and later in early plays of Shakespeare such as *Romeo and Juliet*. It was codified into a strict, mostly *end-stopped, highly rhetorical instrument by poets of the Restoration and the Enlightenment such as John Dryden and Alexander Pope. The heroic couplet dominated English poetry from 1688 to 1776. The direct influence was both French (whose standard line has long been the rhymed couplet—in *alexandrines rather than in iambic pentameter) and Greco-Roman (whose classical meter, the hexameter, could be approximated by heroic couplets). French classical drama (especially the tragedies of Racine and the comedies of Molière) preceded the English classicists somewhat and wielded great influence in the realm of metrical proprieties.

During its heyday, the heroic couplet was used for satirical verse (such as Pope's *The Dunciad*), mock-epic (such as Pope's *The Rape of the Lock*, a passage of which appears below), and verse essay (such

as Pope's *Essay on Man*). Used strictly, however, the heroic couplet tends toward the straitlaced and stiff (despite Pope's venom); the rules, as well as the elegant dance-steps of syntax that adhere to them, keep its rhythmic bounds narrow. Chaucer's looser treatment allows for narrative that is more easygoing.

from THE RAPE OF THE LOCK (Canto II, 19-46)
Alexander Pope (1688-1744)

> This nymph, to the destruction of mankind,
> Nourished two locks which graceful hung behind
> In equal curls, and well conspired to deck
> With shining ringlets the smooth ivory neck.
> Love in these labyrinths his slaves detains,
> And mighty hearts are held in slender chains.
> With hairy springes we the birds betray,
> Slight lines of hair surprise the finny prey,
> Fair tresses man's imperial race ensnare,
> And beauty draws us with a single hair.
> The adventurous Baron the bright locks admired,
> He saw, he wished, and to the prize aspired.
> Resolved to win, he meditates the way,
> By force or ravish, or by fraud betray;
> For when success a lover's toil attends,
> Few ask if fraud or force attained his ends.
> For this, ere Phoebus rose, he had implored
> Propitious Heaven, and every power adored,
> But chiefly Love—to Love an altar built,
> Of twelve vast French romances, neatly gilt.
> There lay three garters, half a pair of gloves,
> And all the trophies of his former loves.
> With tender billet-doux he lights the pyre,
> And breathes three amorous sighs to raise the fire.
> Then prostrate falls, and begs with ardent eyes
> Soon to obtain, and long possess the prize:
> The powers gave ear, and granted half his prayer,
> The rest the winds dispersed in empty air.

How-to Poem A poem in the form of a set of instructions, usually in the imperative: Do this, do that.

The how-to poem tells the reader how to do something. It needs to be as clear as a good instruction manual, but as rich as good poetry in its imagery, rhythms, and imagination. In "What You Should Know to Be a Poet," for example, Gary Snyder advises the novice to learn the names of things, as well as a kind of magic, and goes on to list ordinary, fantastic, and erotic kinds of knowledge. In the how-to poem below, Ted Kooser offers both a recipe and a way of experiencing the details and spaces of one's life.

HOW TO MAKE RHUBARB WINE
Ted Kooser (b. 1939)

Go to the patch some afternoon
in early summer, fuzzy with beer
and sunlight, and pick a sack
of rhubarb (red or green will do)
and God knows watch for rattlesnakes
or better, listen; they make a sound
like an old lawn mower rolled downhill.
Wear a hat. A straw hat's best
for the heat but lets the gnats in.
Bunch up the stalks and chop the leaves off
with a buck knife and be careful.
You need ten pounds; a grocery bag
packed full will do it. Then go home
and sit barefooted in the shade
behind the house with a can of beer.
Spread out the rhubarb in the grass
and wash it with cold water
from the garden hose, washing
your feet as well. Then take a nap.
That evening, dice the rhubarb up
and put it in a crock. Then pour
eight quarts of boiling water in,
cover it up with a checkered cloth
to keep the fruit flies out of it,
and let it stand five days or so.
Take time each day to think of it.

Ferment ten days, under the cloth,
sniffing of it from time to time,

then siphon it off, swallowing some,
and bottle it. Sit back and watch
the liquid clear to honey yellow,
bottled and ready for the years,
and smile. You've done it awfully well.

Hudibrastics   Comic, narrative verse written in rhymed *iambic te-trameter couplets, as in Samuel Butler's mock-heroic poem *Hudibras*, published in 1662.

The effect is close to doggerel, but permitted (even welcomed) because of the satiric nature of Hudibrastics. Rhyme is crucial to the form, and the best rhymes here are the most outrageous and far-fetched. Butler remarks parenthetically,

(For rhyme the rudder is of verses,
With which like ships they steer their courses).

The title character, a knight errant in what were then modern times, takes his name from Spenser's *The Faerie Queen* and his nature from Cervantes's *Don Quixote*.

John Barth's novel *The Sot-Weed Factor*, set in Colonial Maryland, is based on a poem written in Hudibrastics by Ebenezer Cooke (c. 1672-1732):

The Indians call their wat'ry Wagon
Canoe: a Vessel none can brag on.

In his essay "The Prose and Poetry of It All, or, Dippy Verses," Barth remarks, "The Hudibrastic couplet, like Herpes simplex, is a conta-gion more easily caught than cured."

from *HUDIBRAS* (Canto I, 1-14)
Samuel Butler (1612-1680)

When civil fury first grew high
And men fell out they knew not why,
When hard words, jealousies and fears
Set folks together by the ears
And made them fight like mad or drunk

For Dame Religion as for punk,
Whose honesty they all durst swear for,
Though not a man of them knew wherefore,
When gosepel-trumpeter, surrounded
With long-eared rout, to battle sounded
And pulpit, drum ecclesiastic,
Was beat with fist instead of a stick,
Then did Sir Knight abandon dwelling
And out he rode a-colonelling.

I

Iamb or Iambus, iambic *(eyé-am, eye-ám-bic; Greek, "to attack in words"; but Robert Graves says it was "traditionally named in honour of the lasciviously hobbling Iambe" and "may have begun with . . . totem dances which imitated the hobbling of partridge or quail")* A *foot consisting of an unstressed syllable followed by a stress (˘ ´). Iambic words include *arrange, complain, soufflé,* and *revenge.*

Iambic meter, like trochaic, is called duple meter—because each foot contains two syllables. In Ancient Greek, the first iambic verse was composed by Archilochos; originally it was a measure used for *satire. Here is a regular iambic line, the opening of Thomas Gray's "Elegy Written in a Country Churchyard":

> Thĕ cúr- | fĕw tólls | thĕ knéll | ŏf párt- | ĭng dáy.

The line is iambic pentameter, meaning that it contains five iambic feet. Iambic pentameter is the single most important meter in English, used in Chaucer's *Canterbury Tales*, Shakespeare's plays and sonnets, Milton's *Paradise Lost*, and in much of the poetry of Alexander Pope, William Wordsworth, John Keats, Robert Browning, Robert Frost, W.B Yeats, Wallace Stevens, and innumerable other poets.

It is extremely flexible in its rhythm, long enough so that at least one pause (or *caesura) appears in most lines. But this caesura can turn up in different spots within the lines, allowing the poet much melodic freedom. Iambic pentameter's chief use, however, is not in providing music but in permitting speech, the sound of people talking. It dominates the speech of Shakespeare's plays. At the same time it

is an effective measure for giving musical form to thought, so that ideas become more real through the inflections and pauses and diction of a human voice, one whose talk verges on song.

Iambic tetrameter *(teh-trám-uh-ter; Greek, "four measures")* consists of four iambs (˘ ´ ˘ ´ ˘ ´ ˘ ´). Not as weighty or rhythmically flexible as iambic pentameter, tetrameter sounds more song-like, tighter yet airier, compact and capable of both grace and power.

Here are some examples of iambic meter:

Iambic	*Number of Feet*	*Example*
monometer	1	Thus I Passe by And die: —Robert Herrick, "Upon his departure hence"
dimeter	2	While Angels sing And Mortals ring —Thomas Traherne, "On Christmas-Day"
trimeter	3	With sweetnesse of thy breath; O smother me to death: —Michael Drayton, "To His Valentine"
tetrameter	4	The grave's a fine and private place, But none, I think, do there embrace. —Andrew Marvell, "To His Coy Mistress"
pentameter	5	Yet come to me in dreams, that I may live My very life again though cold in death: —Christina Rossetti, "Echo"
hexameter	6	Invention, nature's child, fled step-dame study's blows; And others' feet still seemed but strangers in my way. —Sir Philip Sidney, "Astrophil and Stella" I

An iambic poem, however, is not required to stick to the same line length throughout, although most poems do. Sometimes a poet inserts occasional lines of iambic trimeter in an otherwise pentameter poem,

as in John Milton's "Lycidas." The following poem by Ben Jonson achieves the effects of music, spontaneity, and wit by altering its line lengths as it proceeds. (*See: accentual-syllabic meter.*)

> MY PICTURE LEFT IN SCOTLAND
> Ben Jonson (1572-1637)
>
> I now thinke, LOVE is rather deafe, then blind,
> For else it could not be,
> That she,
> Whom I adore so much, should so slight me,
> And cast my love behind:
> I'm sure my language to her, was as sweet
> And every close did meet
> In sentence, of as subtile feet,
> As hath the youngest Hee,
> That sits in shadow of Apollo's tree.
> Oh, but my conscious feares,
> That flie my thoughts betweene,
> Tell me that she hath seene
> My hundreds of gray haires,
> Told seven and fortie yeares.
> Read so much wast, as she cannot imbrace
> My mountaine belly, and my rockie face,
> And all these through her eyes, have stopt her eares.

Idyll, Idyl (*éye-dul; Greek, "short descriptive poem" or "little picture"*)

1. Short poem depicting rural life or a country scene. The adjective *idyllic* refers to something that is natural, simple, peaceful, and picturesque.

2. Specifically, the name given to *pastorals written by Theocritus (third century B.C.), the apparent originator of the genre. Although his poems deal with the lives and loves of shepherds, Theocritus was in fact an academic poet, associated with the critics of Alexandria, Egypt. Here is the beginning of John Dryden's translation of the third idyll of Theocritus (whose original is unrhymed):

> To Amaryllis love compels my way;
> My browzing goats upon the mountains stray:
> O Tityrus, tend them well, and see them fed

In pastures fresh, and to their wat'ring led;
And 'ware the ridgeling with his butting head.
Ah, beauteous nymph, can you forget your love,
The conscious grottos, and the shady grove;
Where stretch'd at ease your tender limbs were laid,
Your nameless beauties nakedly display'd?
Then I was call'd your darling, your desire,
With kisses such as set my soul on fire;
But you are chang'd, yet I am still the same;
My heart maintains for both a double flame;
Griev'd, but unmov'd, and patient of your scorn:
So faithful I, and you so much forsworn!
I die, and death will finish all my pain;
Yet, ere I die, behold me once again:
Am I so much deform'd, so chang'd of late?
What partial judges are our love and hate!
Ten wildings have I gather'd for my dear;
How ruddy like your lips their streaks appear!

Idylls and other pastoral poems tend to sound artificial, the landscape idealized into a countryside called Arcadia. Daryl Hine asserts that bucolic (or "cowboy song") is a more appropriate term for the poems of Theocritus, but they are traditionally called idylls.

3. A longer narrative piece, such as Tennyson's *Idylls of the King* (which relates various legends about King Arthur, mostly in *blank verse):

And Arthur and his knighthood for a space
Were all one will, and thro' that strength the king
Drew in the petty princedoms under him,
Fought, and in twelve great battles overcame
The heathen hordes, and made a realm and reign'd.

Alfred, Lord Tennyson (1809-1892) explains his use of the term *idyll*: "Regarding the Greek derivation, I spelt my Idylls with two *l*'s mainly to divide them from the ordinary pastoral idyls usually spelt with one *l*. These idylls group themselves round one central figure."

Image, Imagery *(ím-idge; Latin, "likeness, semblance, picture, concept, imitation or copy")* A mental picture; a concrete representation of something; a likeness the senses can perceive.

Ezra Pound says that an image "presents an intellectual and emotional complex in an instant of time." A poetic image transfers itself to our minds with a flash, as if projected upon a movie screen. Many images, such as "a bracelet in a wheel barrow," appeal primarily to the sense of sight. But an image can invoke the other senses too, as in a "sniff of perfume," or a "jangling of banjoes," or a "scratchy blanket," or a "tart cherry." Images serve as a poem's evidence.

Poetry without images, or with too few, seems vacant, generalized, uncompelling. But stale images are no substitute for the real thing, which must hit us as a discovery, however small. Images can be simple descriptions of real life, as in these lines from Geoffrey Chaucer's "General Prologue" to *The Canterbury Tales*:

> A Marchant was ther with a forked beerd,
> In motelee, and hye on hors he sat,
> Upon his heed a Flandrissh bevere hat,
> His bootes clasped faire and fetisly.

NOTE: *fetisly:* elegantly

Images can also be metaphorical, as in these lines from Elizabeth Bishop's "The Burglar of Babylon":

> And the heads of those in swimming
> Were floating coconuts.

And images can be strange and visionary, as in these lines from Charles Simic's "Concerning My Neighbors, the Hittites":

> Their dogs bury themselves and leave the bones
> To guard the house. A single weed holds all their storms
> Until the spiderwebs spread over the heavens.

Imagism A poetic movement invented by Ezra Pound around 1909 and intended as an antidote to the rhetorical excesses of Victorian poetry and the pastoral complacency of Georgian verse.

Pound, along with H.D. (Hilda Doolittle) and Richard Aldington, announced three principles:

> 1. Direct treatment of the "thing" whether subjective or objective.
> 2. To use absolutely no word that does not contribute to the presentation.
> 3. As regarding rhythm: to compose in the sequence of the musical phrase, not in sequence of a metronome.

Imagist poems, strongly influenced by *haiku and other oriental verse, were short, written in free verse, and presented images without comment or explanation. Amy Lowell later led the movement, which expired near the end of World War I. Vorticism, an offshoot from Imagism masterminded by Ezra Pound, survived through a couple of issues of the magazine *Blast!* and was intended primarily to publicize the paintings, fiction, and poetry of Wyndham Lewis.

OREAD
H.D. (Hilda Doolittle, 1884-1961)

Whirl up, sea—
whirl your pointed pines,
splash your great pines
on our rocks,
hurl your green over us,
cover us with your pools of fir.

NOTE: *Oread*: a mountain nymph in Greek mythology.

Imitation *(Latin, "copy")*

1. Translation, especially a free translation or loose adaptation of the original, as in Robert Lowell's *Imitations*, which includes poems based on the work of Baudelaire, Rimbaud, Montale, and others. (*See: translation.*)

2. Method of learning an art, such as poetry. W.H. Auden discusses how a young poet chooses a "master" to learn from. (His choice was Thomas Hardy.) The apprentice tries to mimic the master poet's work, copying the forms and meters and tricks of breaking lines, trying to

catch and match the characteristic tone, choosing similar subjects, or even substituting his own words for the poet's words, noun for noun, verb for verb, in a word substitution poem.

3. In some critical views, the purpose or means of an art, as in holding a mirror up to nature. The poet thus copies or mimics what he perceives in the world, like a camera that reacts chemically to light.

In Memoriam Stanza   An iambic tetrameter quatrain rhymed *abba*, used by Tennyson in his long elegy *In Memoriam A.H.H.*

> from *IN MEMORIAM A.H.H.*
> Alfred, Lord Tennyson (1809-1892)
>
> VII
>
> Dark house, by which once more I stand
>   Here in the long unlovely street,
>   Doors, where my heart was used to beat
> So quickly, waiting for a hand,
>
> A hand that can be clasp'd no more—
>   Behold me, for I cannot sleep,
>   And like a guilty thing I creep
> At earliest morning to the door.
>
> He is not here; but far away
>   The noise of life begins again,
>   And ghastly thro' the drizzling rain
> On the bald street breaks the blank day.

Inversion   1. The reversal of an expected metrical foot, as when a trochee is substituted for one or more of the feet in an iambic line (called a trochaic inversion). Robert Lowell's "The Drunken Fisherman" begins with a trochaic inversion ("Wallow"):

> Wallowing in this bloody sty,
> I cast for fish that pleased my eye

2. A wrenching or disruption of the usual word order in a sentence, as when Tennyson writes "Heavily hangs the tiger-lily" (instead of

"The tiger-lily hangs heavily"). Inversion makes this line more musical, but also more artificial, less conversational. Since Ezra Pound railed against inversion in the early twentieth century, it has fallen from favor, although it recurs in the intentionally wrenched lines of John Berryman's *Dream Songs*.

Irony *(Greek, "dissimulation, pretended ignorance")*

1. A rhetorical figure by which a speaker means something different than what he says (verbal irony).

2. A discrepancy between appearance or likelihood and an actual reality (situational irony).

In Greek comedy, a trickster named Eiron outwitted a braggart named Alazon by feigning ignorance of something and leading him on until he was trapped. Socrates used this argumentative tactic (called Socratic irony) as he asked innocent-seeming questions of his pupils and adversaries in Plato's dialogues. In dramatic irony, a character in a poem or play or story is not aware of the import of what he utters. The duke who speaks in Robert Browning's "My Last Duchess" has no idea how much he is revealing to his guest. (*See: dramatic monologue.*)

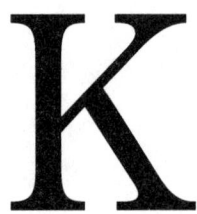

Kenning *(Old Icelandic, "to name after")* A multiword substitute for a noun, such as "whale-road" for "sea."

Kennings appear frequently in Old English verse, such as *Beowulf*, and in related Germanic languages, especially Norse and Icelandic. A kenning is a kind of periphrasis, or roundabout way of using several words instead of one. Instead of "feather," for example, the poet might refer to "joy of a bird." Generally kennings use figures of speech. "Battle," for example, turns into "storm of swords," a phrase which exemplifies both *metaphor (the storm representing a violent clash) and *metonymy (the swords representing men with weapons). This grammatical structure (noun + prepositional phrase) is very common, as in "flame of battle" for "sword." But hyphenated nouns, such as "oar-steed" for "ship," also appear frequently.

A kenning resembles the epithet, such as "loud-roaring" for "sea," which appears in Greek epic poetry. The main difference is that in Greek verse the epithet serves primarily as a formula to plug into a particular metrical pattern, so that the epic poet can say "Grey eyes" instead of "Athena" if he needs two syllables instead of three. (*See: alliterative meter, epic.*)

Kyrielle *(keer-ee-él)* French four-line stanza form, in which each line contains eight syllables and the fourth line is a *refrain.

If the refrain rhymes, the usual schemes for a kyrielle are:

aabB ccbB (etc.)
abaB cbcB (etc.)

The capital letter indicates a refrain (a line that is repeated, perhaps with some variation in the wording). If the refrain is unrhymed, the rhyme scheme may be:

aaaR bbbR (etc.)

Theodore Roethke uses the kyrielle with an unrhymed refrain for some of his light verse and nonsense poems, such as "Dinky."

W.B. Yeats' "The Ragged Wood" rhymes *abaB*, although the refrain line of each stanza is slightly different:

O hurry where by water among the trees
The delicate-stepping stag and his lady sigh,
When they have but looked upon their images—
Would none had ever loved but you and I!

Or have you heard that sliding silver-shoed
Pale silver-proud queen-woman of the sky,
When the sun looked out of his golden hood?—
O that none ever loved but you and I!

O hurry to the ragged wood, for there
I will drive all those lovers out and cry—
O my share of the world, O yellow hair!
No one has ever loved but you and I.

Yeats may not have called this poem a kyrielle. He might have simply considered his stanza a quatrain with a refrain. In any case, the lines are in *iambic pentameter, not in octosyllabics.

The kyrielle below by John Payne rhymes *aabB*.

KYRIELLE / John Payne (1842-1916)

A lark in the mesh of the tangled vine,
A bee that drowns in the flower-cup's wine,
A fly in the sunshine,—such is man.
All things must end, as all began.

A little pain, a little pleasure,
A little heaping up of treasure;
Then no more gazing upon the sun.
All things must end that have begun.

Where is the time for hope or doubt?
A puff of the wind, and life is out;
A turn of the wheel, and rest is won.
All things must end that have begun.

Golden morning and purple night,
Life that fails with the failing light;
Death is the only deathless one.
All things must end that have begun.

Ending waits on the brief beginning;
Is the prize worth the stress of winning?
E'en in the dawning the day is done.
All things must end that have begun.

Weary waiting and weary striving,
Glad outsetting and sad arriving;
What is it worth when the goal is won?
All things must end that have begun.

Speedily fades the morning glitter;
Love grows irksome and wine grows bitter.
Two are parted from what was one.
All things must end that have begun.

Toil and pain and the evening rest;
Joy is weary and sleep is best;
Fair and softly the day is done.
All things must end that have begun.

L

Lai *(also lay)* 1. A brief lyric or narrative poem intended to be sung. The lines rhyme in *couplets and contain eight syllables each. This form, called the French lai, was popular in the Middle Ages. Marie de France wrote the earliest existing narrative lai, and Gautier de Dargies wrote the earliest existing lyric. In current usage, a "lay" is used synonymously, though poetically, with "song."

2. French nine-line stanza, rhymed *aabaabaab*; the *a* lines have five syllables each, while the *b* lines have two syllables each. If there is more than one stanza in the poem, the rhyme sounds will change from stanza to stanza (so that stanza two uses *c* and *d*, stanza three uses *e* and *f*, and so on).

If every next stanza's five-syllable lines pick up the shorter lines' rhyme from the previous stanza, the lai becomes a virelai (or virelay), an interlocking form like *terza rima or the *pantoum. Whenever the virelai reaches its last stanza, the short lines will revert to the original *a* rhyme, making the poem circular.

In a lai nouveau, the first two lines become refrains 1 and 2, and the poem becomes a variation of the villanelle. Only two rhymes (*a* and *b*) are used throughout the poem; refrain 1 recurs as the last line of stanza two, refrain 2 at the end of stanza three, and so on, until the final stanza, whose last two lines are refrains 2 and 1 (reversing the original order).

Language Poetry Poetry that seeks to detach words from their conventional moorings, so that something new and unprecedented, not an imitation of life or the world, emerges.

The Language movement owes much to predecessors such as Gertrude Stein, whose *Tender Buttons* experimented with language used abstractly, nonsensically, freed of its servitude to content and meaning. Other influences include Tristan Tzara, Louis Zukofsky, Charles Olson, and John Ashbery. But as a school or movement it was launched by Bruce Andrews and Charles Bernstein, editors of the magazine $L=A=N=G=U=A=G=E$. Somewhere the equal signs disappeared, a network of periodicals and presses (such as The Figures) sprang up, and Language poetry became a major strain of late-twentieth-century American poetry. Writers associated with the Language movement include Charles Bernstein, Clark Coolidge, Lyn Hejinian, Leslie Scalapino, and Ron Silliman.

Language poetry aims to break away from what we know already, to experiment with what a poem can be, mixing the genres of verse and prose, discovering new measures, coming up with constructs that push beyond the limits of memory, emotion, and tradition that confine and diminish conventional verse. Detractors might argue that much of this so-called Language poetry drones and babbles, a mass of pretentious gibberish, a dead-end of *nonsense verse that is not even funny. But experimental writing necessarily runs many risks, such as pursuing novelty for its own sake, alienating the reader, and courting obscurity. The Language poet rejects conformity and comfortability. Charles Bernstein declares in *A Poetics*, "I care most about poetry that disrupts business as usual, including literary business: I care most for poetry as dissent, including formal dissent; poetry that makes sounds possible to be heard that are not otherwise articulated."

LIFT PLOW PLATES
Charles Bernstein (b. 1950)

For brief scratches, omits,
lays away the oars (hours).
Flagrant immersion besets all
the best boats. Hands, hearts
don't slip, solidly
(sadly) departs.
Empire of sudden letting, soaks
up flaps of fumes, these (his)
fumes. When in the midst

of—days, chartered
whether or not. And suits.
Simple things (thugs)
poisoned with inception.
Such tools as
amount to ill-bred
orientation. Mrs. X
urging Mr. Z to amortize Miss
O. The snowperson snowed
under. On beam, off target.

from THE CELL
Lyn Hejinian (b. 1942)

Lighting by trees
Flattening by depictions of an
    industrialist in a cauldron
A fiction of factors on
    a film
The animals (not dogs) stampeding
    backwards to laughter
It's not in their eyes
Writing by putting a leg
    over a knee is animal
And again it is also
    mineral
It is anatomical to repeat
    but the time isn't right
The times aren't the same
So poetry isn't a reminder
December 10, 1986

Letter Poem *(also called epistle or verse letter)*   A poem written in the
form of a letter.

    Except in the case of an "open letter" or a "letter to the editor,"
most letters are addressed to one specific person by another specific
person—two characters, one speaking and one listening. A letter in
verse can be an actual letter. Marvin Bell and William Stafford
exchanged the poem-letters that eventually became the book *Segues.*
But the letter can also be a vehicle for a *dramatic monologue, in
which a character other than the author speaks. Sometimes verse

letters will include dates, salutations, complimentary closes, and "signatures," but often they will not.

LETTER / Robert Hass (b. 1941)

I had wanted to begin
by telling you I saw another
tanager below the pond
where I had sat for half an hour
feeding on wild berries
in the little clearing near the pines
that hide the lower field
and then looked up from red berries
to the quick red bird briliant
in the light. I have seen
more yarrow and swaying
Queen Anne's lace around the woods
as hawkweed and nighshade
wither and drop seed. A new blue flower,
sweet, yellow-stamened, ovary inferior,
has recently sprung up.
                          But I had the odd
feeling, walking to the house
to write this down, that I had left
the birds and flowers in the field,
rooted or feeding. They are not in my
head, are not now on this page.
It was very strange to me, but I think
their loss was your absence. I wanted
to be walking up with Leif, the sun
behind us skipping off the pond,
the windy maple sheltering the house,
and find you there and say
here! a new blue flower (ovary inferior)
and busy Leif and Kris with naming
in a world I love. You even have
my field guide. It's you I love.
I have believed so long
in the magic of names and poems.
I hadn't thought them bodiless
at all. Tall Buttercup. Wild Vetch.

"Often I am permitted to return
to a meadow." It all seemed real to me
last week, Words. You are the body
of my world, root and flower, the
brightness and surprise of birds.
I miss you love. Tell Leif
you're the names of things.

1801 / Richard Howard (b. 1929)
Among the Papers of the Envoy to Constantinople

May it please Lord Elgin, Earl of Kincardine,
to consider the undersign'd, sole author
and inventor of the Eidophusikon,

for the position so lately rejected
by Mr. Turner. On giving the measure
of its Effects, calm & storm both, sunset

or moonlight, the accurate imitation
of Nature's sounds: approaching thunder, the dash
of waves on a pebbly beach, the distant gun—

my Device was pronounc'd by no less a judge
than Richard Wilson, R.A.—the same who cried out
at the sight of Terni Cascade, "O well done,

water, by God!"—was pronounc'd, I say, by him
"highly successful in agitated seas,"
by reason of the high finish carrying

severally their satellites of colour
into the very center of the Pictures.
As it happens, your Lordship, I visited

the same Joseph Turner known to your Lordship
(I believe) only this week, and found a man
pacing to and fro before his pale muslin

on which the sick and wan Sun, in all the doubt
of darkness, was not allow'd to shed one ray,
but tears. Even as he work'd, pouring wet paint

onto paper till it was saturated,
then tore, then scratch'd, then scrubb'd in a frenzy
at the sheet, the Whole being chaos, until

as if by enchantment, the Scene appear'd then,
great ships gone to pieces in order to fling
magical oranges on the waves—but I

digress: even as he shew'd me two books fill'd
with studies from Nature, several tinted
on the spot—which he found, he said, much the most

valuable to him—this Turner discuss'd
the present urgency of your Lordship's need
for an artist who might draw Antiquities,

with suitable finish, before Removal,
by your Lordship's design, from Athens. He said
he could not, himself, endure the Ideal,

but enjoy'd and look'd for only *litter*—why
even his richest vegetation is confus'd,
he delights in shingle, debris, and mere heaps

of fallen stone. Upon communicating
the intelligence that your Lordship's stipend
must include assistance to Lady Elgin

in decorating fire-screens and the like,
the man turn'd back in some heat to his labour
upon what I took to be that mysterious

forest below London Bridge, where great ships ride,
sails filling or falling, disorder'd too
by the stress of anchorage, all beautiful

though wild beneath the Daemonic pressure
of his inquiry (with so much of the trowel,
surely a touch more *finishing* might be borne!).

Enough of Turner, I have not to speak here
of him, though what I saw was but the *scribbling*
of Painting, surely. What I would say is this:

I venture to suggest in myself a man
your Lordship, and my Lady, most certainly,
might rely upon for accurate Service,

work of a conclusive polish, not a sketch.
There is, may I make so bold, a point at which
in Turner's Picturesque, as Fuseli says,

two spiders, caressing or killing each other,
must have greatly the advantage, in roughness
of surface and intricacy of motion,

over every athletic or am'rous
Symplegma left by the Ancients. I do not
wish to speak further of the man who renounc'd

your Lordship's commission to copy marbles,
muttering (though plain to hear) "Antiquities
be damn'd, by Thames' shore we will die," and went on

raking at the sea with his untidy thumb;
but only to call your Lordship's kind notice
and gracious favour, for the appointed task,

to the creator of the Eidophusikon,
these many years a loyal British subject,
Yours, &c.

Philippe-Jacques de Loutherbourg

Light Verse   Humorous verse, usually rhymed; verse in the service of amusement; rhymed lines that are light as opposed to weighty, dark, or serious.

Poets have used several poetic forms, including *double dactyls, *clerihews, *limericks, and *nashers, exclusively for light verse. But other forms, such as *epigrams, *heroic couplets, *rondeaux, *skeltonics, *sonnets, and *villanelles, have also served admirably for both light verse and more serious poems. Verse that is comic, humorous, or witty need not be light verse, however, as long as it has a certain depth of emotion or range of imagination.

Much light verse is simply doggerel: sing-song, jingling verses, roughly and often ineptly measured (although Goethe's *Faust* contains a number of passages in doggerel—and is hardly inept).

Limerick   A light verse form, often bawdy or scatological, consisting of a five-line stanza rhymed *aabba*.

The pattern of feet (or stresses) in the lines is 3-3-2-2-3, usually in *anapestic ($\smile \smile \prime$) or *amphibrachic ($\smile \prime \smile$) meter. The rhythms, however, can be very loose (befitting a comic form), as in the lines attributed to President Woodrow Wilson (1856-1924):

> I sat next to the Duchess at tea;
> It was just as I feared it would be:
> Her rumblings abdominal
> Were truly phenomenal,
> And everyone thought it was me!

The stanzaic arrangement of the limerick goes back at least to the sixteenth century and the *mad-song stanza, as exemplified by the anonymous "Tom o' Bedlam's Song."

Line *(also called a *verse and a stich)* An aural and visual stretch of words; the basic compositional unit of a poem written in verse.

Aloud, in a song or a recited poem, a line is like a melodic phrase, lasting a certain length before the piece "turns" to the next line or ends. On the page, a line is a typographical unit, a horizontal row of words. If it ends arbitrarily when it reaches the right margin, the text is prose. If, however, it ends where the writer requires it to end, the text is verse (meaning written in discrete lines—or verses—determined by the poet, not a typesetter). In poetry, a line can (and often will) continue beyond the right margin, as in the long-lined poems of Walt Whitman; in this case the continuation is indented beneath the first part of the line.

The poet can determine a line's length in several ways: (1) by using a regular meter, such as iambic pentameter, which requires that a set number of syllables (ten) and stresses (five) must accumulate before the line ends; (2) by ending a line on a rhyme word, whether or not the poem is in meter; (3) by following a *cadence, an unmeasured surge of rhythm; (4) by choosing a line's length visually, making it either similar to the nearby lines or different; (5) by imposing a *line break, either where a pause occurs or between words usually grouped together (such as a prepositional phrase).

Line Break The place where a line ends.

This term applies especially to *free verse, because the poet (and not a metrical imperative) determines when and where to turn from one line to the next. "Break" suggests a sundering, a snapping off of the line, which may come right in the midst of a phrase. One exercise useful in experimenting with free verse is to take a passage of prose

(or someone's poem written out as prose) and break it (or rebreak it) into lines. As Louis Simpson remarks, the poet's "impulse" determines each line break.

The following poem by Adrienne Rich shows some of the ways a poet can break free-verse lines. She can, of course, break where natural pauses occur ("with chords of Joy/ where everything is silence"), although this poem rushes on and omits most punctuation. She can separate phrases or grammatical units: between halves of a conjunction ("impotence/ or infertility"), between adjective and noun ("climacteric/ music"), between adverb and adjective ("entirely/ isolated"), between noun and verb ("the man/ does not want out"), between article and noun ("the/ beating"), between a preposition and its object ("upon/ a splintered table"). She can gradually pull in the lines and then let them out, giving a visual shape like the ebb and flow of tides and a cadence like the lulls and swells of symphonic music.

THE NINTH SYMPHONY OF BEETHOVEN
UNDERSTOOD AT LAST AS A SEXUAL MESSAGE
Adrienne Rich (b. 1929)

A man in terror of impotence
or infertility, not knowing the difference
a man trying to tell something
howling from the climacteric
music of the entirely
isolated soul
yelling at Joy from the tunnel of the ego
music without the ghost
of another person in it, music
trying to tell something the man
does not want out, would keep if he could
gagged and bound and flogged with chords of Joy
where everything is silence and the
beating of a bloody fist upon
a splintered table

NOTE: The fourth movement of Ludwig Van Beethoven's Ninth Symphony sets Schiller's "Ode to Joy" to music.

List Poem   A poem that names or enumerates a series of things; a catalogue, as in many of Walt Whitman's poems.

The genealogies of the Old Testament and the catalogue of ships in Homer's *Iliad* are examples of lists. But, although they may record a roster of names, the lists in contemporary poems more often consist of images and specific details.

THE FAMILY IS ALL THERE IS
Pattiann Rogers (b. 1940)

Think of those old, enduring connections
found in all flesh—the channeling
wires and threads, vacuoles, granules,
plasma and pods, purple veins, ascending
boles and coral sapwood (sugar-
and light-filled), those common ligaments,
filaments, fibers and canals.

Seminal to all kin also is the open
mouth—in heart urchin and octopus belly,
in catfish, moonfish, forest lily,
and rugosa rose, in thirsty magpie,
wailing cat cub, barker, yodeler,
yawning coati.

And there is a pervasive clasping
common to the clan—the hard nails
of lichen and ivy sucker
on the church wall, the bean tendril
and the taproot, the bolted coupling
of crane flies, the hold of the shearwater
on its morning squid, guanine
to cytosine, adenine to thymine,
fingers around fingers, the grip
of the voice on presence, the grasp
of the self on place.

Remember the same hair on pygmy
dormouse and yellow-necked caterpillar,
covering red baboon, thistle seed
and willow herb? Remember the similar
snorts of warthog, walrus, male moose

and sumo wrestler? Remember the familiar
whinny and shimmer found in river birches,
bay mares and bullfrog tadpoles,
in children playing at shoulder tag
on a summer lawn?

The family—weavers, reachers, winders
and connivers, pumpers, runners, air
and bubble riders, rock-sitters, wave-gliders,
wire wobblers, soothers, flagellators—all
brothers, sisters, all there is.

Name something else.

Long Poem A poem whose length and scope exceed those of the
short lyric or narrative poem.

Epics, romances, and verse novels obviously qualify as long poems,
but so do poems of several pages, such as T.S. Eliot's *The Waste Land*.
Edgar Allan Poe, however, denied that a long poem could exist:

> That degree of excitement which would entitle a poem to be
> so called at all cannot be sustained throughout a composition
> of any great length. After the lapse of half an hour, at the
> very utmost, it flags—fails—a revulsion ensues—and then the
> poem is, in effect, and in fact, no longer such. ("The Poetic
> Principle")

Some poets draw a rather arbitrary limit at one hundred lines;
anything over that length would go on too long to sustain its poetic
intensity.

A long poem today could be construed as anything over two pages
in length. More reasonably, a long poem must sustain something
beyond the lyric impulse. Sequences of short poems, or numbered
sections, may characterize the shortest of long poems. Narratives usually require room to tell their stories, and often qualify as long poems.
However, Robert McDowell has identified narrative poems of four to
twelve pages as "middle length." How short is long enough for a "long
poem"? The question is still unresolved.

The most traditional kind of long poem is the *epic, which might
constitute twenty-four books (in the sense of "chapters" or "long sections") and hundreds of pages. Many twentieth-century epics, such

as Ezra Pound's *The Cantos*, reject traditional narrative (except in short bursts) and have experimented with other methods of organization: juxtaposition of scenes and images, alternation of themes. It may be fair to suggest an analogy: a lyric poem (or a short narrative poem) is to the short story as a long poem is to the novel or novella.

Recent book-length long poems include Carolyn Forché's *The Angel of History* and A.R. Ammons' *Garbage* (in eighteen sections made up of couplets composed on adding machine tape).

Love Poem   Poem addressed to a lover, or about the lover, or about the speaker's love, or about love itself.

From Sappho to Catullus to Dante to Shakespeare to Keats to Yeats to many contemporary poets, love has exerted perhaps the primary influence upon poetry, from erotic to romantic to religious to fraternal love, from a love for a particular person to a love for the world—or even a love for poetry. As Ezra Pound says, in a poem he wrote while confined to a prison cage in Pisa in 1945, "What thou lovest well remains/ the rest is dross." Samuel Johnson points out, however, that "the basis of all excellence is truth: he that professes love ought to feel its power."

TO FANNY BRAWNE / John Keats (1795-1821)

This living hand, now warm and capable
Of earnest grasping, would, if it were cold
And in the icy silence of the tomb,
So haunt thy days and chill thy dreaming nights
That thou wouldst wish thine own heart dry of blood
So in my veins red life might stream again,
And thou be conscience-calm'd—see here it is—
I hold it towards you.

Luc-Bat *(Vietnamese, "six-eight")*   A Vietnamese form consisting of alternating lines of six and eight syllables; the end-rhymes of each eight-syllable and six-syllable couplet is echoed by an internal rhyme in the next line, positioned at the sixth syllable; a new rhyme then begins at the eighth syllable. (There are similar rhyming patterns in *Welsh verse.)

Luc-bat occurs in both folk poetry and literary works such as Nguyen Du's *The Tale of Kieu*, a verse novel of 3,250 lines. The following translation imitates the syllabic meter and rhyme scheme of the original: "sum" is echoed by "come"; "blows" and "flows" by "go-"; and so on.

PROLOGUE AND OPENING
OF CHAPTER ONE OF
KIM-VAN-KIEU (THE TALE OF KIEU)
Nguyen Du (1765-1820; tr. John Drury)

In life, a century's sum,
Talent and fate may come to blows.
You pass through ebbs and flows,
Sickened by what is going on.
Something gained, something gone,
Fair cheeks are set upon by spite.

Manuscripts by lamplight
And bamboo texts relate the Ming
Period of Kia-Tsing
When peace was prevailing among
The people. In the Vuong
Family there was a young man, last
Son of a clerk whose modest
But literary past he knew,
And daughters named Thuy-Kieu
And Thuy-Van, both slim, beautiful,
In their two ways equal.

Lyric Poetry   One of the three main genres of poetry (the others being *dramatic poetry and *narrative poetry). It is poetry in which music predominates over story or drama.

Much lyric poetry expresses personal emotion—or at least suggests a real person thinking out loud, however impersonalized that speaker may be. Originally lyric poetry was sung, chanted, or recited to a musical accompaniment. The word *lyric* refers to the poet's lyre, the harp-like instrument the poet or a musician would play. Today that music is more likely to be a suggestion at best, like a vestigal memory. Lyric poetry now tends to be quiet, inward, meditative, mental, while we use the word *song to denote "words and music."

M

Madrigal A brief song performed in parts (by several voices), usually eight to ten lines, as in the Elizabethan playwright John Fletcher's "Take O Take Thy Lips Away."

Mad-Song Stanza A five-line stanza, rhymed *Xabba* with the feet arranged 3-3-2-2-3.

Typically used, since the Renaissance, for songs in the voice of a madman, the form resembles the *limerick, except that the mad-song tends to be in loose *iambic meter (˘ ′), while the limerick favors triple meter such as *anapestic (˘ ˘ ′) and *amphibrachic (˘ ′ ˘). And while both forms indulge in nonsense, the limerick is comic, lightweight, and often lewd; the mad-song is visionary. The anonymous "Tom o' Bedlam's Song" (called "Loving Mad Tom" in Robert Graves' edition) is probably the best-known example. Here is one of its stanzas:

> I know more than Apollo;
> For oft, when he lies sleeping,
> I behold the stars
> At mortal wars,
> And the rounded welkin weeping.

In some editions, however, the lines are arranged in a four-line stanza (and the words differ too):

> I know more than Apollo,
>   For oft when he lies sleeping
> I see the stars at bloody wars
>   And the wounded welkin weeping.

If the song were sung, it would sound the same no matter how it appeared on the page. But is it in five-line stanzas or in *quatrains? Does it use only end-rhymes or does the third line of each stanza contain internal rhyme (as many traditional ballads do)? The stanza could also be arranged as a couplet in the *poulter's measure (a line of six feet followed by a line of seven):

> I know more than Apollo, for oft when he lies sleeping
> I see the stars at bloody wars and the wounded welkin weeping.

It helps the eye when the lines are broken into shorter lengths, and it helps the singer by indicating rhymes and pauses, but it makes no real difference to the listener.

Masculine Ending (*also called rising ending*)   A line that ends with a stressed syllable, such as "Something there is that doesn't love a wall" (Robert Frost). A line that adds an unstressed syllable after the final stress (´ ˘) is called *feminine.

Memory   A source of poetry, limiting if entrusted too literally, debilitating if spent too recklessly. The *muses, the Greek inspirers of the creative arts, were the daughters of Memory, or Mnemosyne. Memory supplies the necessary raw materials of imagination.

Memorization, learning a poem by heart, is one of the best ways to absorb the craft and techniques of poetry. It is a kind of mental ingestion, akin to saving a file on a computer.

Metaphor (*mét-uh-for; Greek, "to carry across"*)   A comparison that likens two different things by identifying one as the other.

In mathematical symbols, a metaphor would require an equal sign, asserting that $A = B$, as in "that strange flower, the sun," a line from Wallace Stevens' "Gubbinal" that equates the sun with a "strange flower." Unlike a *simile, metaphor does not use linking words ("like,"

"as," "such as") to indicate similarity between two otherwise different things.

Metaphor, however, is also the general term for any comparison, including simile, metaphor, conceit, and analogy. In his column in *Natural History*, Stephen Jay Gould writes:

> One day, as I sat at an alfresco lunch spot enjoying a view of the Acropolis, a small truck pulled up to the curb and blocked the Parthenon. I was annoyed at first, but later wonderfully amused as I watched the moving men deliver some furniture to the neighboring house. Their van said Metaphora. Of course, I realized. *Phor* is the verb for "carrying," and *meta* is a prefix meaning "change of place, order, condition, or nature." A moving truck helps you change the order of something by carrying it from one spot to another—and is surely a metaphor. ... A metaphor carries you from one object (which may be difficult to understand) to another (which may be more accessible and therefore helpful, by analogy, in grasping the original concern).

Metaphors, as Gould asserts, are "carriers" which help readers make "imaginative leaps." But it is the poet who must be the moving man, covering that distance, transporting the goods.

I.A. Richards invented the terms *tenor* and *vehicle* to denote the two parts of a metaphor. The *tenor* is the literal subject; the *vehicle* is the figurative connection, the likeness, the thing that is compared to the subject or the carrier—like the moving van Steven Jay Gould saw in Greece. For example, the first stanza of Robert Lowell's "For the Union Dead," contains a metaphor "a Sahara of snow"; the tenor is snow, while the vehicle is the Sahara desert. The terms can apply to similes as well. In Robert Burns' line, "O my luve's like a red red rose," the tenor is "my luve" and the vehicle is "a red red rose."

When a metaphor is extended and elaborated (like the image of "twin compasses" John Donne presents through twelve lines of "A Valediction: Forbidding Mourning"), it is a conceit.

Metaphysical Poets A group of English poets, including John Donne, Abraham Cowley, George Herbert, and Henry Vaughan, who lived during the early seventeenth century and whose poems are

characterized by elaborate forms and rhyme schemes, extensive use of *metaphor and conceit, wit and cleverness, intellectual daring, wide-ranging vocabulary (including scientific terms), and interests in religion and (in Donne's case especially) erotic love.

The term was coined by Dr. Samuel Johnson in his piece on Abraham Cowley in *Lives of the Poets*, 1779-81:

> The metaphysical poets were men of learning, and to show their learning was their whole endeavour; but unluckily resolving to show it in rhyme, instead of writing poetry they only wrote verses, and very often such verses as stood the trial of the finger better than of the ear, for the modulation was so imperfect that they were only found to be verses by counting the syllables.

Johnson adds, "The most heterogeneous ideas are yoked by violence together; nature and art are ransacked for illustrations, comparisons, and allusions. . . ."

Samuel Taylor Coleridge comments similarly on the nature of metaphysical poetry in his epigram "On Donne's Poetry" (1836), which imitates some of Donne's metaphorical ingenuity:

> With Donne, whose muse on dromedary trots,
> Wreathe iron pokers into truelove knots;
> Rhyme's sturdy cripple, fancy's maze and clue,
> Wit's forge and fire-blast, meaning's press and screw.

In this poetry Coleridge sees a camel instead of a winged horse, a cripple in a maze, a torture chamber of meaning—all wrenched and twisted out of natural shape.

In the early twentieth century, T.S. Eliot led a reappraisal and revival of metaphysical poetry. In his essay "The Metaphysical Poets" (1921), Eliot concludes that Donne and some of the others "are in the direct current of English poetry." He also notes that those who "tell us to 'look in our hearts and write'" do not look deep enough: "One must look into the cerebral cortex, the nervous system, and the digestive tracts."

In the following poem, rhymed *abbacdcdee* and using a stress-pattern of 4-2-5-5-4-4-5-5-5-5 in each stanza, John Donne plucks the sun

right out of the sky and positions it in his own bedroom. The images and rich complication of the poem show the love of the physical in metaphysical poetry.

THE SUN RISING / John Donne (1572-1631)

Busy old fool, unruly sun,
Why dost thou thus,
Through windows and through curtains call on us?
Must to thy motions lovers' seasons run?
Saucy pedantic wretch, go chide
Late school boys and sour prentices,
Go tell court huntsmen that the king will ride,
Call country ants to harvest offices;
Love, all alike, no season knows nor clime,
Nor hours, days, months, which are the rags of time.

Thy beams, so reverend and strong
Why shouldst thou think?
I could eclipse and cloud them with a wink,
But that I would not lose her sight so long;
If her eyes have not blinded thine,
Look, and tomorrow late tell me,
Whether both th' Indias of spice and mine
Be where thou leftst them, or lie here with me.
Ask for those kings whom thou saw'st yesterday,
And thou shalt hear, All here in one bed lay.

She's all states, and all princes, I,
Nothing else is.
Princes do but play us; compared to this,
All honor's mimic, all wealth alchemy.
Thou, sun, art half as happy as we,
In that the world's contracted thus;
Thine age asks ease, and since thy duties be
To warm the world, that's done in warming us.
Shine here to us, and thou art everywhere;
This bed thy center is, these walls, thy sphere.

Meter   1. The rhythmic measure of a line of verse. 2. The measure that a group of lines have in common, despite variations. 3. Poetry written in regular, measurable rhythms.

In English verse, there are essentially three elements that can be measured: accents or stresses, number of syllables, and length of syllables. The most common English meter, *accentual-syllabic verse, counts both accents and syllables. *Accentual verse counts only the accents or stresses. *Syllabic verse counts only the number of syllables. *Quantitative verse counts the length of syllables (long or short) as well as their number; although used by poets such as the Elizabethan poet-composer Thomas Campion, and suggested in *The Cantos* of American expatriate Ezra Pound, it is more of a feat or stunt in English than a viable meter; it is, however, the meter of ancient Greek poets such as Homer, Pindar, Sophocles, and Sappho.

"The Neural Lyre: Poetic Meter, the Brain, and Time," an essay by Frederick Turner and Ernst Pöppel, argues that there's a neurological basis—and need—for meter in poetry. They discuss "the three-second LINE . . . tuned to the three-second present moment of the auditory information-processing system." They assert that, in many different languages, a line of verse, however it may be measured, takes about three seconds to utter.

Other explanations of meter describe it as a "breath unit," a memory aid (especially in the oral tradition of bards like Homer), and a musical tempo (such as 3/4 time, the meter of a waltz). Meter imposes order, and hence can seem artificial. But the regularity can induce a kind of hypnotic state in reader or listener, casting a rhythmic spell. It affects the body in the same way music does. On the other hand, too much regularity can quickly become monotonous, tiresome, so poets try to use variation in their rhythms—much as a composer shapes a melody. A drumbeat may accentuate the 4/4 time of a song, but the melody will probably depart from a steady succession of quarter-notes. Instead, some notes will be shortened, some lengthened, and there may be pauses as well. The meter is merely the drumbeat. The actual words of the poem form the melody, which flows musically above the implied, mechanical, ticktock of the meter.

Metonymy *(mih-tón-uh-mee)* A figure of speech in which a thing is represented by something closely asociated with it, like "the White House" used to represent "the President of the United States."

Minor Ionic   A *double foot consisting of two unstressed syllables followed by two stressed syllables (a *pyrrhic and a *spondee, marked ˘ ˘ ′ ′). It is very common in English verse, probably because of phrases constructed as preposition-article-adjective-noun: "*In a dark time* I came into my own" (Theodore Roethke).

Monostich   (*món-uh-stik; Greek, "one line"*) A one-line stanza or poem. Many twentieth-century poets make use of one-line stanzas, either interspersed through a poem or at the end, where a single isolated line is especially emphatic. David St. John's "Iris," for example, begins with a monstitch—

> There is a train inside this iris:

and then alternates couplets and monostichs throughout the poem.

A poem that consists of a single isolated line can be a definition, an aphorism, an image, a fragment, a joke (responding to the title like a punchline), or the kind of inscription one might find on a tomb. But it must stand out, without the interplay and assistance that other lines could provide.

> BYGONES / Charles Wright (b. 1935)
>
> The rain has stopped falling asleep on its crystal stems.

Monosyllabic Foot   A stressed syllable that stands by itself, usually because an unstressed syllable has been omitted, either at the beginning of an iambic line (′ | ˘ ′ | ˘ ′ | ˘ ′ | ˘ ′), or the end of a trochaic line (′ ˘ | ′ ˘ | ′ ˘ | ′), or similarly in anapestic and dactylic lines, or within a line to create a pause, a surprise, or a syncopation ("springing" the line).

An unstressed syllable by itself is not really a foot, although it is very common because of the frequency of the *feminine ending. In scanning an iambic trimeter line with a feminine ending, such as "She's tied | it in | her ap- | ron" (from the anonymous ballad "Mary Hamilton"), the extra unstressed syllable is simply left hanging, like a tassel. One could conceivably scan the last foot as an *amphibrach ("hĕr áp-rŏn"), but this is not usually done.

Movement, The A group of British poets of the 1950s, including Philip Larkin, Donald Davie, Kingsley Amis, and the historian Robert Conquest, known for formal poetry, conservative views, skepticism, and wit. Conquest edited and introduced their work in the anthology *New Lines* (1957). These poets rejected the fragmentation and lyric intesity of Modernist poetry, aiming at an intelligent, compressed, often narrative style. The thrust of the Movement is anti-romantic.

COMING
Philip Larkin (1922-1985)

On longer evenings,
Light, chill and yellow,
Bathes the serene
Foreheads of houses.
A thrush sings,
Laurel-surrounded
In the deep bare garden,
Its fresh-peeled voice
Astonishing the brickwork.
It will be spring soon,
It will be spring soon—
And I, whose childhood
Is a forgotten boredom,
Feel like a child
Who comes on a scene
Of adult reconciling,
And can understand nothing
But the unusual laughter,
And starts to be happy.

Movements and Schools of Poetry Groups of poets banded together either to promote their ideas of what poetry should be—as well as their own poems—or to classify poetry that shares stylistic traits or the same historical period. Generally, the poets themselves organize the first kind of movement, while critics and scholars (who may in fact be poets) recognize the second. Movements led by poets who issued manifestoes and founded magazines include the *Black Mountain School, *Fugitives, *Imagists, *Language poets, *New Formalists, Objectivists (Louis Zukofsky and George Oppen),

*Pre-Raphaelites, and *Surrealists. Movements that may not have codified their programs but recognized their poetic comrades include the *Beats, *Confessional poets, *Deep Image poets, *The Movement, *New York School, *Sons of Ben, and *Symbolists.

Critics have named some historical movements long after the poets wrote, as Samuel Johnson (in *Lives of the Poets*, 1779-81) dubbed Abraham Cowley, John Donne, and similar seventeenth-century poets *Metaphysical. Other historical schools include Neoclassical Poetry (John Dryden and Alexander Pope), Romantic Poetry (William Wordsworth, John Keats, Percy Bysshe Shelley, Lord Byron), the Lake Poets (William Wordsworth, Samuel Taylor Coleridge, Robert Southey), the *Harlem Renaissance, and the Modernists (T.S. Eliot, Ezra Pound, Wallace Stevens, Gertrude Stein).

English poetry is often classified by the name of the reigning monarch, although there is necessarily much overlapping. Thus we have Tudor poetry, in particular that written during the reign of Henry VIII (Thomas Wyatt, Henry Howard, Earl of Surrey); Elizabethan (Edmund Spenser, Sir Philip Sidney, William Shakespeare, Christopher Marlowe); Jacobean, referring to King James I (Shakespeare, Donne, Ben Jonson); Victorian (Alfred, Lord Tennyson, Robert Browning); and Georgian (John Masefield, A.E. Housman, Edward Thomas).

Some movements, such as the *Pre-Raphaelite Brotherhood, Expressionism (Georg Trakl), Dada (Tristan Tzara), and Surrealism (Breton, Eluard, Desnos), are at least equally important as art movements. Surrealism grew out of Dada and Russian Futurism; it began with a manifesto by André Breton.

Movements are like political parties, publicity vehicles that go faster and hit harder than a lone stroller. But William Butler Yeats (himself a member of the Rhymers' Club of the 1890s and a Symbolist) declared, "Out of the quarrel with others we make rhetoric; out of the quarrel with ourselves we make poetry." Movements necessarily involve quarreling with others—the unenlightened, the hidebound, the enemy—and demand rhetoric.

The notion of "strength in numbers" does not necessarily work when it comes to poetic movements. Yeats remarked at a meeting of the Rhymers' Club, "There are too many of us." At best, a movement or school serves to draw attention to deserving work, to persuade

poets to write more inventively, to show readers how to read more attentively, and to change (or restore) the way we look at poetry and the world itself. At worst, a movement bullies in the name of self-aggrandizement, like a literary street gang.

Yeats also says, "All movements are held together more by what they hate than by what they love, for love separates and individualises and quiets, but the nobler movements, the only movements on which literature can found itself, hate great and lasting things." One could argue, for example, that Ezra Pound's *Imagism was based largely upon a hatred of the rhetoric, Latinization, Puritanism, loftiness, manhandled syntax, thunderous blank verse, and sheer length of John Milton's *Paradise Lost*.

Muse 1. The spirit, force, or person that inspires or impels a poet to create.

2. The deity which epic poets such as Homer invoke at the beginning of their poems, specifically one of the Greek goddesses, daughter of Mnemosyne (or Memory), who spoke through the artists she inspired.

Like other epic poems, *The Odyssey* begins with an invocation to the muse (translated here by Robert Fitzgerald):

> Sing in me, Muse, and through me tell the story
> of that man skilled in all ways of contending,
> the wanderer, harried for years on end,
> after he plundered the stronghold
> on the proud height of Troy.

The Greeks recognized nine muses, associated with different arts or sciences: Calliope (epic poetry), Clio (history), Erato (love poetry), Euterpe (lyric poetry), Melpomene (tragedy), Polyhymnia (songs to the gods), Terpsichore (dance), Thalia (comedy), and Urania (astronomy).

In a lecture on "professional standards in English poetry," Robert Graves defines the responsibility of poets:

> the desire to deserve well of the Muse, their divine patroness,
> from whom they receive their unwritten commissions, to

whom they eat their solitary dinners, who confers her silent benediction on them, to whom they swear their secret Hippocratic oath, to whose moods they are as attentive as the stockbroker is to his market.

More specifically, the poet finds this divine inspirer in the bodily form of the beloved, the "personal Muse for whom he has written the poem."

Music Poem   A poem that deals with music in some way, imitating a musical form or a work of music, narrating the lives of real or imaginary musicians, or perhaps examining musical instruments. Of course, many poems consist of words meant to be sung, either written for a particular melody or set to music by a composer.

In one of the following poems, Paul Celan imitates the repetitive form of the fugue. In this intricate musical form, one voice or instrument states a melodic phrase; when a second voice enters and takes up the original melody, the first voice moves on to a new melody that harmonizes with the old one; more voices come in, and the accumulating melodies interweave, repeat, turn themselves upside down, change from major to minor and back again, and perform all sorts of sonic gymnastics. Similar to the fugue is the round, like "Row, row, row your boat." Johann Sebastian Bach wrote the greatest fugues, including a musical treatise, *The Art of Fugue*. The effect is more or less impossible in poetry, since a fugue is polyphonic (several melodies occurring simultaneously), but it can be suggested through patterns of repetition. Dana Gioia's "Lives of the Great Composers" and Weldon Kees' "Round" are other poems that imitate the contrapuntal techniques of music.

In his translation of Celan's "Deathfugue," John Felstiner adds a musical device to the fugue-like recurrences and recombinations of the original. His version gradually switches certain English words back into German, an effect like modulating to a different key in music. These changes are clear and simple, "master" to "Meister," for example. Paradoxically, they reinforce the sense of repetition, simply because we notice the metamorphosis of the words. In a poem about the Holocaust, switching back to German suggests the brutal power of the Nazis. But it also leads the reader back to the original words of Paul Celan, who was both German and Jewish. Felstiner devotes a

chapter of his book *Paul Celan: Poet, Survivor, Jew* to "Todesfuge."

Michael S. Harper's poem below captures the syncopation of John Coltrane's jazz masterpiece, *A Love Supreme*. Another jazz poem, Michael Stillman's "In Memoriam John Coltrane," uses a *haiku stanza as the basis for its riffs. More poems about jazz musicians, meditations on jazz, and improvisations based on jazz appear in *The Jazz Poetry Anthology* (1991), edited by Sascha Feinstein and Yusef Komunyakaa.

Donald Justice, who studied musical composition with Carl Ruggles, has written many music poems, including two "sonatinas" and *The Sunset Maker*, a book of verse and prose centered around music and memories of the study of music:

> One small, tight fist clutching the dread Czerny.
> Back then time was still harmony, not money.

As Ezra Pound remarks, the poet should "behave as a musician, a good musician, when dealing with that phase of [his] art which has exact parallels in music." (*See: blues, song, spiritual.*)

DEATHFUGUE / Paul Celan (1920-1970; tr. John Felstiner)

Black milk of daybreak we drink it at evening
we drink it at midday and morning we drink it at night
we drink and we drink
we shovel a grave in the air there you won't lie too cramped
A man lives in the house he plays with his vipers he writes
he writes when it grows dark to Deutschland your golden hair
    Margareta
he writes it and steps out of doors and the stars are all sparkling
    he whistles his hounds to come close
he whistles his Jews into rows has them shovel a grave in the ground
he commands us play up for the dance

Black milk of daybreak we drink you at night
we drink you at morning and midday we drink you at evening
we drink and we drink
A man lives in the house he plays with his vipers he writes
he writes when it grows dark to Deutschland your golden hair
    Margareta

Your ashen hair Shulamith we shovel a grave in the air there you
    won't lie too cramped

He shouts jab this earth deeper you lot there you others sing up
    and play
he grabs for the rod in his belt he swings it his eyes are so blue
jab your spades deeper you lot there you others play on for the
    dancing

Black milk of daybreak we drink you at night
we drink you at midday and morning we drink you at evening
we drink and we drink
a man lives in the house your goldenes Haar Margareta
your aschenes Haar Shulamith he plays with his vipers

He shouts play death more sweetly this Death is a master from
    Deutschland
he shouts scrape your strings darker you'll rise then as smoke to
    the sky
you'll have a grave then in the clouds there you won't lie too
    cramped

Black milk of daybreak we drink you at night
we drink you at midday Death is a master aus Deutschland
we drink you at evening and morning we drink and we drink
this Death is ein Meister aus Deutschland his eye it is blue
he shoots you with shot made of lead shoots you level and true
a man lives in the house your goldenes Haar Margarete
he looses his hounds on us grants us a grave in the air
he plays with his vipers and daydreams der Tod ist ein Meister aus
    Deutschland

dein goldenes Haar Margarete
dein aschenes Haar Shulamith

DEAR JOHN, DEAR COLTRANE
Michael S. Harper (b. 1938)

a love supreme, a love supreme
a love supreme, a love supreme

Sex fingers toes
in the marketplace
near your father's church

in Hamlet, North Carolina—
witness to this love
in this calm fallow
of these minds,
there is no substitute for pain:
genitals gone or going,
seed burned out,
you tuck the roots in the earth,
turn back, and move
by river through the swamps,
singing: a love supreme, a love supreme;
what does it all mean?
Loss, so great each black
woman expects your failure
in mute change, the seed gone.
You plod up into the electric city—
your song now crystal and
the blues. You pick up the horn
with some will and blow
into the freezing night:
a love supreme, a love supreme—

Dawn comes and you cook
up the thick sin 'tween
impotence and death, fuel
the tenor sax cannibal
heart, genitals and sweat
that makes you clean—
a love supreme, a love supreme—

Why you so black?
cause I am
why you so funky?
cause I am
why you so black?
cause I am
why you so sweet?
cause I am
why you so black?
cause I am
a love supreme, a love supreme:

So sick
you couldn't play *Naima*,
so flat we ached
for song you'd concealed
with your own blood,
your diseased liver gave
out its purity,
the inflated heart
pumps out, the tenor kiss,
tenor love:
a love supreme, a love supreme—
a love supreme, a love supreme—

Myth *(Greek, "a fable")*   Fantastic stories that explain some puzzle of nature—human or cosmic. Myths are the tales we live by, the talismans we wear around our necks and touch for luck, passed along from generation to generation or made up individually as we go along. They can be cultural artifacts (like the myth of Orpheus descending to Hades to rescue his love, Eurydice, but then losing her as he glances back). Or they can be what we conjure up or fantasize to help us live our lives, to find our way out of a psychological labyrinth (as the Greek hero Theseus did).

Poets can retell known myths, interpreting and changing them, or they can invent new ones. Often, though, the poet simply alludes to myth in the course of a poem, invoking the ancient stories, hauling a big catch out of the depths.

EURYDICE / Linda Gregg (b. 1942)

I linger, knowing you are eager (having seen
the strange world where I live)
to return to your friends
wearing the bells and singing the songs
which are my mourning.
With the water in them, with their strange rhythms.
I know you will not take me back.
Will take me almost to the world,
but not out to house, color, leaves.
Not to the sacred world that is so easy
for you, my love.

Myth

Inside my mind and in my body is a darkness
which I am equal to, but my heart is not.
Yesterday you read the Troubadour poets
in the bathroom doorway
while I painted my eyes for the journey.
While I took tiredness away from my face,
you read of that singer in a garden
with the woman he swore to love forever.

You were always curious what love is like.
Wanted to meet me, not bring me home.
Now you whistle, putting together
the new words, learning the songs
to tell the others how far you traveled for me.
Singing of my desire to live.

Oh, if you knew what you do not know
I could be in the world remembering this.
I did not cry as much in the darkness
as I will when we part in the dimness
near the opening which is the way in for you
and was the way out for me, my love.

N

Narrative Poetry   Poetry that tells a story. It is one of the three main genres of poetry (the others being *dramatic poetry and *lyric poetry).

Narrative poetry presents characters and leads them through a plot. Its oldest form is the *epic, such as Homer's *Iliad*. Traditional ballads are also narrative. "The Demon Lover," for example, tells the story of a woman who is seduced and taken away by a man who changes into a demon as soon as their ship reaches the high seas; he sinks the ship to the bottom. The rise of the prose novel diverted more and more of the narrative impulse away from poetry, but some late-twentieth-century poets, such as Louis Simpson, Andrew Hudgins, and Jimmy Santiago Baca, have tried to bring storytelling back into verse.

Nashers   A light-verse form, invented by Ogden Nash, in which lines ranging from very short to (more often) extremely long rhyme comically in couplets.

Some of those comic rhymes will inevitably be *wrenched rhymes*, which the poet forces in some way to fit with the other rhymes. To wrench a rhyme, the poet can simply match words that sound off-key (not quite close enough to take seriously), or alter the spelling of the one rhyme word so that it stumbles into alignment with the other, or add unexpected suffixes—all so that the second rhyme more closely resembles its mate, as in this couplet from Nash's "Kindly Unhitch that Star, Buddy":

> Some people think they will eventually wear diamonds instead of
> rhinestones
> Only by everlastingly keeping their noses to their ghrinestones.

In the same poem, he also rhymes "failure"/"azalea," "seraphim"/ "sheriffim," and "correspondence"/"brunettance and blondance." The effect is like poetic slapstick, as if a line of rambling prose slipped on a banana peel (the rhyme word and its line break) and fell splat on the floor (the rhyme—any which way you can).

New Formalism   A movement that arose in the 1980s to revive formal verse, with the intention of reaching out to a wider public and rejecting the limits of the academy.

Some poets, such as Richard Wilbur and James Merrill, had continued to write rhymed, metrical poems through the period dominated by *free verse (beginning in the late 1950s). But the New Formalists, according to Dana Gioia, "put free-verse poets in the ironic and uncomfortable position of being the *status quo*. Free verse, the creation of an older literary revolution, is now the long-established, ruling orthodoxy; formal poetry the unexpected challenge." In addition to Gioia himself, New Formalist poets include Charles Martin, Timothy Steele, Molly Peacock, R.S. Gwynn, Julia Alvarez, and Gjertrud Schnackenberg.

A related movement, the New Narrative, calls for a return to storytelling in verse. Mark Jarman and Robert McDowell have offered a checklist of what a successful New Narrative poem requires: a beginning, middle, and end; observation; compression of time; containment; illumination of private gestures; understatement; humor; location; memorable characters; a compelling subject. New Narrative poets include David Mason, Frederick Turner, Andrew Hudgins, and Dick Allen. *Expansive Poetry*, an anthology edited by Frederick Feirstein, contains important essays by poets of both movements.

THE NEXT POEM / Dana Gioia (b. 1950)

How much better it seems now
than when it is finally done—
the unforgettable first line,
the cunning way the stanzas run.

The rhymes soft-spoken and suggestive
are barely audible at first,
an appetite not yet acknowledged
like the inkling of a thirst.

While gradually the form appears
as each line is coaxed aloud—
the architecture of a room
seen from the middle of a crowd.

The music that of common speech
but slanted so that each detail
sounds unexpected as a sharp
inserted in a simple scale.

No jumble box of imagery
dumped glumly in the reader's lap
or elegantly packaged junk
the unsuspecting must unwrap.

But words that could direct a friend
precisely to an unknown place,
those few unshakeable details
that no confusion can erase.

And the real subject left unspoken
but unmistakable to those
who don't expect a jungle parrot
in the black and white of prose.

How much better it seems now
than when it is finally written.
How hungrily one waits to feel
the bright lure seized, the old hook bitten.

WHERE IS HOME? / Molly Peacock (b. 1947)

Our homes are on our backs and don't forget it.
But we don't stay in them; we think them.
Homes are from our minds. Once I tried to fit,
repairing through remembering, the stem
of a favorite glass back on its head. No loss.
A man in dirty overalls swung down
from his truck grabbing the bag of shards to toss
into the maw of his truck. To me he was a clown
reaching a powdered hand into the garbage bag
and plucking out the glass intact. Thus in my mind
I'd everything I had. And please tag

along home with me now. The paths are blind
with wet new grass behind the rusty gate
where my low blurry child home lies in state.

New York School   A group of poets first active in New York City in
the 1950s.

Trumpeted by Donald Allen's anthology, *The New American Poetry,
1945-1960*, the New York School paralleled the Abstract-
Expressionist painters of the Manhattan art scene in the 1950s,
especially the "action painters" like Jackson Pollock, who flung and
dribbled paint at canvases laid out flat on the floor. The best-known
"New York" poets include Frank O'Hara, John Ashbery, Kenneth
Koch, and James Schuyler. Their work differs greatly, but they are
all daring, funny, passionate, casual. *Free verse predominates their
work.

The following poem shows the breezy style and the interest in
popular culture typical of the New York School. But the voice is unmis-
takably Frank O'Hara's, hip and urban, funny and emotional and knowing. He would call it an "I do this, I do that" poem. As he says in his
mock manifesto, "Personism," a poet "goes on his nerves."

POEM / Frank O'Hara (1926-1966)

Lana Turner has collapsed!
I was trotting along and suddenly
it started raining and snowing
and you said it was hailing
but hailing hits you on the head
hard so it was really snowing and
raining and I was in such a hurry
to meet you but the traffic
was acting exactly like the sky
and suddenly I see a headline
LANA TURNER HAS COLLAPSED!
there is no snow in Hollywood
there is no rain in California
I have been to lots of parties
and acted perfectly disgraceful
but I never actually collapsed
oh Lana Turner we love you get up

Nonce Form   A poetic form invented for a particular poem.

Fixed forms necessarily begin as nonce forms, although their origins may be murky and undiscernible. However, the *villanelle as we know it began with a pattern invented by Jean Passerat; earlier villanelles, including his own, had simply been imitations of Italian country songs using refrains but with no fixed pattern. The popularity of Passerat's arrangement hardened a nonce form into a fixed form.

A more recent example is the three-stanza form John Berryman devised for his sequence *The Dream Songs*: "eighteen-line sections, three six-line stanzas, each normally (for feet) 5-5-3-5-5-3, variously rhymed and not but mostly rhymed with great strictness."

Nonsense Verse   Playful verse whose words seem to resist ordinary understanding.

Here is a celebrated example of nonsense verse, the first stanza of Lewis Carroll's "Jabberwocky" (1855):

> 'Twas brillig, and the slithy toves
>   Did gyre and gimble in the wabe;
> All mimsy were the borogroves,
>   And the mome raths outgrabe.

Although both Carroll himself and Humpty Dumpty (in *Through the Looking Glass*, 1871) supply glosses for these words, the pleasure in reading and remembering the poem comes not from a translation into the commonplace but from a reveling in the funny, peculiar language.

Carroll's contemporary, Edward Lear, is the other great nineteenth-century master of nonsense verse. But the uses of nonsense stretch back to the *mad-song stanza and to the mad scenes in Shakespeare's *Hamlet* and forward to Modernist experimenters such as Gertrude Stein and James Joyce, Wallace Stevens and Theodore Roethke. Karl Shapiro has even remarked that the "meaning of poetry, as far as language is concerned, is the meaning of *hey-nonny-nonny*"—a popular Elizabethan nonsense phrase.

Nursery Rhyme   A poem or song, typically attributed to Mother Goose, full of rhymes, strong rhythms, and nonsense, telling stories of kingdoms and farms and families.

Nursery rhymes include "Jack and Jill," "Old Mother Hubbard," and "Little Boy Blue." In "Some Remarks on Rhythm," Theodore Roethke writes, "What do *I* like? Listen:

> Hinx, minx, the old witch winks!
> The fat begins to fry!
> There's nobody home but Jumping Joan,
> And father, and mother, and I.'"

In a letter of 1878, Gerard Manley Hopkins discusses *sprung rhythm (which is meter scanned "by accents or stresses alone, without any account of the number of syllables, so that a foot may be one strong syllable or it may be many light and one strong"); he quotes from nursery rhymes to demonstrate this principle: "Here are instances—'Díng, dóng, béll; Pússy's ín the wéll; Whó pút her ín? Líttle Jóhnny Thín. Whó púlled her oút? Líttle Jóhnny Stóut.' For if each line has three stresses or three feet it follows that some of the feet are of one syllable only. So too 'Óne, twó, Búckle my shóe'. . . ."

The poem below by Donald Justice imitates the following nursery rhyme (which traditionally accompanies the tugging and tickling of a child's toes):

> This little piggy went to market,
> This little piggy stayed home,
> This little piggy had roast beef,
> This little piggy had none,
> And this little piggy cried Wee! Wee! Wee! Wee!
> All the way home.

The playfulness of these lines comes from the nonsense (how the piggies lead mundane human lives) and the listing.

COUNTING THE MAD
Donald Justice (b. 1925)

This one was put in a jacket,
This one was sent home,
This one was given bread and meat
But would eat none,

And this one cried No No No No
All day long.

This one looked at the window
As though it were a wall,
This one saw things that were not there,
This one things that were,
And this one cried No No No No
All day long.

This one thought himself a bird,
This one a dog,
And this one thought himself a man,
An ordinary man,
And cried and cried No No No No
All day long.

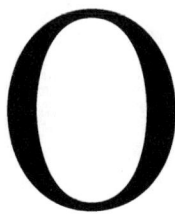

Object Poem A poem about an inanimate object. It may give us a fresh look at something ordinary, or it may transform a strange object into something familiar.

The term is a translation of the German "Dinggedicht," or "thing poem," and some of the best object poems are by Rainer Maria Rilke, such as his "Archaic Torso of Apollo." Charles Simic's "Fork" has two companion poems, "Knife" and "The Spoon."

A NAVAJO BLANKET
May Swenson (1919-1989)

Eye-dazzlers the Indians weave. Three colors
are paths that pull you in, and pin you
to the maze. Brightness makes your eyes jump,
surveying the geometric field. Alight, and enter
any of the gates—of Blue, of Red, of Black.
Be calmed and hooded, a hawk brought down,
glad to fasten to the forearm of a Chief.

You can sleep at the center,
attended by Sun that never fades, by Moon
that cools. Then, slipping free of zigzag and
hypnotic diamond, find your way out
by the spirit trail, a faint Green thread that
secretly crosses the border, where your mind
is rinsed and returned to you like a white cup.

FORK / Charles Simic (b. 1938)

This strange thing must have crept
Right out of hell.
It resembles a bird's foot
Worn around the cannibal's neck.

As you hold it in your hand,
As you stab with it into a piece of meat,
It is possible to imagine the rest of the bird:
Its head which like your fist
Is large, bald, beakless and blind.

Objective Correlative   T.S. Eliot's term for a set of specific objects (images and actions) that will evoke a specific, correlated emotion in the reader. In an essay on Shakespeare's *Hamlet* (1919), Eliot defined it as "a set of objects, a situation, a chain of events which shall be the formula of that *particular* emotion; such that when the external facts, which must terminate in sensory experience, are given, the emotion is immediately evoked."

Occasional Verse   Poem written to commemorate an occasion; a poem commissioned by someone to celebrate some happening, like the Olympian *odes of Pindar or the coronation ode by a poet laureate.

The term is often used dismissively to label a poem as a kind of "work for hire," inspired not by imagination but by something external. However, real poems do arise out of (and for) particular occasions. Dylan Thomas, for example, wrote poems for his birthday. It matters, perhaps, who does the choosing. Ellen Bryant Voigt's "The Last Class" begins:

> Put this in your notebooks:
> All verse is occasional verse.

Occasional verse might also be written on the spur of the moment, about a time of day, for a birthday or a holiday, for a day of the week— anything that represents a quick sketch of the ephemeral, of time fleeing.

Octave *(Latin, "eight")*   An eight-line stanza. An octave serves as the first eight lines of a Petrarchan (or Italian) *sonnet, rhymed *abbaabba*. When used as a stanza in its own right, it is called a brace octave, and can also rhyme *abbacddc*. A common octave rhymes *ababcdcd* or leaves the odd-numbered lines unrhymed: *XaXaXbXb*. *Ottava rima, which Lord Byron uses in *Don Juan*, rhymes *abababcc*. (*See: triolet*.)

Ode   1. A song or lyric, often passionate, expansive, exuberant, rhapsodic.

2. A poem in any of several song-like forms:

• Pindaric or choral ode (used by the Greek poet Pindar and Greek playwrights such as Sophocles): written in triads of three stanzas, a *strophe and antistrophe that are metrically identical followed by an epode that diverges in its meter; the ode may have one or more triads. Wayne Koestenbaum's "Ode to Anna Moffo" is a recent Pindaric ode.

• Horatian ode (as used by or modeled after the Roman poet Horace): regular matching stanzas or metrical units; often in *quatrains such as the *Sapphic stanza, the *Alcaic stanza, or Andrew Marvell's quatrain in "An Horatian Ode upon Cromwell's Return from Ireland" (two iambic tetrameter lines followed by two iambic trimeter lines, rhymed *aabb*):

> 'Tis time to leave the Books in dust,
> And oyl th' unused Armours rust:
> Removing from the Wall
> The Corslet of the Hall.

NOTE: *corslet*: armor, breastplate

John Keats' odes are Horatian in that the stanzas in any given ode have the same number of lines. "Ode on a Grecian Urn" and "Ode to a Nightingale," for example, consist of ten-line stanzas rhymed *ababcdecde*.

• Cowleyan or Irregular ode (also "False Pindaric"; named after Abraham Cowley [1618-1667]): lines of irregular length and irregular rhyme scheme, stanzas (if any) not matching each other in meter, line length, or rhyme; free to be anything but regular. Here is the second stanza of Cowley's "Ode upon Doctor Harvey." The "she" of

this stanza stands for "Coy Nature," pursued by the heroic Dr. Harvey, who discovered the movement of the bloodstream:

> Here sure shall I be safe (said she,)
> None will be able sure to see
> This my retreat, but only He
> Who made both it and me.
> The heart of Man, what Art can e'er reveal?
> A Wall impervious between
> Divides the very parts within,
> And doth the very Heart of Man ev'n from itself conceal.
> She spoke, but e're she was aware,
> *Harvey* was with her there,
> And held this slippery *Proteus* in a chain,
> Till all her mighty Mysteries she descry'd,
> Which from his Wit th' attempt before to hide
> Was the first Thing that Nature did in vain.

The rhyme scheme is *aaaabccbddeffe*; the pattern of iambic feet in the lines is 4-4-4-3-5-4-4-7-4-3-5-5-5-5 (not like any of the ode's other four stanzas). If each stanza followed this pattern, the ode would be Horatian; if the first two stanzas followed it but every third one diverged, the ode would be Pindaric. (Proteus, incidentally, was a Greek god who changed his shape; captured and held long enough, he would stop metamorphosing and reveal the truth, as Nature reveals the circulatory system to Dr. Harvey.)

William Wordsworth's "Ode: Intimations of Immortality from Recollections of Early Childhood" is perhaps the best-known Cowleyan ode. Here are the first two of its eleven stanzas (each with its own rhyme scheme, number of feet for different lines, and indented shape):

> There was a time when meadow, grove and stream, *a* 5
> The earth, and every common sight, *b* 4
> To me did seem *a* 2
> Appareled in celestial light, *b* 4
> The glory and the freshness of a dream. *a* 5
> It is not now as it hath been of yore; *c* 5
> Turn whereso'er I may, *d* 3
> By night or day, *d* 2
> The things which I have seen I now can see no more. *c* 6

The Rainbow comes and goes,	*a*	*3*
And lovely is the Rose,	*a*	*3*
The Moon doth with delight	*b*	*3*
Look round her when the heavens are bare,	*c*	*4*
Waters on a starry night	*b*	*3/4*
Are beautiful and fair;	*c*	*3*
The sunshine is a glorious birth;	*d*	*4*
But yet I know, where'er I go,	*e/e*	*4*
That there hath passed away a glory from the earth.	*d*	*6*

The letters above show how the rhyme schemes differ, while the numbers count the feet in each line. Although these stanzas happen to contain the same number of lines (nine), the other stanzas contain seventeen, twenty-two, twenty, eight, twenty-three, twenty-one, thirty-nine, nineteen, and seventeen lines.

• Elemental ode (invented by Pablo Neruda, sometimes translated as "elementary ode"): short-lined free-verse poems about everyday things; passionate and rhapsodic about the ordinary, lavishing attention and affection on subjects such as watermelons.

The term *ode* is now used very loosely. A sense of rapture, elevation, mystical oneness with nature, and "the voice of the bard" typify poems like Walt Whitman's "Out of the Cradle Endlessly Rocking" and Dylan Thomas' "Fern Hill." In odes the poet usually comments on—and praises—things apart from himself, even though the ostensible subject may be his own childhood.

OLYMPIA 4 / Pindar
(518 or 522-438 or 442 B.C.; tr. Richmond Lattimore)

Mightiest driver of the weariless speed in the lightning's
   feet,
Zeus: the circling Hours, your own,
have brought me to testify
to highest achievements   *strophe*
by virtue of song and the lyre's intricacy.
At friends' good luck the noble will rise to welcome
the sweet message.

O son of Kronos, lord of Aitna,
blast-furnace to hundred-headed Typhon's bulk,
in the name of the Graces
accept this song of Olympic victory,

light at long last from the wide strength of valor.
For it rides the wheels of Psaumis,
who, his brow shaded in olive
of Pisa, comes home, bringing glory   *antistrophe*
on Kamarina. May God be kindly
to his prayers hereafter; I have praise for him.
A keen handler of horses,
he rejoices in hospitality to his friends;
and his face, with clean purpose, is turned toward Concord,
    who loves cities.
I will not steep my speech
in lies; the test of any man lies in action.

So the son of Klymenos
was set free from being scorned
by Lemnian women.
As he won the race in bronze armor   *epode*
and came to Hypsipyle for his garland, he spoke:
"Here am I in my speed.
My hands are as good as my heart.
Many a time even on young men gray hairs
appear, against the likelihood of their youth."

NOTE: *son of Kronos*: Zeus, king of the gods, wielder of lightning; *Aitna*: Mt. Etna in Sicily; *Typhon*: a flame-breathing giant under Mt. Etna; *Psaumis of Kamarina, Sicily*: the victor celebrated by Pindar in this ode; winner of chariot race in the Olympian games of 452 B.C.; *son of Klymenos*: Erginos, one of Jason's Argonauts; *Lemnos*: island in northern Aegean Sea; *Hypsipyle*: Queen of the Lemnian women.

ODES, Book I, ix
Horace (65-8 B.C.; tr. John Frederick Nims)

You see how, white with snows to the north of us,
Soracte looms; how snow's over everything;
    the burdened pines no longer buoyant,
        streams at a stand in the winter weather.
So, rout the cold! Load logs on the andirons

as good hosts should do. Logs! And no rationing
　　your wine, young fellow there! Your Sabine,
　　　　hustle it out from the crusty wine-jars.
Then let the heavens see to the rest of it.
When once they've lulled the winds at their weltering
　　on whitened surf, no cypress quivers,
　　　　never a breath in the ancient alder.
What comes tomorrow, never you mind about.
Each day on waking reckon, "Another!" and
　　chalk up your one more gain. Don't spurn the
　　　　pleasure of love in your time for dancing,
while youth's in bloom, while moody decrepitude's
remote. Now haunt the malls and the stadium.
　　When little whispers stir in starlight,
　　　　make very sure you arrange to be there,
where—who's in hiding?—giveaway laughter from
the dark, a girl's laugh, muffled . . . lovely . . .
　　her bracelet tussled for in fun, or
　　　　ring from a teasingly tightened finger.

NOTE: This ode uses the Alcaic stanza.

ODE TO SALT / Pablo Neruda
(1904-1973; tr. Robert Bly)

I saw the salt
in this shaker
in the salt flats.
I know
you
will never believe me,
but
it sings,
the salt sings, the hide
of the salt plains,
it sings
through a mouth smothered
by earth.
I shuddered in those deep
solitudes
when I heard

the voice
of
the salt
in the desert.
Near Antofagasta
the entire
salt plain
speaks:
it is a
broken
voice,
a song full
of grief.
Then in its own mines
rock salt, a mountain
of buried light,
a cathedral through which light passes,
crystal of the sea, abandoned
by the waves.

And then on every table
on this earth,
salt,
your nimble
body
pouring out
the vigorous light
over
our foods.
Preserver
of the stores
of the ancient ships,
you were
an explorer
in the ocean,
substance
going first
over the unknown, barely open
routes of the sea-foam.
Dust of the sea, the tongue
receives a kiss

of the night sea from you:
taste recognizes
the ocean in each salted morsel,
and therefore the smallest,
the tiniest
wave of the shaker
brings home to us
not only your domestic whiteness
but the inward flavor of the infinite.

Omar Khayyam Stanza *(also called Omar stanza)* A *quatrain rhymed aaXa, derived from Edward Fitzgerald's 1859 paraphrase of *The Rubáiyát of Omar Khayyám* (12th Century). Here is the opening quatrain:

Wake! For the Sun, who scattered into flight
The Stars before him from the Field of Night,
    Drives Night along with them from Heav'n, and strikes
The Sultán's Turret with a Shaft of Light.

Onomatopoeia *(áhn-uh-mah-tuh-pée-uh; Greek, "Making a name")* The use of a word that imitates the sound of what the word means, like *splat, sizzle, buzz* and *puff.*

Expressive sound effects, such as onomatopoeia, have an important place in poetry. In a passage from "An Essay on Criticism," Alexander Pope says:

The sound must seem an echo to the sense.
Soft is the strain when Zephyr gently blows,
And the smooth stream in smoother numbers flows;
But when loud surges lash the sounding shore,
The hoarse, rough verse should like the torrent roar.
When Ajax strives some rock's vast weight to throw,
The line too labors, and the words move slow . . .

The "smooth stream" of words is called euphony *(yóo-fuh-nee; Greek, "sounding well")*: mellifluous sound, pretty noise, a smooth, pleasant, and harmonious flow of words. The "hoarse, rough" words are called cacophony *(kuh-káh-fuh-nee; Greek, "sounding ill")*: unpleasant sound,

a jangle of clashing words, what the Elizabethan songwriter John Dowland calls "hellish, jarring sounds."

Ottava Rima *(aw-táh-vuh rée-muh; Italian, eighth rhyme)* Eight-line stanza form, in which the iambic pentameter lines rhyme *abababcc.*

Adapted, perhaps, from the Sicilian *strambotto* (discussed in the *sonnet entry), ottava rima is credited to Boccaccio in fourteenth-century Italy. It became the heroic form of Italian poetry, used in Ariosto's *Orlando Furioso* and Tasso's *Jerusalem Delivered.* Thomas Wyatt was the first English poet to use ottava rima frequently.

The stanza is flexible and potent, the first two rhyme sounds alternating three times and followed by the "bang" of a couplet using a third rhyme sound. It gives a wonderful sense of buildup and completion, equally suitable for the comic and the serious. Lord Byron's ottava rima stanzas in *Don Juan* are generally humorous, partly because he often uses preposterous, polysyllabic rhymes, usually in the final couplets, as in the following lines from Canto IV:

> Here I might enter on a chaste description,
>   Having withstood temptation in my youth,
> But hear that several people take exception
>   At the first two books having too much truth;
> Therefore I'll make Don Juan leave the ship soon,
>   Because the publisher declares, in sooth,
> Through needles' eyes it easier for the camel is
> To pass, than those two cantos into families.

The example below, which Byron calls "a mere speculation," is not so jocular (though humor is still present in his brief rethinking of Hamlet's soliloquy). William Butler Yeats' stanzas in ottava rima, on the other hand, always sound serious and stately. He uses the form for many of his meditations, including "Among School Children," "The Circus Animals' Desertion," and "Sailing to Byzantium."

> from *DON JUAN* (Canto XIV, 4-6)
> George Gordon, Lord Byron (1788-1824)
>
> A sleep without dreams, after a rough day
>   Of toil, is what we covet most; and yet
> How clay shrinks back from more quiescent clay!

The very Suicide that pays his debt
At once without instalments (an old way
    Of paying debts, which creditors regret)
Lets out impatiently his rushing breath,
Less from disgust of life than dread of death.

'Tis round him, near him, here, there, every where;
    And there's a courage which grows out of fear,
Perhaps of all most desperate, which will dare
    The worst to *know* it:—when the mountains rear
Their peaks beneath your human foot, and there
    You look down o'er the precipice, and drear
The gulf of rock yawns,—you can't gaze a minute
Without an awful wish to plunge within it.

'Tis true, you don't—but, pale and struck with terror,
    Retire: but look into your past impression!
And you will find, though shuddering at the mirror
    Of your own thoughts, in all their self confession,
The lurking bias, be it truth or error,
    To the *unknown*; a secret prepossession,
To plunge with all your fears—but where? You know not,
And that's the reason why you do—or do not.

Oulipo *(oo-lee-póe; acronym for "Ouvroir de littérature potentielle,"* ouvroir *meaning a "workroom in a convent,"* littérature potentielle *meaning "potential literature")*   A poetic movement founded in 1960 by a group of poets and mathematicians, led by Raymond Queneau.

This group explored a number of existing, game-like poetic forms, such as the *sestina (which uses six "end-words," in place of rhymes, in a set order through six stanzas), *cento (poem composed from passages taken from other poets), and *rhopalic verse, which they also call "snowball" (lines in which each word has one syllable more than the previous word, such as "I disdain rhopalic composition unrepentently"). A "melting snowball" would go in the opposite direction, from words of many syllables (or letters) to monosyllabic or one-letter words ("O!"). Here are some of the other forms used by the Oulipo poets:

• holorhyming verse: line in which every syllable must rhyme (for example, "Why sigh, I cry, my sly, shy guy?");

- lipogram: text that does not use certain letters (for example, the poet might eschew or eliminate any words containing the letter "s");
- permutational poem: verse in which the lines can be read in any order;
- tautogram: text in which each word begins with the same letter (like the "A" chapters of Walter Abish's novel *Alphabetical Africa*).

The Oulipo poets also experimented with computer generation of texts and created a number of new poetic forms:

- antonymic translation: a method in which antonyms are substituted for the words of a text, transforming an utterance into its opposite;
- Boolean poem: text that uses the words common to two selected poems to generate a new poem; considering those two poems a "set," the poet draws words from their "intersection";
- Haikuization: a method by which the poet keeps the rhyming parts of a poem but gets rid of the rest, so that the last stanza of Yeats' "Sailing to Byzantium" might become "Never take/ any natural thing./ Make/ enameling/ awake./ Sing/ of Byzantium/ to come."
- perverb: a mixing of the first half of one proverb with the second half of another, such as "The Lord helps those who / gather no moss" or "Still waters / starve a fever"; the word perverb does the same thing: per(verted pro)verb.
- S + 7: a transformation method by which the poet replaces each noun (substantive) in a text with the seventh noun after it in a dictionary. Andrew Marvell's "Had we but world enough, and time,/ This coyness, lady, were no crime" might become, through the S + 7 method, "Had we but worry enough, and timeserver,/ This crab, laetrile, were no crinoline." The results depend upon the dictionary and the accuracy of the noun-counter.

The Oulipo poets are interested in exploiting most rhetorical devices (see *figures of classical rhetoric*) and in word oddities such as palindromes (a sentence that reads the same frontward and backward, such as "Madam, I'm Adam"), portmanteau words (which combine part of one word with part of another, as Lewis Carroll, who coined the term, combined "chuckle" and "snort" to invent "chortle"), and spoonerisms (the switching of initial sounds between nearby words, named after the Reverend W.A. Spooner, 1844-1930, who once said in a sermon, "Our Lord is indeed a shoving leopard"). More of their

methods appear in *Oulipo: A Primer of Potential Literature*, edited by Warren F. Motte, Jr.

Oxymoron *(ok-see-móre-on; Greek, "sharp" + "dull, foolish")* An expression that combines opposite, contradictory qualities, seemingly nonsensical but capturing some psychological or emotional extreme of ambivalence. Romeo's complaint to Benvolio in Act I, Scene I of *Romeo and Juliet* is a good example: "Feather of lead, bright smoke, cold fire, sick health!"

P

Painting Poem Poetry that imitates, describes, critiques, dramatizes, or reflects upon a painting.

Although paintings may be the most common subject of poems about visual art, there are also many poems about sculpture, drawings, prints, and architecture.

Photograph poems are somewhat different, since they are based upon pictures, perhaps snapshots from a family album, that are not ordinarily intended as works of art. Although they respond to images in a visual medium, photograph poems usually deal with artifacts of everyday life, as in Eric Pankey's "A Photograph of My Parents Ice Skating, 1954." Poems that do focus on photographic art, such as the work of Walker Evans or Diane Arbus, are not very different from painting poems. Richard Howard has written two sequences based on portraits of famous artists, such as Charles Baudelaire, by the French photographer Nadar.

Nevertheless, all of these kinds of poems depend upon a second-hand image, rather than the people or places themselves. Plato would call them imitations of imitations. The poem that merely replicates the painting (or other visual work) seems flat indeed. It should add something in its language that takes off from the picture, or talks back to it.

Many painting poems borrow the title of a picture. X.J. Kennedy takes "Nude Descending a Staircase" from Marcel Duchamp. W.D. Snodgrass gives the painter's name along with the title in "Matisse: 'The Red Studio,'" "Vuillard: 'The Mother and Sister of the Artist,'" "Monet: 'Les Nympheas,'" "Manet: 'The Execution of the Emperor

Maximilian,' " and "Van Gogh: 'The Starry Night.' "

Sometimes, of course, different poets will write about the same pictures—just as Renoir and Monet painted some of the same scenes. Anne Sexton wrote her own version of "The Starry Night." Both William Carlos Williams and W.H. Auden wrote poems based on "The Fall of Icarus" by the Flemish painter Pieter Brueghel. (Auden's is called "Musée des Beaux Arts.") Williams wrote an entire sequence called *Pictures from Brueghel,* based on works such as "Children's Games" and "The Hunters in the Snow."

The challenge of writing about a painting is to move beyond mere description. In "A Side of Beef," Jordan Smith speaks in the voice of the painter, Chaim Soutine:

> What money there is
> goes for a side of beef delivered fresh each morning.
> By noon it will have lost those pigments . . .

A poem that's based on a work of art will succeed insofar as it comes to terms with the recognition made by Rainer Maria Rilke as he contemplates a powerful fragment of Greek sculpture in "Archaic Torso of Apollo": "You must change your life." Anything much less than a revelation may sound like make-work, not the work of a "maker."

> STARS WHICH SEE, STARS WHICH DO NOT SEE
> Marvin Bell (b. 1937)
>
> They sat by the water. The fine women
> had large breasts, tightly checked.
> At each point, at every moment,
> they seemed happy by the water.
> The women wore hats like umbrellas
> or carried umbrellas shaped like hats.
> The men wore no hats and the water,
> which wore no hats, had that well-known
> mirror finish which tempts sailors.
> Although the men and women seemed at rest
> they were looking toward the river
> and some way out into it but not beyond.

The scene was one of hearts and flowers
though this may be unfair. Nevertheless,
it was probable that the Seine had hurt them,
that they were "taken back" by its beauty
to where a slight breeze broke the mirror
and then its promise, but never the water.

NOTE: The painting is Georges Seurat's *A Sunday Afternoon on the Island of La Grande Jatte*. Bell likes to say that the poem starts "from a scene like that pictured in the Seurat," except that he "removed the hats from the proper Victorian gentlemen."

Palinode *(pál-i-node; Greek, "singing again")* 1. A poem that retracts or takes back something previously said. In the first palinode, Stesichorus (sixth century B.C.) recants an earlier attack against Helen of Troy. Here is Richmond Lattimore's translation of the fragment:

That story is not true.
You never sailed in the benched ships.
You never went to the city of Troy.

Charles Simic's *"errata"* (which imitates a scholarly book's list of its own errors) is a contemporary palinode. Here are its opening lines:

Where it says snow
read teeth-marks of a virgin

2. A variant of the Greek *ode; a form in which four stanzas are arranged as follows:

Stanza	1	Ode	Strophe A
	2	"	Strophe B
	3	Palinode	Antistrophe B (same form as Strophe B)
	4	"	Antistrophe A (same form as Strophe A)

Pantoum *(pan-tóom; also pantun)* A Malay repeating form, written in *quatrains, in which the second and fourth lines of each stanza become the first and third lines of the next one.
   In the last stanza, ideally, the second and fourth lines repeat the

opening stanza's first and third lines, bringing the pantoum full circle. David Mason's "Gusev," included below, exemplifies this circular structure—and follows the traditional *abab* rhyme scheme. One variation appears in Donald Justice's "In the Attic," which repeats end-words (as in a *sestina) rather than whole lines.

The pantoum was introduced to the West in the notes to Victor Hugo's *Les Orientales*. The poem that Hugo included demonstrates another characteristic of a Malay pantoum: In each quatrain, lines one and two are independent of lines three and four; they deal with different subjects entirely. In the original, rhyme links the disparate halves of each quatrain in a scheme of *abab*.

In the nineteenth century, the pantoum was a popular form in France and England, used by poets such as Charles Baudelaire, Théodore de Banville, and Austin Dobson. In America, John Ashbery's "Pantoum," which begins "Eyes shining without mystery," popularized the form in the late 1950s, especially among the poets of the *New York School.

> MALAY PANTOUM (Les papillons jouent à l'entour sur leurs ailes; tr. John Drury, from the French version of Ernest Fouinet included in the notes to Victor Hugo's *Les Orientales*, 1829)
>
> Butterflies dip and flutter on their wings;
> They fly to the sea, near a chain of rocks.
> My heart has felt ill in my chest
> From my earliest days to the present hour.
>
> They fly to the sea, near a chain of rocks . . .
> The vulture soars on the way to Bandam.
> From my earliest days to the present hour
> I have admired the young.
>
> The vulture soars on the way to Bandam . . .
> And glides down to Patani.
> I have admired the young,
> But none compares to the one I choose.
>
> He glides down to Patani . . .
> Look! Two young pigeons!
> No young man compares to the one I choose,
> Skilled as he is at touching the heart.

EVENING HARMONY / Charles Baudelaire
(1821-1867; tr. Richard Howard)

Now comes the time when swaying on its stem
each flower offers incense to the night;
phrases and fragrances circle in the dark—
languorous waltz that casts a lingering spell!

Each flower offers incense to the night;
the violin trembles like a heart betrayed—
languorous waltz that casts a lingering spell!
A mournful altar ornaments the sky.

The violin trembles like a heart betrayed,
a tender heart unnerved by nothingness!
A mournful altar ornaments the sky;
the sun has smothered in its clotting blood.

A tender heart unnerved by nothingness
hoards every fragment of the radiant past.
The sun has smothered in its clotting blood.
In me your image—like a monstrance—glows.

GUSEV / David Mason (b. 1954)
from the story by Anton Chekhov

The wind has broken free of its chain.
The sea has neither sense nor pity,
and what befalls us falls like rain.
The water's hot as new-made jelly.

The sea has neither sense nor pity.
One dies while playing a game of cards.
The water's hot as new-made jelly.
Above it there are curious clouds.

One dies while playing a game of cards.
Pavel insists he is getting well.
Above the ship are curious clouds
like lions leaping over the swell.

Pavel insists he is getting well
and dies still hating the peasant class.
Lions leaping over the swell
turn to scissors as they pass.

He dies still hating the peasant class
while Gusev lies in a fevered state.
Clouds turn to scissors as they pass
and dead men find it hard to hate.

Gusev lies in a fevered state,
wishing he didn't have to die,
and though he finds it hard to hate
he's saddened when he sees the sky.

Wishing he didn't have to die,
he goes below to suffocate,
saddened now he's seen the sky.
He thinks of snow, the village gate,

and goes below to suffocate,
his dreams increasingly absurd.
He sleighs through snow, the village gate,
sleeps two days, dies on the third.

His dreams increasingly absurd,
he tosses the fever from his bed,
sleeps two days, dies on the third.
They sew the sail-cloth over his head.

He tosses the fever from his bed.
The fever smiles and crawls back in.
They sew the sail-cloth over his head.
Below deck someone's dying again.

The fever smiles and crawls back in.
The wind has broken free of its chain.
Below deck someone's dying again,
and what befalls us falls like rain.

Parody *(páre-uh-dee; Greek, "song sung beside")* A poem that satirizes
or ridicules another poem (by imitating its mannerisms) or a poet (by
lampooning his stylistic tics).

In his "daydream college for bards," W.H. Auden would require
that the only critical exercise be the writing of parodies. *Imitation,
whether for fun or intellectual profit, remains one of the great ways
of learning the craft of poetry.

A pastiche *(pass-téesh; Italian, "pie")* is a kind of parody, denoting

either (1) a hodgepodge of borrowed passages or (2) an imitation of another work, not meant to ridicule. Other words used for designating parodies include burlesque, caricature, lampoon, and travesty.

Lord Byron's parody of Wordsworth's "Peter Bell" appears in *cinquain. In the following parody, Lewis Carroll pokes fun at the rather indestructible "Twinkle, Twinkle, Little Star," by Jane Taylor.

from *ALICE IN WONDERLAND*
Lewis Carroll (1832-1898)

Twinkle, twinkle, little bat!
How I wonder what you're at!
Up above the world you fly,
Like a tea-tray in the sky.

Pastoral *(páss-tur-ul)* A poem that describes country life in an idealized way.

The pastoral began with Theocritus, a Sicilian poet of the third century B.C., who wrote about the lives of shepherds. (A "pastor" is one who leads a flock.) There are three major kinds of pastoral:

• complaint: a shepherd's love song praising his beloved and moaning about her cruelty.

• eclogue: a *dialogue, usually representing a singing contest between two shepherds.

• pastoral elegy: a shepherd's lament for another shepherd who has died. (*See: elegy.*)

Several terms are used interchangeably with pastoral: bucolic, eclogue, and *idyll (or idyl). A *georgic deals with the work of farming and often takes the form of a *how-to poem.

A bucolic (*byoo-kól-ik; Latin, "pastoral," Greek, "ox-herd"*) refers to herders or shepherds in an idealized landscape. In the mystery *Saratoga Haunting*, poet Stephen Dobyns writes, "Traditionally a bucolic setting includes shepherds, farmlands, lush foliage. But even the bucolic can suffer the pangs of modernization and in the present instance the ox has been replaced by a bright yellow backhoe, the herdsman by the backhoe operator."

An eclogue (*ék-log; Greek, "selection"*) is sometimes used as a synonym for a pastoral poem, but it is usually in *dialogue form. Sir Philip

Sidney (1554-1586) includes an eclogue, "Ye goat-herd gods, that love the grassy mountains," which is spoken by two shepherds named Strephon and Klaius, in his *Arcadia*.

Theocritus' pastorals are in fact called idylls. The opening lines of his twenty-seventh idyll present a dialogue between Daphnis, a shepherd, and Chloris, the girl he pursues. Here is John Dryden's translation (written in *heroic couplets, although the original is unrhymed):

DAPHNIS: The shepherd Paris bore the Spartan bride
By force away, and then by force enjoy'd;
But I by free consent can boast a bliss,
A fairer Helen, and a sweeter kiss.
CHLORIS: Kisses are empty joys, and soon are o'er.
DAPHNIS: A kiss betwixt the lips is something more.
CHLORIS: I wipe my mouth, and where's your kissing then?
DAPHNIS: I swear you wipe it to be kiss'd again.
CHLORIS: Go, tend your herd, and kiss your cows at home;
I am a maid, and in my beauty's bloom.

But by the end of this idyll, the shepherd has seduced the girl:

DAPHNIS: The noble deed is done! My herds I'll cull;
Cupid, be thine a calf; and, Venus, thine a bull.
CHLORIS: A maid I came, in an unlucky hour,
But hence return without my virgin flow'r.

The poet comments at the end of the idyll:

First rose the maid, and with a glowing face,
Her downcast eyes beheld her print upon the grass;
Thence to her herd she sped herself in haste:
The bridegroom started from his trance at last,
And piping homeward jocundly he pass'd.

This idyll combines several features of pastoral poetry: a peaceful, beautiful, and isolated rural setting; a shepherd and a girl; a dialogue; some narration by the poet; a lover's complaint; and a seduction that is likened to animal husbandry.

THE PASSIONATE SHEPHERD TO HIS LOVE
Christopher Marlowe (1564-1593)

Come live with me and be my love,
And we will all the pleasures prove
That valleys, groves, hills, and fields,
Woods, or steepy mountain yields.

And we will sit upon the rocks,
Seeing the shepherds feed their flocks,
By shallow rivers to whose falls
Melodious birds sing madrigals.

And I will make thee beds of roses
And a thousand fragrant posies,
A cap of flowers, and a kirtle
Embroidered all with leaves of myrtle;

A gown made of the finest wool
Which from our pretty lambs we pull;
Fair lined slippers for the cold,
With buckles of the purest gold;

A belt of straw and ivy buds,
With coral clasps and amber studs:
And if these pleasures may thee move,
Come live with me, and be my love.

The shepherds' swains shall dance and sing
For thy delight each May morning:
If these delights thy mind may move,
Then live with me and be my love.

NOTE: *prove*: try out; *kirtle*: long dress.

Phanopoeia, Melopoeia, and Logopoeia Ezra Pound's terms for the means by which a poet can "charge language with meaning."

Pound defined them as follows in his *ABC of Reading*:

1. Phanopoeia: imagery, "throwing the object (fixed or moving) on to the visual imagination."

2. Melopoeia: sound, "inducing emotional correlations by the sound and rhythm of the speech."

3. Logopoeia: mental associations, "inducing both of the effects

by stimulating the associations (intellectual or emotional) that have remained in the receiver's consciousness in relation to the actual words or word groups employed."

Place   A poem's setting, location, locale.

Often poetry that isn't rooted to a particular place seems vague, empty. A definite place gives the poem a direct connection not just to the earth, but to the world of the senses, of tangible reality, of concrete particulars, of specific details. And these details are the poet's landmarks and guideposts and lighthouses. Without them the poem is likely to evaporate or shrivel up into nothing. With them it becomes three-dimensional; it happens somewhere; it has its "local habitation."

> RESTORING THE CHATEAU OF THE MARQUIS DE SADE
> Laurie Henry (b. 1958)
>
> Snow falls on Mont Ventoux during the night.
> Perhaps our mountain will be covered next.
> Now just the same two old workmen
> lay stones on the second floor of the chateau,
> the destroyed floor where they did the unspeakable things.
>
> Climbing by on our way to the quarry
> we notice how they work even more slowly than usual.
> There aren't any jobs in Lacoste in the winter.
> Angry French families eat alone by the road.
>
> As we sketch on the walls of the old fort,
> the communist mayor, chef of our art school,
> opens cans of peas and carrots in the kitchen.
> Though he hates the Americans he snaps at his dish washer.
> M. Bouer comes by the kitchen for his salt-free meal.
> Others warn: "Don't breathe in when he speaks."
>
> André Breton signed his name on a wall; we can't find it.
> The new white stones don't blend with the others.
> M. Bouer plans the dungeon for his wine cellar.
> Across the blacktopped road at the dump
> paper and garbage blow into the moat
> as they have since the moat was dug out.

In the cafes in the valley where I never go,
hikers ask directions to the chateau.
All you have to do is keep going up;
between two streets, choose the steeper.

My students carve their names on the walls of a quarry.
One of them wrote me her hate-letter there,
I can tell from the dusty paper.
They can't dig a foot here without hitting stone.

He dreamed of owning the chateau in childhood.
The week he bought it a new wall caved in.
He dreams it's toppled over in the night,
or moved across the valley to Bonnieux.

M. Bouer has now gone to Spain for the winter.
Limestone dust sticks to my skin, stiffens my hair.
Every day my boyfriend writes from New York.
My students need me to change their reservations.
Great Danes guard the arbors in the valley
even when there's nothing left but ash.

When windows blow open on the street
where we thought there were houses,
there is nothing inside but piles of stone.

Plant Poem, Vegetable Poem   A poem that focuses on flowers or trees, fruits or vegetables, fields or forests, photosynthesis or farming, gardens or greenhouses.

Like the *animal poem, the plant or vegetable poem deals with something living but not human. Naturally, the human can spill over into the plant poem and take it over entirely. Like any subject, a plant can serve as a pretext as well as a subject of scrutiny, a starting point for meditations that may lead far afield. But many poems about plants really do maintain their concentration, taking a deep look, lavishing attention on the green world.

ORCHIDS / Theodore Roethke (1908-1963)

They lean over the path,
Adder-mouthed,
Swaying close to the face,

Coming out, soft and deceptive,
Limp and damp, delicate as a young bird's tongue;
Their fluttery fledgling lips
Move slowly,
Drawing in the warm air.

And at night,
The faint moon falling through whitewashed glass,
The heat going down
So their musky smell comes even stronger,
Drifting down from their mossy cradles:
So many devouring infants!
Soft luminescent fingers,
Lips neither dead nor alive,
Loose ghostly mouths
Breathing.

Poem *(Greek, a "made thing")* A text or verbal composition, often written in lines, whose language is compressed and resonant and which conveys an experience, an emotion, or simply an aesthetically pleasing arrangement of words. As Robert Frost says, "it begins in delight and ends in wisdom."

Poet *(Greek, a "maker")* One who creates poems, or one who has created them, or one who thinks and feels like a poet (winged horse at the hitching post), or one who prepares to write poems or attempts writing them or otherwise stays alert for words, images, and experiences that might coalesce into the nucleus of a poem.

There are many synonyms for *poet*. A *bard* (Irish for "poet") was originally a minstrel poet; now, any poet. A *scop* is an Anglo-Saxon court poet. A *makar* is a Scottish poet. The German word, *Dichter,* is interesting because the verb *dichten* (from which it derives) means "to condense" as well as "to write poems." *Minstrel* and *troubadour* both denote Medieval poets who sang of courtly love, but the terms are now used jocularly—and more often for singer-songwriters, like the "Troubadours of Folk."

Poetry 1. The art of composing texts with charged language—songs with their own music. Robert Graves, however, asserts that poetry is

"not an art, but a way of thinking." Howard Nemerov says "poetry is a way of getting something right in language, poetry is language doing itself right."

2. A body of poems, as in "the poetry of Emily Dickinson."

Poetry in Fiction   1. Works of fiction that are considered poetic, such as James Joyce's *Ulysses* and Herman Melville's *Moby Dick*.

2. Works of fiction that contain poems or are partly written in verse, such as Richard Powers' *The Goldbug Variations*, Vladimir Nabokov's *Pale Fire*, D.M. Thomas' *The White Hotel*, E.L. Doctorow's *Loon Lake*, and John Barth's *The Sot-Weed Factor* (and several of his other novels).

Poetry Reading   Public recitation of poetry, often by the author, but also by other poets, actors, and fans of the author.

Readings may take place in coffee houses, auditoriums, private homes, libraries, theaters, museums, classrooms, public memorials, parks, bars, and even stadiums. Most poets read from book or type-script, but some recite from memory. Styles range from plain speaking to chanting to declaiming to singing. Most readers, however, "say" their poems (as Robert Frost put it) in a natural voice, indicating line breaks subtly—if at all.

In the early twentieth century, Vachel Lindsay tramped around the United States, offering a pamphlet, "Rhymes to Be Traded for Bread," and developed the vaudeville style of such catchy populist poems as "General William Booth Enters into Heaven," "The Congo," and "Bryan, Bryan, Bryan, Bryan." William Butler Yeats recorded many poems for radio broadcasts on the BBC—though most were destroyed during World War II. In a surviving remnant, Yeats chants "The Lake Isle of Innisfree." Dylan Thomas' poetry readings in the early 1950s created a sensation, and he recorded many of his poems (and the poems of other poets) for Caedmon Records.

Basil Bunting, who read his autobiographical poem *Briggflatts* to an accompaniment of harpsichord sonatas by Domenico Scarlatti, argues in his book of collected poems for the primacy of reading aloud:

> Poetry, like music, is to be heard. It deals in sound—long
> sounds and short sounds, heavy beats and light beats, the tone

relation of vowels, the relations of consonants to one another which are like instrumental colour in music. Poetry lies dead on the page, until some voice brings it to life, just as music on the stave is no more than instructions to the player. A skilled musician can imagine the sound, more or less, and a skilled reader can try to hear, mentally, what his eyes see in print; but nothing will satisfy either of them till his ears hear it as real sound in the air. Poetry must be read aloud.

Robert Graves, however, asserts in his book *The Crowning Privilege*, that a poem best reveals itself through close, silent reading:

> Although every poem should be suited for reading aloud, with full value given to every sound, pause, and rhythmic idiosyncrasy, a poem read silently in private yields far more of its magic truth than a poem read in a concert hall.

Poetry Slam Competition, usually held in a bar or café, in which poets recite or perform their work, are rated by judges, and may receive titles (such as "Grand Slam Champion") and prizes.

In "The Sidewalk of High Art," an introduction to the anthology *Aloud: Voices from the Nuyorican Poets Cafe*, Miguel Algarín describes the judging:

> Judges, who have been selected whimsically from the audience, are introduced with such "qualifications" as being born in Brooklyn or having never been to a Slam before. These judges will rate the poem from zero ("a poem that should never have been written") to ten ("mutual simultaneous orgasm") using the "Dewey decimal rating system" to avoid ties and "the dreaded Sudden-Death Haiku Improv overtime round." Here we are in the realm of literate humor, with no discerning of "high" and "low," all in the service of bringing a new audience to poetry via a form of entertainment meant to tune up fresh ears to a use of language as art that has been considered dead by many.

Algarín credits the creation of the poetry slam to Marc Smith, "who continues his weekly bare-knuckles events at the Green Mill in Chicago."

The history of poetic competition goes back at least to the ancient Greeks, who held competitions at the yearly Dionysian festival between the tragedies written in verse by poet-playwrights such as Aeschylus and Sophocles. Richard Wagner dramatized poetic competitions, based on historical events and real poets, in two of his operas, *Tannhäuser* and *Die Meistersinger von Nürnberg* (in which prospective master-singers are judged by a "marker," who scratches a mark on his slate for each mistake in versification).

Miguel Algarín mentions other examples of poetic competitions, "from the Greek mythological tale of Apollo and Marsyas to the African griots, from the *Sanjūrokunin sen*, or imaginary poetry team competitions, of tenth-century Japanese court poet Fujiwara no Kinto to the African-American 'dozens.' " He notes that this tradition continues in present-day Puerto Rico,

> ... where El Trovador improvises in the plaza, spontaneously pulling into the verse the life of the folks in the small town, the tragedies that have occurred in their families, the gossip that surrounds their private lives, and the celebratory passages that talk about births, deaths, weddings, and baptisms. All of this is compacted into ten-syllable lines with end-rhymes.

Poulter's Measure   A meter consisting of alternating lines of iambic hexameter (six stresses, twelve syllables) and iambic heptameter (seven stresses, fourteen syllables).

The name derives from the egg seller's practice of offering fourteen eggs, instead of twelve, for each second dozen bought. The lines tend to break into halves (stressed 3-3 and 4-3) so that the lines sound like elongated ballads. The effects of singsong rhythm and monotony led to the meter's demise after the sixteenth century, when poets such as Thomas Wyatt and Sir Philip Sidney still used it on occasion. Here is an example of poulter's measure by George Gascoigne (ca. 1542-1577):

> I could not though I would: good Lady say not so,
> Since one good word of your good wil might soone redresse
>   my wo

Where would is free before, there could can never fayle:
For profe, you see how gallies passe where ships can beare
  no sayle.
The weary mariner when skies are overcast,
By ready will doth guyde his skill and wins the haven at
  last.

Pre-Raphaelite Brotherhood   A group of painters and poets active in Victorian England.

In 1848 several young painters formed an organization called the Pre-Raphaelite Brotherhood, devoted to countering academic, formal art by harking back to the Italian painters before Raphael (in other words, before the sixteenth century). One of the founding members, Dante Gabriel Rossetti, happened to be a gifted poet as well as a painter. The brotherhood lasted only a few years, but the movement it fostered thrived over four decades, adding poets such as William Morris, Christina Rossetti, George Meredith, and Algernon Charles Swinburne. Pre-Raphaelite poetry is characterized by dreaminess, romanticism, and an almost religious view of art. Late in his life, however, Rossetti dismissed the initial brotherhood: "As for the prattle about Pre-Raphaelitism, I confess to you I am weary of it, and long have been. Why should we go on talking about the visionary vanities of half-a-dozen boys?" The movement was also ridiculed as the "Fleshly School of Poetry."

LILITH / Dante Gabriel Rossetti (1828-1882)
FOR A PICTURE

Of Adam's first wife, Lilith, it is told
  (The witch he loved before the gift of Eve,)
That, ere the snake's, her sweet tongue could deceive
And her enchanted hair was the first gold.
And still she sits, young while the earth is old,
  And, subtly of herself contemplative,
  Draws men to watch the bright net she can weave,
Till heart and body and life are in its hold.

The rose and poppy are her flowers; for where
  Is he not found, O Lilith, whom shed scent
And soft shed kisses and soft sleep shall snare?

Lo! as that youth's eyes burned at thine, so went
Thy spell through him, and left his straight neck bent,
And round his heart one strangling golden hair.

Proem *(Greek, "opening, prelude")*   A prefatory poem, such as Hart Crane's "To Brooklyn Bridge," which introduces his long poem *The Bridge*; the opposite of a coda or an epilogue, which is a poetic afterword.

Prose, Free Verse, and Metrical Verse   The three principal modes available to the poet. (One could possibly add *emblematic verse, which is shaped typographically, as a fourth category.)

Prose is what we ordinarily read in newspaper articles, essays, short stories, novels, letters, scientific treatises, and business reports; it is written in sentences and paragraphs and printed (if at all) with a justified right-hand margin, without regard for what words are located on that margin, hyphenating words as needed. Verse is written in lines, although it also uses sentences; a line ends where the poet says it ends, not where a typesetter puts it. Metrical verse is measured or counted in some way: by number of syllables, number of accents, or both; by the length or duration of syllables; by the number of words. Free verse is not measured; it is free of meter and uses *cadence and repetition and rhetorical devices and the naturalness of conversation and the white space of the page to make up for the lack of a regular measure underlying its rhythm.

The following three poems all appear in James Wright's *This Journey* (1982). The first is a prose poem; the second is a free-verse poem; the third is a metrical poem, a *sonnet rhymed *ababcdcd eefggf.*

THE FOX AT EYPE / James Wright (1927-1980)

He knows that all dogs bounding here and there, from the little vales all the way to the cliff-meadows and Thorncombe Beacon and beyond, are domestically forbidden to kill him. So every evening just before the end of twilight he emerges softly from the hedge across the lane and sits elegantly till darkness, gazing, with a certain weary amusement, into the middle distance of the sea.

OHIOAN PASTORAL / James Wright (1927-1980)

On the other side
Of Salt Creek, along the road, the barns topple
And snag among the orange rinds,
Oil cans, cold balloons of lovers.
One barn there
Sags, sags and oozes
Down one side of the copperous gulley.
The limp whip of a sumac dangles
Gently against the body of a lost
Bathtub, while high in the flint-cracks
And the wild grimed trees, on the hill,
A buried gas main
Long ago tore a black gutter into the mines.
And now it hisses among the green rings
On fingers in coffins.

READING A 1979 INSCRIPTION ON
BELLI'S MONUMENT
James Wright (1927-1980)

It is not only the Romans who are gone.
Belli, unhappy a century ago,
Won from the world his fashionable stone.
Where it stands now, he doesn't even know.
Across the Tiber, near Trastevere,
His top hat teetered on his head with care,
Brushed like a gentleman, he cannot see
The latest Romans who succeed him there.

One of them bravely climbed his pedestal
And sprayed a scarlet MERDA on his shawl.
This afternoon, I pray his hidden grave
Lies nameless somewhere in the hills, while rain
Fusses and frets to rinse away the stain.
Rain might erase when marble cannot save.

NOTE: Giuseppe Belli (1791-1863) was a poet, a native of Rome, who wrote many
sonnets.

Prose Poem   A brief work in prose that is considered a poem because of its intense, condensed language or because of some other similarity to poems in verse.

Some poets, such as James Wright, have thought of them more as prose sketches. Often it is difficult to distinguish a short-short story from a narrative prose poem. But this blurring of genres is a blessing to some, an incitement to experiment. *Language poets, such as Leslie Scalapino, move easily from prose to verse. It need not be a problem, except to the harried taxonomist.

Some critics, however, distinguish more harshly. Lewis Turco asserts that a prose poem is anything "not written in verse—in a metrical prosody." By that definition, all *free verse would, in fact, be prose. But we're more permissive here. Anything written in lines, metrical or unmetrical, strict or free, is verse. Anything not written in discrete lines is prose. The lines in prose are nothing but a typographical necessity. Given wide enough margins, a Proustian paragraph could go on for miles. The prose writer does not dictate where one line ends and another begins.

The prose poem began as a conscious form in nineteenth-century France, pioneered by Aloysius Bertrand and Charles Baudelaire. The form represented a kind of reaction against the strict poetic dictates of the French Academy (which is still imperious, having recently prohibited foreign words, such as *le drugstore*, which might corrupt the language). Baudelaire happens to be a master of the classical forms: the *alexandrine, the *sonnet. He wrote companion versions, for example, of "Invitation to the Voyage": one in rhymed verse, one in prose.

In his introduction to *Little Poems in Prose* (also called *Paris Spleen*), Baudelaire asks:

> Which of us, in his ambitious moments, has not dreamed of the miracle of a poetic prose, musical, without rhyme and without rhythm, supple enough and rugged enough to adapt itself to the lyrical impulses of the soul, the undulations of the psyche, the prickings of consciousness?

In his anthology *The Prose Poem: An International Anthology*, Michael Benedikt defines prose poem as:

> a genre of poetry, self-consciously written in prose, and characterized by the intense use of virtually all the devices of poetry, which includes the intense use of devices of verse. The sole exception to access to the possibilities, rather than the set priorities of verse is, we would say, the line break.

In his essay "The Prose Poem as an Evolving Form," Robert Bly says of the prose poem, "Its mood is calm, more like a quiet lake than a sea." He mentions several kinds of prose poem: the fable (both ancient, in the work of Aesop, and contemporary, in the work of Russell Edson and David Ignatow), the "fire-prose" or "illumination" invented by the nineteenth-century French poet Arthur Rimbaud, and the *object poem (as in the work of Francis Ponge and Juan Ramon Jimenez), which "centers itself not on story or image but on the object, and it holds on to its fur, so to speak." Bly adds:

> The fact that no critics have yet laid out formal standards for the prose poem is a blessing. Sometimes a fox and a human being play together best when no loud sounds are heard. When relaxed and aware of no rigid patterns, the mind sometimes gracefully allows itself to play with something equally graceful in nature, and the elegance of the prose poem appears in that play.

Both Benedikt and Bly have written prose poems, and they agree that it is a genre not for beginners but for more advanced writers. (*See: haibun.*)

GET DRUNK (*Enivrez-vous*)
Charles Baudelaire (1821-1867; tr. Michael Benedikt)

Get drunk and stay drunk. That's it; that's the sole solution to our greatest problem. So as not to feel the terrible burden of time breaking your back and bowing you ever closer to the earth, you must remain incessantly, relentlessly, constantly intoxicated.

But intoxicated with what? With wine, with poetry, or with virtue: whatever you prefer. But get drunk!

And if now and then you happen to come to, on the steps outside a palace, amid the green grass of some ditch or in

the dreary solitude of your room; and you discover that your drunkenness is leaving you, or has already vanished, ask wind and wave, ask star, bird and clock; ask every fleeting thing, every flowing thing, everything that can sing or speak or croak or cry out:—ask them: "What time is it now?" And wind and wave, star, bird and clock will all answer: "It's time to get drunk! Yes, if you are not merely to live out your lives as the martyred slaves of Time, make sure you stay drunk, too! With wine, poetry, or virtue, whatever you prefer."

THE COLONEL / Carolyn Forché (b. 1950)

What you have heard is true. I was in his house. His wife carried a tray of coffee and sugar. His daughter filed her nails, his son went out for the night. There were daily papers, pet dogs, a pistol on the cushion beside him. The moon swung bare on its black cord over the house. On the television was a cop show. It was in English. Broken bottles were embedded in the walls around the house to scoop the kneecaps from a man's legs or cut his hands to lace. On the windows there were gratings like those in liquor stores. We had dinner, rack of lamb, good wine, a gold bell was on the table for calling the maid. The maid brought green mangoes, salt, a type of bread. I was asked how I enjoyed the country. There was a brief commercial in Spanish. His wife took everything away. There was some talk then of how difficult it had become to govern. The parrot said hello on the terrace. The colonel told it to shut up, and pushed himself from the table. My friend said to me with his eyes: say nothing. The colonel returned with a sack used to bring groceries home. He spilled many human ears on the table. They were like dried peach halves. There is no other way to say this. He took one of them in his hands, shook it in our faces, dropped it into a water glass. It came alive there. I am tired of fooling around he said. As for the rights of anyone, tell your people they can go fuck themselves. He swept the ears to the floor with his arm and held the last of his wine in the air. Something for your poetry, no? he said. Some of the ears on the floor caught this scrap of his voice. Some of the ears on the floor were pressed to the ground.

Prosody *(próz-uh-dee; Greek, "accent, song sung to music")* The study of sound and rhythm in poetry, of *meter and *versification (how to compose lines of verse).

Prosodical marks include the symbols used to scan verse and note rhyme schemes. Syllables can be stressed (´) or unstressed (˘); or a weak syllable can receive a metrical stress (″); or, for the prosodist who wants to mark four levels of accenting, the medium stresses can be marked secondary (ˋ) and the light stresses marked tertiary (|). In the *quantitative meter used in the classical poetry of Greece and Rome, the length of syllables is marked: long (-) and short (˘). Breaks can be marked: between metrical *feet (|), at a *caesura or pause in the middle of a line (||), for the end of a line (/, when several lines are quoted in a prose sentence), and for the end of a *stanza (//). *Rhyme schemes use the letters of the alphabet to indicate rhyme groups, perhaps reserving capital letters for *refrains (repeated lines).

Psalm *(sawm; Greek, "twitching" or "twanging" [of harp strings])* A sacred song or hymn.

The Book of Psalms, originally written in Hebrew and considered the compositions of King David of Israel, contains 150 of these religious lyrics. The psalms are written in a kind of long-lined free verse whose *prosody is governed by repetition (exemplified in Psalm LXX by the repeated "Let," which begins several lines, an instance of *anaphora) and by variation (in the first line, "O God" changes to "O Lord" and interrupts "Make haste . . . to deliver me" while the latter phrase follows "Make haste to help me"). *(See: biblical verse, free verse.)*

> PSALM LXX (King James Version of The Bible)
>
> Make haste, O God, to deliver me; make haste to help
> me, O Lord.
> Let them be ashamed and confounded that seek after my
> soul: let them be turned backward, and put to confusion,
> that desire my hurt.
> Let them be turned back for a reward of their shame
> that say, Aha, aha!

Let all those that seek thee rejoice and be glad in
thee: and let such as love thy salvation say continually,
Let God be magnified.

But I am poor and needy: make haste unto me, O God:
thou art my help and my deliverer; O Lord, make no
tarrying.

Pyrrhic   A foot consisting of two unstressed syllables ($\smile\smile$).

No English words are pyrrhic, since one of the word's two syllables would have to be accented, however slightly. A pyrrhic phrase such as "in a" requires something stressed to follow it and complete the prepositional phrase. If that something is a spondee, the pyrrhic survives: "in a big town," for example.

Pyrrhic meter is impossible in English, since any noun or verb or even adjective that turned up would be hailed with a rousing stress. And even in a hypothetical poem composed of prepositions, articles, and conjunctions, our speech patterns and rhythmic sense would impose relative stresses every so often. (*See: minor ionic, spondee.*)

Quantitative Meter A meter that measures the length of syllables, long (-) and short (ˇ), and counts their number in lines of verse. The word *quantities* refers to syllable length.

This metrical system was the basis of ancient Greek poetry, adopted by Latin poets and attempted with varying success by English poets such as the Elizabethan lute-song composer Thomas Campion. The various types of quantitative feet (from which English poetry takes its terms for accentual-syllabic feet such as *iamb* and *trochee*) appear in the entry *foot, feet.*

One kind of quantitative meter is called hendecasyllabics (Greek, "eleven syllables"). Here is the pattern of long and short syllables:

$$- \; \smallsmile \; - \; \smallsmile \; \smallsmile \; - \; \smallsmile \; - \; \smallsmile \; - \; \smallsmile$$
$$- \; \smallsmile \; - \; \smallsmile \; \smallsmile \; - \; \smallsmile \; - \; \smallsmile \; - \; \smallsmile$$

In his *Poems in Classical Prosody*, a set of experiments with quantitative meter in English, Robert Bridges (1844-1930) writes these hendecasyllabics in "The Fourth Dimension":

> If this be not a holy consolation
> More than plumpudding and a turkey roasted,
> Whereto you but address a third dimension,
> Try it, pray, as a pill to aid digestion:
> I can't find anything better to send you.

The problem in English is that stress is all-powerful; the first line above is a perfect example of iambic pentameter with a *feminine

ending. But it's only a problem if you try to write English as if it were Greek. (*See*: *alcaics, elegiac distich, ode, sapphics.*)

Quatrain *(kwót-rane; French, "group of four")*   A four-line stanza.

Although quatrains can be rhymed or unrhymed (or partly rhymed), in meter or in free verse, the names given to certain quatrains refer to rhyme schemes—and sometimes to line length. An unrhymed quatrain may be called a tetrastich (especially if it is written in iambic pentameter). Several types of rhymed quatrains are listed below.

• Alternating quatrain: *abab*. The rhyming alternates: lines one and three together, lines two and four together. When the lines are 4-3-4-3 iambic feet in length, it is called the hymn stanza. When the lines are iambic pentameter, it is called the heroic quatrain or Sicilian quatrain (which is used in the Shakespearean sonnet). When lines two and four of one stanza become lines one and three of the next, it is called a *pantoum (although many contemporary pantoums omit rhyming altogether). The following quatrain is in iambic pentameter:

DIVERNE'S WALTZ
Marilyn Nelson Waniek (b. 1946)

Diverne stands in the kitchen as they dance,
laughing and flirting, on the bare parlor floor.
She's taken up the rug, glad for the chance,
at last, to beat it free of sins outdoors.

Her fancy cakes are popular, her punch
has earned light giggles from Miss Atwood's friends.
She'd struggled at Miss Atwood's back to cinch
that tiny waist. *Miss Atwood look right grand.*

Mister Tyler asks for a water-glass of rye:
he's just enlisted, a drop-out from law school.
She notices something dangerous in his eye:
Crazy damn white man, acting like a fool.

Taking her hands, Henry Tyler gives her a twirl
and off they waltz. He swirls Diverne so fast
her head kerchief unknots itself. He smiles
down at Diverne's embarrassment, and gasps:

They blush! Hearing the whispers from the walls,
he sees men grin. His father shakes his head.
But (*That dark rose . . .*) he dances. *What the hell,*
who knows? next week, next month, I could be dead.

• Envelope quatrain: *abba*. The outer lines rhyme with each other; the inner lines rhyme with each other. When the lines are iambic tetrameter, it is called the *In Memoriam stanza, after a poem by Alfred, Lord Tennyson. When the lines are iambic pentameter, it is called the brace stanza or Italian quatrain (as in the first four lines of the Petrarchan sonnet).

NEUTRAL TONES / Thomas Hardy (1840-1928)

We stood by a pond that winter day,
And the sun was white, as though chidden of God,
And a few leaves lay on the starving sod;
    —They had fallen from an ash, and were gray.

Your eyes on me were as eyes that rove
Over tedious riddles of years ago;
And some words played between us to and fro
    On which lost the more by our love.

The smile on your mouth was the deadest thing
Alive enough to have strength to die;
And a grin of bitterness swept thereby
    Like an ominous bird a-wing. . . .

Since then, keen lessons that love deceives,
And wrings with wrong, have shaped to me
Your face, and the God-curst sun, and a tree,
    And a pond edged with grayish leaves.

• Couplet quatrain: *aabb*. Two rhymed couplets join in a single stanza. Trochaic quatrains, such as William Blake's "The Tyger," are usually rhymed in couplets. The following poem is written in what Robert Frost would call "loose" iambic tetrameter.

GOOD HOURS / Robert Frost (1874-1963)

I had for my winter evening walk—
No one at all with whom to talk,
But I had the cottages in a row
Up to their shining eyes in snow.

And I thought I had the folk within:
I had the sound of a violin;
I had a glimpse through curtain laces
Of youthful forms and youthful faces.

I had such company outward bound.
I went till there were no cottages found.
I turned and repented, but coming back
I saw no window but that was black.

Over the snow my creaking feet
Disturbed the slumbering village street
Like profanation, by your leave,
At ten o'clock of a winter eve.

• Even-rhymed quatrain: *XaXa*. Lines two and four rhyme; one and three do not. The opposite, an "odd-rhymed" quatrain (*aXaX*), is rare, but William Stafford's "Clash" is an example. When the even-rhymed quatrain contains lines that are 4-3-4-3 stresses in length, it is called the *ballad stanza.

SOME KEEP THE SABBATH GOING TO CHURCH
Emily Dickinson (1830-1886)

Some keep the Sabbath going to Church—
I keep it, staying at Home—
With a Bobolink for a Chorister—
And an Orchard, for a Dome—

Some keep the Sabbath in Surplice—
I just wear my Wings—
And instead of tolling the Bell, for Church,
Our little Sexton—sings.

God preaches, a noted Clergyman—
And the sermon is never long,
So instead of getting to Heaven, at last—
I'm going, all along.

• Monorhymed quatrain: *aaaa*. All four lines rhyme on the same sound. Few poets use this quatrain, because of the difficulty of finding so many rhymes, over and over again. The repetitions can become tedious, even ludicrous. But the relentless rhyming may be especially suitable for conveying obsession, as in Rossetti's poem below.

THE WOODSPURGE
Dante Gabriel Rossetti (1828-1882)

The wind flapped loose, the wind was still,
Shaken out dead from tree and hill:
I had walked on at the wind's will,—
I sat now, for the wind was still.

Between my knees my forehead was,—
My lips, drawn in, said not Alas!
My hair was over in the grass,
My naked ears heard the day pass.

My eyes, wide open, had the run
Of some ten weeds to fix upon;
Among those few, out of the sun,
The woodspurge flowered, three cups in one.

From perfect grief there need not be
Wisdom or even memory:
One thing then learnt remains to me,—
The woodspurge has a cup of three.

A rhyme sound in one quatrain can recur in the following stanza. Robert Frost uses interlocking rhyme in "Stopping by Woods on a Snowy Evening": *aaba bbcb ccdc dddd.*

(*See: alcaics, ballad stanza, ode* [for some kinds of Horatian ode], *In Memoriam stanza, Omar Khayyam stanza, pantoum, sapphics.*)

Quintilla Spanish five-line stanza containing eight syllables per line and rhyming *ababa, abbab, abaab, aabab,* or *aabba.* Each stanza must have two rhymes (*a* and *b*) and the last two lines may not be a couplet. Originally the quintilla was called a *redondilla.

R

Rap A contemporary form of popular song, invented by African-Americans and dating from about 1976, in which an outpouring of rhymed lines (similar to *skeltonics) are declaimed, not sung, over a driving beat usually provided by a drum machine or by rhythmically scratching a phonograph record.

Nikki Giovanni calls rap "an honest voice of an anguished people." And yet the anger is typically matched by the humor of slangy phrasing, topical wisecracks, and clever rhyming. The form owes a great deal to the fast patter of rhythm-and-blues disk jockeys.

One of the most influential early rap songs was "The Message" (1982), by Grandmaster Flash and the Furious Five. Its lyrics are both flashy and furious, a blend of rage and comic rhyming, as in "Got a bum education, double-digit inflation/ Can't train to the job, there's a strike at the station." (*See: rhyme, song.*)

Reader *(also audience)* 1. The one to whom the poet presents or submits her work. 2. The person that the poet imagines reading her work; the ideal audience. 3. What a poet must be in order to write something worth reading.

Redondilla Spanish quatrain consisting of four eight-syllable lines, usually rhymed *abba*. If rhymed *abab*, it can also be called a *serventesio*. If there are fewer than eight syllables per line (six is a common variant), the stanza is a *redondilla menor*. (*See: quintilla.*)

Refrain A line that is repeated, like the *chorus of a song; also called a burden.

Sometimes, as in Robert Frost's "The Pasture," included below, a refrain will not rhyme with any other lines in a poem. Part of the listening pleasure then comes from one kind of repetition (a string of words) being set off against another (the rhymes). Sometimes the refrain rhymes with one or more lines in each stanza. In "Crazy Jane Grown Old Looks at the Dancers," William Butler Yeats uses a rhyme scheme of *abacacB* (the capital letter representing a repeated line), so that the refrain, "Love is like the lion's tooth," appears at the end of each stanza and rhymes with the second line.

The wording of a refrain can change from stanza to stanza, but at least a recognizable phrase must remain constant. A number of forms require refrains: *ballade, *kyrielle, *rondeau, *rondel, *rondelet, *roundel, *triolet, and *villanelle. In a sea shanty, the leader sings a line and then a chorus of sailors joins in; each stanza uses two different refrains, and the second may be considerably longer than the first, as in the folk song "Shenandoah":

> Oh, Shenandoah, I love your daughter
> *Away, you rolling river*
> I'll take her cross the rolling water
> *Away, I'm bound away,*
> *Across the wide Missouri.*

In a poem not necessarily meant to be sung, the refrain must be interesting in itself. It helps if it can answer each stanza with a different shade of meaning.

THE PASTURE / Robert Frost (1874-1963)

> I'm going out to clean the pasture spring;
> I'll only stop to rake the leaves away
> (And wait to watch the water clear, I may):
> I shan't be gone long.—You come too.
>
> I'm going out to fetch the little calf
> That's standing by the mother. It's so young
> It totters when she licks it with her tongue.
> I shan't be gone long.—You come too.

Regional Poetry Poetry that is firmly, obviously, often proudly set in a particular locale and is saturated with the look and feel of that place. Richard Hugo's Northwest (Washington and Montana in particular), James Dickey's South (Georgia and South Carolina), Ted Kooser's Midwest (Nebraska), and N. Scott Momaday's Southwest (Arizona) represent kinds of regional poetry. So do Thomas Hardy's poems about Wessex, his composite of the southwest part of England, especially Dorset.

Relative Stress A syllable that is accented slightly because of the unstressed syllables around it. This kind of stress usually occurs when a weak syllable falls on a place that would normally be stressed, like the sixth syllable ("in") of Shakespeare's "Th'expense of spirit in a waste of shame." (*See: scud.*)

Renga A Japanese collaborative form, also called linked verse.

This form derives from *tanka, which is arranged syllabically in a stanza pattern of 5-7-5-7-7 (although a tanka is usually complete in itself, even when included as part of a sequence). In renga, the first poet writes the first three lines (the hokku or *haiku), the second poet writes the next two lines (each seven syllables), and they continue trading verses back and forth, a conversation in form, a literary pastime. More than two poets can take part, continuing in a kind of circle. Haiku as a separate form grew out of the practice of renga teachers such as Matsuo Basho, recognized as the first master of haiku. If renga is necessarily a dialogue, a communal exercise, haiku then is the proverbial "one hand clapping" of the Zen koan, the first half of a tanka isolated and answered by silence, an exercise of the solitary self in the midst of the universe.

Repetition The recurrence of words, phrases, lines, or groups of lines, of rhyme sounds, of consonants and vowels, of images and symbols, of themes and ideas.

Repetition is a coming back, a going over, a completion of a circle, an obsessive returning to something emotionally magnetic or rhythmically compelling—and is essential to much, perhaps most, poetry. Its opposite is *variation, changing to something different instead of repeating the same thing. Most often, repetition and variation work

together, as when different stanzas end with the same *refrain. In the following poem, Richard Howard uses a refrain twice in each stanza, but the sixth word of the refrain changes with each repetition.

LIKE MOST REVELATIONS
Richard Howard (b. 1929)
AFTER MORRIS LOUIS

It is the movement that incites the form,
discovered as a downward rapture—yes,
it is the movement that delights the form,
sustained by its own velocity. And yet

it is the movement that delays the form
while darkness slows and encumbers; in fact
it is the movement that betrays the form,
baffled in such toils of ease, until

it is the movement that deceives the form,
beguiling our attention—we supposed
it is the movement that achieves the form.
Were we mistaken? What does it matter if

it is the movement that negates the form?
Even though we give (give up) ourselves
to this mortal process of continuing,
it is the movement that creates the form.

Response   A poem written in reaction to another poem (or, more broadly, to anything); an answer or reply to something the poet has read; a poem written on the same subject as another poem but from a different point of view.

Some responses are written in the voice of a person addressed in the original poem: for example, in Anthony Hecht's "The Dover Bitch," the woman addressed in Matthew Arnold's "Dover Beach" responds to the speaker of that poem.

The following poems respond to Christopher Marlowe's "The Passionate Shepherd to his Love" (in *pastoral*). Ralegh provides the lady's answer, quoting some of Marlowe's details (such as "coral clasps and amber studs"); John Donne, who begins with Marlowe's first line, offers a racier invitation, promising the woman "some new pleasures."

THE NYMPH'S REPLY TO THE SHEPHERD
Sir Walter Ralegh (1552?-1618)

If all the world and love were young,
And truth in every shepherd's tongue,
These pretty pleasures might me move
To live with thee and be thy love.

Time drives the flocks from field to fold
When rivers rage, and rocks grow cold,
And Philomel becometh dumb;
The rest complain of cares to come.

The flowers do fade, and wanton fields
To wayward winter reckoning yields;
A honey tongue, a heart of gall,
Is fancy's spring, but sorrow's fall.

Thy gowns, thy shoes, thy beds of roses,
Thy cap, thy kirtle, and thy posies
Soon break, soon wither, soon forgotten—
In folly ripe, in reason rotten.

Thy belt of straw and ivy buds,
Thy coral clasps and amber studs,
All these in me no means can move
To come to thee and be thy love.

But could youth last, and love still breed,
Had joys no date, nor age no need,
Then these delights my mind might move
To live with thee and be thy love.

NOTE: *Philomel*: nightingale; *kirtle*: long dress.

THE BAIT / John Donne (1572-1631)

Come live with me, and be my love,
And we will some new pleasures prove,
Of golden sands, and crystal brooks:
With silken lines, and silver hooks.

There will the river whispering run
Warmed by thy eyes, more than the sun.
And there th' enamored fish will stay,
Begging themselves they may betray.

When thou wilt swim in that live bath,
Each fish, which every channel hath,
Will amorously to thee swim,
Gladder to catch thee, than thou him.

If thou to be so seen be'st loath,
By sun, or moon, thou dark'nest both,
And if myself have leave to see,
I need not their light, having thee.

Let others freeze with angling reeds,
And cut their legs with shells and weeds,
Or treacherously poor fish beset
With strangling snare, or windowy net.

Let coarse bold hands, from slimy nest
The bedded fish in banks out-wrest;
Or curious traitors, sleave-silk flies,
Bewitch poor fishes' wand'ring eyes.

For thee, thou need'st no such deceit,
For thou thyself art thine own bait;
That fish that is not catched thereby,
Alas, is wiser far than I.

NOTE: *angling reeds*: fishing rods. Other responses to Marlowe's poem include C. Day Lewis' "Song" (beginning "Come, live with me and be my love") and Delmore Schwartz's "The Passionate Shepherd to his Love" (beginning "Come live with me and be my wife").

Rhetoric The art of discourse, the means by which a writer or speaker can persuade and move an audience.

Classical rhetoric constitutes a system through which to compose one's thoughts, "not so much to persuade," as Aristotle points out in his *Rhetoric*, "as to find out in each case the existing means of persuasion." These means include argumentation and style.

Although argumentation—the gathering of evidence, the use of

logic and chains of reasoning, the avoidance and detection of fallacies, the establishing of proofs—might seem more at home in a court of law, it has a traditional place in poetry (enough so that *Symbolist poets rejected the rigors of logic in favor of the suggestiveness of music and imagery). Many *sonnets are constructed on a logical framework, filling in a kind of *if... then ... therefore* structure, as in Sonnet 138 by William Shakespeare (whose logical connective words are *when, thus, but,* and *therefore*):

> When my love sweares that she is made of truth,
> I do beleeve her though I know she lyes,
> That she might thinke me some untuterd youth,
> Unlearned in the worlds false subtilties.
> Thus vainely thinking that she thinkes me young,
> Although she knowes my dayes are past the best,
> Simply I credit her false speaking tongue,
> On both sides thus is simple truth supprest:
> But wherefore sayes she not she is unjust?
> And wherefore say not I that I am old?
> O loves best habit is in seeming trust,
> And age in love, loves not t'have yeares told.
> > Therefore I lye with her, and she with me,
> > And in our faults by lyes we flattered be.

In poetry, *argument usually means the "plot" of a poem, or a synopsis ("plot summary") that may precede it.

Style comprises diction (word choice), syntax (word order), paragraphing, euphony (melodious sounds), and figures of speech (also called rhetorical devices). These figures, which include such essential poetic tools as *metaphor, *irony, and *alliteration, represent ways of transforming either the order or the sense of words, to make the writing more vivid, emphatic, and memorable.

There is also a negative sense of the word *rhetoric*, associating it with bombast, falsity, trickery, empty talk, like the "rhetoric" of politicians. But rhetoric itself is simply the art of expressive speech, and its devices (the figures of speech) provide a wide range of tools for the writer: aids in invention, means of transforming the raw materials of language into imaginative work. (*See: figures of classical rhetoric.*)

Rhopalic Verse *(Greek, "like a club," thicker toward the end, like the club used by Hercules; also called Wedge verse)* A game-like form in which each word in a line is one syllable longer than the word before it. Here is an example: "The circus performer hypnotizes pediatricians." *(See:* Oulipo.*)*

Rhyme *(also rime)* A word that echoes the vowel-consonant combination (or sometimes just the vowel) of another word, as in *rhyme/chime.*

In mathematical terms, most rhymes comprise a constant and a variable. (The exception is *rime riche,* in which the words rhymed are exactly the same—all constant, no variable, except in the meaning of those homonyms.) In the most common type of true or full rhyme, a variable consonant precedes either a fixed vowel and fixed consonant *(brake/shake)* or a fixed vowel by itself *(so/go).*

In *slant rhyme, one of those fixed elements becomes variable *(brake/spoke, brake/brave; so/gay, so/say).* Sometimes both the preceding and following consonants become fixed, sandwiching a changeable vowel *(brake/broke).* Slant rhyme does its work at an angle, tilted away from what a carpenter would call true.

Rhymes can be grouped not only by how closely the words look or sound alike, but also by where they occur and recur. End-rhymes appear at the end of lines. The farther apart they appear, the fainter their repetition will sound. *Couplets, therefore, tend to clang; rhymes separated by one or more intervening lines are progressively harder to distinguish. Rhymes that are end-stopped protrude more prominently than rhymes that are enjambed, in which the sense runs on swiftly to the next line. Sometimes a poet needs the obvious echo, and sometimes will choose to hide or disguise that echo. Rhymes in which at least one of the rhyme words occurs within a line are called internal rhymes. In leonine rhyme, the internal rhyme occurs at the halfway point of a line (often just before a pause, or *caesura) and is echoed by the end-rhyme, as in Alfred, Lord Tennyson's "The splendor falls on castle walls."

Rhymes differ according to the number of syllables that are echoed. The most common kind in English is called single, masculine, or perfect rhyme (also *rime suffisante*), in which the rhyme falls on a single stressed syllable, as in the conclusion of Sylvia Plath's "Lady Lazarus":

> I rise with my red hair
> And I eat men like air.

But the stressed syllable can be part of a polysyllabic word and its stress can be fairly weak, although it must be stronger than the syllable preceding it, as in Thomas Hardy's "The Convergence of the Twain":

> In a solitude of the sea
> Deep from human vanity,

Poets tend to place the monosyllabic word first, before the polysyllabic word whose last syllable rhymes with it.

In double full, feminine, or light rhyme, two-syllable words consisting of a stressed and then an unstressed syllable (such as *thicken/ quicken*) are used for the rhyme sounds, as in Richard Wilbur's "Seed Leaves":

> And making crusty rubble.
> It comes up bending double,
> And looks like a green staple.
> It could be seedling maple,

This kind of rhyming is less common than single rhyme. In Wilbur's thirty-four-line poem, for example, these four lines are the only ones with double-full rhymes.

Rhyming more than two syllables almost always sounds comic. *Triple rhyme* contributes to the humor of Lord Byron's *Don Juan*:

> He learned the arts of riding, fencing, gunnery,
> And how to scale a fortress—or a nunnery.

The list below classifies how the sounds of rhymes are matched. But the poet's ear (and the critic's judgment) are better arbiters of when an exact rhyme is required and when a slant rhyme would be permissible.

Rhyme

• True, full, or perfect rhyme; chime (sounding alike, though possibly looking different):

> Aunt Jennifer's tigers prance across a screen,
> Bright topaz denizens of a world of green.
> —Adrienne Rich, "Aunt Jennifer's Tigers"

> The wrinkled sea beneath him crawls;
> He watches from his mountain walls,
> —Alfred, Lord Tennyson, "The Eagle"

• Eye or sight rhyme (looking the same, sounding different):

> For, unless ways are changing here at home,
> You might not have it if I had not come.
> —Edwin Arlington Robinson, "The Prodigal Son"

• Historical rhyme (once perfect, now sounding different):

> Good-nature and good-sense must ever join;
> To err is human, to forgive, divine.
> —Alexander Pope, "An Essay on Criticism" (II)

Slant Rhyme

(Also called approximate, embryonic, half, imperfect, near, oblique, off, partial, and part rhyme; paraphone or pararhyme)

• Consonant rhyme (final consonant the same, vowel different):

> See the blistered paint
> On the scorching front,
> Or icicle sombre
> On pierhead timber.
> —W.H. Auden, "The Exiles"

Consonant rhyme can be monosyllabic, as in the first couplet of Auden's, or disyllabic, as in the second couplet.

- Assonant rhyme (vowel the same, final consonant different):

> When he came to the king's gate,
> He sought a drink for Hind Horn's sake.
> —"Hind Horn," anonymous popular ballad

Assonant rhyme is especially common in folk songs and in contemporary popular songs, because the vowels echo so audibly, especially long vowels.

- Alliterative or double-consonant rhyme (vowel different, surrounding consonants the same):

> Was it for this the clay grew tall?
> —O what made fatuous sunbeams toil
> —Wilfred Owen, "Futility"

- Rhyming on the weak syllable of a two-syllable word, such as *flower/tatter* or *slimy/gravy*.

Other Rhymes

- Apocopated rhyme (rhyming the penultimate or antepenultimate syllable in one line with the final syllable in the next):

> Till on glass rigid with his own seizure
> At length the sucking jewels freeze.
> —James Merrill, "The Octopus"

- Wrenched rhyme (in which a word is misspelled or mispronounced or garbled in some way to "rhyme" with another word; the effect is usually comic):

> Farewell, farewell, you old rhinoceros,
> I'll stare at something less prepocerous!
> —Ogden Nash, "The Rhinoceros"

- Diminishing rhyme (in which a word loses its preceding consonants as they are repeated):

> What open force, or hidden CHARM
> Can blast my fruit, or bring me HARM,
> While the inclosure is thine ARM?
> —George Herbert, "Paradise" (lines 4-6)

The rhymes, of course, could progress in the opposite direction, building up instead of diminishing.

• Broken rhyme (in which one of the rhyme sounds is the first part of a hyphenated word; perhaps another kind of "wrenched rhyme"):

> I did: through last July's parenthesis,
> I worked, walked, ate, grew brown, wiry and lis-
> some climbing paths. . . .
> —Marilyn Hacker, "Lacoste I"

Alliterative rhyme (*stick/stock*) is an acceptable kind of slant rhyme, pioneered by Wilfred Owen during World War I. Alliteration alone, however, is not very satisfying as a rhyme. The vowel or the final consonant needs to echo.

Finally, some poets who once used rhyme, such as John Milton and Thomas Campion, came to detest it, partly because it was not countenanced by classical tradition (specifically Ancient Greek poetry, which does not rhyme), partly because it seemed merely decorative and ornamental. (Milton's Puritanism was aesthetic too.) And most *free verse (with the exception of Robert Creeley's) eschews rhyming as strongly as it rejects meter: both means of establishing regularity and order, of satisfying expectations rather than constantly diverging.

Rhyme Royale *(also Chaucer stanza, Troilus stanza, rime royal)* A seven-line stanza rhyming *ababbcc*, usually in iambic pentameter.

This stanza form was introduced into English poetry by Geoffrey Chaucer, who used the stanza for *Troilus and Criseyde*, *The Parliament of Fowls*, and several of *The Canterbury Tales* ("The Man of Law," "The Clerk," and "The Second Nun"). Other poets, such as Thomas Wyatt, William Shakespeare, William Wordsworth, and W.H. Auden also have used it. The name may derive from the poems in the stanza form written by King James I of Scotland.

THEY FLEE FROM ME
Thomas Wyatt (1503-1542)

They flee from me, that sometime did me seek,
With naked foot stalking in my chamber.
I have seen them, gentle, tame, and meek,

That now are wild, and do not remember
That sometime they put themselves in danger
To take bread at my hand; and now they range,
Busily seeking with a continual change.

Thanked be Fortune it hath been otherwise,
Twenty times better; but once in special,
In thin array, after a pleasant guise,
When her loose gown from her shoulders did fall,
And she me caught in her arms long and small,
And therewith all sweetly did me kiss
And softly said, "Dear heart, how like you this?"

It was no dream, I lay broad waking.
But all is turned, thorough my gentleness,
Into a strange fashion of forsaking;
And I have leave to go, of her goodness,
And she also to use newfangleness.
But since that I so kindely am served,
I fain would know what she hath deserved.

NOTE: *newfangleness*: fickleness; *kindely*: kindly, naturally.

Rhythm *(Greek, "time, flow")*   The way sounds move against the flow of time. In language, the melody of words together: how they rise and fall, how their pitch changes, how they repeat and vary phrases, how they mix long and short syllables, how the number of syllables rolls out, how the words are punctuated by pauses and silences.

Rhythm must be distinguished from *meter, which may or may not appear in poetry. All writing has rhythm, both prose and verse, although that rhythm may not seem as prominent in expository writing as in a poem. Writing is a temporal art (or act); it necessarily involves words moving against or along with time. Meter, however, is a pattern of measurement, a way of counting words, or syllables, or accents, or the length of syllables. It is like the time signature in music; a piece in 4/4 time has an underlying pattern of four quarter notes per measure; if the melody rigorously followed that pattern, however, it would soon become tedious (especially if the pitch of the notes never varied). Rhythm in metrical poetry resembles the way melody

plays around the steady beat of metronome or drummer: rising, falling, slowing down, speeding up, pausing.

Riddle A poem that playfully or mysteriously hides its subject, describing it but not naming it; a puzzle to be solved by the reader.

A ROUTE OF EVANESCENCE
Emily Dickinson (1830-1886)

A Route of Evanescence
With a revolving Wheel—
A Resonance of Emerald—
A Rush of Cochineal—
And every Blossom on the Bush
Adjusts its tumbled Head—
The mail from Tunis, probably,
An easy Morning's Ride—

Rime Couée *(reem coo-áy; French, "tail rhyme")* Six-line stanza, rhymed *aabaab*, in which the *a* lines (one, two, four, and five) are longer than the short *b* lines (three and six). (*See: Burns stanza, tailed sonnet.*)

Rime Riche *(reem reesh; also rich rhyme)* Rhymes that sound like the same word but mean different things and may be spelled differently, such as *I* and *eye*, or *roam* and *Rome*; also called homophones.

Rispetto *(Italian, "respect"; plural, rispetti)* A poetic form consisting of two *quatrains, usually rhymed *abab ccdd*, often in iambic tetrameter. Originally this Tuscan form, used by Lorenzo de' Medici, contained between six and twelve lines per stanza. Its traditional subject is amorous, paying "respect" to a woman.

Rondeau *(ron-dóe; plural, rondeaux; French, meaning something round or circular, referring specifically to a dance, the "round," for which such lyrics were composed)* A form consisting of fifteen lines (sometimes fewer) arranged in three parts and rhyming *aabba aabR aabbaR*. The *R* indicates a refrain or *rentrement* that repeats the first word or phrase of the opening line.

The terms *rondeau, rondel, roundel,* and *roundelay* were once used interchangeably for certain French forms that use intricate rhyming

on two different rhyme sounds (*a* and *b*) and repeat part of a line, a whole line, or two whole lines as refrains. Although all of these terms denote what are called fixed forms, the original distinctions between them were extremely loose. To further complicate this nomenclature, what we now call a *triolet was once the simplest, shortest kind of rondeau. The chart in which the currently recognized patterns of "Five Similar Repeating French Forms" appear will clarify matters for the reader or writer who prefers strict rules to casual practice. In any case, the terms have now been fairly stable for hundreds of years. (*See: ballade, rondeau redoublé, rondel, rondel double, rondelet, roundel, roundelay, triolet*)

The first, and oldest, of the following rondeaux uses fewer than the usual fifteen lines. François Villon omits three lines (two, seven, and eleven) and rhymes *abbaabR abbaR*. All of these omitted lines would have rhymed on the same sound: *a*. Since there are eight *a* rhymes and only five *b* rhymes (plus the two unrhymed *refrains*) in the full, fifteen-line form of the rondeau, it makes sense to drop some of the *a* rhymes. Dropping the *b* rhymes, however, would magnify the disproportion, rather than alleviate it.

The rondeau by Paul Laurence Dunbar adheres to the standard pattern. In "We Wear the Mask," the "We" refers to African-Americans. And what better mask for a poem about hiding the pain caused by oppression than an intricate French form!

> TO DEATH, OF HIS LADY / François Villon
> (1431-?; tr. Dante Gabriel Rossetti)
>
> Death, of thee do I make my moan,
>   Who hadst my lady away from me,
>   Nor wilt assuage thine enmity
> Till with her life thou hast mine own:
> For since that hour my strength has flown.
>   Lo! what wrong was her life to thee,
>   Death?
>
> Two we were, and the heart was one;
>   Which now being dead, dead I must be,
>   Or seem alive as lifelessly
> As in the choir the painted stone,
>   Death!

WE WEAR THE MASK
Paul Laurence Dunbar (1872-1906)

We wear the mask that grins and lies,
It hides our cheeks and shades our eyes—
This debt we pay to human guile;
With torn and bleeding hearts we smile,
And mouth with myriad subtleties.

Why should the world be over-wise,
In counting all our tears and sighs?
Nay, let them only see us, while
    We wear the mask.

We smile, but, O great Christ, our cries
To thee from tortured souls arise.
We sing, but oh the clay is vile
Beneath our feet, and long the mile;
But let the world dream otherwise,
    We wear the mask!

Five Similar Repeating French Forms

Rondel	*Rondeau*	*Roundel*	*Rondelet*	*Triolet*
A	a	a	A	A
B	a	b	b	B
b	b	a	A	a
a	b	B	a	A
	a		b	a
a		b	b	b
b	a	a	A	A
A	a	b		B
B	b			
	refrain	a		
a		b		
b	a	a		
b	a	B		
a	b			
A	b			
(B)	a			
	refrain			

NOTE: Capital A or B indicates a refrain on that rhyme sound. "Refrain" indicates one or more unrhymed words from the first line. Parentheses indicate a line that is optional. Spaces indicate the usual positions for stanza breaks.

Rondeau Redoublé *(or "double rondeau")*   A form related to the rondeau but longer, in which twenty-five lines are arranged in a pattern of *ABA'B' babA abaB babA' abaB' babaR*. Here's what the algebra means: capital letters indicate refrain lines; each line of the opening quatrain serves once as a refrain at the end of the next four quatrains; refrains *A* and *A'* rhyme, as do refrains *B* and *B'*; a letter rhymes whether it's upper or lower case; finally, the *R* signifies a rentrement made up of the first two words or first phrase of the opening line.

The man responsible for this complication is the sixteenth-century French poet Clément Marot. Jean de La Fontaine and Dorothy Parker also wrote in the form, which is especially suited to light verse.

Rondel *(ron-dél; French, "round")*   A form consisting of thirteen lines arranged in three parts and rhyming *ABba abAB abbaA* (the capital letters being refrain lines). A rondel prime (or supreme) adds a fourteenth line, repeating the *B* refrain.

The rondel differs from the *rondeau in that it repeats whole lines as refrains, rhymes them, and is usually (though not always) two lines shorter; the rondeau, on the other hand, repeats only the first part of the opening line as a refrain and does not rhyme it with anything else. The rhyme schemes differ as well, although both forms use just two rhyme sounds (*a* and *b*). Each form consists of three stanzas.

*Roundel was used synonymously with the other terms, but in the nineteenth century the English poet A.C. Swinburne settled upon a specific pattern and wrote many poems in the form. This confusion in terms can be seen in the following rondel, which is called "Rondeau"—an instance of how freely the terms were used and how similar these forms really are.

RONDEAU / Charles d'Orléans
(1391-1465; tr. Richard Wilbur)

The year has cast its cloak away
That was of driving rains and snows,
And now in flowered arras goes,
And wears the clear sun's glossy ray.

No bird or beast but seems to say
In cries or chipper tremolos:

The year has cast its cloak away
That was of driving rains and snows.

Stream, brook and silver fountain play,
And each upon itself bestows
A spangled livery as it flows.
All creatures are in fresh array.
The year has cast its cloak away.

Rondel Double An expanded form of the *rondel in which four quatrains rhyme *ABBA abBA abba ABBA*. The capital letters indicate refrains.

Rondelet *(French, "little rondel")* A form consisting of seven lines, with a refrain and only two rhymes. The rhyme and refrain scheme is *AbAabbA* (capital *A* = refrain). The refrain lines (*A*) each contain four syllables; the other lines (*a* and *b*) each contain eight syllables.

Roundel An eleven-line variant of the *rondeau, introduced into English by Algernon Charles Swinburne in his *A Century of Roundels*. The term *roundel* is not new; it was used in Geoffrey Chaucer's time to mean a "rondel," as in his "Merciles Beaute: A Triple Roundel." Swinburne's roundel consists of three stanzas rhymed *abaB bab abaB*. The *B* is a short phrase from the first part of the opening line; it is used as a refrain and rhymes with *b* (lines two, five, seven and nine). Metrically, the refrains are short and contain one or two stresses, while the rest of the lines contain four or five (the measure staying consistent throughout a given poem). Swinburne's roundels may be trochaic (like the example below), iambic, or anapestic.

A NIGHT-PIECE BY MILLET
Algernon Charles Swinburne (1834-1909)

Wind and sea and cloud and cloud-forsaking
Mirth of moonlight where the storm leaves free
Heaven awhile, for all the wrath of waking
      Wind and sea.

Bright with glad mad rapture, fierce with glee,
Laughs the moon, borne on past cloud's o'ertaking
Fast, it seems, as wind or sail can flee.

One blown sail beneath her, hardly making
Forth, wild-winged for habourage yet to be,
Strives and leaps and pants beneath the breaking
          Wind and sea.

NOTE: *Millet*: Nineteenth-century French painter.

Roundelay Sometimes used interchangeably with *rondeau, *rondel, and *roundel; in a more general sense, it is simply a lyric with refrain.

Rubai *(Persian, "quatrain")* A four-line stanza rhymed *aaXa* or *aaaa*; usually an occasional poem, spontaneous and witty, but grounded in the mystical Sufi tradition of Islam. A poem made up of three stanzas is called a rubaiyat.

The rubai is also called the *Omar Khayyam stanza, after Edward Fitzgerald's 1859 paraphrase of 101 quatrains from *The Rubaiyat of Omar Khayyam*, a twelfth-century work in Persian. In 1967 Robert Graves and Omar Ali-Shah made a new translation to correct the inaccuracies of the Fitzgerald version. They offer the following comparison of one quatrain:

> *Romanized Persian text*
>
> Gar dast dihad zi maghzi gandum nāni
> Az mai kaduī zi gusfandi rāni
> Wa āngah man wa tu nishasta dar wairani
> 'Aish buwad ān na haddi har sultāni

> *Fitzgerald translation*
>
> A Book of Verses underneath the Bough,
> A Jug of Wine, a Loaf of Bread—and Thou
>   Beside me singing in the Wilderness—
> Oh, Wilderness were Paradise enow!

> *Graves-Shah translation*
>
> Should our day's portion be one mancel loaf,
> A haunch of mutton and a gourd of wine
> Set for us two alone on the wide plain,
> No Sultan's bounty could evoke such joy.

Fitzgerald retains the rhyme scheme but is careless with the sense
and even the spirit of the original. Graves and Shah sacrifice rhyme
for the sake of fidelity to the Persian text.

Rune, Runic Verse *(Old English, "mystery")*   A chant or incantation,
associated with magic. Runes used the letters of the Teutonic alphabet
and were carved on swords, drinking vessels, and stones. Rudyard
Kipling's "The Runes on Weland's Sword" begins:

> A Smith makes me
> To betray my Man
> In my first fight.
>
> To gather Gold
> At the world's end
> I am sent.
>
> The Gold I gather
> Comes into England
> Out of deep Water.
>
> Like a shining Fish
> Then it descends
> Into deep Water.

S

Sapphics, Sapphic Stanza Quatrain in which the first three lines contain eleven syllables and the fourth line contains five syllables; named after the Greek poet Sappho, who lived in the seventh and sixth centuries B.C. and was the best-known practitioner of the form.

In Ancient Greek, the lines are arranged quantitatively, based on the length of syllables (long or short) according to the following pattern:

Feet that can
be spondaic (- -)

‿	‿	‿ ‿	‿	‿	2 and/or 5
‿	‿	‿ ‿	‿	‿	2 and/or 5
‿	‿	‿ ‿	‿	‿	2 and/or 5
‿ ‿	‿				2

In English, the long syllables (-) would normally be accents (′). In approximating the Sapphic stanza, a poet in English can count syllables only (11-11-11-5), or place accents where the long syllables appear in the pattern (trochaic tetrameter, with an extra unstressed syllable in the third foot of lines 1-3 and in the first foot of line 4), or use iambic pentameter in the first three lines (perhaps adding an extra unstressed syllable at some point), or use an accentual count of 5-5-5-2, or simply write three medium-long free-verse lines followed by a short one. Some poets rhyme the lines (although Sappho did not rhyme hers).

The short fourth line is called an adonic. It effectively punctuates the stanza, giving it variety and a quick punch appropriate either for

springing to the next stanza or ending a poem. It is also a natural phrase rhythm in English, appearing frequently in expressions ("Put up or shut up") and names (Abraham Lincoln, Eleanor Rigby, Theodore Roethke).

POEM 1 / Sappho (circa 620-550 B.C.; tr. John Frederick Nims)

On your throne, a marvel of art, immortal
Aphrodite, daughter of Zeus, amused to
lead us on through folly and pain—you'd doom me
    body and soul now?
Come with help, if ever in days gone-by you
heard me praying desperately in the distance—
heard and hurried, leaving your father's home to
    harness your golden
car up. Had it yoked in a moment. Gamy
sparrows flew you quick as a wink around the
dusky earth, their wings in a blur, and sky-high
    diving through cover
spiraled down here. You (your immortal features
hid a half smile stirring the dimple) asked me:
"What's it now, love? Trouble again? And this time
    why the commotion?
What's your wild heart heaving to have, I wonder,
this time? Only tell me her name, the one you'd
have me wheedle round to your love. She's being
    cruel to you, Sappho?
Running off now? Soon she'll be running after.
Won't take gifts? Tomorrow she will—and give them.
Just can't love? Tomorrow she'll love—but you'll see—
    like it or not, dear."
Even so, though! Now's when I need you. End this
tossing, turning! All that I'm mad to have, you
know so well! Then work for it, standing with me
    shoulder to shoulder.

SAPPHICS AGAINST ANGER / Timothy Steele (b. 1948)

Angered, may I be near a glass of water;
May my first impulse be to think of Silence,
Its deities (who are they? do in fact they
    Exist? etc.).

May I recall what Aristotle says of
The subject: to give vent to rage is not to
Release it but to be increasingly prone
    To its incursions.

May I imagine being in the *Inferno*,
Hearing it asked: "Vergilio mio, who's
That sulking with Achilles there?" and hearing
    Vergil say: "Dante,

That fellow, at the slightest provocation,
Slammed phone receivers down, and waved his arms like
A madman. What Attila did to Europe,
    What Genghis Khan did

To Asia, that poor dope did to his marriage."
May I, that is, put learning to good purpose,
Mindful that melancholy is a sin, though
    Stylish at present.

Better than rage is the post-dinner quiet,
The sink's warm turbulence, the streaming platters,
The suds rehearsing down the drain in spirals
    In the last rinsing.

For what is, after all, the good life save that
Conducted thoughtfully, and what is passion
If not the holiest of powers, sustaining
    Only if mastered.

Satire *(Latin, "platter of mixed fruits")* A literary work that ridicules, scorns, mocks, or otherwise attacks the folly or evil of a person, an institution, an idea, or a culture.

Ezra Pound remarks that satire is "surgery, insertions and amputations" and that it "reminds one that certain things are not worthwhile. It draws one to consider time wasted." The Greek soldier-poet Archilochos, who lived in the seventh century B.C. and whose work survives in fragments, is considered the first satirist:

I know how to love those
Who love me, how to hate.
My enemies I overwhelm
With abuse. The ant bites!
(tr. Guy Davenport)

Some of the best and earliest satire appears in the plays of
Aristophanes, such as *Clouds*, which pokes fun at Socrates and other
philosophers. But the terms used to classify the two main kinds of
satire come from two Roman poets, Juvenal (circa A.D. 60-140) and
Horace (65-8 B.C.). Juvenalian satire is a sharp-tongued, morally out-
raged indictment of the evils of society. Its ridicule is fierce. Here is
the opening of Samuel Johnson's "The Vanity of Human Wishes,"
which is subtitled "The Tenth Satire of Juvenal Imitated":

Let observation, with extensive view,
Survey mankind, from China to Peru;
Remark each anxious toil, each eager strife,
And watch the busy scenes of crowded life;
Then say how hope and fear, desire and hate,
O'erspread with snares the clouded maze of fate,
Where wav'ring man, betray'd by vent'rous pride,
To tread the dreary paths without a guide,
As treach'rous phantoms in the mist delude,
Shuns fancied ills, or chases airy good;
How rarely reason guides the stubborn choice,
Rules the bold hand, or prompts the suppliant voice;
How nations sink, by darling schemes oppress'd,
When vengeance listens to the fool's request.
Fate wings with ev'ry wish th' afflictive dart,
Each gift of nature, and each grace of art,
With fatal heat impetuous courage glows,
With fatal sweetness elocution flows,
Impeachment stops the speaker's pow'rful breath,
And restless fire precipitates on death.

Horatian satire is gentler, using laughter more as a medicine than
as a weapon. Here is the opening of the first poem in Horace's first
book of *Satires*:

Maecenas, why is no one living
Happy where he is, whether he chose for himself or fate
For him? Everyone wants to be someone else.
"O blessed merchants!" cries the stiff old soldier,
His body broken by years of hard campaigning.
But the merchant, as the West wind tosses his ship,
Cries, "War is better. And why? There's a battle,
In a moment you're either dead or a hero."
The lawyer swears he'll return to the land, when
A client drags him out of bed at dawn.
The farmer who's signed a bond and is forced to travel to town
Swears the city's the only place.

(tr. Burton Raffel)

Guy Davenport points out that the following satire by Archilochos was "provoked by the superstitious reaction to the solar eclipse of 14 March 711 B.C." As regarding the "late famous general" satirized by Jonathan Swift, there is perhaps no point in searching after his identity, since the poet wanted not to enshrine but to defame. (He is, in fact, the Duke of Marlborough.) As W.H. Auden points out about Alexander Pope's satirical epic, *The Dunciad*:

> [it] should never be read with notes, for to think that it matters who the characters were or why Pope was angry with them is to miss the whole point of the poem, which is best appreciated by supplying one's own contemporary list of the servants of the Goddess of Dullness.

FRAGMENT 113 / Archilochos
(7th century B.C.; tr. Guy Davenport)

There's nothing now
We can't expect to happen!
Anything at all, you can bet,
Is ready to jump out at us.
No need to wonder over it.
Father Zeus has turned
Noon to night, blotting out
The sunshine utterly,
Putting cold terror

At the back of the throat.
Let's believe all we hear.
Even that dolphins and cows
Change place, porpoises and goats,
Rams booming along in the offing,
Mackerel nibbling in the hill pastures.
I wouldn't be surprised,
I wouldn't be surprised.

A SATIRICAL ELEGY ON THE DEATH OF
A LATE FAMOUS GENERAL
Jonathan Swift (1667-1745)

His Grace! impossible! what dead!
Of old age too, and in his bed!
And could that Mighty Warrior fall?
And so inglorious, after all!
Well, since he's gone, no matter how,
The last loud trump must wake him now:
And, trust me, as the noise grows stronger,
He'd wish to sleep a little longer.
And could he be indeed so old
As by the news-papers we're told?
Threescore, I think, is pretty high;
'Twas time in conscience he should die.
This world he cumber'd long enough;
He burnt his candle to the snuff;
And that's the reason, some folks think,
He left behind *so great a s . . . k.*
Behold his funeral appears,
Nor widow's sighs, nor orphan's tears,
Wont at such times each heart to pierce,
Attend the progress of his herse.
But what of that, his friends may say,
He had those honours in his day.
True to his profit and his pride,
He made them weep before he dy'd.

Come hither, all ye empty things,
Ye bubbles rais'd by breath of Kings;
Who float upon the tide of state,

Come hither, and behold your fate.
Let pride be taught by this rebuke,
How very mean a thing's a Duke;
From all his ill-got honours flung,
Turn'd to that dirt from whence he sprung.

Scansion The marking of a poem to note stressed and unstressed syllables, *feet, and *caesurae (pauses). A poem that adheres to some metrical pattern is said to "scan."

Although scansion is held in much the same repute as sentence diagramming, it is useful in reading a poem closely—and subsequently in writing one's own. (*See: accentual-syllabic meter.*)

Scud Vladimir Nabokov's term for an unaccented stress in accentual-syllabic verse.

For example, the first foot in line twenty-seven of Byron's "Mazeppa" (one of Nabokov's examples in his *Notes on Prosody*) is a scud:

And in the depths of forests darkling,

"And in" sounds like a pyrrhic foot (˘ ˘) but could be scanned as an iamb (˘ ´). It is an unstressed syllable but receives a metrical stress. Nabokov calls a line with a scud in the first foot a "first scudder." The line itself is "scudded." Nabokov rejects the notion of metrical substitution or inverted feet, so that, in an iambic line, what we call a trochaic substitution (´ ˘) would be a "tilted scud" (marked ″ -). Nabokov remarks, "Any tilt is a tilted scud, since the stress in such feet is not accented. English theorists term tilted scuds 'inversion of stress'; a better description would be 'inversion of accent,' since it is the word stress that (more or less gracefully) feigns a surrender to the meter. The meter is basic and cannot succumb to the word." Nabokov calls the common *minor ionic foot a "split reverse tilt."

Sentence A group of words that expresses a complete thought or utterance, including at least one subject and at least one main verb (in other words, at least one independent clause); a string of words that begins with a capital letter and continues unwinding until it reaches a period (or full-stop, as the British say).

Most poems feature an interplay between sentence and line, which may coincide but often do not. Sentences can be as short as a single word ("Stop!") or as long as an entire poem. They can be declarative ("I did it."), exclamatory ("I did it!"), interrogative ("Did I do it?"), or imperative ("Do it."). They can be simple ("I did it."), compound ("I did it, and that's that."), complex ("I did it, because I wanted to.") or compound-complex ("I did it, because I wanted to, and that's that.").

The following poem consists of a single sentence that progresses through eight short lines. There is another one-sentence poem in the entry on *Black Mountain School, Robert Creeley's "I Know a Man."

PHOTOSYNTHESIS
A.R. Ammons (b. 1926)

The sun's wind
blows the fire
green, sails the
chloroplasts,
lifts banks, bogs,
boughs into flame:
the green ash of
yellow loss.

Sentence Fragment   A group of words that ends with a period but lacks either a subject or a main verb; a subordinate clause or a phrase or a single word standing by itself. Here are some examples of fragments (in one line of Geoffrey Hill's "Mercian Hymns"):

A pet-name, a common name. Best-selling brand, curt
graffito. A laugh; a cough. A syndicate. A specious
gift. Scoffed-at horned phonograph.

A fragment is a mistake if used carelessly, but a valuable device if used expressively or rhythmically.

Sequence   A group of poems, often numbered; a progression of poems or sections.

The poems in a sequence must be connected in some way, perhaps by title, theme, subject matter, stanza form, range of references,

speaker(s), or an ongoing narrative. A sequence offers a good way to make a *long poem out of a number of short lyrics. Jim Harrison refers to such sequences as "suites," like an orchestral work composed of many brief movements. The best known, and most enduring, kind of sequence is the *sonnet sequence. Recent book-length sequences include Rita Dove's *Thomas and Beulah* and Marvin Bell's *The Book of the Dead Man.*

VEGETABLE POEMS / Katha Pollitt (b. 1949)

1. Potatoes

Blind knobby eyes feeling out
the chinks in the damp black earth
all summer long these tunnel under the fence
to throttle the open field of milkweed and Queen Anne's lace
or live for years in cellars
their softened, mealy flesh
rotting into the earth, indistinguishable from earth
but still flinging up roots and occasional leaves
white as fish in caves.
Feel them, the swollen sac
the baggy elephant skin:
if they are edible, it is only by accident.

2. Tomato

It is the female fruit: the plush
red flesh the fat
sac of seeds and oh
those silky membranes
plump and calm
it fits your palm just so
it is that perfect softball of your childhood
the one you always lost
you can stroke the sleek skin
you can thumb
the comfortable curve beneath:
here's
all soft gum
no sheer
secret murderous teeth.

3. Onion

The smoothness of onions infuriates him
so like the skin of women or their expensive clothes
and the striptease of onions, which is also a disappearing act.
He says he is searching for the ultimate nakedness
but when he finds that thin green seed
that negligible sprout of a heart
we could have told him he'd only be disappointed.
Meanwhile the onion has been hacked to bits
and he's weeping in the kitchen most unromantic tears.

4. Eggplant

Like a dark foghorn in a yellow kitchen
we imagine the eggplant's
melancholy bass
booming its pompous operatic sorrows
a prince down on his luck
preserving among peasants
an air of dignified, impenetrable gloom
or Boris, dying,
booming, *I still am Tsar.*

5. Nettles

Like neighbors not invited to the wedding
these show up anyway: fat stalks
dull hairy leaves
they stand at the edge of the garden and cry *I burn!*
Ugly, but tenacious,
they make themselves useful: in teas,
poultices, cures for baldness and rheumatic complaints.
From us, such homely uses are all they can hope for,
but they too have their dream:
to be the chosen food of their beautiful loves
the peacock
small tortoiseshell
and red admiral caterpillars.

Sestina *(ses-tée-nuh; Italian, sixth)* A fixed form, developed in Provençal by the Troubadours: six end-words are repeated in an interwoven order through six stanzas and in a final three-line envoi (also called tornada) which contains all six words.

After the first stanza establishes a sestina's six end-words (1-6), each of the following stanzas rearranges the previous stanza's end-words as follows: 6, 1, 5, 2, 4, 3. This order can be remembered easily as a weaving pattern that moves from bottom to top and from outside to inside. In *The Spirit of Romance*, Ezra Pound calls the sestina "a thin sheet of flame folding and infolding upon itself." Marilyn Hacker describes it: "A camera on a rotating boom,/ six words spin slowly round and pan the room."

Arnaut Daniel (who appears as a character in Dante's *Purgatorio*) wrote the earliest extant sestina in the twelfth century. It was promptly answered by Bertran de Born's sestina using the same end-words. The original musical setting that accompanied both sestinas still exists. In the early twentieth century, Ezra Pound repopularized the form with his "Sestina: Altaforte," a dramatic monologue based on Bertran's life, but not on any particular poem. Pound's sestina uses the end-words "peace," "music," "clash," "opposing," "crimson," and "rejoicing."

A double sestina consists of two sestinas with a single envoi, using the same six end-words throughout. Once the first set of six six-line stanzas concludes, another starts up. After twelve six-line stanzas, the envoi finally appears. An example is "Ye goat-herd gods, that love the grassy mountains," by the Elizabethan poet Sir Philip Sidney.

The repeated end-words (sometimes called teleutons) do not ordinarily rhyme. But Sidney wrote another sestina, "Farewell, O sun, Arcadia's clearest light," whose end-words are "light," "treasure," "might," "pleasure," "direction," and "affection." Because of the set pattern of end-words, Sidney's rhyme schemes change from stanza to stanza.

Contemporary poets often feel free to alter the end-words of a sestina as they recur, adding or deleting suffixes, using puns or homophones or different meanings, or even using a slant rhyme ("boot" to "boat," for example)—all to make the form more flexible and more surprising while keeping a sense of the repetitive structure. In a sestina that follows, Donald Justice alters the end-words each time

they recur—his poem is appropriately called "The Metamorphosis"—
and omits the three-line envoi.

					End
SESTINA *(Lo ferm voler q'el cor m'intra)*			*Stanza*	*Line*	*word*
Arnaut Daniel (12th Century; tr. John Drury)					

	Stanza	Line	End word
The firm resolve that has entered	1	1	A
my heart cannot be ripped out by beak or nail		2	B
of flatterers who gab away their souls.		3	C
I don't dare batter them with stick or rod,		4	D
alone, without the aid of any uncle,		5	E
and so I'll love my love in grove or chamber.		6	F
When I recollect the chamber	2	1	F
where—my loss too—I know that no man enters		2	A
(and everyone's more strict than brother or uncle),		3	E
none of my parts is still, not even a nail,		4	B
just like a boy about to feel the rod—		5	D
I fear that she might overwhelm my soul.		6	C
If I were hers, body and soul,	3	1	C
and she'd agree to hide me in her chamber!		2	F
It strikes a blow to my heart, more than a rod's,		3	D
that where she is this servant may not enter.		4	A
But I'll remain, close as her flesh and nails,		5	B
ignoring the reproach of friend or uncle.		6	E
The sister of my uncle	4	1	E
I don't love nearly as much—upon my soul!		2	C
If she allowed me, close as fingernail		3	B
to finger, I'd advance into her chamber.		4	F
I'd bow to love that in my heart has entered		5	A
sooner than heed a hard man's flimsy rod.		6	D
Since the flowering of the dry rod	5	1	D
and Adam propagating nephews and uncles,		2	E
I can't believe the fine love that has entered		3	A
my heart has come before in body or soul.		4	C
Wherever she is, in plaza or in chamber,		5	F
my body doesn't stray the length of a nail.		6	B

And my body fastens with nails,	6	1	B
attached to her like bark, the branching rod,		2	D
for she is joy's tower and palace and chamber,		3	F
lessening my love for brother, parent, or uncle;		4	E
in paradise, twice the joy for my soul		5	C
if any man who loves that well can enter.		6	A

Arnaut has posted this song of nail and uncle	Envoi	1	All six end-words (2 per line)
to gratify the soul who weilds a rod:		2	
Sir Desire, famed for chambers he has entered.		3	

NOTE: *Sir Desire*: the Provençal word translated here is *Desirat*, identified in a marginal gloss of an early manuscript as a nickname for Bertran de Born, a fellow Troubadour who answered this sestina with one of his own, "Certainly great vileness enters," using the same end-words. Some scholars, however, think that *Desirat* refers to a lady, the "desired one."

SESTINA / Elizabeth Bishop (1911-1979)

September rain falls on the house.
In the failing light, the old grandmother
sits in the kitchen with the child
beside the Little Marvel Stove,
reading the jokes from the almanac,
laughing and talking to hide her tears.

She thinks that her equinoctial tears
and the rain that beats on the roof of the house
were both foretold by the almanac,
but only known to a grandmother.
The iron kettle sings on the stove.
She cuts some bread and says to the child,

It's time for tea now; but the child
is watching the teakettle's small hard tears
dance like mad on the hot black stove,
the way the rain must dance on the house.
Tidying up, the old grandmother
hangs up the clever almanac

on its string. Birdlike, the almanac
hovers half open above the child,
hovers above the old grandmother

and her teacup full of dark brown tears.
She shivers and says she thinks the house
feels chilly, and puts more wood in the stove.

It was to be, says the Marvel Stove.
I know what I know, says the almanac.
With crayons the child draws a rigid house
and a winding pathway. Then the child
puts in a man with buttons like tears
and shows it proudly to the grandmother.

But secretly, while the grandmother
busies herself about the stove,
the little moons fall down like tears
from between the pages of the almanac
into the flower bed the child
has carefully placed in front of the house.

Time to plant tears, says the almanac.
The grandmother sings to the marvellous stove
and the child draws another inscrutable house.

THE METAMORPHOSIS
Donald Justice (b. 1925)

Past Mr. Raven's tavern
Up Cemetery Hill
Around by the Giant Oak
And Drowning Creek gone dry
Into the Hunting Woods
And that was how he went

At his back the wind
Blowing out of heaven
And at his feet foul weeds
That it was like to hell
And scarcely could he draw
Breath and the ribs did ache

No rest got under the oak
Nor water for the wound
Yet kept the way and drew
Home at length to haven

And the familiar hall
His key into the wards

Then owls cried out from the woods
And terrors of that ilk
So that the bitch at heel
A little moaned and whined
As she some fit were having
That back her long legs drew

Whereat his mouth stood dry
And without any words
Despite his heart heaving
And tongue working to speak
Some name to cast the wonder
Straight from his heart whole

Then bent he to the keyhole
Nor might his eyes withdraw
The while the hall unwound
That thing which afterwards
No man should know or its like
Whether dead or living

Simile A comparison that uses some linking word (*like, as, such as, how*) to make the likeness clear. A figure of speech. A kind of *metaphor (though a true metaphor does not use linking words).

In mathematical symbols, a simile would require an approximate sign ($\approx$), meaning "similar to." In Dylan Thomas' "Fern Hill," there is "fire green as grass," and the poem ends:

Time held me green and dying
Though I sang in my chains like the sea.

A simile generally sounds more casual, and less emphatic, than a metaphor. Instead of a sheer leap, it provides a visible bridge linking two things, indicating a likeness among many differences. It gives both pleasure and information.

Sixain *(síx-ane)* A six-line stanza.
Sixains appear most frequently in the *stave of six (rhymed *ababcc*).

In a *sonnet, a six-line stanza is called a sestet. Other six-line stanzas include the *Burns stanza (rhymed *aaabab*) and the *sestina (except for its three-line envoi).

The following poem by Robert Browning uses an envelope pattern (*abccba*), working inward and then out. The rhyme sounds in the middle are quite pronounced, while those on the outer edges of each stanza are more faintly heard, a nice musical effect.

MEETING AT NIGHT
Robert Browning (1812-1889)

The gray sea and the long black land;
And the yellow half-moon large and low;
And the startled little waves that leap
In fiery ringlets from their sleep,
As I gain the cove with pushing prow,
And quench its speed i' the slushy sand.

Then a mile of warm sea-scented beach;
Three fields to cross till a farm appears;
A tap at the pane, the quick sharp scratch
And blue spurt of a lighted match,
And a voice less loud, thro' its joys and fears,
Than the two hearts beating each to each!

Skeltonics   Rough, bounding verse, usually two accents per line, rhymed several lines in a row, as in the poems of John Skelton (1460-1529). Robert Graves' "In the Wilderness" is a twentieth-century poem in skeltonics.

TO MISTRESS MARGARET HUSSEY
John Skelton (1460-1529)

Merry Margaret,
As midsummer flower,
Gentle as falcon
Or hawk of the tower:
With solace and gladness,
Much mirth and no madness,
All good and no badness;
So joyously,

So maidenly,
So womanly
Her demeaning
In every thing,
Far, far passing
That I can indite,
Or suffice to write
Of Merry Margaret
As midsummer flower,
Gentle as falcon
Or hawk of the tower.
As patient and still
And as full of good will
As fair Isaphill,
Coriander,
Sweet pomander,
Good Cassander,
Steadfast of thought,
Well made, well wrought,
Far may be sought
Ere that ye can find
So courteous, so kind
As Merry Margaret,
This midsummer flower,
Gentle as falcon
Or hawk of the tower.

Slant Rhyme *(also called approximate rhyme, half rhyme, near rhyme, and off rhyme)* *Rhyme that neither looks nor sounds exact. Instead of echoing both vowel and consonant, a slant rhyme echoes only one of them.

With monosyllabic words, if the vowel is the same but the final consonant changes, the rhyme is assonant (*myth/whip, hope/cone, break/cape*). If the final consonant is the same but the vowel changes, the rhyme is consonant (*myth/bath, hope/cape, break/smack*). If the vowel changes but the consonants surrounding it remain the same, the rhyme is alliterative (*myth/math, hope/hype, break/brook*). With polysyllabic words, the same combinations hold true for the final accent, but the unstressed syllable(s) at the end usually stay the same,

dangling like little tails (*Bible: sidle/stubble/babble*). Poets differ in their standards of decency concerning proper or improper slant rhymes. Robert Graves insisted on consonance. Other sticklers require similar vowels (so that *bat/bet*, both containing short vowels, would qualify, but *bat/boat*, one short vowel and one long, would not). Popular songwriters favor assonance because it rings out more noticeably, especially long open vowels. But some poets are casual, careless, reckless, experimental, or especially open-minded—depending on your view of laissez-faire poetics—in their rhyming. As with most poetic issues, a critic may prescribe and proscribe as much as he likes, but precedent is the ultimate law: If the results are poetry, any deviance from standard practice can be sanctioned; If the results are doggerel or drivel, no literary advocate can rescue the offender.

from "FIVE SONGS" (II)
W.H. Auden (1907-1973)

That night when joy began
Our narrowest veins to flush,
We waited for the flash
Of morning's levelled gun.

But morning let us pass,
And day by day relief
Outgrows his nervous laugh,
Grows credulous of peace,

As mile by mile is seen
No trespasser's reproach,
And love's best glasses reach
No fields but are his own.

Song Words fit to be set to music; words and melody combined; a tune, ditty, lyric, *lied, chanson*. Different from a chant, which is declaimed or intoned rather than sung. (*See: ballad, blues, chorus, music poem, rap, spiritual.*)

Some of the devices in the following songs include *refrains (repeated phrases, such as "John Anderson my jo"), *alliteration (the *f* sounds in "Full fadom five thy father lies"), and *onomatopoeia ("ding-dong"). Both songs are rhymed, as are most songs in English.

FULL FADOM FIVE (from *The Tempest*)
William Shakespeare (1564-1616)

Full fadom five thy father lies.
 Of his bones are coral made:
Those are pearls that were his eyes;
 Nothing of him that doth fade
But doth suffer a sea-change
Into something rich and strange:
Sea-nymphs hourly ring his knell:
 Hark, now I hear them,
  Hark, now I hear them—
Ding dong bell.
Ding dong, ding dong bell,
Ding dong, ding dong bell,
Ding dong, ding dong bell.

NOTE: The italicized lines are sung in what is probably the original setting of Shakespeare's words to music, composed by Robert Johnson (who died in 1634), but they are not included in the text of *The Tempest*. Counter-tenor Alfred Deller recorded a fine version of the song.

fadom: fathom, a measure of six (nonmetrical) feet.

JOHN ANDERSON MY JO
Robert Burns (1759-1796)

John Anderson my jo, John,
 When we were first acquent;
Your locks were like the raven,
 Your bonny brow was brent;
But now your brow is beld, John,
 Your locks are like the snaw;
But blessings on your frosty pow,
 John Anderson my Jo.

John Anderson my jo, John,
 We clamb the hill the gither;
And mony a canty day, John,
 We've had wi' ane anither:

Now we maun totter down, John,
    And hand in hand we'll go;
And sleep the gither at the foot,
    John Anderson my Jo.

NOTE: The tune can be found in *Poems and Songs* of Robert Burns, edited by James Kinsley (Oxford University Press, 1969), and heard in a recording by Jean Redpath.

jo: sweetheart; *acquent*: acquainted; *brent*: smooth, unwrinkled; *beld*: bald; *snaw*: snow; *pow*: head; *the gither*: together; *canty*: lively, pleasant; *maun*: must.

Sonnet *(sáhn-et; Italian, "little song"; or perhaps from the medieval Latin* sonitus, *"murmur, soft sound or noise")* A poem of fourteen lines (give or take a couple), usually rhymed, usually written in iambic pentameter; a song usurped by ideas.

A sonnet often presents an *argument, perhaps a romantic plea in the guise of a legal brief. But it may also contain a description of a memorable scene, or a meditation, or a miniature story, or a portrait, or a list. The rhyme scheme and stanza breaks (if any) often determine the structure of the thoughts.

The first sonnets still in existence come from the Sicilian court of Frederick II, sometime between 1220 and 1230. Officials called notaries, who were actually lawyers, wrote and exchanged them, as did the emperor. Fifty-eight of their sonnets survive, at least twenty-six by Jacopo da Lentini (or Giacomo da Lentino, 1188-1240), who generally receives credit as the inventor of the sonnet—although even his name seems in dispute. Perhaps one of his shorter *nonce forms simply caught on at court and came down to us in much the same fourteen-line form. Jacopo and his colleagues preferred a rhyme scheme of *abababab cdcdcd* or *cdecde* (called the Sicilian sonnet). Sometimes they used repeated end-words, as in a *sestina, instead of rhymes. Here is Jacopo da Lentini's "Io m'aggio posto in core a Dio servire" (translated by John Drury):

I find room in my heart for serving God
    so that, at last, I might reach Paradise,
    the holy place where, I have heard it said,
    solace and ease and gaiety suffice.
Without my lady, though, I wouldn't tread

because my pleasure would be stale indeed
if she were not a part of all that bliss.

But no, believe me, I have no intent
of trafficking in sin while going there.
I only want to gaze at her, content
with her sweet look, the deepness of her stare,
so all my consolation would be spent
watching my lady's joy reach everywhere.

The immediate poetic ancestor of the sonnet may be a Sicilian song form, the *strambotto* (consisting of eight lines rhymed *abababab*—the same pattern Jacopo da Lentini uses for his octave, or first eight lines).

Some writers suggest that Guido Guinizelli (c. 1235-1276) adapted the first stanza of a *canzone into the sonnet, which may be true, but he wasn't even alive when the emperor's lawyers wrote their sonnets in Sicily. Other writers have proposed that the Persian *ghazal may have influenced the form and subject matter of the sonnet, but there seems to be no direct evidence for this conjecture.

In English there are two principal kinds of sonnet: the Petrarchan (or Italian) and the Shakespearean (or English). They are characterized by different rhyme schemes and different organizing principles.

The Petrarchan sonnet, named after the Italian Renaissance poet Francesco Petrarca (Petrarch in English, 1304-1374), rhymes *abbaabba* in its first eight lines (the octave) and variously in the last six (the sestet): *cdcdcd* or *cdedce* or *ccdccd* or *cddcdd* or *cdecde* or *cddcee*. Here is Petrarch's "Sonnet CLIX" (translated by Marion Shore):

In what idea, in what part of the sky
did Nature find the shape she copied there,
to form a face so radiant and fair
and show below what she could do on high?

What river nymph has ever loosed to dry
upon the wind such shining golden hair?
When was one heart so virtuous and rare?
although it is the reason that I die.

He who seeks a glimpse of paradise
here upon this earth must vainly seek

if he has never gazed into her eyes;
   nor knows what sweet destruction Love can wreak
unless he hears the way she sweetly sighs,
and hears her sweetly laugh, and sweetly speak.

The Petrarchan sonnet has a two-part structure; the break between octave and sestet is called the volta ("turning" or turning point). It may or may not be indicated by a stanza break. In English this sonnet form is difficult because of the rhyming demands (four different *a* rhymes, four *b* rhymes, and so on).

The Shakespearean sonnet, named after William Shakespeare (1564-1616), rhymes *abab cdcd efef gg*. Here is Shakespeare's Sonnnet 130:

My mistress' eyes are nothing like the sun;
Coral is far more red than her lips' red;
If snow be white, why then her breasts are dun;
If hairs be wires, black wires grow on her head.
I have seen roses damasked, red and white,
But no such roses see I in her cheeks;
And in some perfumes is there more delight
Than in the breath that from my mistress reeks.
I love to hear her speak, yet well I know
That music hath a far more pleasing sound;
I grant I never saw a goddess go;
My mistress, when she walks, treads on the ground.
    And yet, by heaven, I think my love as rare
    As any she belied with false compare.

NOTE: *damasked*: arranged ornamentally; *reeks*: is exhaled.

This rhyme scheme was apparently first used by Henry Howard, the Earl of Surrey, who also introduced *blank verse to English. Its structure is four-part, based on three quatrains and a couplet (although actual stanza breaks are entirely optional). The rhyme is

easier, and there are several possible turning points (although the crux is usually reached with stanza three or the final couplet, which often moralizes or generalizes).

A less common sonnet form, the Spenserian, named after Edmund Spenser (1552?-1599), rhymes *ababbcbccdcdee*. Here is Sonnet 75 from his sequence, *Amoretti*:

> One day I wrote her name upon the strand,
> But came the waves and washèd it away:
> Agayne I wrote it with a second hand,
> But came the tyde, and made my paynes his pray.
> "Vayne man," sayd she, "that doest in vayne assay,
> A mortall thing so to immortalize,
> For I my selve shall lyke to this decay,
> And eek my name bee wypèd out lykewize."
> "Not so," quod I, "let baser things devize
> To dy in dust, but you shall live by fame:
> My verse your vertues rare shall eternize,
> And in the hevens wryte your glorious name.
> Where whenas death shall all the world subdew,
> Our love shall live, and later life renew."

NOTE: *pray*: prey; *eek*: also.

Poets have tried out many other rhyme combinations in their sonnets. In "On the Sonnet," John Keats aspires to a "more interwoven" rhyme scheme: *abcabdcabcdede*. Like the Spenserian rhyme scheme, this Keatsian one is pleasantly interwoven, but too hard to remember easily. Neither form has found much favor.

One advantage of the two principal rhyme schemes, the Petrarchan and the Shakespearean, is that their structures are neat and logical, easy to recall in the act of composition. Many sonnets are spontaneous, such as the fifty-five *Sonnets to Orpheus* that Rainer Maria Rilke wrote in less than three weeks in February 1922, a "breathless act . . . without one word being doubtful or having to be changed." Rilke improvised his rhyme schemes as he went, using a Shakespearean quatrain (*abab*) to begin his opening sonnet, then shifting to the envelope pattern of the Petrarchan (*cddc*) for the next four lines, and

then concluding with a mirroring pattern (*efg gfe*) sometimes used in Petrarchan sestets. He picked what he needed as he went, but he drew from those two great models, writing (or taking down an "enigmatic dictation") furiously, extemporaneously. Of course, many of Rilke's earlier poems had also been sonnets.

The poet is really free to devise any sort of arrangement that works for a particular sonnet. Robert Frost's "Into My Own" consists of seven rhymed couplets, called a couplet sonnet (rhymed *aabbccddeeffgg*). His "Acquainted with the Night" is a sonnet in *terza rima (rhymed *aba bcb cdc ded ee*). Robert Lowell and John Peck have written blank-verse sonnets, dispensing with rhyme altogether. And the poet may choose to alter the meter. One of Shakespeare's sonnets (CXLV, "Those lips that Love's own hand did make") is in iambic tetrameter. Rilke uses various line lengths in his Sonnets to Orpheus. George Meredith's 1862 sequence, *Modern Love*, contains sonnets of sixteen lines each (rhymed *abbacddceffeghhg*). John Hollander's unrhymed sonnets in his book *Thirteens* consist of thirteen lines of thirteen syllables each. In *Firefall*, Mona Van Duyn has written "minimalist sonnets": "I have shortened the conventional iambic pentameter line in varying degrees, some of the sonnets being held to a one-accent line; but I have kept all other conventions of the Shakespearean, Petrarchan, or Spenserian." (Elizabeth Bishop's two-accent "Sonnet," whose first two lines are "Caught—the bubble/ in the spirit level," is similarly minimalist.) Free-verse sonnets, oddly enough, might hardly qualify as sonnets if they departed from the fourteen-line standard. The "little song" can be corrupted only so much.

The sonnet has not always found favor in English. In his dictionary of 1755, Samuel Johnson defines "sonneteer" as "A small poet, in contempt." He remarks of the sonnet: "It is not very suitable to the English language; and has not been used by any man of eminence since Milton." It has, however, been used by many eminent men and women since Dr. Johnson. Since the sonnet came back in fashion, poets such as William Wordsworth, John Keats, Percy Bysshe Shelley, Alfred, Lord Tennyson, Elizabeth Barrett Browning, Robert Frost, Robert Lowell, John Berryman, Gwendolyn Brooks, and Marilyn Hacker have excelled in the form. (*See: curtal sonnet, Eugene Onegin stanza, sonnet sequence, tailed sonnet; sonnets in other entries are listed in "How to Use This Book."*)

WHEN I CONSIDER HOW MY LIGHT IS SPENT
John Milton (1608-74)

When I consider how my light is spent
 Ere half my days, in this dark world and wide,
 And that one talent which is death to hide
 Lodged with me useless, though my soul more bent
To serve therewith my Maker, and present
 My true account, lest he returning chide;
 "Doth God exact day-labour, light denied?"
 I fondly ask; but Patience to prevent
That murmur, soon replies, "God doth not need
 Either man's work or his own gifts; who best
 Bear his mild yoke, they serve him best. His state
Is kingly. Thousands at his bidding speed
 And post o'er land and ocean without rest:
 They also serve who only stand and wait."

NOTE: Milton wrote this sonnet sometime after becoming totally blind in 1651; *talent*: an allusion to the Parable of the Talents (Matthew xxv.14-30) in which a servant buried the talent (a weight of money) that he received from his master instead of investing it; this "unprofitable servant" was cast "into outer darkness"; *fondly*: foolishly.

ON SEEING THE ELGIN MARBLES
FOR THE FIRST TIME / John Keats (1795-1821)

My spirit is too weak; mortality
 Weighs heavily on me like unwilling sleep,
 And each imagin'd pinnacle and steep
Of godlike hardship tells me I must die
Like a sick eagle looking at the sky.
 Yet 'tis a gentle luxury to weep,
 That I have not the cloudy winds to keep
Fresh for the opening of the morning's eye.
Such dim-conceived glories of the brain
 Bring round the heart an indescribable feud;
So do these wonders a most dizzy pain,
 That mingles Grecian grandeur with the rude
Wasting of old Time—with a billowy main,
 A sun, a shadow of a magnitude.

NOTE: The Elgin Marbles are sculptural and architectural fragments, mainly from the Parthenon, brought to London from Athens by Lord Elgin (1766-1841). Since 1816, they have been in the British Museum.

from BLACKS / Gwendolyn Brooks (b. 1917)

PIANO AFTER WAR

On a snug evening I shall watch her fingers,
Cleverly ringed, declining to clever pink,
Beg glory from the willing keys. Old hungers
Will break their coffins, rise to eat and thank.
And music, warily, like the golden rose
That sometimes after sunset warms the west,
Will warm that room, persuasively suffuse
That room and me, rejuvenate a past.
But suddenly, across my climbing fever
Of proud delight—a multiplying cry.
A cry of bitter dead men who will never
Attend a gentle maker of musical joy.
Then my thawed eye will go again to ice.
And stone will shove the softness from my face.

MENTORS

For I am rightful fellow of their band.
My best allegiances are to the dead.
I swear to keep the dead upon my mind,
Disdain for all time to be overglad.
Among spring flowers, under summer trees,
By chilling autumn waters, in the frosts
Of supercilious winter—all my days
I'll have as mentors those reproving ghosts.
And at that cry, at that remotest whisper,
I'll stop my casual business. Leave the banquet.
Or leave the ball—reluctant to unclasp her
Who may be fragrant as the flower she wears,
Make gallant bows and dim excuses, then quit
Light for the midnight that is mine and theirs.

VESTIBULE / John Peck (b. 1941)

All day our paths had crossed, I'd missed you twice
Or three times—then, had come home tired to find
Your sweater on the couch, your shoes kicked off,
The coffee still warm in your waiting cup—
And lightly called your name, only to hear it
Measure the silences; then felt my eyes
Stray back across the sweater's rich abandon,
The shoes more delicate for lying empty,
The porcelain zero of the cup—but then you called,
Upstairs and far away. Your voice brought back
Another room we entered once together,
Catching our breath—bare benches where the Shakers
Sat quiet after field work and prepared
To go together to the larger room.

Sonnet Sequence *(also called a cycle)* A group of related poems in sonnet form (usually fourteen lines of iambic pentameter with a fixed rhyme scheme). The sonnets may be loosely assembled (perhaps according to theme), or they may tell or imply a story.

Many Elizabethan poets wrote sonnet sequences: Sir Philip Sidney (*Astrophil and Stella*), Edmund Spenser (*Amoretti*), Samuel Daniel (*Delia*), Michael Drayton (*Idea*), and William Shakespeare. In the seventeenth century John Donne wrote his *Holy Sonnets*.

A few sonnet sequences, however, are not wholly sonnets. For example, Marilyn Hacker's *Love, Death, and the Changing of the Seasons* (1986) includes several elongated *villanelles and a couple of *rondeaux.

A crown of sonnets (also called a corona or coronet) is a particular kind of sequence. It consists of seven sonnets; the last line of each one must be repeated as the first line of the next; the final line of the seventh sonnet will repeat the opening line of the sequence, so that the crown is (appropriately) circular. The rhyme scheme is not fixed, but some poets choose not to repeat any rhyme sound once it has been used.

A sonnet redoublé (or redoubled sonnet) is a sequence of fifteen sonnets. Each line of the first sonnet serves, in order, as the last line

of one of the following fourteen sonnets. The first sonnet, sometimes called the *texte*, serves as a kind of supply depot for the rest of the lines.

Sons of Ben Poets associated with Ben Jonson (1572-1637), such as Thomas Carew, Robert Herrick, Richard Lovelace, John Suckling, and Edmund Waller. These poets took Jonson's work, known for wit and classical polish, as their model. Their poems are elegant, witty, and convivial. The group met regularly with Jonson in the Apollo Room of London's Devil Tavern. They are also known as Cavalier poets (those who supported the monarchy and Charles I, as opposed to the "Roundheads," the Puritans who supported Oliver Cromwell, such as John Milton).

AN ODE FOR HIM / Robert Herrick (1591-1674)

Ah, Ben!
Say how or when
Shall we, thy guests,
Meet at those lyric feasts
Made at the Sun,
The Dog, the Triple Tun,
Where we such clusters had
As made us nobly wild, not mad;
And yet each verse of thine
Outdid the meat, outdid the frolic wine.

My Ben!
Or come again,
Or send to us
Thy wit's great overplus;
But teach us yet
Wisely to husband it,
Lest we that talent spend,
And having once brought to an end
That precious stock, the store
Of such a wit the world should have no more.

NOTE: The lines are indented to indicate the number of iambic feet they contain: the more indented, the fewer feet. Each stanza is irregular, but they match each other. The Sun, Dog, and Triple Tun mentioned in stanza one were all London taverns.

Speaker *(also narrator, persona)* The person supposedly uttering the poem. It may be a careful way of describing the poet himself. It may be a character. The speaker of Robert Browning's "My Last Duchess," for example, is the Duke of Ferrara. (*See: dramatic monologue, voice.*)

Speech Stress A stress or accent that occurs naturally in the course of speaking—as opposed to metrical stress, which occurs when the metrical pattern dictates.

Spenserian Stanza A stanza, devised by Edmund Spenser and later used memorably in John Keats' "The Eve of St. Agnes" and Percy Bysshe Shelley's "Adonais," consisting of eight lines of iambic pentameter followed by one line of iambic hexameter, the whole stanza rhymed *ababbcbcc.*

> *from THE FAERIE QUEEN*
> Edmund Spenser (1552?-1599)
>
> In her left hand a cup of gold she held,
> And with her right the riper fruit did reach,
> Whose sappy liquor, that with fulnesse sweld,
> Into her cup she scruzd, with daintie breach
> Of her fine fingers, without fowle empeach,
> That so faire winepresse made the wine more sweet:
> Thereof she usd to give to drinke to each,
> Whom passing by she happened to meet:
> It was her guise, all straungers goodly so to greet.
> (The Bower of Bliss: Book II, canto xii, stanza 56)

Spiritual Religious song made up and sung by African-American slaves in the nineteenth century.

Spirituals combined the African call-and-response with biblical stories, often encoding messages of resistance to bondage and even directions for escaped slaves on their way north to freedom, as in "Follow the Drinking Gourd," which tells how to use what we now call the Big Dipper as a kind of compass. The following poem, "Go Down, Moses," implicitly compares the story of the Israelites in Egypt to slaves in the Deep South.

GO DOWN, MOSES / (Anonymous)

When Israel was in Egyptland,
Let my people go,
Oppressed so hard they could not stand,
Let my people go.

Go down, Moses,
Way down in Egyptland,
Tell old Pharaoh
To let my people go.

"Thus saith the Lord," bold Moses said,
"Let my people go;
If not I'll smite your first-born dead,
Let my people go."

"No more shall they in bondage toil,
Let my people go;
Let them come out with Egypt's spoil,
Let my people go."

The Lord told Moses what to do,
Let my people go;
To lead the children of Israel through,
Let my people go.

Go down, Moses,
Way down in Egyptland,
Tell old Pharaoh,
"Let my people go!"

Spondee, Spondaic *(spón-dee, spon-dáy-ik; Greek, solemn drink-offering)* A foot consisting of two stressed syllables (′ ′), such as "hushed crowd" or "skulls crack."

Spondaic meter is virtually impossible in English, since any minor words (such as *and, the,* and *of*) and any polysyllabic words (such as *conflagration*) would introduce unstressed syllables into a line. Spondees sound emphatic. They can be substituted for most iambic feet; for example, "The birds are flying close" could become "Dark birds fly close—thick flocks," three spondees instead of three iambs. A

spondee often follows a pyrrhic foot (two unstressed syllables, a combination called a *minor ionic, as in the phrase "with a rough push").

Sprung Rhythm A term coined by nineteenth-century Welsh poet-priest Gerard Manley Hopkins. Essentially a dynamic term for accentual poetry, the emphatically stressed lines Hopkins found in nursery rhymes and Old English verse. A Hopkins sonnet in sprung rhythm will count five strong accents but will allow a large, variable number of unstressed syllables.

THE WINDHOVER / Gerard Manley Hopkins (1844-1889)
TO CHRIST OUR LORD

I caught this morning morning's minion, king-
   dom of daylight's dauphin, dapple-dawn-drawn Falcon, in his
     riding
  Of the rolling level underneath him steady air, and
     striding
High there, how he rung upon the rein of a wimpling wing
In his ecstasy! then off, off forth on swing,
  As a skate's heel sweeps smooth on a bow-bend: the hurl and
     gliding
  Rebuffed the big wind. My heart in hiding
Stirred for a bird,—the achieve of, the mastery of the thing!

Brute beauty and valour and act, oh, air, pride, plume, here
  Buckle! AND the fire that breaks from thee then, a billion
Times told lovelier, more dangerous, O my chevalier!

  No wonder of it: shéer plód make plough down sillion
Shine, and blue-bleak embers, ah my dear,
  Fall, gall themselves, and gash gold-vermilion.

NOTE: The apparently short lines "riding," "striding," and "gliding" actually belong to the lines above them. The poem is a Petrarchan sonnet.

Stanza *(Italian, "room")* A group of lines gathered together as a unit, like a paragraph in prose. Usually it is surrounded by white space above and below, but stanza breaks can also be indicated by indentations, a metrical pattern, or a recurring rhyme scheme

(such as couplets). Also called strophe and verse paragraph (especially for blank verse groups of irregular numbers of lines, and for free-verse line groups).

Here is a list of terms for various stanzas:

Number of Lines	General Term for Stanza	Specific types of Stanza
1	*monostich	
2	*couplet, *distich	*elegiac distich, *heroic couplet, *ghazal
3	*tercet	*triplet, *terza rima, *haiku, *blues, *tristich
4	*quatrain	*alcaics, *ballad stanza, common meter, Horatian *ode, hymn stanza, heroic quatrain, *In Memoriam stanza, *Omar Khayyam stanza, *pantoum, *rubai, *sapphics, tetrastich
5	*cinquain	*cinquain, *limerick, *quintilla, pentastich, *tanka
6	*sixain	*Burns stanza, *stave of six, *sestina, sestet (in sonnet)
7	septet	*rhyme royale
8	octave	*ballade, brace octave, common octave, *ottava rima, octave (in *sonnet), *triolet
9		*Spenserian stanza

NOTE: The last stanza of a sestina or a ballade (the envoi or "send-off") contains fewer lines than the other stanzas in the poem.

Some stanzas combine different stanzas lengths. A *villanelle, for instance, consists of five tercets and a quatrain.

Stanzas of more than eight lines are simply known as nine-line stanzas, ten-line stanzas, and so on. A long stanza (over eight lines) tends to break into smaller units. The fourteen-line *sonnet, for example, can sometimes work as a stanza, but more often it consists of three quatrains and a couplet or an octave and a sestet.

Stave of Six A six-line stanza in *iambic pentameter or *iambic tetrameter rhyming *ababcc*; a kind of sixain (six-line stanza). The stave of six combines a heroic quatrain and a couplet.

I WANDERED LONELY AS A CLOUD
William Wordsworth (1770-1850)

I wandered lonely as a cloud
That floats on high o'er vales and hills,
When all at once I saw a crowd,
A host, of golden daffodils;
Beside the lake, beneath the trees,
Fluttering and dancing in the breeze.

Continuous as the stars that shine
And twinkle on the milky way,
They stretched in never-ending line
Along the margin of a bay:
Ten thousand saw I at a glance,
Tossing their heads in sprightly dance.

The waves beside them danced; but they
Outdid the sparkling waves in glee;
A poet could not but be gay,
In such a jocund company;
I gazed—and gazed—but little thought
What wealth the show to me had brought:

For oft, when on my couch I lie
In vacant or in pensive mood,
They flash upon that inward eye
Which is the bliss of solitude;
And then my heart with pleasure fills,
And dances with the daffodils.

Stichic *(stíck-ik)* Not divided into *stanzas. A stichic poem is arranged as a continuous block of lines, like a prose work arranged as a single paragraph. The Greek root *stich* means "line," so that a *monostich is a single isolated line, a *distich is a couplet, and a hemistich is a half-line.

Strophe *(stró-fee)*   1. A *stanza, sometimes used to distinguish one irregular in line length.

2. The first stanza of a Pindaric or Greek choral *ode, metrically identical to the second stanza or antistrophe *(an-tíh-stro-fee)*, but metrically different from the third stanza or epode *(éh-pode)*. Sometimes the strophe is called the "turn" (followed by "counter-turn" and "stand").

Subject   What a poem is literally about.

The subject of Wilfred Owen's poems, for example, is the life and death of British soldiers in the trenches during the First World War. Subject should be distinguished from *theme, which denotes what the poet is saying about the subject, his attitude toward it, as Owen's themes are pity, the pointlessness of war, the camaraderie of men.

In *The Triggering Town*, Richard Hugo asserts that a poem has

> two subjects, the initiating or triggering subject, which starts the poem or "causes" the poem to be written, and the real or generated subject, which the poet comes to say or mean, and which is generated or discovered in the poem during the writing.

Substitution *(also variation)*   A *foot that is different from that of the predominant meter of a line; the changing of a foot, replacing the expected foot, such as an iamb (˘ ′) in a line of iambic pentameter, with a different one, such as a trochee (′ ˘) or a spondee (′ ′), that alters the meter's regularity without destroying the meter; a means of making the rhythm of a metrical line more interesting, more surprising, and often more melodic than a line that moves like a metronome.

Surrealism   A literary and artistic movement that grew out of Dadaism and Futurism and stressed the importance of dreams, the unconscious, nonrational thought, free associations, startling imagery, and strange juxtapositions.

André Breton's *Surrealist Manifesto* launched the movement in 1924; its early members included Louis Aragon, Paul Eluard, and Pierre Reverdy. Breton defines surrealism as "Psychic automatism in its pure state, by which one proposes to express—verbally, by means of the written word, or in any other way—the actual functioning of

thought. Dictated by thought, in the absence of any control exercised by reason, exempt from aesthetic or moral preoccupation." Breton also declared that surrealism was based on belief in "the superior reality of certain forms of previously neglected associations," "the omnipotence of dream," and "the disinterested play of thought." Surrealism also thrived in the paintings of Max Ernst, Salvador Dali, Giorgio de Chirico, and René Magritte. One Surrealist, Jean (or Hans) Arp, excelled at poetry, painting, and sculpture. Michael Benedikt's anthology, *The Poetry of Surrealism*, contains translations of Surrealist poems from French.

Robert Bly, however, has said "French surrealism and Spanish surrealism both contain wonderful leaps, but whereas French surrealism often . . . leaps without any specific emotion—many believe that the unconscious does not have emotions—the Spanish poets believe that it does." Discussing Federico Garcia Lorca's *Poet in New York*, Bly goes on to say, "Powerful feeling makes the mind associate faster, and evidently the presence of swift association makes the emotions still more alive; it increases the adrenalin flow, just as chanting awakens many emotions that the chanter was hardly aware of at the moment he began chanting." Bly calls this wild, passionate, associative poetry leaping poetry. Other Spanish surrealists include Blas de Otero and the South Americans Cesar Vallejo and Pablo Neruda (though much of his poetry is not surrealist).

A BRANCH OF NETTLE ENTERS THROUGH THE WINDOW
André Breton (1896-1966; tr. David Antin)

The woman with the crepe paper body
The red fish in the fireplace
Whose memory is pieced together from a multitude of small
    watering places for distant ships
Who laughs like an ember fit to be set in snow
And sees the night expand and contract like an accordion
The armor of the grass
Hilt of the dagger gate
Falling in flakes from the wings of the sphinx
Rolling the floor of the Danube
For which time and space destroy themselves

On the evening when the watchman of the inner eye trembles
   like an elf
Isn't this the stake of the battle to which my dreams
   surrender
Brittle bird
Rocked by the telegraph wires of trance
Shattering in the great lake created by the numbers of its song
This is the double heart of the lost wall
Gripped by grasshoppers of the blood
That drag my likeness through the mirror
My broken hands
My caterpillar eyes
My long whalebone hairs
Whalebone sealed under brilliant black wax

HOME FROM A WALK
Federico Garcia Lorca (1898-1936; tr. Robert Bly)

   Assassinated by the sky,
between the forms that are moving toward the serpent,
and the forms that are moving toward the crystal,
I'll let my hair fall down.

   With the tree of amputated limbs that does not sing,
and the boy with the white face of an egg.

   With all the tiny animals who have broken heads,
and the ragged water that walks on its dry feet.

   With all the things that have a deaf and dumb fatigue,
and the butterfly drowned in the inkpot.

   Stumbling over my face that changes every day,
assassinated by the sky!

Syllabic Meter, Syllabics   A meter in which the number of syllables in a line is counted, not the accents or lengths of syllables; the predominant meter of French and Japanese poetry.

English and American poets such as Marianne Moore, Dylan Thomas, and Kenneth Rexroth began experimenting with syllabic verse in the first half of the twentieth century. It is a meter that often doesn't sound metrical in English: both a plus and a minus. On the

one hand, it imposes an order that is not obvious but gives a sense of regularity more felt than heard. It is a way to regulate the flow of free verse or prose, and to avoid the ticktock of *accentual-syllabic meter. On the other hand, some critics reject it as a true English meter because it is hard to hear as a recurring pattern. Unlike accentual verse, the native meter of the Anglo-Saxons, syllabic meter is imported and arouses some of the controversy still directed at free verse.

A syllabic poem may be measured in two ways. First, it may have the same number of syllables in each of its lines. Philip Levine's "Animals Are Passing from Our Lives," for instance, contains seven syllables per line. In a syllabic poem with uniform line lengths, it helps to vary the number of accents from line to line, as Levine does.

Second, a syllabic poem may use and repeat a consistent stanza shape with differing numbers of syllables in different lines. The first lines of every stanza would have the same syllable count, regardless of how many syllables appeared in lines two, three, and so on. Giving the stanzas a graphic shape by indenting certain lines helps to suggest a regular pattern, an intricate meter that otherwise might be hidden. Each stanza of "The Fish" has a syllabic pattern of 1-3-9-6-8 and rhymes *aabbX* (the *X* being an unrhymed line).

Counting syllables, however, can be tricky. How many syllables are in "interesting," for example. Some people say it with three (like "int'resting") and some use four. In "The Fish," the word "opening" in line five apparently is counted as two syllables (like "op'ning"). But this kind of leeway makes meter flexible. Variation is the brains of repetition.

ANIMALS ARE PASSING
FROM OUR LIVES
Philip Levine (b. 1928)

It's wonderful how I jog
on four honed-down ivory toes
my massive buttocks slipping
like oiled parts with each light step.

I'm to market. I can smell
the sour, grooved block, I can smell
the blade that opens the hole
and the pudgy white fingers

that shake out the intestines
like a hankie. In my dreams
the snouts drool on the marble,
suffering children, suffering flies,

suffering the consumers
who won't meet their steady eyes
for fear they could see. The boy
who drives me along believes

that any moment I'll fall
on my side and drum my toes
like a typewriter or squeal
and shit like a new housewife

discovering television,
or that I'll turn like a beast
cleverly to hook his teeth
with my teeth. No. Not this pig.

THE FISH
wade
through black jade.
    Of the crow-blue mussel-shells, one keeps
    adjusting the ash-heaps;
        opening and shutting itself like

an
injured fan.
    The barnacles which encrust the side
    of the wave, cannot hide
        there for the submerged shafts of the

sun,
split like spun
    glass, move themselves with spotlight swiftness
    into the crevices—
        in and out, illuminating

the
turquoise sea
    of bodies. The water drives a wedge
    of iron through the iron edge
        of the cliff; whereupon the stars,

pink
rice-grains, ink-
    bespattered jelly-fish, crabs like green
    lilies, and submarine
        toadstools, slide each on the other.

All
external
    marks of abuse are present on this
    defiant edifice—
        all the physical features of

ac-
cident—lack
    of cornice, dynamite grooves, burns, and
    hatchet strokes, these things stand
        out on it; the chasm-side is

dead.
Repeated
    evidence has proved that it can live
    on what can not revive
        its youth. The sea grows old in it.
           —Marianne Moore (1887-1972)

Syllable A speech unit consisting of a single, uninterrupted cluster of sound, as brief as a single vowel (such as *I*) or as long as a vowel or diphthong surrounded by consonant combinations (such as *stretch*, *breathe*, and *sphinx*). For example, *clús-ter* has two syllables and the first one is accented or emphasized. A monosyllabic word consists of one syllable (such as *crow*, *speak*, and *bench*). A polysyllabic word consists of two or more syllables (such as *breakfast*, *congregate*, and *impervious*).

Symbol *(Greek, "to throw together")* An image that radiates meanings perhaps hard to express in other words but which can be felt, as in the symbols of dreams.

It is an image that resonates for a person, within a text, or among a people. Symbolic language is figurative (in that the literal image suggests something more), but a symbol differs significantly from a metaphor. In a metaphor, one thing is compared to another so that

its own nature becomes clearer and more vivid; the two things must be otherwise dissimilar, so that the comparison offers a pleasurable surprise ("Why haven't I thought of that before?"). A symbol, however, is an image that plunges to the soul, or the unconscious, of the reader ("I recognize that, but how?"). It does resemble a metaphor, but with one difference: The symbolic image is like a metaphorical vehicle (or likeness) without a tenor (or subject)—or without a single, definable tenor. It is a kite without someone on the ground holding its string.

William Butler Yeats, who viewed the poet's use of symbols as an imitation of the magician's, declares, "It is only by ancient symbols, by symbols that have numberless meanings besides the one or two the writer lays an emphasis upon, or the half-score he knows of, that any highly subjective art can escape from the barrenness and shallowness of a too conscious arrangement, into the abundance and depth of Nature." Yeats also defined symbols as "images that are living souls."

Symbolist Poetry Nineteenth-century artistic and literary movement that raised the symbol to prime importance.

A good example is the use of *leit-motif*, a repeated melodic phrase that suggests some aspect of a character or a theme (such as yearning), in the operas of Richard Wagner. Symbolists rejected argument in favor of music and image, elements that would appeal more to the unconscious mind than to the conscious, aiming for the depths of the soul instead of the mental surface. The movement, influenced strongly by the works of Edgar Allan Poe, began in France and included poets Charles Baudelaire, Arthur Rimbaud, Paul Verlaine, Stéphane Mallarmé, and Paul Valéry. *The Symbolist Movement in Literature*, by Arthur Symons, popularized symbolism in English, including William Butler Yeats among its poets. Yeats, in turn, looked back to the poet-painter William Blake as an earlier symbolist.

CORRESPONDENCES / Charles Baudelaire
(1821-1867; tr. Richard Howard)

The pillars of Nature's temple are alive
and sometimes yield perplexing messages;
forests of symbols between us and the shrine
remark our passage with accustomed eyes.

> Like long-held echoes, blending somewhere else
> into one deep and shadowy unison
> as limitless as darkness and as day,
> the sounds, the scents, the colors correspond.
>
> There are odors succulent as young flesh,
> sweet as flutes, and green as any grass,
> while others—rich, corrupt and masterful—
>
> possess the power of such infinite things
> as incense, amber, benjamin and musk,
> to praise the senses' raptures and the mind's.

Synecdoche *(sih-nék-duh-kee; Greek, taking jointly)* A figure of speech in which a part of something indicates the whole, like "talking head" for "television commentator" or "mouthpiece" for "lawyer."

It is similar to *metonymy, the use of an object associated with something in place of it, like "the crown" to indicate royalty or a monarch. Both of these devices are useful in poetry, in that they focus more closely on something concrete, like a movie camera zooming in on a significant object. (*See: figures of classical rhetoric.*)

Syntax The arrangement of words in a sentence; the tactics of word order. A sentence in an unusual word order would exemplify "wrenched" or "twisted" or "convoluted" syntax. For example, John Berryman writes "Murdered the ruses that would quack me clear/ The orchard squeaks" in *Dream Song* 188.

T

Tailed Sonnet *(also called a caudate [caw-dáy] sonnet)* A *sonnet with a coda.

To the fourteen rhymed lines of a sonnet, the poet adds an extension, beginning with a short line (usually three feet) and following it with a rhymed pentameter couplet. The short line picks up the rhyme of the fourteenth line, thus linking the tail to the rest of the sonnet. The poet can then add a second tail, also beginning with a short line. This full, double-tailed rhyme pattern is *abbaabba cdecde (e)ff (f)gg*—the lines in parentheses being shorter than the lines in the rest of the poem. John Milton and Gerard Manley Hopkins both wrote tailed sonnets.

Tanka *(táhn-ka; also called waka and uta)* Japanese verse form consisting of five lines with a syllable count of 5-7-5-7-7 (or thirty-one syllables in all).

Numerically, a tanka is like a *haiku with two seven-syllable lines added on. As might be imagined, the form is less concentrated than haiku, more casual and conversational, less mysterious, less spiritual. Imagery is important, but there is ample room for statement and declaration too.

Influenced by Chinese poetry a few centuries old, tanka succeeded the "long poem" (or *chōka*), which alternated lines of five and seven syllables. The new form gained popularity in the seventh and eighth centuries. Here is a tanka by Sami Mansei (early eighth century, translated by Steven D. Carter) which illustrates both the syllabic arrangement and the essential nature of the form:

> Our life in this world—
> to what shall I compare it?
> It is like a boat
>   rowing out at break of day,
> leaving not a trace behind.

The following three tanka show how important a part the relations between members of the imperial court, and the words of their poems, played in some of the earliest tanka. Carter's translations differ slightly from the 5-7-5-7-7 syllable pattern of the originals, but they are very close.

Emperor Tenji (626-71; ruled from 668):

> At the broad sea's edge
>   the setting sun casts its gleam
>   on banners of cloud:
> this night, the moon of this night—
> so clearly may its rays too shine!

Princess Nukada (7th Century),
a poem written when she was longing
for Emperor Tenji:

> Waiting for you,
> I languish, full of longing—
> and then the blinds
>   of my house flutter slightly,
> blown by the autumn wind.

Princess Kagami (7th Century)
a reply to the poem above:

> If even the wind . . .
> I think, in envy of you.
> If even the wind
>   would answer my vain waiting—
> of what could I complain?

Tercet *(tér-set or ter-sét; Italian, "third")* Any stanza of three lines; sometimes confined to three lines that rhyme, either consecutively in

a *triplet (*aaa*) or interlocking with another stanza in a pattern called *terza rima (*aba bcb cdc*, etc.); also called a tristich.

There is some disagreement about the terms for three-line stanzas. Paul Fussell, in *Poetic Meter & Poetic Form*, offers a reasonable solution: "Three lines of any length ending with the same rhyme word are called triplets, or, interchangeably, tercets. It is probably better to use tercet only to distinguish three lines organized other than by a thrice-repeated rhyme." A stanza of three unrymed lines could thus be called a tercet (or a tristich). (*See: terza rima for a passage from Dante's* Inferno, *triplet for a poem rhymed* aaa bbb *by Robert Herrick.*)

> THESE ARE THE DAYS WHEN
> BIRDS COME BACK
> Emily Dickinson (1830-1886)
>
> These are the days when Birds come back—
> A very few—a Bird or two—
> To take a backward look.
>
> These are the days when skies resume
> The old—old sophistries of June—
> A blue and gold mistake.
>
> Oh fraud that cannot cheat the Bee—
> Almost thy plausibility
> Induces my belief.
>
> Till ranks of seeds their witness bear—
> And softly thro' the altered air
> Hurries a timid leaf.
>
> Oh Sacrament of summer days,
> Oh Last Communion in the Haze—
> Permit a child to join.
>
> Thy sacred emblems to partake—
> Thy consecrated bread to take
> And thine immortal wine!

Terza Rima (*táre-tsuh rée-muh; Italian, "third rhyme"*) Tercets with an interwoven rhyme scheme, invented by Dante for *The Divine Comedy: aba bcb cdc ded efe fgf*, etc.

When Dante settled on this interlocking form for his religious epic (or what Native Americans might call "vision quest"), he had the Trinity in mind: Father, Son, and Holy Ghost. A kind of Roman Catholic numerology pervades the poem (with its three parts— *Inferno*, *Purgatorio*, and *Paradiso*).

Percy Bysshe Shelley's "Ode to the West Wind" is the best-known English poem in terza rima, but T.S. Eliot, W.H. Auden, and Robert Frost have also used the form.

FRANCESCA OF RIMINI (from *INFERNO*, Canto V)
Dante Alighieri (1265-1321; tr. George Gordon, Lord Byron)

"The land where I was born sits by the seas,
   Upon that shore to which the Po descends,
   With all his followers, in search of peace.
Love, which the gentle heart soon apprehends,
   Seized him for the fair person which was ta'en
   From me, and me even yet the mode offends.
Love, who to none beloved to love again
   Remits, seized me with wish to please so strong,
   That, as thou seest, yet, yet it doth remain.
Love to one death conducted us along,
   But Caina waits for him our life who ended:"
   These were the accents utter'd by her tongue.—
Since I first listen'd to these souls offended,
   I bow'd my visage, and so kept it till—
   "What think'st thou," said the bard; when I unbended,
And recommenced: "Alas! unto such ill
   How many sweet thoughts, what strong ecstasies
   Led these their evil fortune to fulfil!"
And then I turn'd unto their side my eyes,
   And said, "Francesca, thy sad destinies
   Have made me sorrow till the tears arise.
But tell me, in the season of sweet sighs,
   By what and how thy love to passion rose,
   So as his dim desires to recognise?"
Then she to me: "The greatest of all woes
   Is to remind us of our happy days
   In misery, and that thy teacher knows.

But if to learn our passion's first root preys
   Upon thy spirit with such sympathy,
   I will do even as he who weeps and says.
We read one day for pastime, seated nigh,
   Of Lancilot, how love enchain'd him too.
   We were alone, quite unsuspiciously.
But oft our eyes met, and our cheeks in hue
   All o'er discolour'd by that reading were;
   But one point only wholly us o'erthrew;
When we read the long-sigh'd-for smile of her,
   To be thus kiss'd by such devoted lover.
   He who from me can be divided ne'er
Kiss'd my mouth, trembling in the act all over:
   Accursed was the book and he who wrote!
   That no day further leaf we did uncover."
While thus one spirit told us of their lot,
   The other wept, so that with pity's thralls
   I swoon'd, as if by death I had been smote
And fell down even as a dead body falls.

Theme *(Greek, "proposition")* A poem's attitude toward its subject; what it says about its subject.

Sometimes the two words, *theme* and *subject*, are used synonymously, but in poetry the theme is an outgrowth of the subject, the poem's comment on that subject. Sometimes, however, theme is used metaphorically in its musical sense, as a recurrent melodic passage. Thus Theodore Roethke talks about poems that are "written to be heard, with the themes often coming alternately, as in music. . . ."

Tone The emotional spin a poet puts on his words; the edge or attitude in the voice of a poem. When we talk to someone, we can hear his tone of voice—how he says something. Sometimes we can even see it (tongue in cheek, for example). In a poem, tone is the coloration of the words, their shading, their warmth or coolness—as in painting. It is also how they sound, their pitch (high or low), their harmony (sweet or shrill), their volume (loud or soft)—as in music.

Translation The difficult art of capturing a poem in the words of another language.

The translator will often be a poet himself: George Chapman and

Alexander Pope translated Homer from the Greek; John Dryden translated Virgil from the Latin; in our time, Richard Wilbur has translated Molière from the French. The translator's inclusions and omissions, discoveries and losses, compromises and luck will determine the relative success of the translation. Some poets, such as Robert Lowell, refer to their versions of foreign originals as *imitations, permitting themselves the liberty to change the originals for their own purposes, adding images, deleting whole stanzas, rearranging the order. Arthur Waley, a scholar and celebrated translator of Chinese poetry, calls Ezra Pound's version of Li Po's "Exile's Letter" a "brilliant paraphrase." The poet who takes liberties will probably affix a headnote to the poem, something like "after Baudelaire."

Translation is useful to the poet, who can (1) bring new works from another language into English; (2) make newer, more up-to-date versions of already translated works (since, as Richard Howard has remarked, "translations date; originals do not"); (3) have an inexhaustible supply of raw material for poems (even if the originals are someone else's); and (4) write original poems based on, inspired by, or responding to poems from another language.

In the following translations of Catullus, there is a range of approaches. Walter Savage Landor uses rhyme, although the original does not, and adds a third line to the original couplet. Ezra Pound uses the idiomatic "it beats me" as a brilliant play on words, meaning "I don't know," "it hurts me," and "it defeats me." Celia and Louis Zukofsky imitate the sound of the original Latin and use related English words, such as "nescience," for Latin words, such as "nescio." Charles Martin's version is simple, clear, and close to the original. Frank Bidart's version should be called an imitation, since it departs from the original by adding new material. Nevertheless, in finding a new equivalent for what Catullus presents, he revives the poem in the truest sense. After all, for a Roman like Catullus, the image of crucifixion invoked by "excrucior" was as real and immediate as Bidart's image of a fish writhing on a hook.

An Original Poem in Latin and Five Translations

Odi et amo. quare id faciam, fortasse requiris.
nescio, sed fieri sentio et excrucior.

—Catullus (circa 85-55 B.C.)

I love and hate. Ah! never ask why so!
I hate and love. . . . and that is all I know.
I see 'tis folly, but I feel 'tis woe.

—Walter Savage Landor (1775-1864)

I hate and love. Why? you may ask but
It beats me. I feel it done to me and ache.

—Ezra Pound (1885-1972)

O th'hate I move love. Quarry it fact I am, for that's so re
    queries.
Nescience, say th'fiery scent I owe whets crookeder.

—Celia & Louis Zukofsky (1904-1978)

I hate & love. And if you should ask how I can do both,
    I couldn't say; but I feel it, and it shivers me.

—Charles Martin (b. 1942)

I hate *and* love. Ignorant fish, who even
wants the fly while writhing.

—Frank Bidart (b. 1939)

Triadic Line, Stanza   Free-verse lines arranged and indented in three steps.

Much of William Carlos Williams' later work appears in the triadic line, although he's free about altering this pattern. He uses it to demonstrate what he calls the *variable foot, which stipulates that a group of words, whether of one syllable or many, can be metrically equivalent, each foot "variable" in actual length. Skeptics might consider this concept a rationalization, an attempt to graft a metrical basis onto free verse. Hugh Kenner says of Williams, who had suffered several strokes: "Up at dawn, he typed, letter by letter, the left hand guiding and letting fall the right over an electrified keyboard. His eyes followed a line of type with ease but had trouble finding the start of the next line; the three-step indentation he came to favor was in part a way of making a page he could reread." (*See: free verse.*)

"The Descent" was Williams' first poem in his new measure.

THE DESCENT / William Carlos Williams (1883-1963)

The descent beckons
   as the ascent beckoned.
     Memory is a kind
of accomplishment,
   a sort of renewal
     even
an initiation, since the spaces it opens are new places
   inhabited by hordes
     heretofore unrealized,
of new kinds—
   since their movements
     are toward new objectives
(even though formerly they were abandoned).

No defeat is made up entirely of defeat—since
the world it opens is always a place
   formerly
     unsuspected. A
world lost,
   a world unsuspected,
     unbeckons to new places
and no whiteness (lost) is so white as the memory
of whiteness

With evening, love wakens
   though its shadows
     which are alive by reason
of the sun shining—
   grow sleepy now and drop away
     from desire
Love without shadows stirs now
   beginning to awaken
     as night
advances.

The descent
   made up of despairs
     and without accomplishment
realizes a new awakening:
     which is a reversal
of despair.

For what we cannot accomplish, what
is denied to love,
what we have lost in the anticipation—
fa descent follows,
endless and indestructible

Triolet *(tree-oh-láy; French, "little trio")*   Fixed form from the Middle Ages, eight lines rhyming *ABaAabAB* (the capital letters representing repeated lines or refrains).

Originally a kind of *rondeau or *rondel, this form has been recognized as a triolet since the late fifteenth century. Twentieth-century triolets include Robert Bridges' "When First We Met" and Sandra McPherson's "Triolet" (beginning "She was in love with the same danger"). Barbara Howes ("Early Supper") and Dana Gioia ("The Country Wife") have used the triolet as a stanza form in longer poems. (*See: rondeau for a chart that shows the now-fixed patterns of the forms, including the triolet, that began as rondeaux.*)

THE COQUETTE, AND AFTER
Thomas Hardy (1840-1928)

I

For long the cruel wish I knew
That your free heart should ache for me
While mine should bear no ache for you;
For long—the cruel wish!—I knew
How men can feel, and craved to view
My triumph—fated not to be
For long! . . . The cruel wish I knew
That your free heart should ache for me!

II

At last one pays the penalty—
The woman—women always do.
My farce, I found, was tragedy
At last!—One pays the penalty
With interest when one, fancy-free,
Learns love, learns shame. . . . Of sinners two
At least *one* pays the penalty—
The woman—women always do!

Triplet   A three-line stanza rhymed *aaa*.

Some critics apply it as a general term for any three-line stanza, rhymed or not. (*See: tercet for a discussion of the terminology that designates a three-line unit.*)

Poets who write in *heroic couplets, such as Alexander Pope, feel free to insert a triplet now and then. A bracket in the margin typically marks where the three rhymed lines appear. John Dryden likes to stretch out the third line by an extra foot, so that it becomes an *alexandrine (iambic hexameter).

UPON JULIA'S CLOTHES
Robert Herrick (1591-1674)

Whenas in silks my Julia goes,
Then, then, methinks, how sweetly flows
That liquefaction of her clothes.

Next, when I cast mine eyes, and see
That brave vibration, each way free,
O, how that glittering taketh me!

Trochee, Trochaic   *(tróh-kee, tro-káy-ik; Greek, "running")*   A foot consisting of a stress followed by an unstressed syllable (′ ˘). Trochaic words include *basket, hoping, purple,* and *rabbit.*

Trochaic meter, like iambic, is called duple meter—because each foot contains two syllables. The opening lines of William Blake's "The Lamb" are in trochaic trimeter:

Líttlĕ I Lámb, whŏ I máde thĕe?
Dóst thŏu I knów whŏ I máde thĕe?

Trochaic tetrameter consists of four trochees (′ ˘ ′ ˘ ′ ˘ ′ ˘). Often the final unstressed syllable is omitted (′ ˘ ′ ˘ ′ ˘ ′), as in these lines from John Donne's "Song":

Go and catch a falling star,
Get with child a mandrake root,
Tell me where all past years are,
Or who cleft the devil's foot.

It is an emphatic meter, as heard in Longfellow's *Hiawatha* and count-less parodies of it. William Blake's frequent use of trochaic tetrameter, in poems such as "The Tyger" and "Never Seek to Tell Thy Love," suggests both the childlike simplicity and the mystic power inherent in this measure. It is used for incantation in Shakespeare's *Macbeth*:

> *1.Witch.*   Round about the cauldron go;
> In the poison'd entrails throw.
> Toad, that under cold stone
> Days and nights has thirty-one
> Swelt'red venom sleeping got,
> Boil thou first i' th' charmed pot.
> *All.*   Double, double, toil and trouble;
> Fire burn and cauldron bubble.

Acceptable variations include omitting the final unstressed syllable and adding an unstressed syllable at the beginning of a line (used too frequently, however, this variation will convert the trochaic meter into iambic). (*See: anacrusis, catalexis.*)

FALL, LEAVES, FALL
Emily Brontë (1818-1848)

Fall, leaves, fall; die, flowers, away;
Lengthen night and shorten day;
Every leaf speaks bliss to me
Fluttering from the autumn tree.
I shall smile when wreaths of snow
Blossom where the rose should grow;
I shall sing when night's decay
Ushers in a drearier day.

Ubi Sunt *(Latin, "where are")* Poetic theme in which the poet asks "where are" they, where have they gone. The theme began in Medieval Latin, with the formula *ubi sunt* used to introduce a roll-call of the dead or missing and to suggest how transitory life is.

François Villon's *ballade, with the refrain "But where are the snows of yester-year?" is the best known *ubi sunt* poem.

Unstressed Syllable A syllable that is not emphasized, like the *a* in *aghast* or the *ish* in *churlish*.

In an *iambic line, it is hard to find three unstressed syllables together; the ear wants to give the middle one a slight accent. In an accentual line, on the other hand, only the heavy stresses are counted, so a number of unstressed syllables can accumulate before the next loud thump comes along. Syllabic verse and *free verse can also have an indefinite number of unstressed syllables between stresses, a condition close to that of *prose (except for the crucial importance of the line, which controls the rhythm and the syllable count).

Variable Foot   A term coined by William Carlos Williams as a metrical explanation for his own free verse. A variable foot could contain an indefinite number of syllables, all adding up to a single beat.

In practice, Williams' poems in the *triadic line do have the feel of a three-beat meter, but that may derive largely from the visual appearance of the lines, arranged in three steps. In his entry on free verse in *The Princeton Encyclopedia of Poetry and Poetics* (1965), Williams says,

> The bracket of the customary foot has been expanded so that more syllables, words, or phrases can be admitted into its confines. The new unit thus created may be called the 'variable foot,' a term and a concept already accepted widely as a means of bringing the warring elements of freedom and discipline together. It rejects the standard of the conventionally fixed foot and suggests that measure varies with the idiom by which it is employed and the tonality of the individual poem. Thus, as in speech, the prosodic pattern is evaluated by criteria of effectiveness and expressiveness rather than mechanical syllable counts.

Variation   1. Changes in words, phrases, or lines that are otherwise repeated. (*See: repetition.*)

2. A foot that differs from that of the prevailing meter. For example, in a line of iambic pentameter, a trochaic foot would be a *variation,*

as in the first foot of Shakespeare's "Wishing | me like | to one | more rich | in hope" (Sonnet 29), in which "Wishing" is a trochee; also called substitution.

3. A musical term that can be imitated in a set of poetic "variations on a theme"; one of several different views of a subject, as in Wallace Stevens' "13 Ways of Looking at a Blackbird."

Verse *(Latin, "furrow," from the verb meaning "to turn")*
1. A *line of poetry.
2. Poetry written in lines. The opposite of *prose.
3. In a song, a stanza that has different words whenever the same music recurs; as opposed to a *chorus, which repeats the same words, like a *refrain.

Verse Mixed With Prose   A poetic form that includes both prose and verse, or paragraphs and stanzas, or lines and unlined passages.

There are a number of possible combinations: verse-prose, prose-verse, verse-prose-verse, prose-verse-prose, and longer patterns of alternations. Japanese *haibun intersperses *haiku within a prose work, often a travel journal.

TOURISTS / Yehuda Amichai (b. 1924)

Visits of condolence is all we get from them.
They squat at the Holocaust Memorial,
They put on grave faces at the Wailing Wall
And they laugh behind heavy curtains
In their hotels.
They have their pictures taken
Together with our famous dead
At Rachel's Tomb and Herzl's Tomb
And on the top of Ammunition Hill.
They weep over our sweet boys
And lust over our tough girls
And hang up their underwear
To dry quickly
In cool, blue bathrooms.

Once I sat on the steps by a gate at David's Tower, I placed my two heavy baskets at my side. A group of tourists was standing

around their guide and I became their target marker. "You see that man with the baskets? Just right of his head there's an arch from the Roman period. Just right of his head." "But he's moving, he's moving!" I said to myself: redemption will come only if their guide tells them, "You see that arch from the Roman period? It's not important: but next to it, left and down a bit, there sits a man who's bought fruit and vegetables for his family."

Versification   The art of writing in *lines; in particular, the technical aspects of doing so: *rhythm and *meter, *rhyme, *enjambment and *end-stopping, *alliteration and *assonance. (*See: prosody.*)

Villanelle *(vil-uh-nél; Italian folk-song about rural life, from the Latin, "country house")*   A form, usually nineteen lines in length, consisting of five *tercets and a *quatrain.

The first line serves as one *refrain (repeated in lines six, twelve, and eighteen), and the third line serves as another refrain (repeated in lines nine, fifteen, and nineteen). These refrains rhyme with each other and with the opening line of each stanza. The middle lines of each stanza rhyme with each other, so that there are only two different rhyme sounds (*a* and *b*) throughout the entire poem.

The villanelle began as a French adaptation of Italian folk songs about country people. The term had been used widely, for various lyrics with refrains, before the form took its current fixed pattern from Jean Passerat's "Villanelle" after the turn of the seventeenth century. Despite all of the intricate, fussy rules, the villanelle has become a powerful form in twentieth-century poems such as E.A. Robinson's "The House on the Hill," Dylan Thomas' "Do Not Go Gentle into That Good Night," W.H. Auden's "If I Could Tell You," Theodore Roethke's "The Waking," and Elizabeth Bishop's "One Art."

Some poets, such as Leconte de Lisle and Donald Justice, have omitted two of the inner tercets; some poets, such as Marilyn Hacker, have added two or three tercets before the final quatrain. Most poets feel free to alter the phrasing and punctuation of the refrains, changing them as they recur. Enjambment (leading into a refrain, or out of one, or both) can help make this rigid form more flexible and expressive.

The pattern of repeated lines in a villanelle is so distinctive that

some poets feel free to omit some or all of the rhymes. In "Little L.A. Villanelle," Carol Muske rhymes the refrains (which end in "rain" and "refrain") but does not rhyme most of the middle lines: "overflowed," "wipers," "mid-scream," "dreamed," "light," and "faster." Rita Dove begins "Parsley," a two-part poem, with an unrhymed villanelle called "The Cane Fields." (*See: corrupted form.*)

VILLANELLE *(J'ay perdu ma tourterelle) */Jean Passerat (1534-1602; tr. John Drury)	*Villanelle Pattern*	*Rhyme*
My dove has flown away from me:	*Refrain One*	*a*
Isn't there something I can do?	Line 2	*b*
I'll follow her where she may flee.	*Refrain Two*	*a*
You miss your darling's company,	Line 4	*a*
Alas! for me the same is true:	Line 5	*b*
My dove has flown away from me.	*Refrain One*	*a*
As your love proves its constancy,	Line 7	*a*
My faith will show its mettle too,	Line 8	*b*
I'll follow her where she may flee.	*Refrain Two*	*a*
Your moans recur incessantly;	Line 10	*a*
I swear my grief is never through:	Line 11	*b*
My dove has flown away from me.	*Refrain One*	*a*
Now that her beauty I can't see,	Line 13	*a*
Nothing is beautiful to view;	Line 14	*b*
I'll follow her where she may flee.	*Refrain Two*	*a*
Death, so often I've made my plea,	Line 16	*a*
Take now what is given to you:	Line 17	*b*
My dove has flown away from me,	*Refrain One*	*a*
I'll follow her where she may flee.	*Refrain Two*	*a*

THE HOUSE ON THE HILL
Edwin Arlington Robinson (1869-1935)

They are all gone away,
   The House is shut and still,
There is nothing more to say.

Through broken walls and gray
    The winds blow bleak and shrill;
They are all gone away.

Nor is there one today
    To speak them good or ill:
There is nothing more to say.

Why is it then we stray
    Around that sunken sill?
They are all gone away,

And our poor fancy-play
    For them is wasted skill:
There is nothing more to say.

There is ruin and decay
    In the House on the Hill:
They are all gone away,
There is nothing more to say.

DO NOT GO GENTLE INTO THAT GOOD NIGHT
Dylan Thomas (1914-1953)

Do not go gentle into that good night,
Old age should burn and rave at close of day;
Rage, rage against the dying of the light.

Though wise men at their end know dark is right,
Because their words had forked no lightning they
Do not go gentle into that good night.

Good men, the last wave by, crying how bright
Their frail deeds might have danced in a green bay,
Rage, rage against the dying of the light.

Wild men who caught and sang the sun in flight,
And learn, too late, they grieved it on its way,
Do not go gentle into that good night.

Grave men, near death, who see with blinding sight
Blind eyes could blaze like meteors and be gay,
Rage, rage against the dying of the light.

And you, my father, there on the sad height,
Curse, bless, me now with your fierce tears, I pray.
Do not go gentle into that good night.
Rage, rage against the dying of the light.

from FIVE VILLANELLES (I)
Weldon Kees (1914-1955?)

The crack is moving down the wall.
Defective plaster isn't all the cause.
We must remain until the roof falls in.

It's mildly cheering to recall
That every building has its little flaws.
The crack is moving down the wall.

Here in the kitchen, drinking gin,
We can accept the damndest laws.
We must remain until the roof falls in.

And though there's no one here at all,
One searches every room because
The crack is moving down the wall.

Repairs? But how can one begin?
The lease has warnings buried in each clause.
We must remain until the roof falls in.

These nights one hears a creaking in the hall,
The sort of thing that gives one pause.
The crack is moving down the wall.
We must remain until the roof falls in.

READING HEMINGWAY
James Cummins (b. 1948)

Reading Hemingway makes me so hungry,
for *jambon*, cheeses, and a dry white wine.
Cold, of course, very cold. And very dry.

Reading Hemingway makes some folks angry:
the hip drinking, the bitter pantomime.
But reading Hemingway makes me hungry

for the good life, the sun, the fish, the sky:
blue air, *whitewater,* dinner on the line . . .
Had it down cold, he did. And dry. Real dry.

But Papa had it all, the *brio,* the *brie*:
clear-eyed, tight-lipped, advancing on a *stein* . . .
Reading Hemingway makes me so hungry,

I'd knock down Monsieur Stevens, too, if I
drank too much *retsina* before we dined.
(Too old, that man, and way too cold. And dry

enough to rub one's famished nerves awry,
kept talking past the kitchen's closing time!)
Reading Hemingway makes me so hungry . . .
And cold, of course. So cold. And very dry.

NOTE: *Monsieur Stevens*: the poet Wallace Stevens, with whom Hemingway had a fight in Key West in 1936.

Vision   1. Sight; seeing things as they are. 2. Insight into the unexpected or otherwise unseen; seeing things that might be or as they really, more deeply, are. Visionary poetry is prophetic, mystical, a glimpse into the unknown. The Book of Ecclesiastes, Dante's *Divine Comedy,* and Samuel Taylor Coleridge's "Kubla Khan" are visionary poems.

Voice   1. The speaker of a poem. The reader should not assume that the speaker equals the poet.

2. The characteristic sound, style, or tone of a particular poet. Sometimes teachers and critics talk about "finding your voice," as if the poet were born without one and had to set about acquiring one. But William Stafford says, "You already have a voice and don't need to find one." After all, a voice-print is as unique and identifiable as a fingerprint. It might be better to urge the poet to use the voice she was born with, and the words she has learned, to discover what poems she has the power to say.

A poet can, however, speak through the voice of a character, as Robert Browning impersonates a Renaissance painter in "Andrea del Sarto." But this is another sense of the word *voice.* In the same way,

a novelist or narrative poet will let characters speak. It would be foolish to force them all to sound like the writer. A good example of how these kinds of voices work might be Robert Frost's "The Death of the Hired Man." We hear the husband and the wife speak (and the hired man too, through the couple's dialogue); we also hear the voice of a speaker narrating the poem. All of these voices—characters and speaker—comprise Robert Frost's voice.

War Poetry   Poetry about warfare, battles, military life, often written by former combatants; usually written either to glorify war, to recount the exploits of heroes and their gruesome accomplishments, to encourage fellow citizens to march off to battle, to demonstrate the horrors of armed conflict, or to present a gritty, realistic picture of a disproportionately important part of human history. War poems begin with Homer's *epic *Iliad.*

Homer's epic, the *Iliad,* is perhaps the best known of all war poems. But Archilochos, an early Greek poet whose name means "Master Sergeant," was an actual soldier. His work survives in *fragments, as in these lines translated by Guy Davenport:

> My ash spear is my barley bread,
> My ash spear is my Ismarian wine.
> I lean on my spear and drink.

Many war poems, such as Louis Simpson's "Carentan O Carentan," a *ballad set in Europe during World War II, are narrative, recounting stories of particular battles or the routines of military life. But much dramatic poetry deals with war as well. In William Shakespeare's *Henry V* (Act 3, Scene 1), King Henry exhorts his troops to press on with their attack on Harfleur:

> Once more unto the breach, dear friends, once more;
> Or close the wall up with our English dead!
> In peace there's nothing so becomes a man

As modest stillness and humility;
But when the blast of war blows in our ears,
Then imitate the action of the tiger:
Stiffen the sinews, summon up the blood,
Disguise fair nature with hard-favour'd rage;
Then lend the eye a terrible aspect;
Let it pry through the portage of the head
Like the brass cannon; let the brow o'erwhelm it
As fearfully as doth a galled rock
O'erhang and jutty his confounded base,
Swill'd with the wild and wasteful ocean.
Now set the teeth and stretch the nostril wide,
Hold hard the breath, and bend up every spirit
To his full height!

Like Archilochos, many war poets have been combatants. World War I produced—and destroyed—Wilfred Owen, who died a week before the Armistice. In his poem "Strange Meeting," when two soldiers confront each other in the underworld, one declares, "I am the enemy you killed, my friend." Soldier-poets of World War II include Keith Douglas, Randall Jarrell, and Louis Simpson. Yusef Komunyakaa, who served in Vietnam as a correspondent, has written *Dien Cai Dau*, a book about soldiers camouflaged in "tiger suits," men who sit and hold their "helmets like rain-polished skulls."

The following poem, which appears in *Drum-Taps*, springs from Walt Whitman's experiences as a nurse of Union troops and an observer during the Civil War.

AN ARMY CORPS ON THE MARCH
Walt Whitman (1819-1892)

With its cloud of skirmishers in advance,
With now the sound of a single shot snapping like a whip, and now an
    irregular volley,
The swarming ranks press on and on, the dense brigades press on,
Glittering dimly, toiling under the sun—the dust-cover'd men,
In columns rise and fall to the undulations of the ground,
With artillery interspers'd—the wheels rumble, the horses sweat,
As the army corps advances.

Welsh Poetic Forms   The twenty-four "strict meters" of traditional Welsh poetry. The poetry of Wales is renowned for its intricate inter-weaving of sounds, using rhyme (both end and internal), varieties of half-rhyme, assonance, alliteration, and cross-alliteration. We catch bits of this intricacy in the English verse of Welsh poets such as Gerard Manley Hopkins and Dylan Thomas.

In *The Burning Tree*, Gwyn Williams notes that "The millennium from the year 600 to 1600 saw the development and decline of poetry in the strict Welsh meters and the perfection and classification of the sound-echoing devices known as *cynghanedd*. Technically the peak came with Dafydd ab Edmwnd in the middle of the fifteenth century. The twenty-four measures, already classified in the fourteenth cen-tury, were by him tightened up and made more difficult in order to discourage the half-trained practitioner in verse." Williams adds, "let it not be thought that the twenty-four measures have since fallen into desuetude or become merely museum pieces. They have been in con-tinuous use, and a knowledge of them is essential to anyone who hopes to win the chair at the National Eisteddfod. And at least two of the old measures, the *englyn* and the *cywydd*, are in regular use by a very large number of writers to-day."

Cynghanedd (pronounced *kun-yáhn-neth,* the *th* as in "these") is Welsh for "harmony." In verse it is the tight interweaving of either consonants (alliteration) or rhymes (either full or slant). Gwyn Williams cites John Keats' phrase "fairy lands forlorn" as one of the "best examples in English of *cynghanedd*." Without the vowels, the pattern of consonants becomes more obvious: *f-r- l-nds f-rl-rn,* a blend of *f, r, l,* and *n*.

There are three main types of *cynghanedd: cynghanedd gytsain* (alliteration of a series of consonants, also called cross-alliteration); *cynghanedd sain* (alliteration and internal rhyme); and *cynghanedd lusg* (internal rhyme).

In "The Wreck of the Deutschland," Gerard Manley Hopkins uses "certain chimes suggested by the Welsh poetry I had been reading (what they call *cynghanedd*)," as in the lines "Warm-laid grave of a womb-life gray" and "a lush-kept plush-capped sloe." In the first exam-ple, Hopkins repeats a sequence of consonants, a pattern of *w-m l- gr-* (although he also echoes a long *a* in *grave/gray*). In the second exam-ple, Hopkins alternates rhymes and slant rhymes (*lush/plush, kept/*

capped; in addition, *sloe* rhymes with the first and last lines of the stanza, *Oh* and *go*).

In *The White Goddess: A Historical Grammar of Poetic Myth*, Robert Graves defines *cynghanedd* as "the repetitive use of consonantal sequences with variation of vowels" and makes up this example:

> Billet spied,
> Bolt sped.
> Across field
> Crows fled,
> Aloft, wounded,
> Left one dead.

There are three classes of Welsh verse: *awdl*, *cywydd*, and *englyn*. Altogether they comprise the twenty-four "measures" or "strict meters," classified in the fourteenth century by Einion Offeiriad. The awdl ("rhyme, rhymed speech; ode, lay") is a line form. The *cywydd* is usually a couplet form. The englyn was originally a tercet; since the twelveth century six of its kinds have been quatrains using monorhyme or consonance; most of its lines contain seven syllables, although combinations of ten, six, and seven occur.

To give a sense of how Welsh poetry sounds, here are stanzas three through seven from Gwyn Williams' translation of the anonymous "Glyn Cynon Wood":

> If a man in sudden plight
> took to flight from foe,
> for guest-house to the nightingale
> in Cynon Vale he'd go.
>
> Many a birch tree green of cloak
> (I'd like to choke the Saxon!)
> is now a flaming heap of fire
> where iron-workers blacken.
>
> For cutting the branch and bearing away
> the wild birds' habitation
> may misfortune quickly reach
> Rowenna's treacherous children!

> Rather should the English be
> strung up beneath the seas,
> keeping painful house in hell
> than felling Cynon's trees.
>
> Upon my oath, I've heard it said
> that a herd of the red deer
> for Mawddwy's deep dark woods has left,
> bereft of its warmth here.

Each stanza consists of a pair of *awdl gywydd* couplets, rhymed *a* / *a + B* / *c* / *c + B*, so that the lower-case rhymes recur in the middle of the next line and the upper-case rhymes recur at the end of every other line. (Gwyn Williams notes: "The Cynon River is a tributary of the Taff. . . . Rowenna, daughter of Hengist, was given the name Alis Ronwen in a Triad. The English kings descended from her marriage with Vortigern were called Alice's children by the Welsh.")

Rhyme abounds in Welsh verse. Many lines use internal rhymes, either separate from or echoed by end-rhymes. Both full and slant rhyme are allowed, although a particular form may prescribe or prohibit their use. Sometimes a stressed syllable rhymes with an unstressed syllable, as in *sing/talking*. Sometimes the main rhyme does not end a line but is followed by one-to-three syllables. These extra syllables after the rhyme are called *gair cyrch* (pronounced *guyr kirch*), or "reaching-out word." They alliterate or rhyme with syllables in the first part of the next line. For example, one could approximate the effect in English:

> The infantry stormed the **hill**—through *bar*bed *wire*,
> a *bar*rage of *fire* and **shrill**
> bullets and shrapnel that **kill**.

The lines comprise an *englyn penfyr*, whose rhyme scheme can be notated as *A + gair cyrch* / *A* / *A*. The main rhymes (*A*) are "hill," "shrill," and "kill." The *gair cyrch* is "through barbed wire," which is echoed at the beginning of the next line by "barrage" (alliteration) and "fire" (rhyme). Both kinds of echoing occur in the example, but only one is necessary. *Gair cyrch* resembles the *qafia*, or refrain of a

few syllables, that follows the main rhyme in a Middle Eastern form called the *ghazal.

Frequently in Welsh verse, successive lines begin with the same consonant, a technique called *cymeriad* (pronounced *kuh-máre-yad*). Another kind of cymeriad occurs when the final word of a line is repeated near the beginning of the next line.

The contemporary poet writing in English may find it useful to experiment with some of these Welsh techniques: any of the intricately rhymed line and stanza forms; the standards for using slant rhymes (matching similar kinds of vowels—short, long, or diphthong); the sound interweaving of *cynghanedd* (especially alliterating a sequence of consonants). If nothing else, it would be good training in the orchestration of sounds. Listed below are twenty-four strict meters of Welsh poetry:

• Gair cyrch: 1-3 syllables *after* the Main Rhyme; alliterated or rhymed in the first part of the next line;

• Main Rhyme: indicated by a capital letter;

• Other rhymes: indicated by lower-case letters; may be internal rhyme or (in *englyn proest gadwynog*) a slant rhyme;

• / = line break (two or more letters between virgules indicate internal rhyme).

To approximate the Welsh sounds of these terms, say:

    ch   as in the Scottish *loch*;

    dd   like the *th* in *these*;

    th   like the *th* in *thin*.

In the pronunciation guides below, *th* must indicate both of these last two sounds. Usually it represents "dd" and sounds like the *th* in *these*; but "thoddaid" includes both (its beginning is unvoiced, as in *thin*, while its middle is voiced, as in *these*).

Englynion (8 kinds)

e. = englyn (eng'-glin; plural englynion)	Syllables per stanza	Rhyme and sound devices
e. penfyr (pen'-veer)	10-7-7	A + gair cyrch /A / A ("short-ended")

e. milwr (*mih'-loor*)	7-7-7	*A / A / A* ("soldier's englyn")
e. unodl union (*ee-noh'-dl een'- yon*)	10-6-7-7	*A + gair cyrch / A / A / A* ("straight one-rhyme englyn") 1st 2 lines = shaft (*paladr*); 2nd 2 lines = wings (*esgyll*); each line uses *cynghanedd*.
e. unodl crwca (*ee-noh'-dl croo'-ca*)	7-7-10-6	*A / A / A + gair cyrch / A* ("crooked one-rhyme englyn") Like the *e. unodl union*, but "wings" come before "shaft."
e. cyrch (*kirch*)	7-7-7-7	*A / A / b / b + A* 1st *A* rhyme stressed, 2nd *A* rhyme unstressed: *throw/window*; 2nd *b* rhyme comes in the middle of 4th line.
e. proest dalgron (*pro'-est dal'- grawn*)	7-7-7-7	*A / A / A / A* Slant-rhymed using either all short vowels (*hat/hit/bet*) or all long vowels (*hate/height/beat*) but not a mixture of both.
e. lleddfbroest (*clethev'-broist*)	7-7-7-7	*A / A / A / A* Slant-rhymed using diphthongs: *boil/fuel/vial/vowel*.
e. proest gadwynog (*pro'-est god- win'-og*)	7-7-7-7	*a / A / a / A* 1st line slant-rhymed with 2nd and full-rhymed with 3rd; 2nd line full- rhymed with 4th: *rod/dead/nod/led*.

Cywydd Measures (4 kinds)

c. = cywydd (*cuh'-with*)	*Syllables per quatrain*	*Rhyme and sound devices*
awdl gywydd (*ow'-dl guh'- with*)	7-7	*a / a + B* 2nd *a* rhyme comes in the middle of line 2; main rhyme (*B*) recurs at end of next couplet. (Sometimes considered a single 14-syllable line.)

c. deuair hirion (*die'-ire here'-* *yon*)	7-7	*A / A* masculine + feminine rhyme: *sword/forward*
c. deuair fyrion (*die'-ire veer'-* *yon*)	4-4	*A / A*
c. llosgyrnog (*clos-geer'-nog*)	8-8-7	*a / a / a + B* 3rd *a* rhyme comes in the middle of line 3; main rhyme (*B*) recurs at end of next tercet.

Awdl Measures (12 kinds) (*ow'-dl*)

Line Forms	Sections per line	Syllables per section	Rhyme	Cross alliteration
rhupunt (*ree'-pihnt*)	3-5	4	*a a (a a) B*	last 2 sections
cyhydedd hir (*cuh-hih'-* *deth here*)	4	5-5-5-4	*a a a B*	

In both of these forms, a second line would rhyme *c c (c) B*. The internal rhymes stay within a line, while the end-rhyme connects not internally but with an adjacent line.

Stanza Forms	Syllables per line	Rhyme and sound devices
cyhydedd fer (*cuh-hih'-deth* *ver*)	8-8	*A / A*
byr a thoddaid (*bir ah thoth'-* *ayd*)	10-6-8-8 or 8-8-10-6	*A + gair cyrch / A / A / A* or *A / A / A + gair cyrch / A*
clogyrnach (*clog-ir' nach*)	8-8-5-5-3-3	*A / A / b / b / b / A* (The last 4 lines can be a single line, like a rhupunt)

cyhydedd naw ban (*cuh-hih'-deth naw bahn*)	9-9	*A / A* (can go on for many lines with same rhyme)
toddaid (*toth'-ayd*)	10-9	*A + gair cyrch (b) / b A* (Used with *cyhydedd hir* or 9-syllable couplet)
gwawdodyn (*gwaw-dod'-in*)	9-9-10-9	*A / A / A + gair cyrch (b) / b A*
gwawdodyn hir (*gwaw-dod'-in here*)	9-9-9-9-10-9	*A / A / A / A / A + gair cyrch (b) / b A* (More 9-syllable couplets can come first; the *gair cyrch* must rhyme, not just alliterate—hence the *b*.)
hir a thoddaid (*here ah thoth'-ayd*)	10-10-10-10-10-9	*A / A / A / A / A + gair cyrch (b) /b A*
cyrch a chwta (*kirch ah choo'-ta*)	7-7-7-7-7-7-7-7	*A / A / A / A / A / A / b / b + A* (six 7-syllable lines followed by *awdl gywydd*)
tawddgyrch cadwynog (*towth'-girch cahd-win'-og*)	8-8-8-8	*a b / b C / a b / b C*

Irish verse, another branch of Celtic prosody, uses similar forms and rules in its traditional poetry. The central metrical structure of Irish verse is the *rann*, or four-line stanza, often written in seven-syllable lines and rhymed *abab* or *XaXa* (although the unrhymed *X* may consonate with *a*). Alliteration is somewhat different than in English: Vowels as well as consonants may alliterate, and any stressed word with a different sound will block the alliteration. Consonance also differs from the English sense, so that in consonant words the vowel lengths are the same and the consonants belong to the same

class. An English approximation might match short vowels (or long vowels) and consonant groups such as plosives (*b, p; t, d; g, k*), nasals (*n, m, ng*), or liquids (*l, r*). Examples of this kind of consonance might include *reed/late* and *dim/pun*.

Irish meters may specify (1) the number of syllables in different rhyme words (an *a* rhyme might consist of three syllables, while *b* might consist of two), (2) consonance between rhyme words and the last words of unrhymed lines, (3) the position and frequency of alliteration and internal rhyme, and (4) alliteration from the end of one line to the beginning of the next. Sometimes the odd-line rhymes are stressed and the even are not. Eleanor Knott gives the English example of *bit/rabbit*. The stressed rhyme is called *rinn*, the unstressed one *airdrinn*. (Notice how the terms demonstrate the technique.) In all of these Irish meters, the poem begins and ends with the same syllable, word, or line, a technique called *dunadh*.

For further information on Welsh and Irish forms, see Gwyn Williams' *An Introduction to Welsh Poetry*, Tony Conran's *Welsh Verse*, Eleanor Knott's *An Introduction to Irish Syllabic Poetry of the Period 1200-1600*, and Lewis Turco's *The New Book of Forms*.

Word A signifier; the basic unit of the sentence—and of language; the atom of a body of discourse.

A word consists of one or more syllables, clusters of sounds that may or may not be strung together. *Word*, for example, consists of a single syllable; *language* consists of two syllables, the first accented (láng-uage); *vocabulary* consists of five syllables, with a primary accent on the second and secondary accent on the fourth (vo-cáb-u-lár-y). Each syllable, however, contains individual sounds called phonemes, which may or may not correspond to the letters. For example, *word* and *worth* both contain four phonemes, but *worth* has an extra letter (*th* is a single phoneme).

In addition to its sounds (a matter of pronunciation) and its visual appearance when written (a matter of spelling), a word has one or more meanings and one or more functions within a sentence. The meaning is what the word signifies, what it conveys to someone who speaks the language. Even a nonsense word may have meaning—though a meaning perhaps dependent on sound, like a dog's bark. The function of a word depends on how it is, or can be, used in a

sentence. Accordingly, each word serves as a part of speech: noun, verb, adjective, adverb, preposition, conjunction, pronoun, article, interjection. In different contexts, a word can serve as different parts of speech. *Rope*, for example, can serve as noun, verb, or adjective:

> She twirls the rope.
> They rope the steers.
> They cross over a rope bridge.

The following lines from Christopher Marlowe's *Doctor Faustus* include all nine parts of speech:

> *The clock strikes twelve.*
>
> *Faustus.* It strikes, it strikes! Now body, turn to air,
> Or Lucifer will bear thee quick to hell!
> O soul, be changed into small water-drops
> And fall into the ocean, ne'er be found.

In the lines spoken by Faustus, the parts of speech are as follows:
- noun (person, place, thing, or idea): *body, air, Lucifer, hell, soul, water-drops, ocean*;
- verb (action or state of being): *strikes, turn, will bear, be changed, fall, be found*;
- adjective (modifying a noun): *small*;
- adverb (modifying a verb, an adjective, or another adverb): *Now, quick, ne'er*;
- preposition (forming a transition from a noun or verb to something that modifies it): *to, into*;
- conjunction (joining words, phrases, or clauses): *Or, And*;
- pronoun (substituting for nouns): *It, thee*;
- article (indicating something—*a, an,* and *the* are the only ones, used before nouns or noun phrases): *the*;
- interjection (or exclamation, an utterance like a cry or a shout or a gasp or a curse): *O*.

PERMISSIONS

"Tourists" from *Great Tranquility: Questions and Answers* by Yehuda Amichai. Copyright © 1983 by Yehuda Amichai. Reprinted by permission of HarperCollins Publishers, Inc. and Yehuda Amichai.

"Photosynthesis" is reprinted from *The Selected Poems: 1951-1977* by A.R. Ammons, by permission of W.W. Norton & Company, Inc. Copyright © 1977, 1975, 1974, 1972, 1971, 1970, 1966, 1965, 1964, 1955 by A.R. Ammons.

"A Branch of Nettle Enters through the Window," by André Breton, translated by David Antin, *The Poetry of Surrealism*, edited by Michael Benedikt, 1974. Reprinted by permission of the translator.

"The Exiles" from *W.H. Auden: Collected Poems* by W. H. Auden, edited with Preface by Edward Mendelson. Copyright © 1934 by The Modern Library, Inc. and renewed 1962 by W.H. Auden. Reprinted by permission of Random House, Inc. and Faber and Faber Ltd.

"That Night When Joy Began" from *W.H. Auden: Collected Poems* by W. H. Auden, edited with Preface by Edward Mendelson. Copyright © 1937 and renewed 1965 by W.H. Auden. Reprinted by permission of Random House, Inc. and Faber and Faber Ltd.

"Stars Which See, Stars Which Do Not See," by Marvin Bell, from *Stars Which See, Stars Which Do Not See*. Copyright © 1977 by Marvin Bell. Reprinted by permission of the author.

"Get Drunk" by Charles Baudelaire. Originally appeared in *The Prose Poem: An International Anthology* published by Dell/Laurel Editions, edited by Michael Benedikt. Translation by Michael Benedikt, © 1976. Used by permission of Michael Benedikt.

"Lift Plow Plates," © 1983, 1992 by Charles Bernstein. Used by permission of Roof Books, from *Islets/Irritations*.

"Enriching the Earth" from *Farming: A Handbook*, copyright © 1969 by Wendell Berry, reprinted by permission of Harcourt Brace & Company.

"Catullus: Odi et Amo" from *In the Western Night: Collected Poems 1965-90* by Frank Bidart. Copyright © 1990 by Frank Bidart. Reprinted by permission of Farrar, Straus & Giroux, Inc.

"Sestina" from *The Complete Poems* by Elizabeth Bishop. Copyright © 1979, 1983 by Alice Helen Methfessel. Reprinted by permission of Farrar, Straus & Giroux, Inc.

Robert Bly, "Driving Toward the Lac Qui Parle River" from *Silence in the Snowy Fields* © 1962 by Robert Bly, Wesleyan University Press by permission of the University Press of New England.

Poem by Matsuo Basho and four poems by Kobayashi Issa from *The Sea and the Honeycomb: A Book of Tiny Poems*, translated and edited by Robert Bly, Beacon Press. Copyright © 1971 by Robert Bly. Reprinted with permission of Robert Bly.

"Home from a Walk" by Federico Garcia Lorca from *Lorca and Jimenez: Selected Poems*, translated by Robert Bly, Beacon Press. Copyright © 1973 by Robert Bly. Reprinted with permission of Robert Bly.

"Ode to Salt" by Pablo Neruda from *Neruda and Vallejo: Selected Poems*, translated by Robert Bly, Beacon Press. Copyright © 1971 by Robert Bly. Reprinted with permission of Robert Bly.

"piano after war" and "mentors" from *Blacks* by Gwendolyn Brooks, © 1991. Publisher, Third World Press, Chicago, 1991. Reprinted by permission of the author.

Four poems, reprinted from *Traditional Japanese Poetry*, Translated, with an Introduction, by Steven D. Carter with the permission of the publishers, Stanford University Press. Copyright © 1991 by the Board of Trustees of the Leland Stanford Junior University.

Carmen 85 ("Odi et Amo") by Catullus, translated by Charles Martin, *The Poems of Catullus*. The Johns Hopkins University Press, Baltimore/London, 1989, p. 122.

Carmen 85 ("Odi et Amo") by Catullus, translated by Celia & Louis Zukofsky. Louis Zukofsky, *Complete Short Poetry*, 1991. The Johns Hopkins University Press, Baltimore/London, 1991, p. 310.

"The Last Woman with Lotus Feet" from *Dwarf Bamboo*. Copyright © 1987 by Marilyn Chin. Reprinted by permission of The Greenfield Review Press.

The poems by Basho entitled "sweeping the garden," "the autumn coolness," and "what with fleas and lice" are reprinted from *One Man's Moon* translated by Cid Corman by permission of Gnomon Press.

Robert Creeley, "I Know a Man," from *Collected Poems of Robert Creeley, 1945-1975*. Copyright ©

INDEX

Abecedarius, 17-18
Abstract language, 1
Abstract poetry, 1-2
Academic verse, 2-3
Accent, 3
Accentual meter, 3-5
Accentual-syllabic meter, 5-7
Acrostic, 7-8
Adjective, 313
Adverb, 313
Alcaics, alcaic stanza, 8-9
Aleatory poetry, 53-55
Alexandrine, 9
Allegory, 9-10, 103
Alliteration, 10-13, 99
Alliterative meter, 13-16
Alliterative rhyme, 232
Allusion, 16-17
Alphabet poem, 17-18
Alternating quatrain, 217-218
Ambiguity, 18-20
Amphibrach, 20
Anacrusis, 20-21
Anadiplosis, 100
Anapest, anapestic, 21-22
Anaphora, 22-23, 100
Anastrophe, 100-101
Anglo-Saxon meter, 13-16
Animal poem, 23-24
Antanaclasis, 104
Anthimeria, 103
Anthology, 24-25
Anti-poem, 25-26
Antonomasia, 104
Antonymic translation, 191

Apocopated rhyme, 232
Aposiopesis, 101
Apostrophe, 26, 103
Apposition, 101
Approximate rhyme, 231-232,
258-259
Argument, 26
Ars poetica, 26-27
Article, 314
Assonance, 27, 101
Assonant rhyme, 232
Asyndeton, 101
Aubade, 27
Audience, 27, 222
Automatic writing, 27
Auxesis, 103

Ballad, 28-29
Ballad stanza, 29-31
Ballade, 32-33
Beat, 33
Beat poetry, 33-34
Biblical verse, 34-36
Black Mountain school, 36-38
Blank verse, 38-40
Blason, blazon, 40
Blues, 40-43
Bob and wheel, 43
Boolean poem, 191
Broken rhyme, 233
Burns stanza, 44-45

Cadence, 46-47
Caesura, 48
Calligramme, 85-87

More From Story Press!

The Fiction Dictionary by Laurie Henry. The essential guide to the inside language of fiction. These are terms from yesterday and today—plus those just being coined for the language of tomorrow. You'll discover genres you've never explored, writing devices you'll want to try, fresh characters to populate your stories. *The Fiction Dictionary* dusts off the traditional concept of "dictionary" by giving full, vivid descriptions and by using lively examples from classic and contemporary fiction . . . turning an authoritative reference into a can't-put-it-down browser. *#48008/$18.99/336 pages*

Idea Catcher from the Editors of Story Press. This spirited journal will help you open your eyes to the creative possibilities of your everyday world. On every page, you'll find something to stimulate your senses and spark your imagination: inspirational writing "prompts," insightful quotes from well-known writers, and short anecdotes about how authors "caught" the ideas that became great works of literature. #48011/$14.99/160 pages

The Art and Craft of Novel Writing by Oakley Hall. Using examples from classic and contemporary writers ranging from John Steinbeck to Joyce Carol Oates, Hall guides you through the process of crafting a novel. In example-packed discussions, Hall shows what works and why. You will learn the key elements of fiction and gain inspiration along the way. *#48002/$14.99/240 pages/paperback*

The Best Writing on Writing, edited by Jack Heffron, is the first in a series that will showcase the most provocative new articles, essays, and lectures on fiction, nonfiction, poetry, playwriting, and the writing life. These 27 illuminating and thought-provoking selections are a lively feast of the well-written word and how it is fashioned. *#48001/$16.99/208 pages/paperback*

The Best Writing on Writing, Volume 2, edited by Jack Heffron, is the year's best collection of memorable essays, book excerpts, and lectures on fiction, nonfiction, poetry, screenwriting, and the writing life, all from 1994. The selections feature such luminaries as Joyce Carol Oates, Margaret Atwood, Justin Kaplan, Charles Baxter, and Maxine Kumin, to name a few. *#48013/$16.99/paperback*

Turning Life Into Fiction by Robin Hemley. Writers' lives, those of their friends and family members, newspaper accounts, conversations overheard—these can be the bases for novels and short stories. Here, Robin Hemley shows how to make true stories even better. You'll learn how to turn journal entries into fiction; find good story material within yourself; identify memories that can be developed; and fictionalize other people's stories. Exercises guide writers in honing their skills. *#48000/$17.99/208 pages*

Address Unknown by Kressmann Taylor. Commemorating the 50th anniversary of the liberation of World War II concentration camps, this gripping tale portrays in letters the terror of Nazism as it unfolds between an American and his former business partner in Germany. It serves as a sobering reminder that history can repeat itself. *#48006/$12.99/64 pages*

Fiction Writer's Workshop by Josip Novakovich. In this interactive workshop, you'll explore each aspect of the art of fiction, including point of view, description, revision, voice, and more. At the end of each chapter you'll find more than a dozen writing exercises to help you put what you've learned into action. *#48003/$17.99/256 pages*

New York Magazine Crossword Puzzles by Maura B. Jacobson. One of America's favorite puzzle-constructors brings you an assortment of her witty and inventive puzzles. Each collection contains fifty stimulating puzzles, reprinted from *New York* magazine, with themes ranging from literature and famous films to the Bible and the Oscars. *Volume 1:#48004/$9.99/64 pages/paperback Volume 2:#48005/$9.99/64 pages/paperback Volume 3:#48009/$9.99/64 pages/paperback Volume 4:#48010/$9.99/64 pages/paperback*

These selections are available at your local bookstore or directly from Story Press. To order from Story Press, send payment, plus $3.50 postage and handling for one book, and $1.00 for each additional. Ohio residents add 5.5% sales tax. Allow 30 days for delivery.

Story Press
1507 Dana Avenue
Cincinnati, Ohio 45207
or call: 1-800-876-0963

VISA/MasterCard orders call TOLL-FREE
1-800-289-0963

6555